A Call from

A journey around the edge of Europe

by

Andrew Earnshaw

MAPLE
PUBLISHERS

A Call from the East

Author: Andrew Earnshaw

Copyright © Andrew Earnshaw (2023)

The right of Andrew Earnshaw to be identified as author of this work has been asserted by the author in accordance with section 77 and 78 of the Copyright, Designs and Patents Act 1988.

First Published in 2023

ISBN 978-1-915796-68-4 (Paperback)
      978-1-915796-69-1 (eBook)

Cover Artwork: The Mamayev Kurgan. Painting by Talana Gamah.

Rear Cover Photograph: The open road: heading east in Turkey

Book layout by:
      White Magic Studios
      www.whitemagicstudios.co.uk

Published by:
      Maple Publishers
      Fairbourne Drive, Atterbury,
      Milton Keynes,
      MK10 9RG, UK
      www.maplepublishers.com

A CIP catalogue record for this title is available from the British Library.

This book is a memoir. It reflects the author's recollections of experiences over time. Some names and characteristics have been changed, some events have been compressed, and some dialogues have been recreated, and the Publisher hereby disclaims any responsibility for them.

Reviews of the first book in the series: *Far Horizons: Across the Great Divide*

"This is really well done. Terrific descriptions and typical dry British humour. I've been in many of the same locations and enjoyed reliving my own travels through the author's eyes."

"Very well written and enjoyable book - the chapters are quite long but well partitioned to allow you to take a break or read straight through. I like the amusing stories and the vivid descriptions of the author's experiences, particularly with the local fauna."

"A super book. Well written on the lighter side of motorcycle travel."

"Good read and lets you know how vast & diverse America is both size wise & culturally, makes you feel like taking your own trip to wherever."

"Although this is a book about a motorcycle journey, it is more about the journey than the motorcycle. So while other riders will definitely find plenty to relate to in the bikey-bits, it's just as entertaining for people who don't ride motorcycles."

"So there I was hiking through the Galapagos Island's on my Honeymoon and all I could think about was where can I find a place to sit down and continue reading 'Far Horizons'. I'm actually serious.. I've read every motorcycle travel book I could get my hands on and I must say, this is the best one I've read yet!!"

"I loved the book. Having travelled many of the miles that Andy did, it was interesting to hear the thoughts of someone who has never seen them before. I enjoyed Andy's style, it was like sitting over coffee or a beer and having a great chat with him."

This book is dedicated to my pillion rider
and navigator: Diane Earnshaw

Contents

Foreword

On the 24th of February 2022, the Russian armed forces invaded Ukraine. This book was undergoing its final preparations as the tanks rolled over the border. Suddenly, the context of our journey through the lands that were now war-torn became very clear. In 2012, when we undertook our trip, there were signs that all was not well. These are captured in observations we made and the comments of people we met.

I wasn't sure how to proceed with publishing the book. Should I go back through the draft and update it, taking into consideration the events of 2022? Or should I leave it as it was written, with comments added after the fighting in 2014? In the end I decided to retain the content as it was originally written, with the exception of changing the names of people we met and befriended in Ukraine. Strange to observe, when proof-reading the written word, that we came away from eastern Europe with the realisation that it was a tinderbox, waiting to catch fire and explode. And sad to say that some of our observations became prophetic.

I would like to thank the following people – dear friends – who have provided valuable assistance: Stuart Robinson and Neville Mallett (proof reading and assisting with editing and punctuation), Danara Kalenova (translation), and, of course, my navigator and pillion rider - Diane Earnshaw. I would also like to thank Talana Gamah for the wonderful cover artwork, oft mistaken as a photograph when people see it hanging on our wall. And finally, Ed Curry, who we first met in America, for his sage advice, packages of useful equipment and constant encouragement.

Both Diane and I would like to thank the myriad people we met upon the road. People of many nationalities who blessed us with great kindness, proving the fact that, despite the terrible circumstances we see around us, nearly all humans are fundamentally decent. If you remove obvious racial differences, the accents and language variations, the tools we humans use to apply stereotypes, our observations are that we are (pretty much) all the same. I hope you enjoy the journey. And, if you are a motorcyclist, fair weather to you and safe riding!

Chapter 1
Organisation

In September 2009, I tumbled out of a four-month motorcycle tour of North America, back into the litter-strewn garden that is England, feeling disjointed and slightly dispossessed. In truth, just before abandoning the bike to the shipping agents in Baltimore, I was sorely tempted to head towards Arizona to while away the winter months. But such lotus-eating was out of the question; the bank manager was waiting for me, cudgel in hand. Funds were at a critical level and I needed to find a job as quickly as possible.

In the back of my mind, I knew that I'd been badly bitten by the long-distance travelling bug and my aspirations for a second big trip were shared by my better half, Diane. An outline developed for a journey that would push the envelope a little, without taking it too far. Western Russia seemed to fit the bill: the roads were likely to be poor but passable, and accommodation would probably be cheap but easily found. The idea of visiting Russia had been developing before the last trip ended and, over the next year or so, we started to flesh out our ideas.

An outline route began to emerge. I reckoned the farthest east we could go without breaking the pillion, bike, or rider would be somewhere west of the Urals. Volgograd seemed an obvious choice. We started to explore the possibility of riding north to south through Russia, then heading for Syria via Turkey. After that a touch of vagueness crept in. Should we try to ride through Jordon and Egypt then return to Europe via North Africa? Or should we dip into Syria then return through Turkey? At this point, the Arab Spring blew up and took our plans with it. Far from heading for Syria, it rapidly became *the* country to avoid.

One day, shortly after finding out that Syria was a no-no, I listened to a radio programme describing Georgia. The received impression was of a deeply forested and mountainous country, where the men were men and goats might have good reason to keep a watchful eye over their shoulders. It sounded edgy and mysterious. It found its way onto the itinerary. But the more we researched going there, the harder it seemed to be able to make it happen. There were all sorts of tensions between Russia and Georgia following their recent war with each other. The border with Russia to the north of Georgia was closed, an awkward nuisance when attempting route-planning. A few of my more knowledgeable confidants at work (mostly Russians) threw up doubts and questions – like: 'why on earth do you want to go there? Why?' It just made me more determined. It's a Yorkshire thing.

By the end of 2010, the plan was emerging nicely from the mists of general confustification. We decided to travel northwards through Scandinavia to cross into Russia via one of the northern border crossings. Then we would head from north to south via Saint Petersburg and Moscow to Volgograd. After that, we would try to find a legitimate way to enter Georgia, where we would pootle around in the deep, dark, mountainous forests, ending up on the border of Azerbaijan. This would mark the mid-point of our little adventure.

From Georgia, we decided to work our way back home through Turkey, before picking up the coast of Europe and threading our way, more-or-less, right the way around the edge of the continent, arriving eventually in northern Spain, where we would board a ferry across the Bay of Biscay, making landfall roughly five months after our departure. We would almost certainly find ourselves wet, cold and close to bankruptcy at this point. Not for the first time in my life, would I find myself penniless in Portsmouth. In the slightly modified words of Ace Rimmer of the cult sci-fi comedy *Red Dwarf*: Smoke us two kippers, we'll be back (sometime) before Christmas.

Chapter 2
Disorganisation

Thursday the 28th of June, 2012. Approximate time 09:05am.

In about seven hours, a large Scandinavian ferry will judder away from the jetty at Harwich, destination Esbjerg, Denmark. If, as planned, we wish to be on board that ferry, we need to leave home four hours from now. Our motorcycle needs to be successfully loaded and sitting on an even keel, packed with five month's-worth of clothes, assorted camping equipment, tools, travel-associated sundries, pillion passenger, and pilot. Unfortunately, here on the day of departure, we find ourselves running into difficulties packing the bike.

Up on the top floor of our house, Diane is calmly carrying out final checks on her part of the clothing pile and carefully filing the necessary documentation. Like every good administrative assistant, she has everything carefully laid out on the bed and is sorting it into neat piles before packing it; soft items are carefully tied with elastic bands and paperwork is filed in order of importance before being placed in a waterproof, tear-proof wallet. She has taken her role extremely seriously. On one of my few trips up there, I try to look similarly efficient by saying, 'Don't forget to pack a photocopy of my paper driving licence Hun.'

Meanwhile, I'm grafting away in the car park around the back of the house attempting to pack the bike. I haven't taken my role quite so seriously and, as a consequence, I need all the remaining few hours left to accomplish my task.

There are a few problems that need to be faced in this one-sided battle with time, space, mass and the pull of the planet. I have a Toyota Hiace van packed to the rafters to my right and a large red motorcycle sitting on its centre stand to my left. Despite the threat of rain, the ambient temperature is rising by the minute and my frustration with myself is climbing too. The key problem I face is the same one I experienced in Los Angeles three years ago. Packing the bike for solo riding is relatively easy. Whatever won't fit in or on the panniers can be heaped up in soft baggage on top of the pillion seat. But when a pillion passenger is added into the equation, that extra space evaporates. I discovered this in a car park alongside the Queen Mary when Diane joined me on the trip around America.

I think we're going to miss the ferry.

The minutes tick their way inexorably. Each attempted variation ends in failure and another bit of kit is deemed superfluous and thrown back into the van. Then finally, at around one o'clock, I seem to have cracked it and manage to heave the creaking bike off its centre stand and on to two wheels with a big 'flump' as the suspension attempts to cope with the down force. Diane comes down to view the result. I climb aboard for a test ride around the car park.

Oh my God! I can't steer it! It's turned into a monocycle!

I can hear you saying, 'why on earth didn't you carry out at least one full and proper complete dry run before now?' And, to be honest, you would have a reasonable point, fairly made. The whys and wherefores of my failure are many-fold and complex - is my lame excuse. Summarised in a sentence they add up to: 'we were working too hard and were situated at the wrong end of the country for all of that', admittedly a less than convincing pair of reasons. Right now though, we've discovered a simple fact: riding two-up for five months around distant lands apparently requires more gear than we have available stowage space to accommodate; so even more things have to go. Moreover, we must ditch them and re-pack within the hour or we will miss the ferry. It's as simple as that.

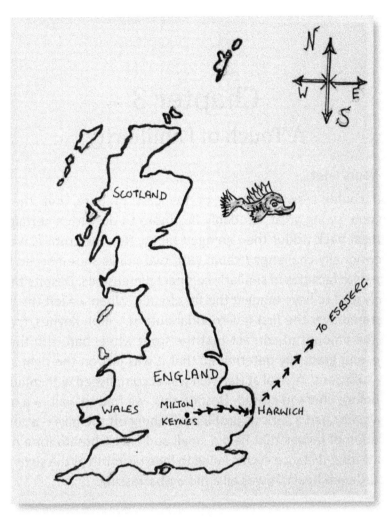

The start of the journey – Milton Keynes to Esbjerg, Denmark.

Chapter 3
A Touch of Familiarity

A few hours later....

You couldn't swing either of my cats in here, but then the expression 'swing a cat' probably has more to do with a certain type of nautical back tickler than an aged tabby. No. The truth is we have a dimensionally challenged cabin with two bunks shoe-horned into it and en-suite facilities of similarly compact dimensions. Despite this, I'm certainly glad to have made it this far already. When we left the house, we teetered over the first few roundabouts in Milton Keynes, trying to gauge the amount of contact that the front wheel had with the road surface, and gradually determined that it was just on the right side of 'barely sufficient'. Arrival at Harwich was accomplished with minutes to spare before check-in closed. Despite this, we had to wait in a queue. My Navigator had a serious problem climbing off the bike – a complex negotiation of moves that held a small audience's breath for a minute or two. A long-distance cyclist failed to hide his mirth at the sight of our over-burdened beast. It was all a tad embarrassing.

14

We repair from our cabin to the restaurant/bar area as the ferry heaves gently over a lazy swell. The problem that we face is a couple of weeks away and is commonly known these days as *The Russian Federation*. There's no way that I'm going to manage the bike/luggage-mountain on anything like off-road situations. Something will have to be done to lighten the load. Not necessarily straight away, but sometime soon. Like tomorrow, or maybe the day after. In the meantime, we can relax and be amused by the ship's entertainment officer who, as it turns out, is rather good. After a slightly shaky start to his set, he quickly has all the children enthralled and their parents visibly concerned about the part of his show that involves 'audience participation'. After watching for a while, munching on a very expensive but otherwise delicious chicken sandwich, we beat a tactical retreat back to our cabin.

***

A grey morning arrives, peeping through the porthole, which is letting in as little light as possible. Shortly before arrival at Esbjerg, we pass a jack-up drilling rig being towed out to sea. It reminds me of a dead spider floating on its back in the bath. By the time we arrive in the port it has started to drizzle with rain. The call for passengers to head to the car deck leads to a disorganised shambles of bag ferrying – no pun intended – on our part. By the time everyone else is loaded up and ready to roll, we're still trying to work out which bag goes where. We are the last bikers to leave the ship, but we do catch everyone up at the passport booth, where bored customs officials carry out a cursory passport check, then wave us through.

On the way out of town, we pass the tallest chimney in Scandinavia, part of a relatively clean coal-fired power station. At the other end of the environmental spectrum lie the huge storage yards dedicated to a newer, cleaner power source: wind turbines. Their graceful sails are carefully stacked ready for shipment. The bike settles into its pace with the valve gear of the flat twin engine rustling away quietly in the breeze as the skies lighten and the rain spits its last drops onto the screen. Esbjerg slips behind in the sulky, overcast distance. We are properly on our way!

I've flown over Denmark many times when I lived and worked here in the early noughties, commuting into Copenhagen from Stansted Airport. From the air, it is a lovely country, littered with varying sizes of islands, all of which have a patchwork quilt of farmland, woodland and copses; ringed by indented, low-lying coasts and deserted beaches. The towns are few and far between; some are vibrant university towns, others are small and quiet (possibly even boring).

From the perspective of riding a motorcycle on the main road that links the west of Denmark to the east, the main impression is that the land is seriously flat. The highest point (anywhere) is a mere 561 feet, a fact that probably explains why lots of Danes use bicycles. In the main, the motorcycle riding experience is one of droning through wide countryside interspersed by the odd coppice, small stands of wind turbines and the occasional farm emitting the wafted scent of silage. Away from the motorway, many of the roads are exceedingly straight. It isn't a particularly inspiring place to ride a motorcycle, if truth be told. In 2003, I kept a bike here for a few months and the chicken strips on the back tyre were SERIOUSLY EMBARRASSING.

To prepare for the trip I've been attempting more in the way of maintenance on the bike than I did previously. I decided that the nightmare scenario of suffering a puncture, alone in a country where national recovery services are a nonentity, was just too worrying to contemplate and booked myself on a BMW 'Adventure Maintenance' course run by the Paris Dakar racer Simon Pavey. When, during the course of the course, if you get my meaning, I was asked by Simon where I intended to go, and replied, 'Russia', he chuckled mirthfully in his offbeat Aussie manner and quipped, 'I think you'd better get yourself on our Off-Road Riding Skills course. The roads over there are effing appalling.'

I didn't mention to him that I would be riding with five-month's-worth of supplies and a pillion on board, but comments like this from a Paris Dakar Rally legend should, I suppose, be taken seriously. The course was excellent and is highly recommended to anyone contemplating something similar, or, dare I say it, more adventurous. It showed us how to do all the jobs that are needed to keep the bike running on an extended and punishing overland trip. But most importantly, we learned how to carry out that most challenging of ordeals: repair a puncture in a tubeless tyre or, if the chips are really down, replace the tyres. It left me quietly confident that I could handle such an occurrence (no doubt time will tell). It also left me with a pannier weighed down by a bead breaker, bead setter, assorted tyre irons and lots of CO_2 canisters to help re-inflate the pesky blighter.

Mr Pavey would scoff at these precautions. 'All you need to break a bead is a side stand,' said he, deftly demonstrating how this cunningly simple piece of knowledge was brought to bear on a recalcitrant punctured hoop. I was impressed. My fellow classmates were impressed. We all had a go. It only occurred to me months later that this method is fine if you're in the company of one or more like-minded riders, preferably Paris Dakar heroes, built like brick outhouses but absolutely useless if, like us, you gently explore the world as solo rats of the road. I have seen it demonstrated solo by an American on YouTube, who physically heaved his bike up to accomplish the task, but he was probably once a gunnery instructor in the Marine Corps, so that doesn't count. But Mr Pavey is forgiven, because now I can fix a puncture and the bike has a centre stand. I just need to be able to break the tyre bead to remove the tyre without pulling one or more vital muscles, hence the rather nifty American bead breaker sitting in the right-hand pannier. At the time, I ignored his sage advice regarding off-road riding skills and just thought, 'surely it can't be that bad, can it?

***

Our immediate plans are to find a campsite outside Copenhagen, visit the city tomorrow, then head for Sweden. We'll ride up the eastern seaboard, stopping off in Stockholm before making a lunge for the border with Finland. Our route will then take us down to Helsinki where we hope to find a ferry service that will spirit us over to Tallinn. When we get there, we will have landed a short day's ride from the Russian border. It's just a rough plan and it sounds quite simple, but the distance isn't to be sniffed at – I guess it will be well over a thousand miles. The Danish sector is likely to be the easiest and shortest.

Danes are, in the main, well paid and enjoy a good lifestyle. They are fond of waving their red and white flag, which is the inverse of the flag of England, and show no embarrassment at running it up a flagpole outside their house. They pay a shed-load of tax – for example up to 180% on new cars and motorcycles, a single fact that rules Denmark out of my list of desirable places to permanently reside. If I paid that much tax, I'd still be saving for the bike I'm now riding. That said, the roads are excellent, although typically populated by old bangers due to the crippling rate of vehicle tax. One of my Danish friends once told me that every time they resurfaced the road outside his house he went and asked the workers, 'why are you repairing a perfectly good road?' To which they shrugged and said, 'now is the time for it to be done.' Arriving at a fuel stop, we check out the map posted on the wall inside the petrol station and I point out the town of Roskilde to Diane. 'This is where we're heading. We're going to take a left turn fairly soon,' I declare, adding, 'I do hope the famous rock festival isn't on!'

***

Camping Roskilde

As we arrive at Roskilde, two observations can be made: firstly, there are a lot of teenagers wandering around with strange hats on. Occasionally, an open-back vehicle goes past packed with them, cheering at passers-by and drinking out of beer bottles and cans. These are students who have graduated to wearing funny hats. Secondly: there are other visitors to the town who seem to be lugging camping gear and crates of beer on little trolleys. It doesn't bode too well.

My fear is that the campsite will be fully booked by festival-goers. Such fears subside when we arrive at the site. The office is run by a slightly strange, youngish bloke with a punk-meets-rockabilly hairstyle who speaks excellent English and asks me if we hold membership of some kind of obscure Euro camping organisation. I respond that we do not. 'You really have to be a member to camp here,' says he. 'I really only want to camp for a couple of nights and then be on my way, heading out of Europe,' I reply. He shrugs his shoulders and replies slightly downheartedly, 'OK then.' Super! That seemed to work quite well.

Our pitch overlooks a fine body of water, with the campsite nestling up a slight incline in amongst the trees, which form windbreaks for the caravan and campervan pitches. Some of the caravans display signs of having spent many a season on the site, having been fenced off with well-planted gardens and the odd flagpole in front of them. There's no doubt about it, Danes, like their German cousins, are a very organised race. I think all the disorganised ones pitched over to England circa 800AD and landed in Yorkshire. I content myself in musing that they were the adventurous, good looking, cricket playing ones who would never, ever buy a static caravan.

Once the tent is erected, we can relax and settle down. We have some food, but we've already decided we need to eat it all to reduce the top weight, so we light up our Trangia stove and pile everything into a pan and scoff it in short order. The wind picks up as the shadows start to lengthen. I decide to have a go at flying my kite. I bought it in Oregon and haven't unpacked it since purchasing it. Whilst it is doing a very fine impression of a kestrel, I relax a bit and look around, taking in the fine scenery of the place and observing (with a curled upper-lip) what appear to be festival-goers, who are arriving and putting up the kind of crappy pop-up tents you buy at a supermarket, before cramming them full of beer cartons. I turn around to be faced by a lady on exercise who has had her little circuit of the campsite interrupted by a kite that has gracefully stalled into the ground leaving the string across her pathway.

The look on her face is one of tight-lipped admonishment. How dare I put a trip hazard directly across her intended route? Sheepishly, I wind the string in and remove the offending cordage whereupon she smiles sweetly and says 'thank-you' in English, before resuming her power walk with terrier in tow. I think that's enough of kite flying for one day. I have, in fact, just suffered a minor example of Danish public chastisement. I once saw a woman berate a window cleaner in Copenhagen for having the temerity to put his ladder up on the pavement she wanted to walk on. Try doing that in Gillingham or Southend!

The evening descends with all the usual sounds of a campsite. People in caravans are watching telly, the prospective concert-goers are getting drunk and playing music and the most magnificent sunset splashes rich tones of red, orange and purple-blue to the west as the wildfowl land in the lake to roost. Tonight, this is a very beautiful place on earth.

In the deep of night, the wind picks up further and the tent flaps and shudders, rocking about. I get up and check the guys. Everything is fine and I eventually nod off into a nice deep sleep.

*** * ***

The purpose of our visit to Copenhagen is to sample some of the sights and to chill out a bit – enjoy some of the café culture that flourishes there. Our first stop is a district of the city called Nørrebro. I lived here between 2003 and 2004. The area was once quite notorious, having been the communist enclave of the city and synonymous with radicalism in its early days, but nowadays it has softened a little and become quite fashionable, whilst still feeling slightly edgy.

A key feature of Nørrebro is that its name is completely unpronounceable to anyone other than a Dane. In fact, I stopped taking taxis from the train station because I couldn't pronounce either the district or indeed the street that I lived in. All I got from taxi drivers (most of whom were Turkish, as it happened) was a blank stare. It was much easier to walk. Arrival at my old address, 10 Birkegade, which I think means Birch Street and is pronounced something like 'Beerkergellluue', reveals that my old motorcycle parking space is still there and still available. This is the old Jewish quarter, a fact confirmed by numerous examples of the Star of David on the buildings and the presence of the Jewish cemetery, which sits just over a red brick wall at the end of the street. Thankfully, the people who once lived here escaped virtually without loss of life over to Sweden during World War II, spirited away from the Gestapo in a remarkable and famous operation.

The housing is made up of high tenement buildings with shops beneath them, which crowd in on the bicycle and car-lined street. We have a meal in a cool little café-bar-cum-laundromat, then we head into the city centre to try to find the National Museum, which has a remarkable collection of Bronze and Iron Age bog bodies with nondescript names like 'the woman from Huldremose'. At this point we manage to get lost. I thought I knew the city reasonably well. I've ridden around it many times before. On one occasion, I pulled up at a set of traffic lights, glanced at the car next to me, which turned out to be a limousine, and came face to face with Queen Margrethe II and her uniformed equerry. I'd like to say she smiled at me, but she didn't. The truth is she completely blanked me. Meanwhile, the passage of a few years has left me bereft of my navigational skills.

Having failed to locate the museum, we take an extended tour around the various districts: past the fine central train station, the Tivoli gardens, the famous Rådhuspladsen town hall square, and the wonderful churches scattered around the city. Copenhagen is a particularly charming capital city, modest in size, but brimming with character. We eventually find our bearings and head towards the harbour and a fortification called Kastellet, the site of Copenhagen's most famous resident: The Little Mermaid.

Down by the harbour it is particularly hot. There are hundreds of tourists. Almost to a man, woman, and child they are Japanese or Chinese and they all want to scramble down to be photographed alongside the Little Mermaid. As luck would have it, the tide is out. Diane is keen to photograph the statue. Personally, I think she's a touch over-rated – the mermaid that is, but I guess Copenhagen just wouldn't be the same without her.

***

Day 3 of the grand Russian odyssey. Our mission today is to take the short hop over to Sweden via the bridge that links the two countries and to head in the direction of Stockholm. With our gear loaded, Diane decides to stretch her legs and walk to the campsite entrance, leaving me to pootle over to the reception office on the bike to hand in the electronic gate barrier tag. Inside, the punk rockabilly smiles warmly and commences the checkout procedure. Suddenly his face changes, with furrowed brow. 'Weren't there two of you when you checked in?' asks he. I nod gravely. 'Do you think I've murdered her in the night?' I respond. The effect is like applying an electric shock. His face lights up and he lets out a huge guffaw. 'Yes! Yes! You've killed her, haven't you?' he cackles (a little too much like Gollum for my liking) then roars with laughter, almost bent double. 'Buried her in the woods in a nice shallow grave.' I respond. He has lost the power of speech.

Diane enters the office to be confronted with one bemused motorcyclist and one hysterical campsite receptionist who points up at her from his doubled contortion and squeaks, 'Oh, you're still alive!'

Before we take our leave of Denmark, there is one small mission to undertake. Roskilde is home to a world class attraction: the Viking Ship Museum. On display there are preserved examples of Viking longboats pulled up from their watery graves beneath the brackish waters of the Roskilde fjord, and that's enough to make a visit worthwhile. Not content at displaying the originals, the Danes have studied their history to the n'th degree and have started building replica ships with exactly the same tools that were available to the average shipwright in 900AD, or thereabouts; the results of their loving endeavour are objects of immense beauty. I defy anyone who stares upon one of these stunning vessels not to be moved by their graceful lines and the intoxicating aroma of wood, hemp and tar. The finest example of these is the largest built so far, a copy of one that is displayed inside the museum, an ocean-going vessel, built originally in that most Nordic of Viking cities – Dublin. The voyages that the Vikings undertook in their longboats were quite extraordinary – I noted when I rode to the northernmost part of Nova Scotia that they'd beaten me there by a thousand years and it's interesting to also note that they wandered far and wide down the rivers of Europe, ending up in many of the places that we hope to visit. All done pre- Garmin.

Chapter 4
To Tentipi or not to Tentipi

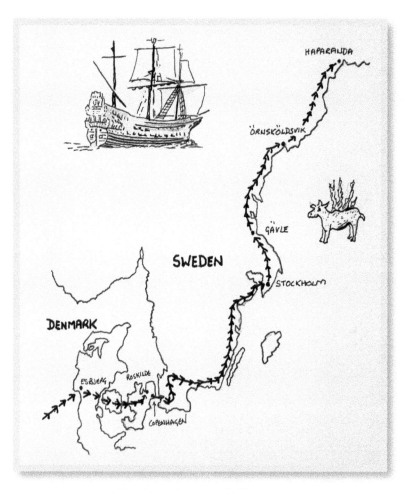

Northwards towards Finland.

One of my favourite possessions is Swedish. It nestles in my affections just below, in pecking order, my motorcycles and my Fender Telecaster electric guitar - which I play quite poorly. The object in question is a Tentipi.

There are many sizes of Tentipi. You can go and camp in the Arctic winter in one, lighting up your wood-burning stove that can be accommodated safely within – breaking every camping rule in the book. Alternatively, you can hire a mahoosive version of the same basic design and hold a hundred-person wedding reception inside its canvas cover, complete with central, hog roasting kitchen. But you can't fit one on a motorcycle and tour for five months. It would eat into all your space for clothing, food and tools. Which is a crying shame. A Tentipi is a perfect all-season home from home in my humble opinion.

It seems strange that, by simply passing over a bridge, we find ourselves in a land of unfamiliarity, in contrast to across the water where everything was vaguely familiar. Riding off the ferry into Esbjerg felt a bit like coming home again, whereas taking the awesome and magnificently splendid bridge-cum-tunnel that stretches its concrete muscle and steel sinew over the straights between Denmark and Sweden feels like entering a land far removed from our islands. In contrast to Denmark, it is immediately and noticeably sparse in its human population, yet vast in the local population of pine trees.

The Øresund bridge is a wonder of technological achievement, recently made famous by the fictitious discovery of a conjoined body at its exact centre in the Scandi Noir series, *The Bridge*. When we arrive at its exact centre, of bodies there are none. Instead, we find ourselves buffeted by very nasty side winds, causing the bike to wobble alarmingly, a reminder that we have too much top weight too far behind the natural centre of gravity of the bike. I chide myself that something *must* be done about our baggage mountain at our next overnight stop. The weight of a Tentipi would have crippled the whole going concern.

Garmy, our errant satnav device, has gone absent without leave. During the rushed run-up to departure, I purchased a map-set from the website and tried to download it. I was a bit miffed that my previous map-set, which is only two years old, wouldn't load from my computer to the device. It appeared to be loading but then, after spending hours transferring data, suddenly popped up a screen message on the device to the effect of: 'bugger off mate, this map set is out of date.' I was not amused. Various attempts at loading the new maps failed, apart from ones that spoke Russian. The result of this data transfer carnage is that, as soon as we arrive in Sweden, we end up hopelessly lost.

A quick stop at a petrol station presents an opportunity to buy a printed map - a rather cunningly designed one that folds perfectly whilst managing to present exactly the optimum regional information on each of its waterproof pages. What's more, it fits perfectly into the map holder on top of the tank bag. It manages to achieve so many things that no other map that I've had the pleasure of owning has ever done before. A glance reveals an error in my navigation immediately. In bypassing the town of Malmö, we've somehow missed the turn off for the road to Stockholm.

Fortunately, all is not lost. We don't have to turn around and start all over again because the map shows that there are quite a few back roads that work their way over to the road to the capital. All we have to do is turn left, no – sorry! – right, at the next opportunity.

It is a very beautiful summer's day. Sweden stretches out to both sides and ahead of us – a wide, flat, open landscape of neatly tended farmland interspersed with the odd conifer forest or two. The farms and houses are, by and large, immaculate. After riding for quite some considerable time, we are still just a few miles from the bridge, but by gradually working our way through and around the small villages and towns, we eventually meet the road to Stockholm; not the one we originally wanted, but hey-ho, beggars can't be choosers.

After riding on for an hour or so, an opportunity to stop for the night offers itself in the form of a road hostelry called *Bella's Place* at the small settlement of Bromölla. It's a bit early in the afternoon, but we decide to call it a day. We have a mission to accomplish: to root through our luggage and ditch as much of it as possible. As we teeter in around the corner, Bella's reveals itself to be a rather grand diner and motel complex, themed comprehensively on America circa 1955.

The staff in the restaurant speak a little less English than I'd expected, but we manage to ascertain that there are rooms aplenty and, within a few minutes, we're offloading our bags in what appears to be a virtually brand-new themed room, which honours a boxer from the fifties called Ingermar Johanssen, a Swedish ex-World Champion who I've never heard of before. His photos, which adorn the whole of one the wall opposite the bed, reveal a rather handsome chap with an impish smile, the possessor of a fearsome right punch from a fist, one of a pair that he nicknamed 'toonder and literning'. Given the evidence of the photos on the wall, he was quite a lady's man.

We commence the cull.

'Do you realise we have seven torches?' I enquire of my Navigator. We have seven torches but only one head torch, so one of us is going to struggle to read at night in the tent.

Meanwhile, outside the room, my super-rocket gas stove is happily burning away the excess gas that we've managed to cram into the panniers, increasing Sweden's greenhouse emissions quite significantly, but what else can I do? I'll have to plant some trees when I get back home. While the gas is depleting itself, I strike up a conversation with our neighbour from the adjacent cabin.

'You look like you're heading a long way,' he says, after apologising for the noise made by his grandchildren who are staying with him. I give him a summary of our plan to ride north to south through Russia and then try to make our way to Georgia. His eyebrows involuntarily raise themselves. 'You need to be careful in Russia,' he says. 'Russia isn't safe. It's full of gangsters and the government is bad. I don't like Putin. The roads are terrible. You will probably get robbed.'

The food in Bella's place is excellent fast-food fare. The whole place is an amusing insight into what Swedish people think Americana is, or should be, all about. And, honestly, they've done a terrific job. It reminds me of the set of Jack Rabbit Slim's, venue of the famous dance scene in 'Pulp Fiction'. The one where Travolta showed he could still dance a bit.

***

We depart Bella's at precisely the final checkout time of 11am, having offloaded our surplus gear onto a rather nonplussed waitress. I'm not sure what she'll make of the pot of Marmite we've presented to her.

The bike feels more controllable, no doubt about it. It is still heavy, but much more rideable and there is a reduced tendency to 'teeter' around tight corners with the steering now feeling as if it is actually connected to the front wheel again. The road passes through a wide, spacious country, past immaculate buildings with characteristic red and white painted barns.

One surprising feature is the lack of a decent dual carriageway to help push the pace along. The road is a mixture of single carriageway interspersed with regular stretches where one side is dualled and the other left as single carriageway, a feature that requires very careful drivers who finish their overtaking well before the carriageway returns to single. It's a design that would be downright lethal in Milton Keynes, England.

Very gradually, we pass into a more remote and slightly wilder country, with a lot more forestry apparent and, presumably, the occasional chance of sighting a moose or two. The Swedes have been very thoughtful regarding the matter of moose. They've erected wire fencing for the entire length of the road, apart from the odd gap, before which they've erected signs showing a moose crossing the road. How do the moose know not to turn left or right while crossing the road? Are they all fully signed-up members of the Tufty club? These are mysteries known only to Swedish road engineers. They should share their secret with the Canadians, because moose cause regular carnage in Canada. I once heard that a wayward moose made the dangerous crossing to Denmark, without using the bridge. The Danes apparently panicked completely, no doubt fearing similar carnage on their fine, well-laid roads. Only when the moose was eventually captured, did they allow their children out again. It tickled me pink but might not be true.

***

Over the next two days we ride on the same road, heading northwards just a few kilometres inland from the Baltic Sea, passing along a coastline that is rarely visible. The distance to Stockholm is well over 600 kilometres and the pace is slow. Our overnight stop at a small town called Gamleby is notable for two things. Firstly, the town is shut when we arrive, and secondly, its campsite is cunningly hidden behind a military camouflage manufacturing plant operated by SAAB. When we eventually manage to locate the site, we opt for a log cabin in an attempt to avoid the bloodsucking mosquitoes which quickly render our 'guaranteed to work' midge repellant completely useless.

The next day, after suffering numb-bum syndrome mile after mile on relatively deserted roads, the traffic density gradually increases and the road mans itself up on the outskirts of Stockholm as we pass a massive truck factory to our left. We're stopping off in the capital with a singular purpose: to visit the Vasa Ship Museum. I heard about it a few years ago from a magazine article. Apparently, it is a 17th Century warship that sank in the shallow waters of the Baltic and remained almost perfectly preserved until it was heaved up from the depths and moved into a museum.

Our fabulous concertina map states categorically that there is a campsite just a few miles ahead. Being a born skeptic, I'm finding this information a trifle rich. I mean what city worth its salt puts up with a campsite slap-bang near its cultural heart? Turns out the map is correct. We pass a sign for the site and hang a right, miss the next sign and then get lost in an area of nondescript housing.

***

Wednesday 4th July. Stockholm is a relatively large city and navigation is complicated somewhat by the geography of it, scattered as it is over a group of islands that once provided a strategically placed, fortified location, protecting the seaborne entrance to the hinterland of early Sweden. Being of such significance, the city grew in its importance to the point nowadays where almost a quarter of all Swedes live within its metropolitan boundaries. This explains why there are very few of them scattered around the rest of what is quite a large country – ranked 55th in the world by area. So far, we have barely met or spoken to any Swedes. It's like someone has turned the sign on the door to 'closed'. Last night, we ventured into the city centre in a bid to familiarise ourselves with the lay of the land. The road we were following terminated at the waterfront and, having parked the Mutt up, we wandered over a small bridge to a beautiful white, fully-rigged steel sailing ship called the AF Chapman. It was built in Whitehaven, Cumberland in 1888 and now serves as a youth hostel, with an open café. Here, we sipped tea and propped our feet up for a wee while. A relaxing end to a busy day's riding.

Today, we are hunting down the Vasa. We've decided to pack the bike and ride to the museum, trusting that it will be safe to park the ensemble in public. Then, after visiting the museum, we'll seek an exit from the city to the north. Having carefully laid an imaginary bread crumb trail along our route last night, navigation into the city goes surprisingly smoothly, way beyond my usual standard of lostishness.

We thread our way through busy shopping streets thronged with sharply-dressed young city workers and tourists, past a pleasant quayside alongside which many boats of various vintages are tied up. Then we hang a right to the place where the museum hides. Unfortunately, I spot the entrance to the car park too late and need to execute a prompt 'U' turn. Doing so nearly results in the end of the trip – something that Diane is totally unaware of, as it happens.

Having negotiated the 'U' turn and headed back the way, I wait at a junction for the traffic travelling in the opposite direction to subside. Momentarily, I get confused by the direction of traffic. Sweden once drove on the left, just like the UK. But they decided to switch to the 'wrong' side and carried out the change on the 3rd September 1967. Momentarily confused, as I'm sure many Swedes were in 1967, I fail to check to my left. Then, perhaps following the years of being taught to 'look both ways before proceeding', I happen to glance to the left as I start to feed the clutch out. That moment of hesitation gains a fraction of a second for the tram that has been silently approaching at a fair old rate of knots to whistle past my nose giving me a heart stopping shock. I instantly feel guilty. It felt almost as if someone 'up there' nudged me and made me glance to the left. Without a doubt, had I not done so, one, or both of us would now be squished.

This is a lesson. Riding for months in foreign countries carries many unknown risks – the anticipated road conditions not the least of them – so I really need to concentrate on honing every possible riding skill and not become lazy or overconfident. I'm still chiding myself as we locate a parking spot, keeping the bike upright to allow Diane to climb off before leaning it onto its side stand and hopping off myself. It turns out she was completely unaware of how close she was to becoming flat.

From the outside, the Vasa ship museum is a little faded. Repair work is being carried out to the structure adding to the feeling that it isn't quite at the top of its game. When we eventually manage to find our way the long way round (no pun intended) to the front door, we find a considerable queue. If I wasn't so keen to see what's inside, I would probably at this point decide to call it a day, return to the bike and head off to our next destination somewhere to the north. But this is something on the bucket list. My navigator, meanwhile, has no real inkling of what we're about to see and is forced to put up with the queue with her normal patience and good humour.

By the time we reach the doors, I can't wait and am very eager to part with my hard-earned dosh and get inside. I'm like a four-year-old waiting for the pantomime to begin. Inside it is vast, dark, and hushed. A beautiful deep scent of ancient wood mixed with a smidgen of je ne sais quois pervades the hall as eyes adjust to take in what is simply an astonishing sight. The hairs on the back of my neck tingle and stand on end, sending shivers down my back. Shiver my timbers!

The Vasa, Stockholm

Built between 1626 and 1628, around the time when Charles 1st took the throne of England, the Vasa is an amazing artifact, not least due to its condition, which is virtually perfect, but also because it is so beautifully crafted. I've never seen anything like it before in my life. Sad to learn, therefore, that this wonderful ship managed to sail but a few hundred yards on its maiden voyage before heeling over and dragging many of its crew to their death in the cold waters of Stockholm harbour. The Swedish King wanted to know who was responsible and very few (if any) were man enough to point the finger at his majesty himself. Instead, they floundered around looking for someone else to take the blame.

Beautifully crafted the ship may be, but hydro-dynamically effective is another matter completely. At the time, the Dutch were the foremost shipbuilders in Europe. They'd perfected a method of building warships that allowed them to propel them down the slipway far quicker than their main rivals, the English, and were taking rude delight in regularly whupping the Royal Navy's ass. So, it's hardly surprising that the Swedes turned to the Dutch to help them design what they hoped would be the most powerful warship of its day.

Unfortunately for the Swedes, the Dutch were very adept at designing ships that could navigate shallow waters, whereas the Swedes wanted something impressive to cow the enemy into rapid submission. The resulting vessel had suitably imposing, high decks, and not much below the water line – perfectly good when tied securely to a jetty, but almost guaranteed to make like a performing porpoise at the first gust of wind on open waters and, especially so, if it hadn't been properly filled with ballast.

The first sign of a slight breeze on departure caused the vessel to heel over alarmingly right in front of the huge crowd that had gathered to watch it sail. The ship righted itself before being caught by a second gust that delivered the coup-de-grace. Many sailors in those days couldn't swim. Others were trapped below as the water rushed in through the open lower gun ports or were crushed by objects like gun carriages breaking free. In all, around thirty people lost their lives from a crew of around a hundred and forty. The museum has some of the skeletons of these unfortunates on display and have skillfully reconstructed the faces of some of them, including two women, thought to have been sailing for a short distance down river before being put ashore.

The reconstruction of the human wreckage is haunting, so realistic are they, and so cleverly exhibited. If you turn around in the darkened display room, they almost look as if they're about to speak to you. The building that houses this treasure, derided somewhat by me on my trip around the outside of it, is very well designed inside with lots of different floors that allow you to view the ship very closely at different deck levels. A wide range of artifacts from the wreck are displayed in different rooms on each level. A sheave from a block sits in one display case next to one that has been cleaned. It has just been lightly brushed but looks brand-new – and beautifully made. Another treasure is mounted on a wall – one of the main sails, threadbare and gossamer with age, but it's a miracle really that we can look upon it at all, having survived over 350 years beneath the waves.

The wooden fabric of the Vasa has been preserved by the injection of polyethylene glycol, which I think probably adds to the intoxicating smell of the whole ship. There are rumours that all is not well in this method of preservation – we can only hope that this is unfounded and that generations in future will be able to stare in awe, as we both do while we wander around it. It is, quite simply, a treasure from the deep, not just in Swedish, but also global terms. If you get a chance to see it, don't hesitate to do so.

***

Breaking free of Stockholm turns out to be the simplest of tasks. The road north is well signposted and the traffic system works too. The road we're following, the E20, heads in a north-north-westerly direction, avoiding a bulge of land that sticks out into the Baltic Sea. It's only when you peruse the map that you realise that Stockholm is quite far south, which means we have many miles to cover to reach the border with Finland. The distance from Malmo to the Finnish border is just over a thousand miles, the same distance as London to Naples. We cast our way northwards across wide, flat farming countryside under a blue-dome sky, dotted with the odd white cloud.

Despite the distances to be covered, it will be a short leg today. Our sights are firmly fixed on the city of Gävle, which constitutes a hundred-mile hop. Arriving at our destination, we bear right and cruise into town, past green parks and modern low-rise apartment blocks, then along slightly worn streets lined by modern shops and offices laid out in a grid pattern. Diane is on hotel watch. It doesn't take too long to spot one, a plain building dressed in pink and grey concrete, sitting opposite a slab-faced concrete car park. Gävle, it would seem, is a refreshingly 'normal' city – a place that holds few pretentions. I like it already.

It is famously known as the city of the goat. I kid you not. Every year they make a huge straw goat around Christmas time. Every year some arsonist or other attempts to, and apparently often succeeds in, burning down Billy. This points to a long history of resident pyromaniacs, because the city has burnt itself to the ground on a regular basis throughout its history, something that explains the wide grid pattern that its streets have more recently adopted in an attempt to just stop burning down.

***

The task of loading the bike in the morning is complicated by the need to remove it from the car park opposite the hotel, where it was left last night. When I proffer the ticket to the machine it speaks Swedish to me and then proceeds to eat the ticket! I stand for a good minute, gobsmacked, before noticing an intercom button and press it with little hope of anyone responding. Sure enough, there is the sound of a phone ringing in some unoccupied office somewhere in the belly of the adjoining shopping mall.

I let it ring for a couple of minutes. A guy approaches with a ticket for his Volvo and says something to me in Swedish. 'The machine has eaten my ticket', I reply. 'Oh, well they will answer.' he replies nonchalantly before tactically withdrawing to a different machine. I wait for a few more minutes and am close to deciding to tramp off and start looking for someone, when the line clicks and a voice says something in Swedish. 'The machine has taken my ticket', I shout into the microphone. There is a confused pause, then a reply - 'Someone will come.' For my troubles, I receive a free ride out, which almost makes the hassle worthwhile.

Arriving at a small lay-by outside the hotel, I find that a huge coach has squeezed itself into the available space, leaving just enough room to shoehorn the Mutt behind it. I ferry the two hard pannier cases down first – a task that must surely extend my arms an inch or two closer to ape-dom. As I wrestle with fitting them to the bike, a guy appears alongside, lights a fag, and asks me in English where we are heading. When I reply that we're on our way to Finland and then on to Russia, he puffs his chest out and replies with some pride, telling me that he's Finnish. 'I've lived in Sweden so long that people think I'm Swedish, but I'm not, I'm Finnish. I drive this tour coach for the band,' he says nodding towards a group of long haired, Bohemian Russell Brand types who have gathered outside the hotel, commenting further that they are 'very famous' in Scandinavia and the former Soviet Balkan states. Have Abba reformed? Are the two blokes still pug ugly?

'You'll like Finland', he states emphatically. 'We're far more friendly than the Swedes. They won't let me park my bus close to the hotel', he continues with a look of disgust. 'I ignore them and park where I want, pretend I don't understand all their stupid rules – we'll be gone today, heading on the ferry for a gig in Estonia'.

I reflect on this. The Swedes do seem to have been vaguely remote and stand-offish so far. This is completely at odds with my experience of Swedes who I've met through work. They have always been quite humorous and charming. Maybe we've just come at a bad time! The bus driver explains to me that he needs to warm the engine up. 'You can't drive these things away immediately – got to let the oil work its way around the engine. But there'll be a lot of smoke from the exhaust and you're gonna get choked by it, so I'll wait a few minutes to let you get packed and out of the way', he explains helpfully, as he lights up a fresh fag, opens up the back of the engine bay and proceeds to check the fluids. 'That lot expect me to get off on time', he nods towards the Bohemians, 'But they can wait for a minute or two.'

'It's going to take a lot longer than a minute to load this baby!' I think, ruefully, heading back up for the next load of baggage.

***

Out on the highway, we notice a lot more motorcycles heading in the opposite direction, a significant percentage of which are of the 'adventure' genre of bikes like the one we are riding. Their riders extend a downward pointed finger, the continental version of biker's greeting each other on the open road. I wonder if there's been some kind of meeting up ahead? We're heading into much wilder territory, with fewer settlements, deep forests and the appearance of exotic-looking insects splattering themselves onto the bike's screen. We scan the forests for moose sightings, but fail to spot any of the enigmatic and retiring beasts.

After the excesses and relative comfort staying in a hotel last night – and the part excess of hiring a cabin a couple of nights before, we decided on this afternoon's leg that we really ought to be looking to pitch the tent tonight – and as many nights as possible thereafter. Once we arrive in Russia, we expect official camping opportunities to dry up. Around 4pm we spot a likely looking sign.

Forty minutes later finds us with the tent erected, the bedding unpacked and unraveled, and a nice bottle of red open and breathing in our plastic cups. The site is situated in the village of Överhörnäs, population of around 600 souls, situated alongside a gorgeous stretch of typically deep blue water, close to the larger city of Örnsköldsvik, which translates roughly to 'Cold Eagle Bay'. It seems to be a place almost lost in time.

I'm pleased to say that our campsite routine is falling into place. On arrival, it is my job to approach the booking office and try to make myself understood, whilst Diane remains by the bike so as not to scare the natives. At this particular campsite, the person attending the office was a very cheerful young lady who spoke almost perfect English and made us feel very welcome. Once we'd paid our dues and found our pitch – 'camp anywhere' being the options today, we set about pitching our tent. Diane is very particular about the spacing of the pegs around the doors. I'm less so and let her complete the initial theodolite survey and placement in peace. The result: a zip that whisks around the door opening as if lubricated by the finest light oil found in Christendom. After that she moves into the tent, unpacks everything and sets up the bedroom compartment with inch-perfect precision while I play 'Kumbaya' with my little Trangia stove, methylated spirits and matches. It's like firing up a Mamod toy steam engine but, perchance, not quite so satisfying since it lacks a miniature whistle. Such is the joy of camping.

In a search for victuals earlier on, we rode into the little town that nestles amongst the trees across the water, built mostly of pleasant wee houses with broad shallow-pitched roofs, the town possesses a small supermarket with an expensive wine selection. Heading back on the return journey, I inadvertently missed the entrance to the camp site, turning instead with a false flourish into the gravel drive of one of the prim, well-kept bungalows that are scattered hereabouts – much to the bemusement of the owner who, was just taking his lawn mower out of the garage. There, we were stuck. The bike had buried itself into the gravel, nose first, and it took hell 'n all to get it turned around and vacate the poor fella's property. Rather than assist us, the owner just stood in front of his garage with his hands on his hips.

Back at the campsite, as the evening settles over the lake that laps the edges of the camp site, we find ourselves finally being accepted and acknowledged. The various caravan and motorhome owners give a little nod or wave as we pass by, to and from the shower block, almost imperceptible, but welcome nonetheless. I feel like I could spend more time here, despite the population of mosquitoes who are a gentler breed than their Canadian cousins, but still partial to the odd nip. It would be great to be able to explore more – maybe head inland towards Norway – but we can't. We're a full-on day's ride from the Finnish border and that's where we are heading. The rock band bus driver this morning asked me whether I was heading to Lapland. 'It's not far out of your way,' he commented, 'maybe sixty of your miles the road you will take to reach the Arctic Circle. Turn left should you,' he declared in Yoda speech. 'See Santa's worker elves and find there endless daylight will you.'

My ears pricked up big time and I've quietly been studying the map ever since.

**

There's no doubt about it, the nights are getting perceptibly shorter as we travel northwards. Waving goodbye to the nice lass in reception, we head off, in good order, into a land that is slipping further and further towards a feeling of wilderness, reminding me of the incredible beauty of the ride in 2009 around the northern fringe of Lake Superior.

Once topped up, the tank on the bike allows a whole day's riding, and we've become accustomed to putting in long shifts in the saddle, rarely stopping for a break. We pass houses that are noticeably more modest than those down south. It leads me to wonder if the wealth here is really and truly as evenly distributed as we are led to believe.

Around midday, we find a small service area with a fuel station and a restaurant across the road. It's baking hot, something of a surprise this far north. Fittingly, the restaurant has a Mediterranean theme with an outdoor 'al fresco' dining area. Two nights ago, we were received quite royally by the Turkish proprietors of the late-night kebab café we popped into and this is the same. It's nice to take a break, but I find myself itching to get back on the bike. There's something addictive about long-distance motorcycling that captures you and won't let you go, despite the discomforts. For a pillion I suspect it isn't the same, missing the engagement with the machine – and I have to say that, on four wheels, I feel none of it. Despite my itchy feet, Diane needs time to rest and recuperate, so we take a leisurely break.

Our first waypoint today is the small city of Umeå, a centre of education originally settled by the Sami people, the indigenous population of Northern Scandinavia. The modest uplands of this northeastern part of the country reveal themselves occasionally on the horizon, but, by and large, the area is quite flat and typically farmland or forest - increasingly forest. There are also many small lakes, presumably left over when the glaciers of the Ice Age retreated. They all squiggle like little tadpoles in a northwesterly direction, pointing in the direction from whence, I suspect, they came.

Our day's journey is the longest of the trip so far, as we push determinedly for the Finnish border. The intention is to look for a hotel on the Swedish side then plunge into Finland first thing in the morning. Major settlements are few and far between. In the late afternoon, we pass through the largest one for a while, a town called Skellefteå. It's a modern town, with a relatively modest population (around 32,000) and famous for a few things of note: it has a gold mine – well kind of – the main ore is actually copper. Home for a pretty decent ice hockey team, it is also the source of one of the world's oldest pair of skis which are over 5,000 years old, a fact that I don't recall David Vine ever mentioning.

Skellefteå isn't notable for its architecture though, at least not as far as we can see riding through. It has a typically boxy feel. Functional, clean and not very inspiring. This, of course, is only a mite ironic coming from a resident of Milton Keynes, the home of concrete cows.

***

The adjectives modern, functional and boxy can't be applied to the Stadt hotel, our overnight hostel in the delightfully named town of Haparanda, which nestles right on the border of Sweden and Finland. If the hotel literature is to be believed, it was once *the* most exciting place to be in Europe – bizarrely claiming to have been the only point of contact (in espionage terms) between Europe, Russia, Persia and China, populated by spies and anarchists. I have difficulty digesting this claim. How and why did Persia and China manage to get involved?

Before I mock too strongly though, it is interesting to note that this town and neighbouring Tornio are where Lenin and his entourage of self-imposed exiles crossed the border into the Russian Empire during the February revolution, so they really do have a place in history here. I'm not sure if he stayed at the hotel – I guess they would know if he did and would advertise the fact. Then again, for a while he shaved off his beard and went around in disguise. That might have fooled everyone, including the reception staff of the Stadt.

Despite being slightly faded, the hotel has quite a grand old feel to it, with a wide sweeping staircase and a stunningly beautiful, wood-paneled function room on the first floor, lit by wonderful crystal glass lamps. We sneak in there and have a nosey-around, feeling slightly surreptitious. It really is very special, dating from the turn of the twentieth century and providing a hint of the early grandeur that was most likely appreciated by your average run-of-the-mill anarchist or revolutionary. Most of them came from wealthy families after all, not least Lenin himself.

Such desperados are quite hard to find in the bar nowadays. Following a meal out on the sun terrace, we repair there to discover quite a lively scene – populated by a significant proportion of the town's youth. The barmaid strikes up a conversation with us, asking what we think of Haparanda and Sweden, in general. In reply, I enthuse about Stockholm and our visit to see the Vasa – for me a high point of the past few days. 'I don't like Stockholm,' she says, surprising us a little and reminding me of the robot in *Hitchhiker's Guide to the Galaxy* who doesn't like oceans. 'We are poorer up here and those who live in the south don't care about us. We're a lot more friendly up here. I found Stockholm to be a very unfriendly place when I lived there.' It turns out that this typically blonde 'Swede' is actually of Finnish parentage but has lived in Haparanda for most of her life. So, very strangely, we have largely passed through a huge country and have managed to strike up conversations with hardly any of its inhabitants. We have tended (perhaps by accident) to meet Finns – all of whom end their conversation with 'you'll really like Finland, we're all very friendly!' Since this is our next stop, much like the television weatherman Michael Fish opining to a worried lady that the Great Storm of '87 'wouldn't be too bad', I take this to be a most positive forecast.

Chapter 5
Stir-Fried Rudolph

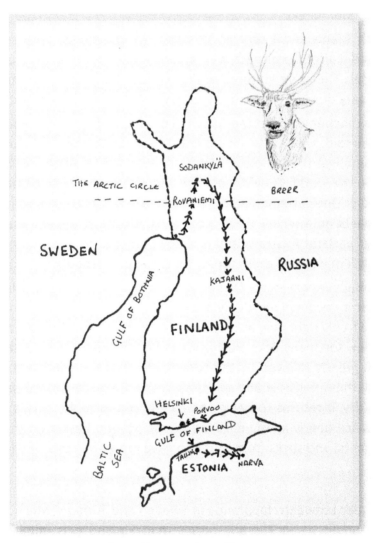

From Haparanda to Narva.

In the eighteen months prior to our departure, we spent a considerable amount of effort researching how to reduce our clothing pile for the trip. This involved visiting outdoor pursuit emporiums and discussing the merits of various types of clothing with hirsute young salesmen. These cheerful, ruddy-cheeked souls all gravitated towards the wonders of one product above all others: Merino wool. Underclothes fashioned from Merino wool, they declared, can be worn 'for weeks' without smelling; and by that, I think they meant 'for a period greater than or equal to four weeks'.

Both Diane and I took in this gem of knowledge with a thinly disguised, curled-lip disgust, as if a rancid ram had been placed under our noses. The more cultured of the outdoor types also admitted that it was 'very quick drying and can probably be washed overnight'.

The clincher was that Merino wool has the ability to keep you warm when it's cold, and cool when it is hot. The sheep that wear and produce it are amongst the happiest, comfiest, sweetest smelling and filthiest sheep in the world. They dry out the very instant they climb out of the sheep dip. One salesman admitted that he'd only taken a single pair of underpants on a recent three-week long adventure expedition to the remoter parts of Australia and had not bothered to wash them once. 'Actually, I'm wearing them today,' he exclaimed proudly.

I remain unconvinced. Diane swears by her Merino gear, whereas I find that it becomes decidedly prickly when I perspire – and I'm doing so quite freely right now as we depart the Hotel Stadt. I feel like a sheep with a few too many ticks. Having loaded up the bike and paid the hotel bill, I'm greatly relieved by the cooling effect of the wind as it passes through the riding gear and spirits away the discomfort. Once the wool shirt is dry, it returns to being completely comfortable. This is a good thing, since nearly all my eggs are in one Merino basket on the shirt, underpants, and socks front. But I do have more than one of each.

***

The border between Haparanda in Sweden and Tornio – which sounds like it should be in Tuscany rather than Finland – is initially a bit nondescript. Our first mission is to find a petrol station and top Mutley up with fuel. We very quickly spot one on the roadside. It turns out to be fully automated. Diane hops off the bike as we wait in a small queue to get to the pumps. When we do get there, we find that not one of our credit/debit cards works. Arriving in Finland has revived memories of the financial meltdown that hit me in Canada in 2009!

A lady from one of the cars approaches.

'Are you having difficulties?' she asks in very passable English. When I explain that my card isn't working, she tells me it's quite a common problem. 'You could try down at the gas station over there,' she says pointing over to a garage that was previously hidden from view amongst the small forest of young trees. 'Or you could try your card in the bank over there if you need cash.' All very helpful – within a few minutes, we are topped to the brim with fuel and our wallets are stashed with spare spondoolies. A few miles further on, we locate a left turn onto the E75 that heads northwards towards the Arctic Circle, courtesy of a map bought at the garage.

I'm jingling like an over-stuffed piggy bank. Denmark and Sweden both have their own currencies, in Denmark the Krone and in Sweden the Krona. Demark has its currency pegged to the Euro, whereas the Swedish Krona is a free-floating currency. It goes wherever it likes in a most airy-fairy manner. Finland, on the other hand, is fully signed up to the Euro. The result of all this Scandinavian monetary mayhem is that we have lots of loose, useless change in our pocket. For a trans-European traveller the Euro makes a lot of sense. For the unfortunate Greeks, right now, it makes no sense at all.

***

It comes as quite a surprise that Finland initially feels different to Sweden. My impression is that the roads aren't quite so well maintained and the general feel is a bit less sterile. Quite quickly, the land opens up to broader fields – many with a strange little wooden hut in them, some built with angular walls and quite steeply sloping roofs, presumably to safeguard against heavy snowfalls. This openness only lasts for a while though, and soon the road we are following starts to pass through millions of slender young birches that line either side, with their white trunks gleaming ghost-like in contrast to the darker, taller conifers.

The horizon ahead reveals a dark leaden bank of clouds that are far too well-developed for my liking, no doubt foreboding heavy rain, if not a thunderstorm. It's time to break out the wet weather gear, prompting a roadside stop at a conveniently placed bus stop that sits in a tiny settlement of low-lying, single-storey houses. As soon as I remove my helmet, I feel a mosquito nip.

Having both taken one of our boots off to thread on the first leg of the over suits, teetering close to a fall, then taken the other one off after placing the now wrapped one back in the other boot, we are rain-protected to waist height. The fairer of the two of us then has an enormous wrestle to complete the task of wriggling the suit over her shoulders and then doing up the zip. In fact, she can't do the zip up without external assistance, resulting in me almost lifting her off the ground with each upward tug. It's another case of bad preparation. We bought a lot of new gear and failed to test all the possible combinations. Diane's rain suit doesn't fit over her BMW 'Charlie' suit. On the plus side, mine fits quite well, and I do feel quite smug about that detail point.

***

If Diane's suit had been any tighter, we'd have needed the sort of crane used to lower Henry the Eighth onto his charger to get her back on the pillion. But, thankfully, we did manage to get her weather-protected because, a few miles down the road, we hit first a bit of light rain, followed by a torrential downpour. This starts to ease off a little as we arrive at the first sizeable town since Tornio - the town of Rovaniemi. I shout back to Diane that it might be worth stopping for a meal – a bit early in the day perhaps, but there aren't any major towns on the map for quite a few miles.

Since crossing the border, we've entered the region of Lapland, the northernmost part of Finland. Rovaniemi is the capital of Lapland, and as such is considered to be a city, with a municipal population of just over 60,000. The part of the city we ride into has a drab feel to it – the rain may not be helping. Twenty-two thousand miles of travel on my own little world tour has taught me that very few people live in gloriously splendid surroundings. Most of us live in 'normal' towns, villages and cities. You make the best of what you've got, and this is the best there is for the people of Rovan... Rovanienemeri. I'm sober and I can't pronounce it or spell it.

As we park the bike next to a row of shops, people are dashing by to get out of the rain. We clump through a pedestrian-only street that reminds me of Gillingham shopping centre. Despite the rain, a group of men are sitting outside a bar, drunk, loud, and possibly offensive. I think they may be expressing the view that our mothers have dressed us funny, but since we can't understand them, we just ignore them. A little further on, still in shouting range, we see a Chinese restaurant and take a peek in through the window before ducking inside. The interior is quite dark, with a bar at the far end and a large, impressively stocked fish tank complete with nervous-looking fish. The carved cork dioramas and (hopefully) fake ivory figurines behind the bar are singularly impressive.

Whilst we peruse the menu a couple of young girls arrive and sit themselves nearby, chattering in animated fashion as if they haven't seen each other for a while. I'm guessing that they are in whole or part Sami, that is to say native Lapps, since they aren't blonde or at all Scandinavian looking. Fittingly, the menu also has a local twist: stir-fried reindeer! That must be some size of wok they're wielding back there beyond the bead screen! I find the reindeer option to be too tempting and decide to 'go for it'. Diane sticks to tradition with a nice beef chow mein.

Rudolph is served in strips of meat with an intensely rich sauce that is almost overpowering and certainly wasn't derived from reindeer stock cubes. He is also pretty tough and chewy. Monika on Masterchef would not be impressed. Beef would probably have been a better option. From now on the reindeer hereabouts are totally safe, as far as I'm concerned – unless I find myself starving above the Arctic Circle and the only other option is to eat the pillion passenger.

***

Quite by surprise, about ten miles north of Rovaniemi, we meet a series of signs advising us that we have arrived at the home of Santa Claus.

Unfortunately for Santa, his place of abode turns out to be a cross between the Pleasurewood Hills theme park at Lowestoft and Notcutts Garden Centre Christmas grotto in Norwich. Conveniently, Shell, the oil giant, has placed a petrol station opposite Santa's front gate - just in case the reindeer are a bit winded come the 26th of December and he feels the need to get his 4x4 out of the garage.

I'm quite at a loss to understand why someone so secretive as Santa, a man who sneaks down chimneys for goodness' sake, would want to advertise both his homely abode and his elf-staffed workshop in this fashion. We decide to give the old boy a miss and press on. Having done so we are rewarded by further sign-posting that tells us we have crossed the Arctic Circle. Hooray! Beyond this point, the road heads across an increasingly remote vista, occasionally enlivened by the odd lake and tiny settlement. The land is very slightly undulating, but not enough to see far beyond the millions of trees that line the road and march into the distance. I wouldn't go so far as to describe the view as scenic but, in European terms, this is a big, wild country.

We are heading towards a town called Sodankyla – another unforgiving tongue-teaser. I traced it on the map last night and noted that it sits comfortably north of the Arctic Circle, about thirty miles or so at a guess, and is also well on the way to the very northernmost tip of Europe. But, most importantly, it also sits at the junction of another road that cuts east and then runs south, threading its way via various towns and linking roads right the way to Helsinki. That will be our route for tomorrow. We are heading inexorably towards our date with the Russian border.

✳✳✳

The town of Sodankyla is pleasant enough. It comprises houses that are typical of the area, mostly single storey with wide shallow roofs, set in wooded surrounds. In fact, the whole town feels like it 'lives within the forest'. The Finnish, Swedish and Norwegian armies train their soldiers in arctic warfare here. I guess they must be twiddling their thumbs a bit right now. There's a fairly large hotel here too, but we're a lot more interested in following the signs for a campground, which sits towards the edge of town alongside the river, just left of midge valley.

We alight the Mutt and approach the site office, past a rustic and slightly decrepit sign made up of white painted logs arranged in an 'A' frame, to take our place in a queue behind two other bikers from Switzerland. 'Are you riding the Nordcap?' the taller of the two asks me, whilst signing papers and showing passports. I have absolutely no idea what he's on about, quite a common problem when conversing with the Swiss, I find, so I respond with, 'Nope, we're riding to Helsinki,' hoping this is not a stupid retort. It causes a slightly confused, befuddled look. The mosquito assault commences.

The Swiss riders have booked a cabin, something that very quickly reveals itself to be a damn fine choice. By the time we arrive at the tent pitching area, we are somewhat distressed by the howling storm of vexatious little bloodsuckers pursuing us. And we haven't even started to pitch our tent yet. Fortunately, I have come prepared. The misery of the assault that took place on the moose hunting mission in Maine during the American stage of the expedition has left an indelible mark (well, around three hundred single mosquito bite marks at the time, to be precise). We have, neatly stashed in our top box, close to hand, our own individual mosquito head nets, which are donned along with brimmed hats, seconds after our helmets are removed. Repellent bought in Western Scotland, carrying a cast iron guarantee that it will put paid to any biting beastie's attention, is slapped over hands, necks and anywhere else that springs to mind, and, with that, we are ready for a short sharp spell of tent erection. Diane is quickly out with the theodolite.

A pair of Brit wusses.

47

I do have to admit that we must look like a pair of complete plonkers. I'm faintly aware that some of the seasoned Scandinavian die-hards are looking over, shaking their heads and muttering under their breath, 'must be a pair of Brits'. I don't care. Let 'em laugh. Shortly after completing the tent erection, we are joined by new neighbours in the shape of a very plucky young French couple on cycles, who would like to put up their micro-tent but are being attacked mercilessly by their own personal swarm. I pop over and lend them our Scottish repellent, which is gratefully received. They're not getting the head nets. Sorry. Entente cordiale runs to midge repellent and no further.

***

After doing our bit for European relations, our quest for food takes us into the town centre where we find that a fast food outlet (possibly the only one for a hundred miles) has just closed and is being vacated by the local town youths. I wonder what life is like for youngsters hereabouts? This lot look bored silly, it has to be said. Maybe things improve when the first snows fall and the skidoos can come out of the shed.

Diane spots that the joint is selling a variety of insect repellence products. After a short debate, we settle for a strange, square, green, asbestos looking coiled wick device that gets her vote, with mutterings of 'having used one of these in Aviemore', and a good old standard can of fly spray. My money's on the can of spray. The wick on the green coil has to be lit and then smolders – never a good idea in a tent one would think, but desperation brings forth many an iffy solution and anything that kills, maims or sternly deters tent entry in the mosquito department gets my seal of approval.

On arrival back at base camp, still starving, Diane sets about lighting up the 'coils of fear and loathing', while I give the whole interior a good old blast from the can. Before she manages to light the second coil, a veritable rain of exoskeletal flying objects relinquish their grip on the tent nylon and plunge to the trampled grass to commence their bizzy-buzzing death throes. I've said before that I don't like killing things, even insects, but this is war!

Diane's method transpires to be far gentler and kinder than mine. It involves making a stink in the tent, not unlike a ganja den. Mosquitoes are clearly upstanding citizens of the insect world and are repelled by clouds of 'Red Leb', opting not to enter the den of iniquity, preferring to head off and find some French blood instead. Having thus kippered our tent, it will no doubt attract the attention of sniffer dogs at border checkpoints and ferry ports from here to Georgia and we will likely be detained for questioning. Visions of snapping white rubber gloves haunt the smoky atmosphere.

Quite without realising it, we have entered the land of endless summer daylight, just a few days or so after the summer solstice occurred. Having spent a couple of hours in the camp bar, quaffing the local Lapin Kulta Export lager (which is quite nice), playing darts and pool and gorging on salted peanuts to stave off starvation, we return to the stinking pit called our tent at kicking-out time. It is perfectly light and could be almost midday. The tent is relatively midge-free and completely so in the mesh-protected inner sleeping kaboosh. I can't adequately describe how much of a relief that single fact is.

***

The morning doesn't dawn. That's the problem with endless days. And residents will have to contend with endless nights surprisingly soon. Tent packed, we bid farewell to the voracious midges and get the hell out of town, heading south. Our road is long and gently undulating as it winds its way through youthful forests, swaying pastures and the occasional settlement. The oft ruddy houses have wooden walls and felt roofs. They sit in sizeable plots, mostly laid to rich, green lawns – fed by the plentiful rain and mowed not too caringly. The verges grow high with grass and wild flowers, including millions of dandelions that have only just turned to feathery orbs. They scatter their winged seeds in the sigh of disturbed air we leave in our wake. Before long, we find ourselves passing deep through the forests and arrive at an impressive sign marking the Arctic Circle. It's constructed from three logs arranged almost like a tepee frame with a circle enveloping it, the circle faintly reminiscent of 'The One Ring' – except I'm fairly sure the script that adorns it only makes passing reference to 'and in the darkness bind them', because right now Lapland is devoid of darkness.

The Finnish coach driver in Gävle, back south a few days ago, told me that we will find a line drawn on the road at such crossing points and that the local men have a pleasant custom of urinating on both sides of the line. I suspect this was a wind-up, in the hope that the strangely dressed Brit would, in due course, reveal himself to a coach load of retiree blue-rinse tourists, hose down the road and get arrested for indecent exposure and urinating in public. As we depart, I lean back and shout to Diane airing my disappointment at the paucity of reindeer in this neck of the woods, and Finland in general. The only one I've seen, so far, found itself swimming in black bean sauce.

Blow me down if we don't swing gently around the next corner to be met by a solitary, scrawny, moth-eaten individual wandering cautiously up the other side of the road. As we approach and pass him, he vacates the road for the safety of the verge, then (in the mirrors) retakes the highway. The only thing his mother didn't teach him well, was that he should walk on the side of the road that faces the direction of traffic, a small detail in an otherwise impeccable road safety performance. We soon pass many more of these gentle animals, all of whom appear unafraid of the traffic and either take charge of the road or shelter amongst the trees on the roadside. They look a bit raggedy – very obviously still losing their winter coats. And the antlers of the finer males of the species are clearly quite itchy too because they spend a lot of time rubbing them on the nearest useful scratching object. We decide not to park up in their immediate vicinity.

I was advised by my friend the coach driver, that veritable mine of useful information, to be very careful out here. 'The reindeer like standing in the road because the traffic blows the mosquitoes away,' he advised. They have my sympathy. A bit later in the tale we're going to meet the world champion of this horse fly-ridding technique.

We pass many motorhomes, of varying ages and states of repair, one amusingly being led up the road by its own little posse of reindeer, resembling a large white Santa's sleigh. As the reindeer/motorhome convoy approaches (at a steady two miles per hour) we slow down. A juvenile reindeer, who obviously hasn't fully learned the rules, breaks away and crosses over to the forest on our side, attracted by some juicy morsel in the verge, causing a ripple of consternation in the remaining family whole. While the rest of them proceed to make their way up the road to a forest trail over to our left, father reindeer goes over the road, picks up the reluctant youth and guides him back over. And there they all patiently wait, allowing the traffic to pass, with the occasional flick of the head to ward off the biting insects, before heading back to the relative comfort of the highway. I now feel particularly bad for having eaten one of them.

***

Motorhomes are extremely popular hereabouts and many motorcycles are in evidence today too, short summer refugees enjoying our splendid pastime. Around midday, we pull into a petrol station, joining a group of other bikers. A lady pillion wanders over and chats with us about our bike. Her husband currently rides a Honda Blackbird but is considering trading his bike in against one like ours. She also mentions the Nordcap and asks us if we visited there, explaining (when questioned) that it is the most northerly navigable point in Europe sitting at the confluence of Norway, Finland and Russia. Every year, people flock there to witness the Solstice, including many motorcyclists. This information provides a small moment of epiphany, explaining the flow of bikers heading south when we rode through Sweden, doubtless returning from the solstice festival, something that probably involved the use of ritualistic pagan devices and naked maidens. I usually end up arriving a day late for such events.

The towns we occasionally pass through, are low-rise, modern places with the occasional factory or retail outlet, visible through thin screens of trees. Finland is famous as a leader in technology, Nokia perhaps being its most famous global brand. But, passing through this part of the country, you are struck by one of the primary older industries: forestry. In the recent historical past, forestry provided tar, used originally for waterproofing sailing ships and washing babies with a pungent version of soap. The tar was derived from the sap of trees and was used in much earlier history as a medication for diseases of the mouth and gums. Finland is the source of the world's oldest piece of chewing gum, made from this tar, dating from many thousands of years ago, and spat out on a forest trail by someone who should have known better.

As the day slips into late afternoon, the weather turns, leaving a variegated grey blanket of cloud across the sky and ushering in quite a strange sight. It's a field full of dummies all dressed up in various articles of mixed coloured clothing and all with large straw-mop heads. They are vaguely reminiscent of the scarecrows of Novia Scotia, met in the twilight of the last trip. Lying alongside the 'Silent People', as they are known, is an interesting and somewhat ramshackle establishment called the Niitty Kavihla Field Kitchen, staffed by two cheerful and suitably nutty young ladies and comprising a rustic log cabin shop and an outlying cooking gazebo. It is weird, it is strange, but it serves up a stonkingly good jumbo sausage in a roll. My dietary health obsession is overcome by the smell of the spitting sausages that are griddled over a fire pit made up of three huge concrete rings, which might have (in another life) been components for a storm drain.

The dummies in the field are the work of an artist and dancer called Reijo Kela. He hasn't fully explained the significance of them and leaves the onlooker to make up their own mind. Since they are also called 'The oddity of highway 5', it looks like the onlooker is pretty much as nonplussed about the whole thing as we are but, to help us on the path of enlightenment, he has let on that they are something to do with identity and our place in the greater scheme of things. Where I'm from it would simply be called *Fly Tipping*.

Best pork sausages this side of the Dolphin Chipper, Aberdeen.

Back at the kitchen, we are entertained by the one young lady of the two who speaks English, with a description about life in this thinly populated part of the country. 'Have you seen many moose?' she asks. I reply that we haven't seen ANY moose and, furthermore, that it is something of a disappointment. 'There were five or six of them on the road outside my house this morning,' she confides, proceeding to give me directions to where she lives, which strikes me as particularly trusting. 'We get everything here. In winter, packs of wolves come over from Russia.'

It transpires that we are just a couple of miles from the Russian border, something I hadn't noticed on the map due to a fold. Interestingly, the young cook's comment is a perfect example of the western view of Russia. Bad things come from there, cold arctic winds, wolves, bears and the occasional Stalin or Putin. I wonder if the Russian view of the west is that 'In spring, packs of wolves come from Finland'.

In the late afternoon, we arrive at the city of Kajaani. Once we've left the main route, we find the city to be typical of many before, especially in the rest of Finland and Sweden: modern, nondescript, clean and boxy. The drabness of the buildings is, by good fortune, offset by the magnificent natural surrounds. The city has been built on the banks of the river Oulu, which flows from Lesser Lake Rimpilansalmi (go on, try to say it, I dare you) towards Lake Oulu. It provides for a very scenic landscape, rich in trees and water. I have to say that the local architects would get a 'should have tried harder' vote from this particular voyager though. Our hotel for the night is a case in point. It's a slab fronted, pale fawn rendered building that feels heavily reminiscent of the old and defunct Eastern Bloc. Thankfully, the rooms inside don't reflect the outside of the building (although they are very small) and we settle in for a comfortable night, so long as we don't stub our toes on luggage.

*** *** ***

We often find ourselves passing through places like Kajaani without the opportunity to explore them and can only comment on the view from the saddle. I regret this more with Finland than with Sweden and Denmark because I find myself wishing I had more time to explore here. Finland has a long history of occupation by both the Swedes and the Russians. As such, it has had its fair share of battles. These, in part, led to the rise of a movement for independence, not least because the residents were fed up of being invaded. Kajaani boasts the remains of a strategic castle, built by the Swedes and blown to smithereens by the Russians.

The morning reveals horrible weather. Very heavy rain has moved in, prompting me to park the bike under the cover of the hotel entrance , allowing me to pack it without getting completely drenched. Once we hit the road, splashing out of town like a pair of already bedraggled rats, it just gets worse and worse. We plow on regardless and cover a few miles, until the downpour becomes torrential and deeply uncomfortable. Suddenly, out of the gloom, a sign appears promising fuel and food. We decide to pull in and take a break. Maybe this torrent will ease off a bit in the next half hour or so.

Having topped up the fuel, we head over to the adjacent eatery, noting on our way that half of the motorcyclists of Finland have taken refuge within. There are a few amused glances as we struggle to peel off our awkward oversuits. The Finnish bikers have, to a man and woman, equipped themselves with two-piece wet suits. These are far easier to take off and put on again. Here, I have to admit a bit of stand-off with our friend Ed over in the USA, who questioned me at some length about what we were going to take on the trip.

Some of you may recall, that Diane and I met Ed and his wife Sandy in Yellowstone National Park during the trip around North America. I then met them sometime later at the Sturgis motorcycle rally. Ed has provided a deep well of biking related advice and knowledge ever since. After I returned from the US, our already firm friendship deepened, with both he and Sandy taking a tour of the UK with us and us returning to Sturgis to stay with them for a second time over there. During this time, I have only ever known him to be wrong once. That occasion, detailed in the previous book, *Far Horizons,* involved the firmly held belief that Walmarts would stock a BMW oil filter for my bike. His flumoxation, on discovering that they didn't, is a treasured memory that still raises a little chuckle on recollection and always will.

On the subject of wet weather riding suits, he was absolute in his conviction. 'You need to take a two-piece suit,' said he by e-mail, with a hint of a command. 'They are much easier to get in and out of and they keep everything out. I buy mine from a cheap store and they're very good and never let me down.' I recalled some kind of yellow thing that he donned in a fit of inclement weather in Spearfish Canyon back in 2011. As usual, I had my doubts. I've spent all my adult years riding and six of those have been spent commuting twenty-five thousand miles a year into London, suffering countless downpours, snow, ice, a frozen goatee and everything else in between. My experience has been that even one-piece suits generally leak, so what hope is there of keeping the elements out, donned in something that has a gaping, yawning gap in the middle? It's just that all these Finns seem to be so dry. And all their suits look so cheap.

It dawns on me that Ed may well have a point. And when I consider my poor little navigator's wrestling exertions just to get the oversuit over the suit, I'm beginning to feel that further investigation is required – in fact, it needs to take place before we leave Finland. The rain starts to ease off as we scoff a lazy meal. We return to the (somewhat grubby) steed and press onwards and downwards – geographically speaking.

Very gradually, the lands are opening up. The further south we go, the more evidence there is of population increase – in relative terms that is. We start to see evidence of land clearance. Vast swathes of forest cut back, with huge mounds being built from the massive root-balls that have been torn from the earth. We eventually take a wrong turning and discover, with some dismay, that we've done got lost. In attempting to remedy the situation we run into a police roadblock.

I ease down to walking pace as one of officers of the law strolls over and raises his hand speaking Finnish. 'I'm sorry, I don't understand you,' is the best I can do in reply.

'You must take a breath test,' he says, not in a particularly assertive way - more like a matter of fact. He pulls out an electronic palm-size tester and fixes a nozzle to it. 'We have a zero tolerance in Finland and are testing everyone,' he says presenting it to me. 'Blow hard until I say stop.'

Getting pulled up thus by the Finnish police can really ruin your day. They have zero tolerance to alcohol in the blood or for speeding. The law in Finland applies a fine for traffic offences based on the earnings of the driver. Everyone's earnings are held in a database (though not mine – ha!) allowing the officer on duty to access the data and apply a fine. Famously, the highest fine went to the boss of Nokia, who was nabbed for speeding and kipper-slapped to the tune of €116,000. He was travelling at 47mph in a 31mph zone on his Harley. Suddenly, driving a sleigh attached to eight reindeer starts to make a lot of sense.

***

After a long day of hard mileage, we arrive at the town of Porvoo quite late in the evening. According to the maps, there is a campsite situated somewhere in the town across the river and we are determined to find it. This leads to a lot of frustrated riding around, following signs that seem to lead to nowhere in particular – at least nowhere that looks like a camp site. Eventually, after many circuits around the same part of town, we discover a road through a patch of woodland and are almost surprised to find that the campsite does actually exist. It's just well hidden, though not quite as well as the camouflaged one in Sweden.

We draw to a halt outside the reception office and are immediately greeted by a very, very drunk man, wielding a half empty glass of lager in one hand and an empty beer bottle in the other, regaling us in Finnish before eventually asking us in slurred English where have we come from? When I explain to him that we've ridden from England, he asks how far have we travelled? The truth is I don't know. 'Maybe two thousand miles,' is my best, almost certainly inaccurate guess. This news has the effect of cementing our friendship for the duration of the check in procedure, our short stay in Porvoo, and possibly even for life. We might even get married at some later date.

***

Tuesday 10th to Wednesday 11th July. We're going to spend two days camping in Porvoo. Day one will be spent carrying out a spot of 'make and mend', with a trip into town to sample the delights on offer. We have a few things on our shopping list, but a pair of cheap two-piece rain suits lies right at the top. The town of Porvoo is split by its high street between a historic old town and a slabby, Scandinavian newer district. The old side is a very quaint place, built mainly of brightly-painted shiplap clad wooden houses that often lean at quite bizarre angles along the cobbled streets. The new town is notable for boasting one of the highest concentrations of Toyota Hiace vans in Europe, from what I can see, which just goes to show how sensible the population of Porvoo really are. Toyota Hiace vans are *the* most reliable vehicles in the world. Now I've declared this, my van has probably instantly collapsed on its suspension in the car park, back at our house.

Our mission to find improved weather protection leads us to a Yamaha dealership sitting in the coniferous forest on the edge of town where we are welcomed very warmly by a young salesman, who takes us straight to the shelf that holds the two-piece suits that every biker here wears. It doesn't take long to realise that the extra-large size will fit me, but the large size are out of stock and Diane, small as she is, will not fit into a medium because of all her other riding gear.

'If I order one up today for you, we will have it in two days,' the salesman says helpfully. I point out that we intend to depart on that day. 'I can guarantee we will get it by 9am,' he replies, 'If you don't turn up, we'll put it into stock.' The deal is struck. I'm really starting to like the Finns. They're down to earth, pleasant, helpful and friendly - even more so when drunk.

***

Back at the campsite, we head up to the patio bar area at reception where alcohol 'may be consumed' and very often is. Beer in hand, we get chatting to a rather enigmatic chap who has parked his large American pick-up truck across from the bar and is sipping a coffee and generally taking life easy. He reminds me of the Esteban Vallejo character in the brothel scene of *Kill Bill 2*, possessed of a knowing smile and the experience of his many years.

After initial introductions and the usual 'where are you going, where have you been', he tells us a few things about where we've just visited. 'I used to be an engineer in the paper-making industry,' he tells us. 'I've worked all over the world setting up paper making plants.' It turns out that he worked very close to where I once lived in Kent, working at the paper mill at Aylesford. It seems like he didn't mind the UK, although he once worked in Southend-on-Sea, which he found 'a bit rough'. It's difficult to argue that one. His praises are really reserved for just one country in the whole world: New Zealand, where he lived and worked and where he very much intends to return to for at least one more year of his life.

I ask him about the forest clearances that we noticed on our way southwards, remarking on the huge piles of roots that lined the roadside at regular points. 'It's an ecological disaster,' he replies, matter-of-factly. 'The big lumber and papermaking companies don't care about the land or the wildlife and are drying out the ground and ripping up huge areas of forest. It's a disaster for the moose.' I recall my time in Maine, hunting moose with the mad moose lady. 'Yes, they need ponds, don't they?' I reply. 'They do. And they are all being drained just so they can plant more trees to rip out a few years later. It's a catastrophe. They hide it from us by leaving a bit of forest near the road, then drain all the lands behind that.' We should take note of this when companies declare paper to be ethically sourced from renewable stocks. The ponds aren't being renewed. Fauna will suffer.

Our conversation is quite wide-ranging. He tells me that he likes to hunt, but his father hated guns and wouldn't allow them in the house. 'Have you heard about the war in 1939 with the Russians?' he asks. I nod and say I know a bit about it: that the Russians were fought to a standstill by the Finnish ski troops and their hit-and-run tactics, but the Russians won in the end.

'My dad was one of those ski troops,' he replies. 'He said that he killed many, many Russians and that it affected him deeply. He hated guns and any form of killing after that.'

***

The route to the bathroom, which is patrolled by stealth mosquitoes (if you hear one it has already bitten you), wends its way past the smokehouse barbeque station, then past a water point, through some trees to a point where a young Russian couple are camping in their old Opel car. They have a large dog on a lead tied to the car door handle and are listening to loud music, sitting on fold-up camping chairs and, by the evidence on the return journey, gradually getting sozzled on vodka. No-one is camping near them for a good thirty yards or so. The lack of proper camping equipment and Russian plates on their battered car is sufficient. They are outcasts.

Diane and I have no such problem. It seems that the Finns can spot a Brit from a hundred yards since we are nearly always addressed immediately in English. At an evening stop by the smokehouse, we are urged by a group, comprising two couples, to use their barbeque fire, which is well lit in the grating. Iaana, the younger of the two ladies, is around my age and speaks very good English. Her husband makes excuses and leaves shortly after our arrival, telling us that he must travel home for work in the morning. Iaana tells me that Vesky, the old man of the remaining couple, doesn't speak English but has been admiring our bike. 'He kept wandering over to it today,' she laughs. Her translation helps us to make a conversation with the older couple who want to know where we are travelling and where we've been already. I tell them that we've travelled through Scandinavia and are now heading across to Estonia and then on to Russia.

'I have travelled a lot in Russia,' Iaana says, 'and have found the Russians to be very friendly people. Ordinary Russians are no problem at all. You just need to be careful about the Mafia. And the roads are very, very bad.'

We share each other's drinks and chat animatedly as the night deepens, the fire crackling in the fireplace. We talk about Finland.

They are proud of their country and its achievements: 'We have the best education in Scandinavia and are the richest of the Scandinavian countries.' This is a bit of a surprise to me. I thought perhaps that Norway held the most wealth and certainly Sweden feels a bit wealthier than Finland.

***

In the morning, as I'm preparing the bike for our day trip to Helsinki, checking a few things over and treating it to a good clean, Vesky pops round and gives it (another) good look-over. I point out the main features of it out to him and fire it up. His eyes sparkle and he pats the tank, muttering something that I think means 'fine machine'. He's particularly interested in the stickers on the top box and realises with surprise that the bike has been around North America. He takes a few shots of bike and stickers on his camera.

In a fit of rare forward planning, we've decided to find the ferry terminal, memorise the route to it and buy our tickets to Estonia in advance, thus avoiding any 'drama queen' moments from the rider tomorrow morning. As a bonus, we can add another famous capital city to our bag. So, after a strange 'ham salad sandwich in black bread' breakfast at the reception-bar, we head off over the bridge, through the town, past the Yamaha dealers and hang a left on the main motorway into the city, which lies about thirty miles away.

The road sweeps along rolling countryside before entering a typical urban sprawl, populated by large retail outlets and suburbs. The city centre has a strange halfway feel of both grand and yet quite stark architecture, with tall buildings, long shopping streets and loggerjam traffic. Following signs for the ferry terminal becomes quite demanding. There happens to be more than one terminal and we are looking for the Estonian ferry line. Our route there takes us past a long square, bordered by up-market shops, then dog-legs away from the city centre into a slightly poorer set of streets that, for some reason, remind me of Edinburgh. Amazingly, without satnav and by merely following road signs, we find ourselves outside the ferry terminal, parked up and ready to buy tickets.

The young Estonian man behind the counter in the terminal speaks impeccable English, something that almost leads me into a disastrous trap! Having sold me the ticket, he summarises the itinerary. 'This is your ticket for two people and one motorcycle and please carefully note that the ferry leaves at two-thirty and you must arrive early for boarding.'

Normally, by this time in proceedings, I'm not paying much notice at all. He's already told me it leaves at two thirty and I've taken a mental note. It's good timing for us. No rush to pack the tent, we can take it easy and still turn up with plenty of time to spare. It took about an hour and a quarter to get here and the traffic was bad. Leaving the campsite at around 10 should be fine and will leave time to pick up the wet weather suits.

I glance down at the ticket which very clearly says: 'Departure Time: 1:30pm'

'This says 1:30.'

'No 2:30'

I show him the ticket. 'It says 1:30'

He looks at it. 'No, it says 2:30'

'In English this is ONE-THIRTY,' I repeat.

He looks confused and embarrassed and goes bright red. I suddenly feel very bad and take the ticket back from him. Confusion reigns, so we leave it at that.

I later found out that he was using the correct Scandinavian expression of time – 30 before two. My very, very bad.

We now have plenty of time today to explore the centre of Helsinki, a fine city with (as previously mentioned) some rather interesting architecture, especially the buildings built in the art-deco era. The central main railway station is a case in point, perhaps built a little early to be deemed 'art-deco', but impressive regardless of that fact. Built in red granite in 1919, it features a tall tower topped with green copper sheet and sports a magnificent arched entrance. Two monolithic statues of men holding lanterns guard the entrance, managing to look a tinsy-winsy bit too Trollish for my liking, but strangely photogenic nevertheless. The BBC voted this wonderful building one of the world's most beautiful railway stations. Personally, I would place Mexborough station a notch or two higher, but I don't think anyone from the BBC has ever visited Mexborough, despite it being the birthplace of Brian Blessed.

It's important, when visiting a great capital city like this, to end the day with a spot of high-brow culture. We manage to do so at a wonderful, circular Swedish theatre (like a small white Albert Hall) chinking fine bone china in the café attached, and slurping the tea contained within, knowing that it cost its very own weight in gold. I nearly fainted at the till when they asked for the money and made a right fool of myself by double-checking the till receipt before having to wind up my dropped jaw like a drawbridge. The staff were not impressed. They turned up their noses at my Yorkshire fiscal prudence, proving unequivocally that snobbery exists everywhere you meet human beings and inflated prices. Even in Scandinavia.

***

Thursday the 12th July. There are two days left before our Russian visa commences. Sailing for Tallinn today will allow us one day to visit the sights of that city, then we will depart for the border. It gives us a day to navigate to St Petersburg, where Diane has pre-booked us into a rather swish hotel. Our visa is limited to one month. Bearing in mind the dire warnings regarding road conditions, it makes sense to maximise the number of days we allot to travelling in Russia, just in case we run into difficulties. Up until today, we've been wending our gentle path through Scandinavia with a weather eye on the critical date of the 14th July. Now it's time for the plan to come together.

We arrive at the motorcycle dealership, turning off along its rough gravel car park. Wandering inside, we are greeted by the young salesman. 'I have your suit! It arrived this morning as expected.' As we exchange funds for suits, I ask him if the staff would be able to use two lightly worn oversuits that we now need to discard. 'Sure, I think the race guys would love them.' I noticed a couple of race bikes parked up outside the workshop and am chuffed that the suits will get some use on wet days at the circuit. They might even help win the odd race!

Riding into Helsinki is now just sufficiently familiar to ensure that we arrive at the ferry terminal in good order and, having had our passport checked, we're waved through to park up in a substantial queue of bikes. 'There's an event going on over in Estonia on the Russian border,' a friendly German rider advises us. 'That's where we think we'll go. Are you heading that way?' I tell him that we probably won't. We need to find postal services to send stuff back home and it would be a shame to by-pass Tallinn. Moreover, I want to arrive at the Russian border in good shape – not hung over, or deaf from heavy metal capers and all-night rev-limiter bashing. Perhaps age is creeping up on me. I wonder if the band we met in Gavle were heading for the bike rally?

'I wonder where he's going?' the German interrupts my thoughts, nodding at a young thick-set biker in front of us who is standing alone besides his Suzuki Intruder, dressed in combats, tattoos aplenty, semi-mohican haircut, and the cut of a Scandinavian Motorcycle Club (MC). The loading staff signal to us to fire up and move towards the ramp in pairs and we happen to pull up next to the club member, an opportunity to strike up a little friendly conversation methinks. I'm itching to ask him where his club is located and, after a few moments of thinking the better of it, I lean over and shout – 'do you speak English?' After a momentary glare, he shouts back 'No!' - clearly a lie, but how big a porky is not worth investigating.

The big surprise, as we look around after lashing the bike down to the rings in the ship's deck, is that there are a lot more 'heavy duty' club riders around, sporting their different cloths on the back of their cut-offs. In fact, we 'ordinary' civvie bikers are considerably in the minority. Our non-communicative friend appears to be lonesome amongst them and sits just across the way from us in the bar, glowering away and keeping himself clear of all the others. The main intrigue for me comes from one of the most heavily represented clubs who are wearing all the right gear but, despite that, they don't quite look the part. Basically, they look like a convention of chartered surveyors and their wives, all clean-cut with immaculate leathers and very polite with it too. It all makes for interesting people-watching.

⊶⊷⊶◆⊷⊶⊷

Chapter 6
A Minor Hitch in the Planning Department

The voyage across from Finland to Estonia is relatively short. It isn't much further than Dover to Calais, if at all. The ferry is slightly rough around the edges with a bar that seems to be attempting to replicate an English pub, all dark wood and Wiltonesque carpet. It's reasonably lively too. The beer pumps are on overdrive. But after an hour or two, it all comes to a premature end as the passengers are piped to the car deck. Half an hour later and we've disembarked, flown through customs and are picking our way cautiously into the city of Tallinn, a short distance from the dockside, on greasy roads that haven't dried out from the recent showers. We spot a hotel almost immediately, off to our left. It would be difficult to miss, as it's a rather large tower. Quite a posh one if front lobby appearances are to be believed.

Our first impressions of Tallinn are predominantly positive ones. The old city rises up on a hill, girded by many old buildings and churches that line the medieval streets of what was once a bustling Hanseatic trading centre. It's a walled city that is accessed along an old roadway that is flanked by two gate towers and lots of market stalls. Tourism is clearly very important to Tallinn.

The traffic is in a completely different league from what we've experienced so far. We were warned about this by our recent Finnish acquaintances who, in a fit of Scandinavian solidarity, considered Estonia to be a paler shade of the darker Russian whole. They warned us that Estonian drivers are nutcases; cats of the craziest variety. The Estonians, on the other hand, seem to be trying to project the image of a brave new nation, firmly ensconced in the warm and loving embrace of the European Union (whose flag flies everywhere). They just haven't managed to convert to European Union driving standards yet – it's a work in progress.

An early evening meander into town reveals a veritable labyrinth of thoroughfares, squares and back alleys constituting a charmingly preserved centre. On the periphery of that are quite a few decaying reminders of a more recent past: boarded up, blackened sandstone-built factories that could have leapt straight from the pages of Dickens' 'Hard Times'. In the main touristic streets, there are many lively bars and restaurants, ideal venues for stag nights and suchlike, fronted by pretty girls dressed in a kind of Bavarian national dress. We grab an evening meal in one of the restaurants before heading in search of cheap vodka.

I have it on good authority from an ex-colleague who retired from the British Army some time ago, that proper Russian vodka is a fine substitute for methylated spirits – not for drinking, you understand, but for the seasonal firing up of spirit stoves like the Trangia. I've decided to experiment with this knowledge, just in case we are unable to buy pukka camping stove spirit across the border. We find a suitable vodka emporium a short walk across the asymmetric roundabout opposite our hotel, strategically placed next to a sizeable park. Feeling a little furtive, like a client in a '60s barbers seeking 'something for the weekend', I wander around the liberally-stacked shelves while Diane checks out the local liqueur, which is called 'Vana Tallinn'. The really high-end vodka has a lower alcohol percentage – nowhere near enough to get a spirit stove going, but the lower end stuff is cheap as chips and appears to have the required octane level to fire up the Queen Mary's boilers. Guessing there won't really be a problem transporting small quantities of vodka into Russia, a few Euros change hands and we depart with me trying to hide the offending liquor in its brown paper bag from public view.

Back at the hotel, I'm curious to see if this clear, high-octane spirit will indeed do the business. So, I dig out the Trangia and, making sure that the snuffer cap is nearby, I give it a go. Not a chance. Not even a splutter. The British Army would've gone without if they relied on this stuff. Besides that, I can't see the Russians handing it out anyway. They'd have chucked a few hand grenades and said, 'go and get your own vodka'.

***

I awake with a thumping headache. Across the bedroom on the dresser sits a half empty bottle (a half-bottle at that). If I'd drunk Brasso filtered with cotton wool, I doubt the result would have been any worse. The only thing missing this morning is a well-placed park bench.

Once the Anadin Extra headache tablets kick in, we are free to wander through Tallinn to explore some of the sights and culture that abound. One of the most prominent of the churches on the hill is St Olav's, which sports an impressive spire at 123 metres. Scandinavian in design and execution, the interior is very simple, painted in white with rather beautiful flourishes in the design of the arches and the lamps. It's an example of early Scandinavian interior design minimalism; IKEA with an ecclesiastic twist. Ethnically, despite what the Finns say, most Estonians are part of the Finnish race, distinct from the other Scandinavians and regularly invaded by them over the centuries. This church marks the settlement here of Danes in the eleventh century.

One of my tasks for the day is to post anything non-essential back home. This leads to an amusing hour or so in the city's main post office. It turns out to be a red letter day for philatelists in the hallowed halls of Tallinn post office. I have a passing fascination with collecting stamps. The only badge I was awarded in my failed cub-scout career was a hobby badge based on my stamp collection, put together in its entirety by my dad. Skip said that my stamp collection was the finest one he'd ever seen put together by a cub-scout. Yep, that would be right. A thirty-seven-year-old ex-cub-scout called David.

I find myself strangely drawn to the antics of the local collectors, who exhibit varying degrees of insanity. One individual is particularly noteworthy. He's bought a huge number of stamps and postcards and has taken them over to a table for a frantic rush of licking and stamp application. It seems like he's in a race against time because he then needs to get the assistant behind the sales desk to apply the ink stamp. A furious, whispered argument ensues as he demands that the assistant stamps the covers and returns them to him. The post office official is reluctant to help the poor guy in his quest to make a bob or two. In the end, he relents and surrenders the ink stamp with a 'go do it yourself' gesture. The philatelist is furious by this point and storms over to the table, accidentally tripping and dropping everything on the floor. Oh dear me, what a wonderful palaver!

When my turn arrives to approach the counter, I find myself face-to-face with the sternest woman I have ever met. She studies my customs declaration for an inordinate length of time then studies me with unblinking eyes, making me fidget. I don't want to blink first. Instead, I want to make her smile. It would feel like a small victory, but despite my best attempts at bogus flirtation, I fail miserably and get totally blanked as she applies the required postage, lips tightly pursed. I do hope Russian lady officials are less stern than their Estonian counterparts.

***

During our tour of the city today, we came upon the church of St Nicholas – a very old church which is now a museum, having been badly damaged by the Soviet air force in the closing days of the Second World War. It contains a most interesting artefact: a painting on a long series of panels called the Danse Macabre, the main character of which is the figure of death.

Death, in the form of a skeleton, propositions each character he meets to follow him. All of those propositioned thus try to give reasons in verse why they shouldn't follow. Starting with the Pope, then the Emperor, he works his way down through society until the point where some fool decided to store the whole thirty metres of the masterpiece in a damp storeroom, allowing it to rot away. This is one of two paintings by a thirteenth century artist called Bernt Notke; the other one was held in Lübeck, Germany and was destroyed in 1942 by bombing. With some good fortune, a series of photographs were taken of the destroyed version before the war and the portion on display in Tallinn corresponds perfectly with the ones in the photographs, so historians are quite sure that both were the same. Death dances with the entire strata of medieval society, ending up with a baby, demonstrating the egalitarian nature of the Bubonic Plague. It's a gruesome subject, but a unique bridge to the past.

Another mysterious artefact cropped up at a much smaller and older church in the centre of the city, called the *Church of the Holy Spirit*, part of a medieval hospital complex. The church has the same simple, white interior as St Olav's, with a dark wooden balcony around two of its walls. A particularly elaborate clock adorns the exterior and the altar screen, which is beautifully carved, is the work of the aforementioned Mr Notke, who seems to have had a very productive plague-free stay in the city. The thing that leaps out at me, though, is a large Royal Navy ensign that hangs from an angled flagstaff in a prominent position. An information board at the back of the church explains the relevance of this item in the church. Below the ensign are a series of brass plaques, 'sacred' plaques no less, memorials to the men of the Royal Navy and newly-formed Royal Air Force who gave their lives in the Estonian War of Independence, 1918-1919.

"I am sure that without the arrival of the British fleet in Tallinn in December 1918, the fate of our country and our people would have been very different – Estonia and, I believe our other Baltic states would have found themselves in the hands of the Bolsheviks." *General Johan Laidoner.* It wasn't to last. Estonia was invaded and annexed by the Soviet Union in 1940, then captured by the Germans in 1941 before falling again under the Soviet Union in 1944, finally regaining independence in 1991.

✳✳✳

Tomorrow is the big day! We need to take an early breakfast then pack everything carefully – to make sure that all the documentation we need is ready to hand; then we can head for the border in good time. I've read all sorts of horror stories about endless queues at the Russian border and don't want to risk being at the back of one of those babies. Our crossing point sits at the town of Narva. In a fit of prudence, I decide it might be worth looking the place up and trying to find out a bit more about how to get vehicle insurance.

A spot of internet investigation during the preparation phase revealed that insurance is sold at the border. In fact, due to recent agreements between the European Union and Russia, my UK insurance policy is completely valid. But seasoned travellers on the various forums warned that this shouldn't be trusted and that your average Russian traffic bobby out in the sticks will almost certainly never have heard of the agreement. Such information seems invaluable and worth taking into consideration, as does the advice that it is illegal for a Russian policeman to shout at a civilian. He can shoot you, but he has to do so quietly, preferably using a silencer, and above all without rancour.

In the back of my mind, I'm not entirely sure we will be successful tomorrow. I keep having visions of being turned away over some small technicality. Perhaps my answers on the visa application (and subsequent interview at the consul's office in Edinburgh) will have been picked up negatively: did I do military service? Yes. Did I learn to use weapons? Well yes, that's what you do in the military. What about explosives? Jeez, where does this end! Yes I did, but only little ones. Nuclear weapons then? What about those bad boys?

Then there's Diane's time spent in the Air Cadets. Why didn't they ask her about that?

***

Saturday 14th July. Today is a big changeover day for the cruise liners and holidaymakers. Loads of people are busy checking in and checking out of the hotel making it a hive of activity in half a dozen languages. Our packing proceeds reasonably smoothly. The baggage situation is much relieved by the large shipment of clothes, equipment and souvenirs sent back home. Confidence is high, mixed with a degree of nervous tension about getting through the border. Once everything is packed, we decide it would be prudent to carry out a final inventory of our documentation, making sure the important documents are ready to be presented.

Pilot: 'Passports'

Navigator: 'Check. Both here'

Pilot: 'Vehicle registration document'

Navigator: 'Check'

Pilot: 'Driving licence paper copy'

Navigator: 'Photocopy here'

Pilot: 'Original?'

Navigator: 'That's at home.'

I'm aware, after about eight seconds, the time it takes to tell someone they've been voted out of Strictly Come Dancing or Master Chef (why it takes that long is beyond me) that my mouth is wide open and my eyes are staring in disbelief, all of which is quite rude and not making my travel companion entirely comfortable.

'I distinctly remember you saying, "make sure you pack a copy",' she states emphatically.

My mind goes back to the day of packing. She, carefully putting the paperwork together; me running hither and thither with my arse on fire trying to pack the bike. I do clearly recall on a trip to the top floor of the house saying, 'don't forget to pack a copy of my paper driving licence,' meaning let's take a copy of it as well as the original – exactly what we've done with the vehicle registration documents. Diane, it would appear though, has done *exactly* what I requested.

We teeter on the very precipice of an enormous Mexican stand-off. For a few seconds, I wonder if it would be possible to blag our way through another eighteen or so countries without an original paper driving licence. The fact is, I've never been asked for my driving licence – paper or plastic - on any of my foreign trips, whether they be business or pleasure - except when I've had to hire a car. Even the Finnish police neglected to ask to see my driving licence. If we get stopped, maybe I could flourish the plastic licence and, if asked for the paper one, say that the original 'was accidently washed with my underpants and socks in the sink at the last hotel chief'. Then I recall a singular attempt to flunk homework, at age fourteen, by proffering that it had been 'eaten by the dog'. Mr Roy Turton, pupil bane and maths teacher extraordinary, was having none of it and the repercussions were severe. I decide it's just not worth the potential hassle. Picking up the mobile, I dial 'home' and drag daughter, Suzannah, out of her Saturday morning lie-in.

***

Our next problem is accommodation. There's no way we will be crossing the border for at least two days, so we need to extend our stay either here in Tallinn or somewhere nearer the border. A quick conversation with reception rules out this hotel – they're full and we need to vacate promptly at eleven. It dawns on me that we could have gone to the bike festival, after all. We could ride there now, but we'll just get a single night's camping then be forced to pack up and find somewhere else.

We decide to ride out of the city centre, heading towards the border. Hopefully we'll find somewhere to stay in that general direction. Within a few minutes, we find ourselves in a much more run-down area, replete with signs of the old communist era: badly built apartment blocks, the earlier post-war ones embellished with fake grandeur and concrete casts of the hammer and sickle, the newer ones just very badly built. Further out, on the road to Narva, we pass the remnants of heavy industrial plants, long closed, and a huge railway yard. Then the road picks itself up, becomes thoroughly modern and spits us out into open farmland, dotted with woodland. Clearly, the European Union has helped Estonia build a very decent highway heading all the way back to Russia.

Diane and I haven't really spoken to each other for at least an hour and a half. I'm in a monumental huff and she's having none of it - our first proper argument of the trip. On the face of it, I'm searching for hotel or motel accommodation where we will be able to provide an address for Suzannah to Fedex or TNT the offending article of documentation into our sweaty paws. In truth though, I'm using the riding of the bike to calm myself back down. As the miles rustle by, I rationalise that really this is entirely my fault. It's a classic case of not saying what you actually mean, something of which I have past history.

Chapter 7
A Wee Stopover

After about forty minutes of droning up highway number 1, we pull into a roadside stop for a coffee and a calm down, exchanging the odd nip to even things out before discussing the options. 'Maybe we can find something out this way. We can watch out for hotel signs,' I offer, in an attempt to break the ice. A little further up the road, we spot signs for a motel, but, to be frank, it doesn't look that appealing. Then a bit further on, we see signs for more accommodation, directing us off the motorway and onto the back roads, a diversion that throws us at least fifty years back in time.

We pass quietly along a small road that winds its sinuous path through dark forests bordered by deep green grass and bracken. At regular intervals, we pass groups of people heading into the forest with baskets and buckets, without doubt heading off to do a bit of mushroom picking. I'm sure of this because I've seen it before in Poland. Whatever the gains of throwing off the Soviet yoke, it's beginning to dawn on me that Estonia still has strong flavours of the old eastern bloc, just like Slovakia when I travelled there in 2007. There are plenty of poorer people driving ancient cars hereabouts – in stark contrast to Finland.

A few miles further on, we sweep around a corner and are greeted with the unexpected sight of a grand Palladian mansion – its glorious, crumbling façade towering above the road. There are signs for a hostel, which appears to be situated in one of the outlying buildings. We dismount and investigate on foot.

The site of the house and all its respective outbuildings is vast, taking up a fair proportion of the village it lies in. What appears to be the old coach house has been renovated and all the signs for the hostel seem to point to this building. What an intriguing place to spend a few days! However hard we search though, there doesn't seem to be an entrance. Eventually, we spot people entering the mansion via a side entrance and wander over to investigate. It turns out to be a small shop. I try asking a lady if the hostel is open. She shrugs and indicates that someone further inside can speak English.

It turns out that the hostel closed some time ago – this is the only part of the huge complex that is open to anything, the rest is derelict. I wonder what happened to the original owners of this fine house? I imagine it being evacuated in the turmoil of the Soviet invasion at the end of the war. Or maybe it was abandoned before that in the 1920's. Whenever it happened, it has reached a point where something needs to be done, or the decline will be terminal. It reminds me of Wentworth Woodhouse near Rotherham. When I was a kid, it was still a grand occupied mansion, but it became disused and fell into decay. It was eventually bought and now there's hope that it will be saved from further ruin. I hope that happens here, too.

＊＊

We took directions back in the shop, but within minutes we find ourselves quite lost. We don't have a working map and the road skirts a few villages, made up mostly of simple houses – a far cry from what we've been used to over in Finland and Sweden. We are passing through a remote and rather lovely part of Estonia that feels almost timeless. We pass the occasional car and tractor along narrowing roads that all but peter out. Then, just as it seems like we might have to turn around and go back the way, we emerge in a village built predominantly of wooden-walled, tin-roofed houses. The village turns out to be situated on a sea-inlet. Sitting adjacent to the ancient quayside we discover an incongruously swanky restaurant, which happens to advertise a few rooms. We decide to check out if they have any vacancies.

It seems to be a refuge for the upper classes of Tallinn – a kind of wacky, hip bolt-hole away from the city. I'm not entirely sure what they'll think of us two! When I pop through the door, my fears are quickly confirmed. After looking a bit confused, the staff inside say, 'I'm sorry, we are fully booked.' It's a shame, because I think it would be a terrific place to spend a couple of days.

Back at the bike, we ponder our options under the curious gaze of the staff within the restaurant. 'There was a hotel on the outskirts of Tallinn, just before the railway complex. Maybe we should head there,' I ponder. Diane agrees. Following our little tiff, we are heading back into safer waters.

***

The next four days are spent languishing in a hotel called the Susi, which is situated in an industrial area on the edge of the city. It is notable for its 1980's décor, external glazed lift and a half-body statue of a wrestler called Aleksander Aberg who, the plaque states: 'within 17 years pinned more than 5000 wrestlers to the floor and never lost a competition'. Tallinn's very own Big Daddy. Our first night's sleep is disturbed by a bunch of Russians who have spilled from the bar into the room next door in order to drink vodka and carouse until dawn, whereupon they start snoring. Just like my pillion, who has gently snored through the whole episode and wakes up wide-eyed and bushy tailed.

Since we have time on our hands, we decide to carry out further exploration of Tallinn, opting to visit an art museum called the Kumu, which is housed in a quite extraordinary, modern complex of buildings. The collection within covers a fascinating chronology of Estonian history in the form of paintings and sculptures that reflect the periods of influence either under occupation, or as an independent state. I do find the brutally modernistic art of the Soviet period quite compelling. But my favourite section of the museum is the room of busts, an installation of hundreds of mimetic sculptures of human faces, mounted on shelves on the wall and on plinths on the floor. The effect is downright spooky.

***

I decide to give the bike a good check over and clean, and in doing so, I find that the wiring to one of the funky crash-bar spotlights has been ripped from its normal place of residence, probably when I tied the bike down on the ferry. After a bit of humming and hawing, I realise that I don't have the means to fix the wiring in the toolkit (a bit of an omission), so I decide to run it down to a large DIY retail store that sits adjacent to the supermarket down the road from the hotel. I can buy the necessary bits 'n bobs and fix it in their car park. This gives Diane time for a bit of retail therapy while I pull out the tools and start to take the light apart.

It turns out that the spotlight is an over complex affair. I do like German engineering, but I prefer it to be pre-1980 – a time when they seemed to manufacture things with an eye for uncomplicated quality (although there are some exceptions). Luckily though, once the light has been disassembled, it turns out that the two wires have been ripped straight out of their connector, presenting an opportunity for a simple fix. All it takes is a bit of 'hole opening' using the handy little pawl in my Victorinox multi-tool, followed by stripping the wires back, bending them over and securing them with superglue. I think a couple of blobs of chewing gum would also suffice, but I don't have any.

With the Superglue hardened, I tentatively offer key to ignition, turn it, start the engine and flick the sidelight switch (which also has an earlier botch fix using a clipping from an old credit card) and am delighted by a fully recovered shaft of illumination. Marvellous stuff. I think it's the first time I've ever managed to successfully stick anything other than my own skin using Superglue.

***

Back in the hotel room, we spend quite a lot of time on the internet. I'm researching facts about Estonia and Diane is very sensibly trying to plot a route to our next hotel in St Petersburg, which she's had to re-book at great expense.

Following independence, Estonia embraced capitalism with passion and quite quickly became a land of high economic growth, low debt, and falling unemployment – a kind of Baltic tiger, similar to the Irish one, minus Father Ted. Along with just about everyone else in Europe though, the train hit the buffers big-style in 2008 with negative growth and rising unemployment. Fortunately, the country has worked hard to develop its industry and has exploited vast beds of shale gas for self-sufficient energy. You get the feeling that they have the nous to see the current hard times through and emerge into a bright future.

If there is one concern, it isn't the current economic crisis in the EU. It sits just over the horizon to the east. In my last job, I became friendly with a young consultant from Estonia. When she told me that's where she hailed from, I became quite excited, telling her that we were intending to ride to her homeland on our way to Russia and asking her questions about the country, to which she shrugged and replied, 'I don't know. My parents are Russian. Ask me about Russia.'

Right now, Russia and Estonia still have a disputed border. It was supposed to be ratified, but the Russians decided not to do so. The country has a significant number of ethnic Russians, just like my ex-colleague, within its population. Narva, the town we hope to travel to in two days' time, is essentially a Russian town, situated within the borders of the EU. Its population of around 65,000 numbers less than 3% of ethnic Estonians and the region it resides in has tried to hold referendums in the past with a view to becoming autonomous. Reading about this on the Internet, I get the distinct feeling that there are untied strings still flapping around in the post-Soviet break-up breeze and I wonder how things will look from the other side of the disputed border. If you were Russian, would you really want to live in Estonia?

**

After three days of kicking our heels, there's a ripple of excitement in the camp. Whenever we've consulted the Fedex website, it has charted the bizarre meanderings of our errant driving licence. A proper little tourist it is. It spent an enjoyable overnight stay in Paris, then decided that Stockholm was well worth a visit. But now, the website tells me it is in a van heading across Tallinn. As the clock works its way past midday, we are finally cheered by the sight of a delivery van turning up outside the hotel lobby and can breathe a sigh of relief as we tear open the white plastic envelope to reveal the wayward green-and-white licence.

Our journey tomorrow will initially take us the 125 or so miles to Narva, then a further 90 miles to St Petersburg, no doubt after quite a wait at the border. Realistically, we can expect to reach St Petersburg bang on the evening rush hour. We don't have much in the way of maps right now but, if all goes well, the Garmin should miraculously spring to life somewhere near the Russian border because, although we failed to download the European maps, the Russian ones seemed to load OK.

***

Thursday 19th July. We have eaten five days into our visa, sitting around waiting for the driving licence, but, at last, we are ready to rock and roll! Loading the bike is an exciting event. The weather is fine. Warm, with blue skies and just a few high-altitude wisps of cloud. A right turn onto the dual carriageway outside the hotel puts us straight on the road to Russia! I'm hopeful that the first leg to the border will take just a couple of hours. It's a fine stretch of road but, after droning along nicely for three quarters of an hour, such hopes are dashed as it turns into single carriageway.

A mixture of flat farmland and occasional forest flashes by on both sides. We pass wind turbines and spot a stork nesting on the chimney of an isolated farm building. Occasionally we hit road works. I used to hate it in the old days when the tarmac was ripped up and left with those wiggly grooves cut into the surface. The skinny motorcycle tyres in those days used to love following the grooves. I didn't. Nowadays, things are a bit better in the tyre department, but the Estonians have taken groove-cutting to a whole new level and the bike feels positively rubberised as we pass over them. At one point, the road has disappeared completely whilst work proceeds on building a new junction. All of which has slowed us down significantly.

Having negotiated all the road works, we pass closer to the coast and catch a glimpse of the rich blue of the Baltic Sea. We've topped up on fuel at a super-smart, brand new petrol station and are now ready for the border. Arriving at Narva, we quickly locate another petrol station. If the information on the internet is correct, they should sell Russian vehicle insurance. Leaving Diane to watch over the bike, I pop inside and ask if they sell it.

I receive a confused shrug. All attempts to point to the bike and indicate 'paperwork' are met with the said shrug and 'Niet'. Searching the shelves of the station shop also draws a blank – they don't sell insurance packs and they don't even have any maps of Russia. We spent a considerable amount of time in Helsinki scouring the map section of numerous bookshops for Russian maps. Nothing. Searching Tallinn revealed the same. So, no insurance and no paper maps either. The pressure on our little Garmin is starting to mount.

There isn't much we can do about the insurance. I know full well that I have the required documents and if we get stopped and our documentation isn't accepted, we'll just have to deal with it then. The staff in the petrol station do provide some advice though. When I ask about the border, they tell me to go to the 'waiting area' and indicate the direction to take. We pootle around the town looking for the 'waiting area', passing around a road loop in a careworn industrial part of the town. Eventually we find what we're looking for – a large compound with an office hut at the entrance that, at first sight, appears unmanned. We pull in behind a Russian biker on a battered Suzuki with a broken front mudguard.

Our new Russian biker friend speaks very passable English and tells us that we need to go to the entrance hut. None the wiser, we head over there with our document package. The documents are surplus to requirements, we just need to pay a fee. A few euros lighter and armed with a ticket, we are directed to a second hut on the far side of the yard to hand in the ticket. The man in the bothy seems to be Russian. He tells us we can head straight for the border. As we climb on the bike, we notice that our brolly, formerly tucked under the straps that hold the baggage on top of the panniers, has gone walkies. Nice.

The Russian biker kindly offers to show us the way to the border. We climb on board and latch on to him as he scoots off in brisk fashion, heading towards the centre of, what turns out to be, quite a pleasant town. And there lies the Estonian side of the border, a modern border post staffed by smart people in Scandinavian-style border guard uniforms.

A guy approaches and asks us to climb off the bike and present our documents at the customs post, where they are studied closely. It takes a while, giving time to look around at two fortifications that stare at each other across the river border. On this side, the black, white, and blue national flag of Estonia flies bravely above the ramparts. Across the river, on the Russian side, their red, white, and blue tricolour does likewise, but on an older, larger castle. S'funny that. I don't, in my mind, associate medieval castles with Russia – although they did go around blowing them up in Finland. While we wait, a steady stream of people arrive on foot from the Russian side, along with the odd car. Things seem to be moving very, very slowly.

Our Russian friend gets the green light and thumbs his bike into life, riding off at the same pace as before. He isn't hanging around, that's for sure. He told us at the waiting area that he was heading to Moscow – quite a haul. 'I will arrive very late,' he said resignedly. I'm thinking he will arrive very late tomorrow; perhaps that's what he meant.

About ten minutes later, we too get the go-ahead and can mount up and ride down the hill to the bridge. As we pass across its delicate span we leave the European Union and plunge into Russia.

Chapter 8
Sandra Victoria

The border post on the Russian side is large, modern and spacious, with booths sitting under a covered gantry and offices over to the left. A man in uniform waves us down and directs us to park out of the way next to one of the booths, having a careful look at our number plate. His uniform is reminiscent of the old days of the Soviet Union – especially the broad-rim hat that adorns his head. Everything is done by polite gesture and few words are spoken. For some reason, I notice that his uniform isn't really what I would call a uniform. At a distance, all the badges make it look so, but on closer inspection it is more utilitarian, as if designed by Dickies the overall manufacturers – quite neat really, and, admittedly, a strange detail to notice. I approach the booth clutching all our paperwork.

Blow me down and take me to the foot of our stairs if the person peering back at me, from within, isn't Posh Spice herself. Then she smiles and I realise she isn't Victoria, but actually could be Sandra Bullock. Well, Sandra Bullock minus maybe fifteen or twenty years. I say 'Hello' and am relieved to find that she speaks a little English. 'Passport please, and passport for vehicle.' There's that lovely smile again. She too sports a uniform, but one that's a slightly more civilianised version than the one worn by the male official. She's embellished the whole affair with plenty of jewellery, including a Gucci lookalike watch. I also notice that she has very elaborate and carefully painted fingernails. It all helps to make things feel a bit more normal and less imposing than perhaps they could be.

She explains that I need to fill in a rather large form. 'You must fill this in here, here, and here: value goods, computers, money, you must like to be careful. I sorry – English very poor,' she says, flashing again that slightly self-conscious smile. I've got the drift and say, 'thank-you very much and your English is much better than my Russian.' Not a great riposte.

However, lame comment aside, I thought that went extremely well. Diane and I are directed to a steel table next to the booth, adjacent to where the bike is parked. I commence form-filling. A Russian car driver who speaks virtually perfect English strikes up a conversation with Diane as I carefully write our passport details, vehicle details and a list of all the things we are bringing into the country. After about ten minutes of taking it steady and making sure there are no mistakes or omissions, I join the queue and hand the form in.

Sandra places the blunt end of her pen in her mouth as she studies the form carefully, then notices something and frowns. My heart skips a beat. 'I am sorry. This is not correct,' she says very apologetically. 'You see, this should be here.' She hands the form back through to me and I can see my mistake instantly. Despite the assistance of Diane's new friend, I've filled in each of the lines of the form one line below where I should have done so. A new form is produced apologetically, and I return to the table feeling like a complete dork.

It only takes five minutes to complete the form this time, just copy and paste really – with the friendly assistance of the English-speaking driver, making sure we get everything on the correct line this time. And gosh! Aren't the Russians nice! I head back again to the booth, imagining the ignominy of a fall at the next fence – having to fill it in for a third time. It really would be a case of putting on a pointy hat and taking to the stool in the corner if that happens! But no! This time Sandra goes further and starts carefully studying each entry, then comparing the paperwork we've handed in and ticking things too. It's a very close check. The world seems to be holding its breath. Still reading carefully, her right hand puts her pen down and slowly reaches for something... an ink stamp! It's at this moment that you know you are through. Roll the stamp in ink then bang, bang, bang, apply more ink and bang! She gathers up all our paperwork, shuffles it into order, and hands me a new form with a smile.

'This form very, very important. You must give to customs when you leave. Or motorcycle cannot go.' Then she smiles again very warmly and says, 'Welcome to Russia.'

Chapter 9
Plenty Ladas

All right I admit it, I found myself being charmed by a Russian border official. Very bad. We have been stopped just short of the final barrier for no apparent reason, a good opportunity for Diane to give me a well-deserved cuff, but it isn't forthcoming. This part of the procedure is overseen by another girl, this time blonde, who is also wearing a sexed-up uniform and brandishing a walkie-talkie. We are the only traffic in the queue to enter the country, but it seems as if we are too much for the infrastructure to handle, so we have to wait. And wait. And wait a bit more.

We still have a fair way to go today, and I guess we've taken a little over an hour to get through the border. When I recall all the horror stories on the Internet, it seems to me that we've had an easy run. I'm just hoping we don't fall at the final fence and sit here for the next six or seven hours. The girl answers the radio. I get ready to start the bike. Nope, hold on there bald eagle. It was a false alarm.

Five minutes later, another call. Without smiling, she indicates over to us with the flick of a radio aerial – we can go. The final barrier is raised, the bike chuckles into life and we pull up the hill into the small town of Ivangorod. Within thirty seconds we've spotted our first Lada.

***

The first thing that strikes you on riding into Russia, isn't a sudden decline into a broken society. Russia isn't broken – well not immediately, discernibly broken. The first noticeable difference is the conversion from our European alphabet to the Cyrillic one. Everything immediately becomes indecipherable. After that, it's the cars and vans, which are completely different from anything we're used to. Estonia had the faint whiff of the former Soviet empire, but Russia proper, unsurprisingly, has it in bucket loads.

I must admit, I expected the road to completely disappear half a kilometre back the way and it hasn't. In fact, it hasn't really deteriorated that much at all. The houses look like houses and the shops look like betting offices. That's about it for now. We thrum quietly through town with me marvelling that the road is actually quite good. Seems like we were being spun a line after all. As we leave the environs of Ivangorod, we start to pass a huge queue of trucks that are heading to the west; mile after mile of articulated lorries stuck in what looks to be a never-ending line, the drivers standing around in bunches or hanging out of the windows having a chat; some are cooking on the side of the road.

Approaching the edge of the town, we pass the odd house, a petrol station, youthful trees, open untended fields with giant stands of cow parsley that are on the point of breaking into white blossom. Shortly thereafter, the road takes a turn for the worse and enters a period in time dating back to around 1935. There are occasional glimpses of objects frozen in time: abandoned buildings, telegraph poles that have probably never managed vertical mode and an intriguing concrete and steel structure that looks like a huge ramp. But the road! Oh my God, the road!! It has turned into a concrete and tarmac patchwork quilt interspersed by potholes, super potholes, ruts, ridges and melted marzipan folds. The bike skips, lurches, slams and jars as we try to weave our way around the mayhem, mostly unsuccessfully. Simon Pavey was bang on the mark and would almost certainly not be impressed with my riding skills! I have remained with my posterior firmly clenching the seat. Simon teaches people to stand up while they are riding in conditions such as these.

I read in my Internet research about a group of people, Germans I think, who travelled to St Petersburg in modern motorhomes. For some reason, I recall this and wonder what happened when they hit this lot. I imagine the interior of the motorhome detaching itself from the exterior and the whole lot smashing up, along with all the crockery, into matchwood and ceramic shards. Then it dawns on me that I have the suspension set to 'sport' and I stab the switch on the handlebar to put it to normal, hoping it will make a difference. It doesn't. I shout back to Diane that we will probably have a wrecked bike in one month's time. No wonder all the Russian bikes and cars look so worn out.

After a while, we appear to be arriving at a junction. There aren't really any major markings, but a sign appears, indicating a left turn, directing us to Санкт-Петербу́рг, wherever that is. Then, even more helpfully, another slightly wayward sign says Sankt-Peterburg, so I pull over to the centre of the road and turn off, followed by an old truck of uncertain vintage. At this point, what I thought was about the worst road I've ever ridden on, deteriorates quite dramatically. I catch a glimpse in the mirror of the truck weaving alarmingly all over both sides of the road, trying desperately to avoid lorry-sized holes. Surely this can't be the E20 - the main road to the metropolis of St Petersburg – it can't be can it? Having passed through a stretch of forest, we emerge at a wide river, spanned by an old concrete bridge, the structure of which is eroded and chipped in many places, revealing the ridged steel skeleton reinforcing bars within. Repair work is being carried out on the bridge at the far end. Something must have gone horribly wrong for it to warrant a repair job. I decide that this just *cannot* be the main route and decide to turn back and check the signs shouting back to Diane, 'Did you see the signs for St Petersburg back there?'

'I didn't see any signs,' she shouts back. I'm thinking that my navigator might have suffered some kind of wiring failure due to the road conditions. We pick our way back to the main road and turn right, heading back towards the border. It's tempting to keep going and join the queue of trucks. Sandra would be surprised as we hand in our form, the ink barely dry, and say, 'Thanks for the lovely welcome but we've decided not to stay. Byeee.' Having pulled into the mud at the edge of the road, we peer back at the sign. It waves its wayward finger in the direction of the broken-most road. That's it then! It really is the road to SP.

***

We find ourselves stuck behind a large truck that is grinding up a hill with dark forest on either side. Suddenly, the truck lurches to the right and drives off the road onto the soft verge. Peering ahead, the reason becomes instantly clear. The verge is of far better standard than the road. We follow suit. The driver, though, has had a chance to glimpse us in the mirror and politely pulls over to let us pass at the next opportunity, brushing the forest branches in his effort to let us through. How kind!

A few miles later, the traffic picks up. The mixture of vehicle brands is quite interesting: there are plenty of cars from the Far East – mostly the cheaper Daewoos but, not surprisingly, there are a significant proportion of Ladas.

I have a soft spot for Ladas. They provided cheap, affordable transport for many UK drivers in the wake of the late '70s and early '80s, the years of punk rock, stagflation, the miner's strike, Maggie and the Falklands. My own mode of four-wheeled transport was a cut-and-shut Austin Allegro (All-aggro), the interior of which had been eaten by my dog, a remarkable hound called Lucy. For very little money I could have taken a loan out and bought a brand-new Lada Riva.

The problem in doing so was that a Lada, in our youthful eyes, had become the sole preserve of flat-capped pigeon racers who walked the odd whippet – people who had upgraded from a Honda C90 via a Reliant Regal. Cheap meant unreliable and prone to rusting at the drop of a hat. Ironically, a Lada Riva would have been the ideal car for me for two fundamental reasons: firstly, even in those days I had a penchant for older engineering and the Riva was based on a Fiat design dating from 1966, and secondly: I only drove cars for utility purposes – my main passion was always two-wheeled. A Lada Riva (or VAZ-2107 to give them their Russian name) would probably have been ideal – I just lacked sufficient bottle to go and buy one and thus destroy the tiny shred of street cred that I mistakenly thought I possessed, continuing to drive my lurcher-chewed Austin Allegro instead.

We find ourselves passing through villages and then a small town. The houses are usually single storey affairs within a patch of land that is oft laid very neatly to vegetable growing. Some have chickens scratching around their periphery. The town is a dour place with old blocks of flats and wire link fences, not particularly appealing to western sensibilities. At one junction, a car appears to the right as we approach and swings out onto the right-hand side slip road. As we ride past, he accelerates and undertakes us. It isn't done in an aggressive manner, but it does serve a reminder that the standard of driving might be a little 'different' from now onwards.

The roads might be atrocious, but in the back of my mind I know that we're making acceptable progress. The miles are ticking over, and the occasional sign does indicate that we're on the correct road. The main downside on the navigational front is that Garmy the satnav has donned a Russian bearskin hat and taken to communicating in the native vernacular. A complete waste of time and effort giving him the maps in the first place. The bike, heavily loaded as it is, seems to be coping with just the occasional huge CRASH as the suspension bottoms out in a pothole. After a couple of hours, the traffic increases and we observe clear signs that we're approaching a city, passing through outlying suburb towns with proper pavements and a slight improvement in the quality of tarmac. It becomes quickly apparent that my earlier fears of hitting St Petersburg bang on the rush hour have fully transpired.

As the pace slows to a dribble, we crawl past parklands, broad traffic junctions and crowded bus stops. I realise that I have no way of knowing where I'm going. The satnav continues to deliver its navigational advice in Cyrillic and might as well be on Mars. The result: we are hopelessly lost on arrival. Put simply, we need to find a map, and we need to find one right now! The opportunity for salvation shows up on the right-hand side in the shape of a modern petrol station. We pull in and dismount. I'm not going to bother topping up with fuel right now – we have plenty of 'good stuff' purchased near the border in Estonia, so I make a beeline for the kiosk shop, which looks not dissimilar from its western counterparts. The petrol station is busy, with people pulling in and out at regular intervals. I wander around the small shop looking for maps and quickly locate one. It's a hardback book with a comprehensive street plan of St Petersburg in Cyrillic – a kind of A-Z guide no less. Not quite what I was looking for, but certainly better than nothing if we do get hopelessly lost – or perhaps I should say 'hopelessly more lost than we are right now'! Time to try out my visa credit card. It works!

* * *

Back at the bike, we try to suss out where we are. It's just impossible. The one thing I can recall from our internet surfing in Tallinn is that most of the outer roads radiate into the city centre. I can also see that there is a large ring road. I think we should just press on and see what transpires. We ride a bit further on, then spot the unmistakeable sign of a major junction with the ring road. This turns out to be a very impressive stretch of concrete and tarmac, with traffic fair barrelling along its sweeping curves. At one point we flash past an avenue of futuristic street lights. They look really very, very impressive. It turns out that we've been taking all the right turns – Diane recognises where we are and taps me on the shoulder, pointing and shouting, 'It's along there!' Unfortunately, the waypoint that she's recognised turns out to be a gigantic roundabout snarled in the most humungous bottleneck of traffic.

It's been a long old day, I'm growing a little weary in the saddle, and I really did not want to end up trying to negotiate what we now face. It's called Vosstaniya and it seems to have been purposefully designed to cause the maximum carnage possible in the shortest space of rush-hour time. The work of Beelzebub and his lower minions, it is approached by a confusing myriad of roads, pouring in cars, buses, vans and trucks, most of them apparently in the wrong lane. At its centre, a lone traffic policeman brandishes a baton to little effect and is clearly pushed to the limit of the law in <u>not</u> shouting at or shooting citizens. I decide to nudge forward and force our way through, ignoring the furious horns and total chaos around us. We creep around it in little fits and starts and in doing so, it dawns upon me that Russian drivers are actually quite courteous.

In fact, we're getting quite a bit of attention from many of the drivers. A man with his family packed in a car points us out to his kids. They smile and wave. We wave back. Gradually we work our way around and, by some miracle, pop out at the other side on the correct road. Diane is getting even more excited. 'I know where we are!' she shouts. 'the hotel isn't far from here.' It feels almost like Luke Skywalker and r2d2 on their mission to destroy the Death Star, except it isn't really like that – Diane has no robotic features, bleeps, or whistles. At least none that I'm aware of.

The navigator, bless her, has garnered a rich source of information on our 'down-time' in the Hotel Susi. She re-booked the hotel and has been merrily ditching the yellow man in the surrounding area on Google street view and memorising the result. She's a very gifted navigator. Such forward planning is an anathema to me and I regularly poo-poo it. But she ignores me studiously and now it's paid off. Well, almost. 'I think we've just passed the road,' shouts Diane. I pull into the side and we get our bearings. It turns out we are very close to our destination. How so, I have no idea, but there we are. Somehow, we've ridden here more or less directly, completely clueless, apart from the final kilometre or so. It's a minor miracle!

***

At the hotel, we are met immediately by security. As Diane pops in to check us in (a reversal of normal procedure), I stay with the bike and manoeuvre it into a useful space adjacent to where the guards are patrolling. The first guard to approach indicates that I should park it a little further down the way around the corner where it is more visible to CCTV. Seems like a good idea.

Whilst I'm in the process of doing this, a second guard approaches and indicates to me that I should park around the back of the hotel in a more open car park. 'Is rules!' he declares firmly.

'Is not very good rules,' thinks I.

I point to the CCTV.

'Niet, not allowed.'

It would appear that rules are written to be followed, so I climb back aboard, fire up the bike and ride it around the back. Diane appears with a key card. We are all checked in and can relax for two whole days and three nights. Heaven. The room is superb, sitting high on one of the upper floors, with a luxurious bed. My travelling companion has done us proud. Returning to the bike, it's time to detach the panniers and haul them up to the room – quite a task, they're very, very heavy. A man approaches.

'Do not park here! Is not safe,' he says.

'I was told to park here by your security guard!' I reply, slightly miffed.

'Is not safe. I am manager. You park round there,' he says indicating that I should return the bike to its original location under the CCTV.

'I tell guard.'

Back in my original parking spot, under the watchful eye of a young chef and his receptionist girlfriend, I lock the bike and cover it. I've brought a lightweight cover to hopefully make the bike less obvious when it's parked up. I think a well-tied cover is the first barrier to a traveller's bike being molested by scumbags. Whether it will give protection in Russia remains to be seen. The first and best line of defence is provided by the staff of the hotel really (as long as they aren't in league with the scumbags). Then there's the large yellow alarm lock that is attached to the front disc brake. After that there's the bikes own alarm – which, frankly, is a trifle feeble. And finally, the steering lock and immobiliser. You might think this is way too heavy a set of precautions, but believe me, the skill and outright cunning of a motorcycle thief is often quite astonishing.

Diane and I were well minded of the need for this level of security by a seasoned Scottish traveller during our first shake-down trip to Switzerland back in 2008, when the bike was virtually brand-new. We met a guy who was riding a Honda Gold Wing and offered him a beer whilst chatting by our tent.

'I see you don't lock your bike,' he said after a while nodding over to the Mutt.

'Not here, I don't think anyone will nick it next to the tent,' I responded.

'You can never be too sure,' he said. 'I've travelled in Eastern Europe a lot and it's different there. I stopped in a hotel in Poland and they told me it wasn't safe – told me to push the bike through the hotel and park it in the generator room chained to the generator. I thought, 'this is a bit over the top,' but did as they said. In the morning, I found that someone had tried to hack off the chain. I realised that the hotel manager had told the thieves where the bike was, but they were beaten by my chain, the idiots. You can't trust anyone out there.'

'Oh I don't know,' I replied, 'I've travelled there too and never had any problem.' I could tell by his face that he'd marked me down as a lightweight.

The next morning, we awoke to find our erstwhile friend had taken an early departure and so had our eggs. Removed from under our flysheet — no doubt to teach us a lesson. Next time, I will chain my eggs securely to a generator.

***

Our first foray into St Petersburg reveals a city of great beauty. The Nevsky Prospect runs straight as a die down to the huge square that is flanked on its far side by the Winter Palace. It was down this very road that the revolutionaries marched on the Winter Palace in 1917. The little I know about the city is that it was built by Peter the Great, rising out of the mosquito-blighted marshland and built to be his capital.

One of our first stops is at the Church of Our Saviour on Spilled Blood. The long queue of people waiting patiently to enter the inside of the church testifies to its popularity, and possibly to its significance too. We spot it after briefly stopping to photograph the beautifully elaborate glass frontage of a grand restaurant, refurbished to its former glory. Then, stepping around a corner, we are stopped in our tracks by the sight of the church. The building is fabulously ornate, built in red brick with the iconic onion domes that dazzle with gold, blues, yellows and pale green; it is a wonderful feast for the eye.

It was built between 1883 and 1907 on the spot where Emperor Alexander II was mortally wounded by a bomb. In the attack, he was initially completely unharmed by a grenade thrown by a revolutionary. I'm not sure if it was bravery or gross stupidity, but Alexander decided to get out of his carriage and give the assailant a good ticking off. The scene sounds Pythonesque, if truth be told: 'he is not a revolutionary! He's a very naughty boy'. He was then mortally wounded when a second bomb went off, thrown by one of the other revolutionaries who was also killed in the act of lobbing the bomb. Anarchic competence did not seem a strong point in those days, but then I'm not sure how well organised we should expect anarchists to be.

The church is flanked on one side by a canal. On the other side, the precinct is fenced in by elaborate railings set in a brick wall that emulates the main building, having tiny onion domes atop red brick pillars. Beyond that lies a serene area of parkland consisting of a patchwork of bright green grass and dark tree-dappled shadows.

In the midst of all the detail and opulent decoration that adorns the outside of this remarkable building, the one thing that captures me the most is the construction of the onion domes. Some are constructed of small, multi-coloured pyramids set in geometric patterns; others are twisted like a loosely wrapped turban. The top of the onion gives way to a gold leaf pommel that is supplanted by a Russian suppedaneum (orthodox) cross made up of a small cross beam at the top symbolising the sign 'INRI', then the main cross beam, with a third smaller, slanting beam that represents the foot board, the angle of the beams pointing to the two thieves on either side of Christ, one penitent and the other not.

It is interesting to note that, after the war, the restorers of the church left a small segment of wall untouched, displaying the fury of shellfire or bombs that scarred the surrounds of an original stone plaque, the splinters having torn away the fabric of the plaque and peppered the surrounding brickwork. This is a reminder of the horrific conditions the city endured during the siege of Leningrad (as it was then called), between September 1941 and January 1944.

Once we can avert our gaze from this treasure house of symbolic tragedy, we notice that there is a very lively street market just outside the precinct of the church. We wander over and drift around a couple of stalls, ending up paying a little too close attention to one that is selling good quality, hand-painted Matryoshka dolls. The stall owner, a trim blonde lady who I would guess to be in her late forties, eyes us up and then makes her opening gambit. 'Deutche? Amerikan?' she asks. 'No, we're British,' I reply. 'Ahh British!' she says, with just a hint of relish. I think we have been scanned and targeted and are now pretty much nailed. She just needs to close the deal.

It turns out that she has a very relaxed sales technique, backed up by excellent English. In fact, she doesn't really try to sell us anything at first. When we started talking to her, she seemed a little severe, but she opens up very quickly, with a wide smile and razor-sharp wit. This is our first proper insight into the character of many Russian people. As with the dolls, you just have to peel back the first layer and then they will quickly smile and engage with you. When we explain to her that we are touring through Russia, she tells us of a place we really should try to visit, a place that lies some way out from St Petersburg, deep in the forest, with ancient wooden churches and surrounding buildings. 'It would be such a shame not to see it,' she says.

The nesting dolls are, unsurprisingly, one of the main souvenirs to be found on all the stalls, but equally prominent, and to my mind far more collectable, are the lacquered boxes. I notice that some of them bear intricate paintings of an owl and end up buying a very expensive example, being an owl myself, at least in football supporting terms. We depart with our precious little cargo leaving a rather delighted stall holder who beams, 'I will shortly close my stall and go to meet my daughter,' graciously missing out: 'now that I've sold twice my daily quota.'

***

A leisurely wander along the canals and back streets that run parallel to the Nevski Prospect finally deposits us alongside a series of very grand old buildings that lead us to the Winter Palace. One in particular stands out, with heroic, muscled figures forming the pillars of a vast portico. We are just a few hundred yards away from the quite extraordinary sight of the Winter Palace, which for some reason, I was expecting to be white. I suppose it's a reasonable mistake to make. In fact, it is predominantly pale green with its columns and baroque flourishes painted a contrasting white and gold. It hasn't always been so. Surprisingly, this colour is the one favoured for such buildings by the Soviets. It's a colour that you see in many parts of Russia, along with pale blue.

I'd been under the misapprehension that the Winter Palace had been built by Peter the Great but, yet again, I'm wrong. The palace before us is actually the fourth incarnation and has been under fairly constant modification, in some form or other, from the 1730's onwards. The vast frontage of the palace faces directly onto a massive square, that stretches away into the distance across to the Building of the General Staff and Guards Corps Headquarters, a wide-fronted crescent of a building with a broad, central archway, topped by a statue of victory standing in a quadriga — a stylised Roman racing chariot. The Alexander column rises from the centre of the square, made of red granite, it is the tallest of its kind in the world, but not quite as tall as Nelson's whose hat pips it by a few feet. Well done Horatio!

**

On our little walk around the perimeter of the Winter Place, we find ourselves running into all manner of people hawking various tourist 'experiences', predominantly boat rides down the nearby Bolshaya Neva, one of the wide arms of the River Neva. A salesman, with a strong American accent, surprises me with a robust and cheerful charm offensive, 'Hey Man! Where're ya from? You American?' he shouts. I find myself suckered into a reply, 'No I'm a Brit.'

'A Brit! Hey, love your beer man.'

As we walk a bit further on, I'm left wondering if he really said that or did I mistake what he said and he was actually complementing me on my goatee – which has been growing too long, if I'm honest, and now makes me look a bit like a gnome. It's anybody's guess. I am slightly hard of hearing these days, Diane even more so. But what was an American doing selling boat trips in St Petersburg? Russia is starting to be quite an intriguing place.

**

We make our way into the Winter Palace with the intention of buying a ticket for a tour. It turns out we're too late – a huge disappointment. In the end, we decide that we'll come back tomorrow and commence our wander back to the hotel and maybe find somewhere for a bite to eat.

On our way back, we pass through some pleasant parkland before happening upon a very grand building with a broad, neo-classical front festooned with doric columns picked out in white against pale yellow. It turns out to be the Russian State Museum and there is sufficient time remaining for us to pay up and wander through its spacious and rather beautiful galleries. The building itself is the former palace of a Grand Duke but, over time, it has become the repository for many art treasures originating from various sources. It reminds me of one of my favourite museums back in London: the Wallace Collection, where the surroundings and fabric of the building are the equal of the treasures held within.

The paintings of ordinary Russian life are wonderful. I love the feeling of character that radiates from them, but balance this with the knowledge that these were painted for the aristocracy, who subjugated the peasants to serfdom pretty much right up to the revolution, although Peter III did make it illegal to kill your serf in the 18th century. What comes across though, is the deep love that Russians hold for their country and how beautiful and varied the landscape is. All the rich, diverse, ethnic variations of life are lovingly captured in the artwork on display.

Russians are also very fond of folk tales. One of my favourite items in the whole museum is a beautifully carved miniature, portraying a folk story called 'How the mice buried the cat'. I spend a lot of time transfixed by this miniature marvel.

The cat appears to be dead and the mice are carrying it away on a sled, some acting as horses dragging the sledge along, others playing musical instruments or marching, one smoking a pipe. In one of the folk versions of the story, the mice have found the cat to be asleep and, thinking their old adversary is dead, are celebrating its passing with a lavish funeral. The cat is trussed up on the sledge like Gulliver; eventually awakening, he eats all the mice. That story is probably the origin, but examples such as this carving are much more subtle.

Here, the cat is an allegory for Peter the Great, who banned the playing of musical instruments by the peasantry and introduced sales of tobacco for taxation purposes. The carving mimics his funeral, with an identical sled to the one used in his procession to the grave, pulled by big mice – or even rats, equal in number to the funerary horses that pulled Peter's sled. The peasants are celebrating the death of the Tzar, but they won't be freed from tyranny, not for quite a few years, and then, very shortly after, they will regain it under Stalin.

***

Today is the 21st July, our second and final full day in St Petersburg. Time to visit the Winter Palace! I'd also like to visit the famous ship of the revolution, which my map tells me is called the Aurora. As we walk down the Nevsky Prospect, we notice that the weather isn't quite as nice as yesterday and could augur some rain before the day is out. We pass a sports shop selling a nice line in Russian Olympic team sport and leisurewear, a reminder that the games will soon commence back home in London.

The Winter Palace is a grand example of the Italian Baroque style of the enlightenment period. The main staircase that takes you on the start of your journey into the building is quite stupendous, dripping in gold, yet subtle in style. Quite what the revolutionaries made of it all when they rushed in here can only be imagined. You could stand and stare at it for a very long time; and we do.

***

I could wax lyrical about every corner of this magnificent building. It displays an opulence that was denied to all but a tiny, elevated proportion of the Russian population. Strangely though, some of the views from the high sash windows are peculiarly intimate with the streets below. The windows give a panoramic view of the streets, the bridges, and the broad expanse of river. One may doubt that such intimacy with normal life would have occurred when the palace was occupied by the Tzar or empress, but there's a painting of Catherine the Great opening one of the windows to address the crowd during the insurrection that led to her being placed on the throne. So, of that, I'm not entirely certain.

The details in the palace are exquisite – I particularly like the door handles cast in the intricate shape of a bird's talon, which grips a ruby red, multi-faceted crystal of glass. And the floors in some of the rooms exhibit marquetry of the highest possible quality. The library is very personal and contained, whereas many of the rooms are vast.

A beautiful example of the artwork found in the Winter Palace.

Out on the river, a variety of pleasure vessels and ferries plough their industrious watery furrows. Some of these vessels display the Soviet penchant for the modernistic, resembling refugees from a Captain Scarlet television episode. The perception in the west is that Russian manufactured machinery is badly made and likely to break down at any minute. I'm guilty of it myself. When I saw a Soyuz spacecraft exhibited in the National Space Museum back home in Leicester, I thought it was incredibly crude compared to the intricate and elaborate spacecraft built in the United States, and had to remind myself that, in fact, it worked extremely well. One thing's for certain: the Russians were more than capable of building an amazing palace and equally awesome churches, even if the Italians did help them out here and there. Just like they did with the Ladas.

***

Our walk from the Winter Palace to the Aurora takes us across a huge bridge spanning the river. A few spots of rain start to intrude just after we leave the palace; by the time we reach the middle of the bridge the spots have turned into a steady downpour. We haven't brought our wet weather gear with us – a bit of a faux-pas, we just have one small umbrella. At the end of the bridge, we discover a small park by the roadside and take shelter along with little groups of other tourists under the trees, waiting for the increasing downpour to subside.

This side of the river has a variety of interesting attractions: a large fort, a modern representation of a sailing ship that houses a restaurant, a huge hotel and wide thoroughfares. But beyond that, heading in the direction of the old warship we are looking for, we discover a series of back streets that hark back to the days of communism and perhaps earlier still – downbeat, gritty streets, frowned over by dilapidated old buildings, the walls plastered with posters advertising punk bands. We stop off at a coffee bar to attempt a quick 'dry-out' whilst eating a pastry hot dog. Peering out through the window provides a snippet of ordinary life. A woman in a pinafore is sweeping the entrance to what looks like a down-at-heel general grocery shop, greeting people who wander in for a paper.

When I think of all the comments and stern warnings about the risks of travelling in Russia, I wonder if it is wise to step off the beaten tourist path. But despite the more downbeat nature of the streets, it doesn't feel particularly dangerous. The people here seem perfectly normal and are just going about their lives on a rainy Saturday in July. It's quite obvious we are foreigners and tourists, but no one pays us the slightest bit of attention.

***

The rain eases off a little, allowing us to complete the short walk to another part of the river that lies at an angle to the one we crossed earlier. In the distance we can see our target, an old pre-dreadnought cruiser, one of very few ships of that age still in existence.

I've always felt that these steel ships built at the end of the nineteenth century appear to be crude and un-seaworthy, preferring the improved lines of the ships developed after the revolutionary British battleship HMS Dreadnought. But having now cast my eyes upon one of the breed, I have to say that she looks very grand and stately, at least from the oblique stern quarter that we approach her from.

She sits some way out into the river, her three tall funnels providing some proportion to her length. Painted a darker grey than that used by the Royal Navy, with contrasting green at the waterline, she is in superb condition. Her freeboard is relatively high and dotted with many dozens of portholes and she has relatively little in the way of superstructure – just a small bridge and plenty of funnels. At the very prow and stern are two light guns, the remainder of her main armament sitting below main deck level along her flanks. Right forward, two sizeable anchors sit on little plinths securing them to the side of the ship, presumably offering some level of redundancy. A small red star is picked out near her prow.

The Aurora remains a commissioned ship in the Russian Navy and is manned by serving sailors. You can't just wander aboard. The gangway to the ship is secured off and a sizeable group of visitors are made to wait until the previous party depart. There is no charge for the visit. Above us the skies are steadily clearing, leaving just an odd spit or two of rain.

It seems like some people here have been waiting a while and some of the natives are a bit restless. They remonstrate with one of the sailors who approaches the end of the gangway to open the rope and let someone leave the ship. He's having none of it. I get the impression that they have just managed to secure a longer wait. After a while they angrily depart the scene. Maybe their charabanc is about to leave. As soon as they've gone, the sailor reappears and opens the gangway with a cheery smile, ushering everyone in. Cute.

Once aboard the ship, the surprises continue. Not only is she rather beautiful, but she is indeed lovingly cared for. Everything about the fabric of the vessel is immaculate. An assembly of paint pots, chipping hammers and brushes tucked around a corner bear testament to the continual upkeep. The caulked wooden decks, that are gently drying from the recent rain, lead to an open doorway into the interior, which is surprisingly bright on account of both the lighting and the many portholes and would be instantly recognisable to a modern matelot. In fact, to me, the Aurora almost feels homely.

She was launched in 1900, well before the revolution and around the same time that the Church of Our Saviour on Spilled Blood back across the river was completed. She was designed to be part of the Pacific fleet, but lived her early life in the Baltic. When the Russo-Japanese war broke out four years after her launch, she sailed with elements of the Baltic fleet on a trip right round the world to reinforce the Russian elements of the Pacific fleet.

On their way down the North Sea, the Russians ran into the British fishing fleet on the Dogger Bank. The Russians were highly nervous about the risks from the new-fangled torpedo boats that were threatening to usurp the balance of power wielded by the great fleets in the form of battleships and cruisers. They weren't alone in this fear and it is often forgotten that Great Britain at the time was aligned with Japan. On the night of the 21st October, the Russians mistook the fishing boats for attackers and panicked. The result was a tragic loss of life in the fishing fleet and a rather shot up Aurora. Her chaplain was killed in the crossfire, after the ship was targeted by her own side on what nowadays would be called a 'blue on blue' incident.

After a number of other mishaps, she found herself in the middle of one of the most one-sided sea battles in history, the battle of Tsushima, the only totally decisive battle between steel battleships and the last one that resulted in one fleet surrendering to the other at the scene of the battle. Aurora, her captain dead, managed to escape to Manila where the Americans interned her until the termination of the war.

For the Russians of course, this early history probably just underlines how corrupt and incompetent the navy was under the rule of the Tzar. Aurora's fame doesn't rest with the ignominy of defeat at the hands of the Japanese or of internment at the hands of the Americans. It rests on the fact that the gun on the forecastle fired a blank shot that provided the signal for the storming of the Winter Palace. It was from this very spot that the October Revolution, arguably the greatest revolution in history, commenced in 1917, at least according to popular Russian history.

Sailors will be sailors, and one thing they love is when the public visit their ships. On the Aurora the crew are treated like movie stars. Everyone wants a photo with them on the forecastle of the ship, lined up with their arms around their guests in front of the famous 6-inch gun. The visitors are just ordinary families with kids and smart phones and the scene would easily be repeated in many other countries from the west or the east. We could quite easily be stood on one of the ships I served on during 'Navy Days' in Plymouth circa 1977.

The cruiser Aurora

Chapter 10
Some Motels are rougher than others...

Sunday 22nd July. After a long day's ride, we find ourselves dismounted from the bike, slightly dishevelled, eyeing up our first Russian motel. I'm not entirely sure where we are.

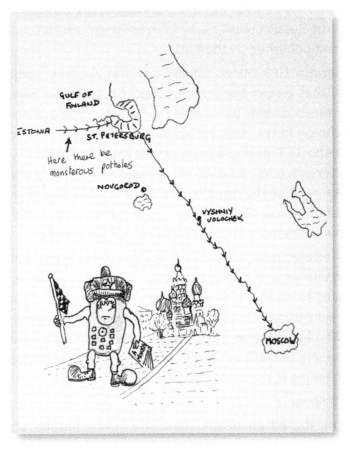

From Saint Petersburg to Moscow.

Earlier in the day, with the bike packed and breakfast attended to, we departed our hotel in the late morning sunshine. Before departure I decided to set the bike's electronic suspension to 'off road maximum', a setting confirmed by a picture of a high mountain appearing on the LCD display screen beneath the rev counter. Within minutes we were lost. We'd wandered off in the wrong direction, ending up in a factory district that was very clearly going nowhere. I cursed a little into my helmet. I decided before departure to ditch the map of St Petersburg in favour of a new hard-bound atlas covering the whole of Western Russia on its many pages, discovered in a bookshop a few hundred yards down the Nevsky Prospect from the hotel. It is reminiscent of the old 1960's RAC atlas that my dad still has in his bookcase, the obvious difference being that the Russian version is written in Cyrillic. And it covers Russia. And it wasn't published by the RAC.

The Garmin GPS 60csx satnav, our troublesome combat-ready carbuncle, that graces the screen support bar on the bike, did rise a little to the occasion. By zooming right out, I could see where we were in relation to the basic geography. That, however, was about the sum of its efforts. Entering an address for Moscow into its 'where to?' function merely led to a lot of thinking, head scratching, and absolutely zero pointing-out of the route to Red Square. After fifteen minutes of contemplation, it quietly folded up its own internal atlas and declared 'I've run out of memory and need to lie down for a while.'

Our failed electronic navigational guide resulted in us pulling up to a halt at the entrance to a large park opposite a sport stadium, with our map book open on top of the tank bag and hopefully the correct way up. This we did under the curious gaze of a group of young mothers and toddlers who appeared to be just about to enter the park playground. I was genuinely flummoxed, but in equal part had the nagging feeling we were heading in the correct direction.

'Can I help you?'

We both looked up to the sight of a young mother and buggy-strapped toddler. She'd sussed that we were English speaking and she spoke our language rather well. An older man who was passing by also stopped to help and then another lady who also spoke a little English.

'We're trying to find the road to Moscow,' I replied to our small gathering. A swift translation was made for the benefit of the old man who, with eyebrows raised, nodded his understanding.

This led to an interesting situation, because it seemed that none of them drove a vehicle, and, in fact, not one of them knew how to locate the road to Moscow.

'My husband is biker, he will know!' said the lady who arrived last, deftly poking the keys on her mobile with her thumb at the same time. I was quite impressed that she used the term 'biker'. After a short conversation in Russian, she turned back to us and assured us that indeed we were on the correct road.

'My husband says road ahead go like this (excellent impression of a 'fork') and you must take road to right then see signs for Moscow. Road not far from turn, maybe three kilometres.' Everyone seemed very happy with this and waved us on our way, each person's good turn for the day having been delivered with warm friendliness.

***

At first sight, the motel we have thankfully found quite late in the afternoon looks reasonable. It has a white plastic shiplap frontage with a sign on it declaring it to be a motel and a café to boot. The frontage also has little flower borders fashioned in concrete and painted white. The reception area is a dubious combination of pink with green borders and sports a curved wood and faux marble reception desk. All well and good, so far, then.

The lady in charge of the motel looks at me very, very sternly as I attempt to read from my phrase book. She makes no indication of recognising anything I've tried to say, speaking to me in Russian in the way we Brits talk to foreigners, speaking slowly to improve word recognition. After a moment of embarrassing silence, during which she stares fixedly at me, she indicates that I should follow her. We walk down a hallway and she unlocks a door. In my attempt to say, 'one room for two people for one night', did I actually say, 'one room, the two of us for an hour?'

She points to a threadbare room containing two beds with distinctly meagre, thin mattresses, a clapped-out armchair, and a display cabinet that would suit a 1940's terrace-home parlour but has no part to play in the functioning of a motel bedroom. I'm part disappointed, part delighted. Negotiations are going swimmingly well, and we haven't understood a single word each has spoken so far. Outside the room, she points over to a door on the opposite side of the hallway and says, 'Niet!', wagging her finger and leaving me none the wiser as to what happens behind it. Then she signals that I should follow her back up the corridor. We pass through the reception area and down a corridor on the other side of the motel, where I'm introduced to the toileting and bathing facilities. Enough said about them for now.

Right then. Time to close the deal! Back at reception she holds up one finger then flicks it to signal 'one night only and then you, my friend, are offski' and writes down the cost, which is really, exceedingly cheap.

A lively little joint come sundown...

Back at the bike, I explain to Diane that we have a room for the night. Not a nice room, but a roof over our heads, nevertheless. I decide not to mention toileting facilities. The situation is an improvement on the one we found ourselves in about forty-five minutes ago and I don't want the fact that there is a shared shower and toilet to be a deal breaker, even though Diane will be sharing toilets and a communal shower, sans door, with myself and twenty or thirty truck drivers who are right now assembling their vehicles in the vast yard behind the motel.

***

On the road down from St Petersburg, a few things had slotted into place. Firstly, the suspension was a huge improvement once it was set to 'off road maximum'. The bike started to float over the potholes and ruts with the grace of a greyhound on a beach, allowing us to relax and enjoy the ride. We passed through many little villages, all of which seemed to have but one main thoroughfare – the main highway itself. It was like being cast back in time.

The quaint houses were similar to those we saw on the journey to St Petersburg, nearly all wooden and mostly brightly painted, single storey affairs with tin roofs. Many had varying degrees of carved elaboration and almost all had rich, well-stocked vegetable gardens. On the edges of such settlements, it was very common to pass lines of people selling fruit and vegetables by the roadside, or even at the ends of their gardens. One of the favourite foodstuffs appeared to be strings of nuts coated in something that looked like toffee – looking like horse chestnut shish kebabs.

Secondly, it quickly became apparent that the Russians share the same penchant for interspersed dual and single carriageway main roads, as do the Swedes. The difference is that, here in Russia, the dual carriageway sections allow the locals to build up speed to around eighty-seven miles per hour (or faster if they aren't in a Lada) and then head straight for the oncoming traffic at the end of the dualled section in a desperate attempt to pass everything in front before the road returns to single carriageway. Their lack of skill and judgement in this suicidal manoeuvre is astonishing. The worst exponents drive large Japanese or European 4x4's with blacked-out windows. There are no Swedish road safety crash barriers to hinder their progress. On the plus side, I get the distinct impression that they aren't deliberately trying to kill themselves or anyone else. There's no real aggression. They just drive like complete loons.

***

Once in our room we both look around it in dismay. The sheets look clean, that's fair enough. The tiny towels, on the other hand, appear to be around thirty years old and are cunningly fashioned from water resistant cardboard and sandpaper. They would make excellent match strikers. There is an air-conditioning unit of indeterminate age that is only good for resting a can of coke. The room is stiflingly hot and there are a few mosquitoes waiting patiently for lunch, up near the ceiling. I decide I'm going to head off for a shower.

The shower room is communal, allowing for multiple standings. The place is terribly worn and tired, but thankfully the water is hot. Every ten minutes or so, the lady manager appears to give it a good clean, spraying it with something that smells like urine and mopping the residue. I return to the room.

'Showers hot.'

'I am NOT going in that shower,' replies my pillion.

'I think it's clean. It just doesn't smell clean. They're spraying something on it that smells like cat pee.'

Eventually, Diane agrees to take a shower, so long as I guard the entrance.

***

Wind back the clock a few hours. Whilst still on the road, we saw a sign for a hotel and decided to investigate. By my reckoning, we had covered just over half the distance to Moscow and, since the shadows were lengthening ever so slightly, we decided it was a good time to stop. The road had improved quite dramatically with evidence of a fair amount of improvement work going on, but as soon as we pulled off the highway and headed towards a small town, it deteriorated in very dramatic fashion.

To our left we passed a prison. I have now decided against any form of crime whilst transiting Russia. Then, when we arrived at the little town, the road decided it had had enough. A roadblock told us to go elsewhere. Up ahead, we could glimpse some road-laying machinery, so clearly this was a temporary blip, but it meant that we had to take a back road to our left and, put very simply, a back road in Russia means no road at all. We lurched from pothole to pothole on the packed earth that served as a track, generally following all the other traffic in the hope that it was heading to the town centre.

As luck would have it, we managed to pick our way to the hotel without too much ado. The town had a few Soviet-era apartment blocks that were close to derelict, plenty of nicer little houses with gardens, a very well-kept church and a rather imposing slab-fronted building advertising itself as the hotel. Having parked the bike with Diane standing guard, I wandered through into the reception area, fingering my phrase book, to be faced by a long desk with two women sitting at different ends of it. Both were poker-faced in the very, very extreme. More poker-faced than you could wish to encounter, even in your darkest dreams.

I attempted to say 'hello', then follow it up with the phrase in the book, 'I would like to have a room for one night, two people, please and thank-you.' I'd addressed the thinner of the two ladies, the one nearest me who appeared to be the 'administrator'. She stared back at me as if I'd just dropped my kegs and coiled one down on the scrap of carpet by the desk.

What then transpired was a kind of Mexican stand-off. I stared at her and she stared at me. Then I looked at her colleague who was also staring silently. After what seemed like a minute the second, larger lady delivered the coup-de-grace, quite simply and with one word: 'Niet'.

Back at the bike I tried to explain to Diane that there was no room at the inn. 'I think they're fully booked, but then again I can't be sure. I don't think they liked me. Maybe they're full of road workers.'

As we rode away, I was overcome by the strange feeling that we had escaped lightly.

$$***$$

Out at the bike, I check over a few things and contemplate that we are probably better off in this motel. The room might be worse than anything I've ever stayed in and the café is decidedly strange, but the ladies that staff the joint have warmed to us and now all smile as we pass to and from the shower, the café and the bike. It appears that they think we're American.

If we were American, we would be in a good position to carry out a bit of espionage. Every ten minutes or so a Russian fighter aircraft passes over on its final approach to land. It seems to be doing a series of 'bumps and starts', no doubt part of an evening test flight. I say this because I think I would be able to recognise one of the latest generation of MIGs or Shukhois, but this one is a bit different. It has the angled, chiselled lines of something newer, and very smart and capable it looks too.

***

It's around eleven thirty and I have to repair to the loo. I've been trying to get to sleep in the stiflingly hot room, bed sheets thrown back - partly due to the heat and partly through a groundless fear of bed bugs. The room is just so tired and faded, with itchy, wafer-thin pillows and the smell of years of dust, that I can't believe the only beasties around are the swatted mozzies that now lay lifeless, having been dispatched some hours ago. I pull on a few clothes and slip out of the room into the dark corridor, becoming aware of the unmistakeable yet muffled din being generated by a party that's going on inside the café over at the far end of the building. Quelle surprise!

Rounding reception brings me abruptly face-to-face with two vodka-soused local ladies of indeterminate age who are holding each other up rather better than their undersize dresses are holding them in. It's a bit of a shock to all three of us. They both coo and purr in slurred Russian, their words thankfully a complete mystery to me as I shrug and say weakly, 'sorry I don't speak Russian.'

My arm is rubbed affectionately by one of the two in the queue.

'американский', she declares with warm appreciation. It sounds to me like 'Amerikanski'

'Niet!' I respond firmly. 'Engliski!'

This causes a lot of shrugging, probably because it isn't a real word in Russian, but more likely down to pronunciation. A request for translation is shouted to the current occupant of the cubicle, the third member of their trio. 'Lon-don' comes the muffled reply along with a fit of inebriated giggling and the sound of clothes being rearranged and the flusher being operated. The 'ker-ching' is almost palpable, but by the time I exit the loo a few minutes later, they've given up on me and headed back to the cafe. Loud cheers greet their entrance.

＊＊＊

At around 5 a.m., the truck drivers fire up their engines in a mechanical dawn chorus, waking us in the stifling heat of the room as they grind past the end of the motel out onto the open highway. By the time we rise and drag ourselves through to the café, the whole place looks like nothing has happened for weeks. The tables are clean with little flower vases on them, the odd traveller is in for breakfast and there is nary the slightest whiff of vodka. It's as if the bawdy house of the night before was just a fading dream.

I calculate that our journey today will be a relatively easy drone towards Moscow, arriving there in the mid-afternoon, an estimated distance of about 250 miles, something achievable if the roads don't deteriorate spectacularly. The weather is fine and the temperature rising rapidly as I cart everything out to the bike and commence the loading routine. We trundle through a mixture of attractive countryside and patches of forest, occasionally passing broad expanses of water. The villages that we ride through are similar to the past few days: in the most part, cast back in time with rustic wooden houses, but perchance a little less so than yesterday. A tiny smidge of modernity has crept in. Away to our left, we pass the only campsite that we've seen thus far. Its derelict state tips a nod to the wisdom of overnighting in a motel. Any motel.

In between dicing with our fellow travellers, there is ample time to enjoy the scenery and gradually gain appreciation for the average Russian trucker. They can be split into three distinct groups, as far as I can see. The first group are relatively rare. They drive in the comparative luxury of a European truck, mostly Scanias, Volvos and German MANs – living it up, so to speak. Then there are the drivers of smaller trucks that are clearly of Soviet origin and quite often come in a shade of fetching pale blue, with a white 1960's-style bumper arrangement up front. A significant proportion of these carry water and the rest are farmers with produce piled to the point of suspension failure, grinding along at a modest forty miles an hour or so. Finally, we come to a very numerous group, driving a truck that I find myself quietly impressed with – the truck brand in question is the Kamaz.

Kamaz trucks appear in various configurations, the most common being a traditional articulated variant and, less often, a large mineral wagon with rakish lines. The trucks themselves appear to be angular refugees from the 1970's, but many are clearly a lot newer than that, some being brand new. Drivers of Kamaz trucks cover huge distances and presumably sleep in an upright position. They don't have the nice comfy sleeping compartment beloved of their western-equipped comrades. Nor do they have the elaborate artwork of western trucks, preferring a limited choice of a few flat colours of drab green, mid-blue, yellow or orange. A bit like the 1970s output of British Leyland.

The austerity of the Kamaz has its roots in planning by committee – getting the job done without the trappings of luxury, but getting the job done, regardless. I'm surprised to note that many of the truckers driving them are quite young. They don't have the benefit of air conditioning so usually have the windows open and are oft-most found to be stripped to the waist with a sun-tanned arm resting on the window frame as you sweep past them. I'm becoming a bit concerned that Diane may be developing a crick in her neck. When a truck breaks down or has a puncture, they pull off the road and fix it right there by the roadside. If the damage is severe, they strip the thing down to its skeletal state, then get a brew going and wait for spares amidst the scene of vehicular carnage. This occasional image of self-reliance helps to explain the huge ramps in roadside parks we noticed almost immediately after crossing into Russia. The ramps allow drivers to carry out inspections and maintenance. We occasionally spot the odd Lada driver using them for an oil change.

Russian vehicles are built to survive the road conditions, where roads can be found. It's no surprise to find out that Kamaz trucks have been a dominant force in the Paris-Dakar rally truck section for years.

You can find videos on YouTube of them doing amazing things. I think we should start importing them. I like austere vehicles. My 1957 Ariel was built shortly after rationing ceased. Its primary purpose was to get people to work and to haul the family in a sidecar at the weekend if one was hitched on to it. Of all my bikes, it is the one that will always start – first or second kick.

The drivers of these Russian trucks are a hard-working bunch – and hard-drinking, if last night was anything to go by. They are also friendly to those who are short of sight. Their registration numbers are plated in the usual fashion but, for some reason known best to Russians themselves, they also have the registration number plastered in huge letters and numerals on the back of the truck. What's that all about?

***

Another feature of the journey that intrigues the alien traveller (well, me at least) is the 'disappearing road'. The highway we are travelling on is variable in its quality as it flits twixt meadow, hamlet and forest, but we are managing a steady sixty miles an hour on it, which I consider to be good going. In large part, this is courtesy of the effectiveness of the BMW's off-road suspension setting, which is coping admirably. I don't know why I didn't think of switching to it before we arrived in St Petersburg. But, on passing minor junctions we can see, more often than not, that the road simply disappears into an abyss of rutted mayhem some ten or twenty metres after the turn. Unfortunate travellers who have turned into one of these junctions can be seen rolling in drunken fashion over the potholes, swerving manically to avoid them wherever possible.

Roughly every twenty-five or thirty kilometres or so we pass police stations that bear the initials ДПС. This has nothing to do with Nelson Mandela. It stands for DPS, Dorozhno-Postovaya Sluzhba, 'Road Inspection Service'. A few years ago, shortly after the collapse of the Soviet Union, gentlepersons badged thus were apparently not averse to stopping foreign travellers and demanding fines from them. It was reading such scare stories on the web that led me to baulk at entering Russia without my driving license paper copy, the less said about which the better. Thankfully, times appear to have changed. As the traffic slows down on the approach to each station, a policeman can be seen facing the oncoming traffic with baton in hand. A revolving baton means 'continue on your way, good citizen' whereas one held out straight means, 'pull in comrade, you look pretty suspicious to me, an inspection is required'. So far, we have only met batons of the twirling variety.

It occurs to me after passing a few of these stations, that the whole country could be put into 'lockdown' mode very quickly. Essentially, the DPS stations give the opportunity to create roadblocks throughout the network. It's very different from western Europe.

At around 4p.m., we notice a change in the road conditions and especially in the weight of traffic. We start to pass large industrial and retail centres. We have been counting the kilometres down to Moscow and have arrived at the outskirts of the great city. The road passes through quite pleasant suburbs with parks, shops, kiosks and crowded bus stops. Traffic lights at junctions usher in long queues in the swelteringly dry heat. In most part, the traffic is orderly, but occasionally someone loses their patience and tries a trick or two to get to the front of the queue. There are a few opportunities for us to filter, but I err on the side of caution. The bike is very wide with its panniers and still overloaded, so I decide to sit it out in the queue behind trucks that are belching fumes, open to the stares of commuters who are crammed into buses. Each stop provides time to drink in something new. At one junction, we sit opposite a large park complex with an impressive memorial in the brutally modernistic Soviet fashion, replete with wreaths. It's so different that it draws the eye before the lights change and it's time to progress to the next new sight.

As we work our way in towards the centre of the city, the roads improve measurably. We pass over a bridge high above the Moscow River, catching a glimpse of a surprising occupant of a berth over to the right – the view broken by flapping blue and white banners on poles that adorn the bridge. The object of interest is an old Soviet-era frigate, a Krivak to be precise, to give it the name NATO assigned to it, covered in dark red lead paint on her upperworks. I'm more than a little surprised to see a ship of this size so far inland, but there it sits, the Druzhnyy, which means 'Friendly'.

So, what is the *Friendly* doing here, so far from the sea? Well, the intention is to turn her into a floating museum. How they got it here is a complete mystery to me. The Moscow River is a tributary of the River Volga, a river that drains into the Caspian Sea, a sea that is land locked. But the ship was built in Kalingrad on the Baltic Sea. Maybe it has wheels under the keel.

***

Diane is now in meerkat mode, hotel hunting. As we pass down a wide dual carriageway, deep in the heart of the Moscow rush hour, it's clear that she's having no luck at all. We flash up our little friend on the handlebar and ask it to check the status of accommodation. After the degree of reluctance shown in even finding Moscow, it's a faint surprise to find it diligently putting its shoulder to the task, no doubt browsing the Moscow A-Z. The result is a modest list of options. We decide to head for the Moscow Nova hotel, the sister to the one in St Petersburg.

As we plunge deeper into the city, it reveals itself to be a surprisingly modern, clean and rather grand place. Why surprising? Well, I suppose my own preconceptions are conditioned by the western negativity that is directed towards our old potential foe and onetime ally. My expectations were that Moscow would be drab, uniform and particularly badly built. But it isn't. It is full of life and vigour with signs everywhere of a recent economic boom – new skyscrapers, neon advertising and lots of shopping opportunities. And the traffic is hurtling around at breakneck pace. There are plenty of Ladas, but the number of top-of-the-range Mercedes, BMWs and Range Rovers, not to mention Ferraris, make it feel, quite frankly, richer than Knightsbridge. Then again, Knightsbridge is full of wealthy Russians.

Our route eventually brings us in a theatrical swoop around a very recognisable landmark: the red walls of the Kremlin. The wide thoroughfare sweeps around it, then over a bridge. I'm watching the Garmin like a hawk, counting down the hundreds of metres to the turn off to the hotel. Just as we reach the junction, it switches screen and declares itself to be 'recalculating'. I search the mirror for the missed turning, but I can't see it. We're forced into another circuit of the ring-road.

The second time around, exactly the same thing happens – then a third. By now, I'm getting really pee'd off – mostly with myself, but also with the Garmin, and am cursing quite vigorously in the helmet. I'm as nippy as a cow-poked Yorkshire terrier. It transpires that the software, which has only recently become available, is mapping itself a few tens of metres from true geographical accuracy. When the speed of the cut-and-thrust traffic is taken into consideration, I find myself unable to predict the turn to the hotel with any safety and we keep missing it. In fact, the whole situation feels quite dangerous – the large executive cars are taking no prisoners around here. Thoroughly defeated and frustrated, we head out of the centre and return to Meerkat mode.

***

After a great deal of searching and a few false leads from the Garmin, we eventually turn up outside a very posh-looking hotel: the Moscow Radisson Blu. In fairness to our electronic guide, it did eventually direct us to a hotel, but the place in question was in a very run-down district with one or two abandoned cars providing hints that this may not be the best of choices. Then, just a half kilometre or so further on, we turned up completely by chance outside the security gates of this great tower. Clearly, we have a choice: feast or famine. Weighed down with fears for my credit card, I trudge up through the beautifully tended gardens leaving my navigator with the bike.

When I return to the bike, joyfully clasping a posh electronic key card, the said navigator is deep in animated discussion with a young Russian motorcyclist who seems a little embarrassed as I approach closer and quickly takes his leave with a wave. Diane fills in the details of her encounter:

'I'd put my helmet on the ground and the biker rode past. He rode right up there and then did a big 'U' turn, riding pell-mell back the way before doing another 'U' turn. He seemed to be asking me if I was OK and pointed to the helmet on the ground, he seemed very worried. I think a helmet on the floor means biker in trouble and he just wanted to make sure I was OK. Isn't that nice?'

Our hotel of choice is strategically placed adjacent to the huge Kursky train station and a newish shopping mall. A metro station gives us a link with just a few stops to the city centre and the area around the Kremlin. A cluster of upmarket shops adorns the lobby of the hotel, one selling Fabergé eggs. Cheap, it ain't.

One of the benefits of staying in a slightly upmarket joint is the level of security afforded to vehicular parking, which is of the top order. So, we can relax and enjoy our day sightseeing tomorrow. A slight downside is that we can't really afford to go blowing more money away in the hotel restaurant, so we head past the station and check out the supermarket in the mall, walking past lines of street traders and taxi drivers on our way there. I find myself faintly surprised by the number of younger women strolling around, dressed up to the nines, with high-end boutique bags draped on their arms – a sign of extravagant wealth in any city. They all look like supermodels.

The supermarket is stocked to the rafters with exceedingly fine fare. The vodka section is astonishing in its variety and so is the wine section. But, more impressive still, is the range of food on offer. I would place the quality roughly in line with Waitrose back home. We're able to pick up some nice bites to eat and wine to wash it down with. When we arrive at the cashier's desk though, we start to struggle. A question is asked in Russian, we shrug apologetically. Moments like this are doubly difficult because you've ground the whole queue behind to a halt and are left facing a bemused cashier who thinks you've just flown in from planet Zog.

'Can I help you?'

The person asking is a tall and rather distinguished gentleman, queuing behind us, who speaks impeccable English. I explain that I have no clue what I'm being asked.

'The young lady is just asking if you need a bag,' he says.

He helps to guide us through the process, then wishes us well as we prepare to depart, bags in hand. In my fertile imagination, I wonder if perhaps he's a spymaster – maybe a professor of English who works part-time for the intelligence services in the daytime and sips Martini at American Embassy functions at night, trapping the unwary with his easy charm.

***

We start the morning with a nice coffee in an open-air café near the railway station.

Strangely it doesn't feel like we've travelled too far to get here. It's common knowledge that this vast country, with its deep forests and endless steppe and marshes, has managed to swallow up huge armies throughout history. In fact, notwithstanding the awful road from the border to St Petersburg, we haven't found either the distance or the road conditions to be too bad. If we'd set off early and found the correct route out of St Petersburg, then we could have managed the trip between the two great cities in one leg – around 400 miles or so. But I don't think you could do it in an afternoon and wonder how the rider we met on the Estonian border fared.

The other notable surprise is the great strides that Russia has taken in modernising itself. It is probably doing so a bit late in the day, following the slump in fortunes after the end of the cold war, but the over-riding impression, especially in Moscow, is of a country on the upswing, no doubt in large part due to the wealth of oil and natural gas reserves. The *nouveaux riche* are not difficult to find, hereabouts. If they're not bowling around in their executive cars, then they're easily spotted at our hotel – a steady stream of plump, dark haired, middle-aged men, dressed in high-end fashion, with a young model wife or girlfriend on their arm. The hotel is stacked top to tail with them, and the car park is full of their BMWs and Mercs.

Outside the two great cities, the situation feels a world apart. A few things have struck me so far. The first is that the road we were travelling on intersected a largely flat, but often quite beautiful land. At the time we were riding through it I thought about the latent potential for food production, for some reason. So much of it is still forested. It occurred to me that Russia could probably quite easily feed the rest of the world if its agriculture were to be developed to the same degree as, for instance, the corn belt in America – and if it had sufficient farmers to produce the food. Then again, chopping down forests is probably the last thing we want to do in these days of global warming. Maybe we should ask the Russians to plant *more* trees instead.

***

One of the greatest cultural gulfs we have crossed is a gaping chasm in the concept of health and safety. It started in Tallinn and has been on a downward spiral ever since. We've travelled from one of the most risk-averse safety cultures on earth headlong into one that shrugs its shoulders, takes a deep draught of vodka and just gets on with it.

Central reservation barriers are only an occasional feature. The humble road sign is an endangered species along with road markings. If you can't overtake, then man up for goodness' sake and undertake, preferably on the verge, but make sure you are on your cell phone when you do it. Bald tyres on old cars are a given.

You must give way to approaching motorists. You may do so at the very last nanosecond before a 140mph closing speed head-on collision occurs, but you must do so, all the same. Our experience so far has been that Russian drivers are perfectly courteous if they are driving something in the mid to lower end of the cost bracket. It may feel like they are trying to kill you, but they aren't. Anyone in a BMW less than ten years old doesn't care one way or the other.

And so it begins. Diane has noticed that I appear to be developing an unreasonable, irrational, almost pathological hatred of BMW cars and their drivers. She has noted this carefully and is now honing a suitable response called the 'sharp twin-sided rib dig' to be used in the event of bad behaviour by the pilot. It is slightly less efficacious than Bruce Lee's one-inch power punch, but it does have the desired effect.

Chapter 11
The Kremlin

I've been looking forward to riding the Moscow subway, which is famous for its architecture and cleanliness. If I'm completely honest, the metro station we depart from outside the Kursky railway station isn't gobsmacking, but it does have some pleasant features and frills. The lights shine from huge circular recesses in the roof, perfectly symmetrical as they march the length of the platform. The roof is supported by columns faced with glazed tiles, giving the whole space a light and airy feel. Yet the colours are sombre fawns and browns. It manages to be both restrained and quietly celebratory.

We are, of course, heading for the Kremlin but, to do so, I think we need to make a line change. Not being too fluent in Cyrillic and struggling to make sense of the metro map, we decide to alight a station or two early and walk the rest of the distance which I estimate to be about half a mile at the most. Our chosen station spits us out adjacent to what appears to be the defence ministry – a huge building, richly decorated with symbols of its communist past. Uniformed officers pass to-and-fro, bearing attaché cases. We thread our way down a hill and along the main road that we circuited repeatedly last night, then through an underpass where kiosks sell cheap touristic treasures including plastic AK47s and MIG jets.

***

The Kremlin has a busy ticket office. Most of the visitors are Russian, but we end up queuing with a couple whom I assume to be American, but could be Canadian. Time to be a bit careful! In an unusual fit of tactical sensibility, I ask them where they've travelled from and it turns out that they are indeed from the land of the maple leaf.

One thing that strikes me particularly about this couple is the casually negative way they talk about the country they are visiting, complaining about the queue and the price of the ticket, as if they expect bad service and a broken society, a preconception that I'm ashamed to say we both held on our arrival a few days ago (and, in fairness, partly reinforced by the state of the roads and accommodation). The price for a full tour of the Kremlin is quite costly and we won't be taking it, that's for sure, but I have to keep reminding myself that this is one of the most expensive cities in the world. I ask them when they arrived, and they say they flew in yesterday. It's their first trip to Russia. We both tell them that we found St Petersburg to be a fantastic city, to which they reply, 'Oh really?' Yes, really!

***

A Kremlin, I am reliably informed, is a fortification within a city. THE Kremlin is the one in Moscow. Apart from the famous red walls that are often seen on television, the rest of the buildings are a curious mixture of different architectural styles, originating from many different periods. Buildings have been erected and torn down over hundreds of years on the site, many of those that survived being of Italian design. The result reeks of quality.

Access to the citadel involves passing through a tower then crossing a long, flat-cobbled bridge. The original moat was enormous. We have joined a steady stream of Russians, young and old, who are making their way to the tower gate at the other end. The Trinity Tower is a very impressive square structure, surmounted by an enormous, iconic red star. Entering through it transports you into another world beyond the teeming metropolis. It's a world of competing rhyme and reason: cultural, religious, atheist, aged, modern, royal and revolutionary. From its origins, steeped in royal and Christian orthodox symbolism, it gradually developed into modernism, via the mock grandeur of the Senate building to the austere monochrome of socialist centralism, in the shape of the State Palace.

The buildings are complemented by beautiful parkland and gardens, making the Kremlin one of the most interesting and attractive places I've ever set foot in – a genuine surprise.

The churches here are numerous. Their walls are combinations of pale stone and ones painted white. One church has rather beautiful domes clad in silver, providing a pleasant contrast to those painted gold. Each church has its own character, depending on its age. The arched doorway of one being richly decorated with twisting, woven plant stems and leaves, interspersed with mythical animals picked out in gold relief against a steel blue background. It bears flaky testimony to its age with the wear of years.

I must shamefully admit that my knowledge of this fortress was limited mainly to the images of the May 6th processions, when the Politburo sidled out above Red Square on the top of Lenin's mausoleum to witness the parade of armour and missiles that we in the West feared so much. Lines of soldiers and tanks trundled and marched past, followed by civilians waving bunches of flowers. After the parade, the politburo members presumably then sidled back in here for a tot of the hard stuff. During the cold war years, the abiding images of Red Square, for me, were the walls and towers of the Kremlin and the low, slab-sided pyramid of Lenin's tomb. The glorious buildings within the walls never registered at all. It's almost as if there was a trick of the eye, but I suspect it is more to do with the Soviet authorities airbrushing the religious buildings out in an act of careful editing.

Joseph Stalin went a step further than airbrushing. His brush of choice was a truckload or ten of dynamite, used to demolish the Cathedral of Christ Saviour, a few hundred yards outside the walls - to make way for a monumental Palace of the Soviets. Quite an achievement for someone who nearly became a priest. Marble from the demolition of what was the largest Orthodox Church in the world found its way into the buildings of the Metro, which was under construction back in 1931. Sadly, having blown the cathedral to smithereens, the state then ran out of money and couldn't proceed beyond the digging and building of foundations. When these filled up with water the authorities opened them as the world's largest open-air swimming pool.

***

There are two wonderful, particularly photogenic objects in the grounds of the Kremlin. The first is an elaborately carved cannon of massive proportions, the Tsar Cannon. It is over 19 feet long and about 10 feet high, weighing a tad under 40 tons and built in 1586, it has never been fired in anger – which is nice – but has been fired on at least on one occasion. A replica of this gun was recast in 2001 and donated to the city of Donetsk in Ukraine.

The Tsar Bell is just as richly decorated and similarly hugely proportioned but, unlike the cannon, it is broken and has never been rung. It stands over 20 feet high and is the largest bell in the world. It broke during casting when the wooden frame around it caught fire. Cold water was poured onto the conflagration and a fragment weighing over 11 tons dropped off the bell. A classic case of 'oops - it came off in my hands chief'.

***

After taking a short break for lunch in the formal gardens, watching a little sparrow hunt for insects in amongst the bright red and green begonias, we start to make our way back towards the entrance/exit tower. I was of the impression that sparrows are seed eaters, but it transpires that the common house sparrow has been found to eat 838 different foodstuffs, including insects. Clearly it shops at Sainsburys, rather than Lidl.

On our way out, we have a good look around the outside of the more modern State Palace. It was built in 1959 to host the congresses of the Communist Party and is now used for theatre events and pop concerts. It has managed to weather this transmogrification with a certain degree of dignity – from Nikita Khrushchev to Mariah Carey via Gorby and Boris Yeltsin. Peeking through the mirrored windows provides a glimpse of the understated grandeur that must have impressed the comrades as they arrived from the outlying republics, making them feel important and part of something to the greater good. The acoustics in the hall are reputed to be amongst the finest in the world.

***

Outside the old citadel we take a left and head through an attractive park, making our way in an anti-clockwise direction towards Red

Square. This involves a pleasing stroll along the river with the huge walls on our left, travelling across the view used by the BBC whenever there is a political interview with someone from Russia. We wander past the huge walls and their towers and then hang another left, up a slight incline into Red Square, to be greeted by the iconic sight of the Cathedral of Vassily the Blessed, or to give it the name most of us recognise, St Basil's.

As a child, I always thought the cathedral looked like it was made from icing sugar, and I have to say that seeing it in the brick doesn't take that impression away. It is much older than the Church of Our Saviour on Spilled Blood in St Petersburg and is more elaborate, sporting a proliferation of onion domes, each of which is decorated differently. I'm especially enamoured by the dark green, pale green one that has a spiral twist. On the one hand it reminds me of an ancient Persian's headgear, on the other an ice cream cone – flavour: pistachio. I have to grudgingly admit that the domes of Moscow have just pipped the wonderful spires of Copenhagen in the 'wow' factor. It's a close-run thing, but I'm voting for the onions.

To our left, the walls of the Kremlin run for the entire length of the square, interrupted by the magnificent Spasskaya tower, the main entrance to the Kremlin, and also by Lenin's Mausoleum. To the right, the view is dominated by the façade of the State Department Store, or GUM as it is known, famous for endless queues of shoppers waiting patiently for meagre pickings in harder times, but thankfully, 'tis no longer so. In total, it stretches for 794 feet and occupies a site that was traditionally a trading quarter. The square was formed when the Italians, who were designing the Kremlin walls and towers, advised the authorities that there needed to be a decent functional 'killing ground' on this more vulnerable side of the citadel. Gradually, over time, the killing field metamorphosed into a market and, later still, the site of ceremonies and banquets, which I think is something of an improvement.

The term 'Red' doesn't really mean the colour red, even though quite a lot of the buildings are red brick. In older days they were whitewashed. It doesn't reflect an association with communism, either.

In fact, the true meaning is 'beautiful'. We are standing in 'Beautiful Square', the centre of Moscow and, in many ways, the centre of Russia, since all of the main roads into Moscow lead to this spot and all the main roads radiate from Moscow to the rest of the country. And it really is a beautiful place to take a breather and soak it all in.

When we arrive at Lenin's tomb, a very embarrassing lapse in the trip-planning department rears its ugly head.

One of my major intentions on this five-month sojourn was to pop by and see Lenin. But, as we arrive opposite the dull red granite mausoleum, we can see that it is fenced off with barricades and closed. There are no goose-stepping guards – just a single, loosely-uniformed blonde girl, who is paying attention to the texts on her mobile phone. It turns out that the tomb closes at 1pm sharp. We've travelled 3,000 miles for a date with Lenin and arrived 90 minutes late!

Where one moment disappoints, another provides reward. At the end of Red Square, we arrive at another square called Manezhnaya, coming face-to-face with an impressive statue of Marshall of the Soviet Union Zhukov, captor of Berlin and joint victor of Stalingrad, mounted on a horse in full military regalia, exactly as he was when he took part at the victory parade in Moscow in 1945, riding a white stallion called Idol. I don't think he arrived to inspect the troops with a pigeon on his head, but there's one perched up there today.

The square is a focal point for stalls selling the usual souvenirs, ranging from matryoshka dolls to brightly coloured football scarves, including a Manchester United one. It's a loud and vibrant place, with some kind of mini pop concert being played behind the market stalls. But, a short distance away, we discover a man selling something altogether more interesting. On a table in front of him, he has a fine range of Russian military badges. And they aren't your common-or-garden ones either. They date from throughout the years of communism and include some that are very rare and collectable: Second World War tank crew badges, submarine captain badges and jet fighter pilot badges amongst others. We have discovered Soviet era badge heaven. My wallet is instantly out, a rare occurrence indeed.

━━◆◇◆━━

Chapter 12
Manoeuvres in the Dark

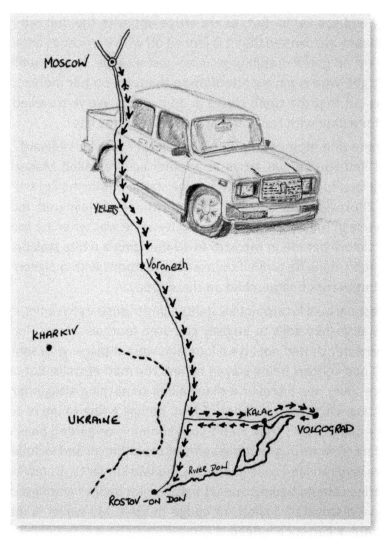

"Volgograd is relatively safe, avoid Rostov at all costs!"

We have one final mission to undertake before we depart Moscow; one we hope to achieve on the way out of the city. We want to find the Harley-Davidson shop and purchase a few of their very collectable 'T' shirts.

I've been trying to discover the route on the internet and have loaded it into the Garmin. Initial indications seem favourable, as it appears to point us in the correct direction, so we proceed with a degree of confidence. It appears that we need to ride out of the city to the ring road and hang a right, ride along the ring road for a few miles, then work our way back in towards the centre of the city. Somewhere down that road, we will find the Harley dealership on our left-hand side.

The first stage of the journey proceeds as planned. Having negotiated the ring road, we ride down a broad and thoroughly modern dual carriageway – the Leninisky Avenue – and arrive *tout de suite* at a point where the Garmin waves his little chequered flag, signaling arrival. But, all we've done is arrive at a set of traffic lights opposite a large office tower block. We peer over at it and conclude that our wee electronic friend has been uttering porkies again. The events on arrival in Moscow, where we kept missing our turn-off to the hotel, do not inspire confidence in Garmy's accuracy. So, we ride on a bit further, only to realise that the road is veering off, away from the city and not at all where we wish to go. At the first opportunity, we pull over and try to find a way back, eventually ending up in a busy little suburb of cheaper, worn-down housing, opposite a ramshackle car workshop. Moscow is very expensive and plush in the centre but, like many cities, her underskirts are a trifle tatty around the edges.

After a spot of faffing around, we manage to complete our 'U' turn and head back the way we came, right past the place where the Garmin is still merrily waving its flag, jumping up and down shouting, 'it's here, it really IS here!' We both stare over again. Nothing! So, we travel right out, across the ring road and try to execute another, altogether more risky 'U' turn in the heavy midday traffic, before pulling over to examine notes taken from the internet. I find myself to be very, very confused.

'I'm sure we went the correct way,' I muse, not without the odd seed of doubt. It feels like we're lost, but all the evidence points to that not being the case. I'm in half a mind to just get back on the ring road and ride hell-for-leather for the south.

Despite that feeling, we decide to have one last go, because the 'T' shirts really are very collectable. We trundle back down now familiar territory. And then, suddenly, Diane gives a shout and a tap on the shoulder, 'There it is!' We have arrived at the most heavily disguised Harley-Davidson dealership in Orthodox Christendom. The Garmin was right all along: the shop sits underneath the tower block, camouflaged by a cunningly placed MacDonald's restaurant and a wee dip in the surrounds. How could I doubt my little friend? It sits there in its wee cradle with a smug countenance awaiting its next mission, atlas in electronic hand.

***

Our route, if the map is to be believed, and I think it probably is, should take us down the M4 to a point where it divides into two. At this point we need to take the M6 – the road to Volgograd. At least I think it's the road to Volgograd. I had originally formed the idea of trying to strike eastwards, riding down along the river Volga, but now I'm not so sure. The fact is that nothing is going to happen if we can't navigate out of Moscow, but at least the signposts are readable, and we are generally heading in the correct direction.

We decide to stop at a petrol station to top up with fuel. Having filled the tank right up to brimming and paid in the shop, I wander back out across the forecourt to meet up with Diane. On arriving at the bike, we're approached by a young guy who has just filled his Suzuki SV650 with fuel. He speaks English and asks us where we are heading. We explain that we're heading south to Volgograd, after which we intend to make our way to Georgia. I'm half expecting him to ask why we want to go there, but his eyes light up and a big grin stretches across his face. 'I'm from Georgia, it is my home!'

Back on the road, we find the traffic to be very heavy and progress to be painfully slow. Our diversion to buy 'T' shirts has proven to be fatal in terms of achieving a decent mileage today. We're heading in the correct direction, but we've lost the day. A decision has to be taken: press on a bit further or call it a day and find a hotel. The truth is that we are less than likely to find accommodation once we've departed the outskirts of Moscow, and I'm not too keen about the possibility of searching for a hotel or motel in the dark. Diane is even less enamored with the thought of tent erection at the roadside. We pull off the main highway at a town called Domodedovo, totally unaware that one of the main Moscow airports shares the same name. It's a bit like pulling into Staines without spotting Heathrow. We do, however, spot a sign indicating that we are approaching a hotel.

Progress is slow. We head right through the town, thinking with a shake of the head that we must have made a mistake and missed the hotel. Then suddenly we pass a second sign saying: 'Green Park Hotel' and promptly miss the entrance. After executing a quick 'U' turn we head up a small road that takes us into pleasant, predominantly coniferous woodland before depositing us outside a large sprawling complex that is part hotel and part holiday retreat. This I did not expect.

***

The lady in reception is slim, middle aged, with blonde hair and the typically severe look of Russian receptionists with which we've recently become familiar. Much to my surprise, when I open my mouth, her pursed-lip glower turns into a broad, welcoming smile. A few minutes later, I skip out to the car park like Gollum with a fish in his mouth, and declare to Diane, 'It's quite nice and we're in!'

The route back to reception is a strange one, indeed. The entrance is a nondescript side-door that was pointed out helpfully by staff from the restaurant, first time around. Beyond that, we negotiate a series of wide corridors with light tiled floors, before passing through a door into a relatively dark, windowless reception room situated in the bowels of the building. The administrator/receptionist is sat behind a dark wood counter, still smiling sweetly.

The Hotel check-in procedure in Russia involves a lot of form-filling, the purpose of which is to register us with the local authorities. Diane has read the rules on this and has been fulfilling her administrative duties to the letter – something I personally would probably have forgotten to do, had I been travelling solo. In the previous hotel, it was done without us having to ask and so it is in this one, but if a hotel fails to ask, then Diane is fully primed to demand it of them. She's like a terrier after a squeaky toy. This *has* to be done and it *will* be done. It just takes a bit longer to check in as forms are filled in, passports copied, and ink is applied to stamps. Ink stamps are popular in Russia. Diane makes sure she has copies of the documentation and I have little doubt that she has it all carefully filed away, ready for the day that batons cease to twirl and the ДПС ask us for our paperwork. Thank goodness! At least one of us is properly organised!

The receptionist summons a lady, who takes us on a lengthy and slightly confusing journey along numerous corridors, up flights of stairs before opening a door into a surprisingly light and immaculately clean room, sizeable in proportion, which is decorated in the style of the 1980's. It's a huge effort to haul all the gear up from the bike, but I think the decision to call it a day was the right one.

***

Thursday the 26th of July 2012. The opening ceremony for the 2012 London Olympic Games takes place tomorrow.

The morning dawns, showing early signs that it will be a hot day. The builders are already busy working on a new-build extension to the hotel as we load up the bike ready for departure. Today's journey will transport us into the unknown. Google maps didn't allow us to use the little yellow man last night to check out the road conditions or the scenery we'll pass through. And, to be perfectly honest, even if it did, I probably wouldn't check it out. I don't even know the distance to Volgograd. I did take note of it when working out an itinerary as part of the visa process, but that's well in the past. I think I calculated that it would take three days to get there. Neither of us realise right now that we will be in the saddle for one of the longest rides we have undertaken to date.

It's a short ride to a junction with the M4 motorway, a road that manages to throw up a variegated mix of surface quality as it wends its purposeful way southwards. The traffic is light and the countryside increasingly vast, flat and open. The road is the central feature, carving through the seemingly endless plain like a pair of scissors cutting through a taught cloth.

The first problem of the day rears its ugly head very quickly. It's exactly the same problem that beset us shortly after crossing the border into Russia: I'm completely unable to make out the wording on the road signs. If I could slow down or stop and have time to ponder them carefully, I might be able to sort one or two place names, but right now the only name I can understand at all is the one for Moscow on the rare occasions that a junction allows for a 'U' turn. So, we trundle on for a fair amount of time, taking in the sights whilst we head into the unknown.

A couple of features have become apparent. Firstly, the road is now in remarkably good shape. In fact, it seems almost brand-new and appears to have been laid to a standard that would rival the very best roads in Denmark. The second feature – one that crops up every few miles or so – is a little less appealing: every now and again we pass a small, brick-built block. The brick block coincides with another feature. It seems that you can pull up and decide to cross the motorway on foot to make your way to the block, where presumably you can relieve yourself in whichever way you see fit. I make a mental note: 1) make sure to use the facilities at each and every fuel stop and 2) take regular fuel stops. I do not wish to sample the brick shithouses and I'm sure my partner will be of the same accord.

***

Talking of fuel, something strange has happened to the Mutt. We're tooling along at a steady seventy to seventy-five miles an hour and it doesn't seem to have much in the way of reserve power when I open it up. It's feeling a little winded. It doesn't take too much pondering to work out what's going on. I read on a few web blogs that the fuel here varies greatly in quality. We've ridden far enough to flush out the last

129

vestiges of decent fuel from our final fill up in Estonia and my big red mule, loaded up beyond its comfort level and starved of decent RONs, is now feeling decidedly asthmatic. It also feels ever so slightly rougher than normal.

Gradually the lands depart from being extremely flat and start to undulate a little, the road flowing nicely along the folds. As time ticks over, we happen across a fuel stop with a café attached and decide to pull over to get a bite to eat.

The establishment we have happened upon is in a state of mixed disrepair. The forecourt surface is poor without being fatally treacherous. To the left is a small and welcoming café, serving standard Russian café fare: savoury pastries, small pizzas, limited salad options and Lays crisps. Around to the right and set back from the main café and petrol station are the toilets – state and condition currently unknown.

In the café, we join a few fellow diners and settle for pastries, crisps and coffee. The indecipherable map book is drawn forth for consultation.

I estimate that we've been on the road for about an hour and a half and try to trace that in kilometres, index finger tracking along the E4, passing our intended turn to the east and plunging down into the depths of the south. I suspect we are at least seventy miles off track having blithely sailed past a series of signs that would have directed us in the correct direction if we'd been able to read them.

A middle-aged couple sitting at an adjacent table notice our furrowed brows and offer to help. The husband speaks a little English. I explain to him that we are heading for Volgograd, but that I think we've missed the correct road junction. He tries to help us pinpoint our position on the map, but seems to have difficulty himself, summoning the girl from behind the counter. She too doesn't seem to know where she lives. While they are deep in discussion pondering the map, a group of motorcyclists bustle into the room and immediately take an interest. One of them, an impressively big fella, speaks superb English and introduces them all as being members the Moscow branch of the Honda Gold Wing Owners Club.

'We have ridden to the Nordcap and are now riding to the Black Sea,' he declares. 'We don't know exactly where we will end up, but there is a big motorcycle rally on the Black Sea so we may end up there.'

'We rode up to the north of Finland too,' I reply. 'But we didn't get as far as the Nordcap, we're heading down to Volgograd and then on to Georgia. We think we missed our turnoff, and we want to see where we are on the map.'

He checks the map very closely and points to it. 'We are here.'

He explains to me that all is not lost. 'You can ride south on this road and turn off down here,' he tells us pointing to a junction far to the south. 'This road takes you to Rostov on Don, but that turning will take you to Volgograd.'

So, there we have it. Put simply, I can't read the maps. There's absolutely no point in me placing the map in front of my nose in the plastic window that sits on top of the tank bag. It would probably constitute a hazard if I started trying to decipher it. Robert Baden-Powell would not have been impressed by this cock-up. He'd have drummed me out of the cub-scouts for sure, long before I decided to quit of my own accord.

As a final friendly gesture, our Honda-riding friend writes out his mobile number. 'If you need help or just translation, phone me anytime.'

In the words of an advert from the 1970's: 'You meet the nicest people on a Honda.'

In the words of a 'T' shirt I wore at the time: 'I'd rather eat worms than ride a Honda'. But I've mellowed quite a bit since and have, in fact, joined the Legion of the Damned a while back and bought one.

Having sorted out our route, we head out to take advantage of the water closet facilities, wandering from the relative comfort and cleanliness of the café to the toilet block. A couple of the Russian lady bikers are exiting in hurried fashion, hands over their mouths and eyes staring – indicating to us not to go in there. But we persevere and enter the broken-down block. Just in from the entrance a lady sits behind a desk with a bowl on a table collecting payment of a few roubles. After paying, we turn our separate ways: left for gents and right for ladies. I worked for a while in palliative care – a job that removes most vestiges of delicacy regarding toileting. But nothing has quite prepared me for this. All I can say is that I'm very happy on two counts. Firstly, I only wanted a 'Jimmy Riddle' and secondly, men do that standing up. Diane emerges from her experience a whiter shade of pale. 'You'll never guess what it's like in there,' she says. I don't really want to know.

***

Before we departed, the 'Wing rider told us that we were welcome to ride along with them if we wished to do so. 'We stick to about a hundred and forty,' he said. I declined graciously, 'we're riding a bit slower than that – we've got a heavy load.'

It was a weak excuse. Closer to the truth lays the fact that I don't generally like riding in groups and, right now, the Mutt feels like an asthmatic, overburdened donkey at 130 kph. Three of them are riding Gold Wings, one couple being two-up. Then there's a solitary lady who is riding a rather smart, yellow Can-Am trike of the sort ridden by Jeremy, the huge, mad lunatic we met on the way up to Seattle, as documented in *Far Horizons*.

Since we're getting a head start on them, I decide to wind the Mutt up to see how it feels. Very soon, we are sweeping along, up-hill and down dale, sitting in relative comfort behind the screen. The bike is coping reasonably well but it really doesn't feel like it has much left in reserve. I keep an eye out for our friends and drop the speed back to around eighty miles an hour. We drone on for a considerable period without any sign. The traffic has increased a little. Occasionally, we pass the odd truck or car and, far less frequently, a car passes us by. There are no signs of police patrols. The road remains good quality. Eventually, I spot some single, bright lights in the mirrors and ease back a little to seventy-five miles an hour. The lights grow, until they blend and form with the shape of the vehicles bearing them. Our friends have caught us up.

They sweep past gracefully with a blast of the horn and a kick of the leg or a wave. The lady on the Can-Am doesn't wave. She's hanging on for grim death just like Jeremy was at that speed. I think the trikes are designed for more stately progress than this, despite being able to rip along fast enough. Later into the afternoon, we pause for a top-up of fuel and there they are, all lined up outside the next café on the road, no doubt having a coffee and afternoon snack. We fill up and press on.

***

Mid-afternoon and the road ceases to be a motorway, becomes clogged with traffic, and enters the sizeable city of Voronezh. Initially, this doesn't present too much of a problem – it's a nice change after a few hours of plugging along the motorway. But the traffic through the city becomes very slow as we pass further into it, leaving me to start ruing the lack of a bypass. It's a pleasant enough city though, quite green, with plenty of trees lining the streets. We pass through an area lined with older Soviet-era apartment blocks then into one with more modern ones. Towards the centre of the city, the buildings are appreciably older and some are clearly pre-Revolution. Right in the centre of the town stands an impressive, white civic building that has a tower as its central feature, not unlike the gate tower in the Kremlin. A star and wreath adorn the pinnacle. Maybe the authorities are hedging their bets on a return of communism.

My initial thoughts are that we should perhaps look for accommodation here. It's around 3pm and I'm not sure how easy it will be to find something further down the road. Motels hereabouts are a rare as rocking horse poo. We're sitting in a traffic jam in what appears to be the main shopping street, so I pull over and feed 'accommodation' into the satnav. It comes up with a hotel nearby, down a junction to the left. This takes us into an area that appears a bit dog-eared. I don't recall selecting the 'take the roughest route' option! After a modest degree of faffing around, we pitch up outside a derelict building that may or may not have been a traveller's rest at some point in its life. Right now though, it's a home for chirruping sparrows. We decide to give up and press on.

***

The road-building effort hereabouts is quite phenomenal. I've certainly not seen anything like it before, anywhere else. Endless streams of Kamaz trucks pass by, heading to and from the sites where the roads are being laid. Occasionally, we pass a truck that has broken down and has been torn apart by the roadside. When we pass roadworks, we discover a veritable flurry of activity, something we don't typically see at home. We once travelled past more than forty miles of traffic cones on the M6 south of the Scottish border and didn't see one single road worker.

But before I get too misty-eyed about the Russian effort, I should make mention of the flag wavers. It works something like this: You drive or ride at a steady 80 m.p.h. in a stately fashion down the road, being overtaken by BMW 4x4s ,until you happen upon a contra-flow section where the traffic crosses a space in the central reservation to let the workers lay a new section of tarmac. All well and good so far, but then the fun begins... Approaching the crossing point, there are no warning signs, no flashing lights and absolutely zero lorries with illuminated arrows and impact resistant rears. No. There's just a bloke in hi-vis overalls. He's standing in the carriageway in front of two or three carelessly cast traffic cones, nonchalantly waving a little flag in the general direction of the temporary gap in the Armco. The only safety consideration is: how quickly can he move if someone is on their mobile and not paying attention? Which covers around 90% of the oncoming traffic.

At one particular contra-flow section, it's all gone spectacularly wrong. The guy waving the flag is doing so with a little more urgency than normal. The reason rapidly becomes clear. A massive mineral truck has missed the contra-flow turning and has proof-tested the brand new crash barrier in no uncertain terms, flattening a good fifteen yards of it before coming to rest at a jaunty forty-five degree angle. Hopefully, there was a brick privy close by for the poor flag waver!

***

5 p.m. – I'm starting to get a little concerned. The motorway has disappeared like a will o' the wisp and we're grinding along in a queue behind a family in a Lada Samara. We pass through a series of small towns. The broken and part-rutted roads are choked with traffic as we

pass large trading complexes – an eclectic mix of stalls selling fruit, bread, toys, mobile phone repair services and eateries. We're now feverishly looking for accommodation. The distance between towns is huge and I'm becoming seriously concerned that this is our last chance saloon.

Suddenly we spot lodgings. The family in the Samara dive to the right towards the entrance. They're clearly on the same mission as us and spotted it at the final moment. I'm less decisive. We both stare across as we drive past. I think I would rather sleep next to the bike in a field than in that place. We scan both sides of the street to no avail. Seems like it was the only place in town. Rough as hell, with a car park jam-packed full, so most likely no room at the inn anyway. As we mosey out of town the shadows are appreciably lengthening. The sun is low in the sky. Rough calculation? Two hours before it hits the horizon. Tops.

∗ ∗ ∗

One hour later. Service has re-commenced in the motorway department and we're now cracking on at pace as the sun makes its final lunge to the west. The verge of the motorway is huge. People have pulled over in their Ladas and are sitting in folding chairs watching the world go by, drink in hand. I shout over to Diane, 'Maybe we should pull over and camp for the night.' She isn't keen. I can't blame her.

Eventually, we happen across a sizeable lorry park and pull to the side of the road. The park is similar to many we've passed today – littered with a dozen or so food outlets varying from people grilling meat on half-barrel barbeques to small trailer cafes like the one we're walking over to. The huge layby is packed with dozens of trucks parked in tight rows, clearly laid up for the night. There is nary a cloud in the sky. The sun finally disappears. It's chilly and we need warming up. I need a burger or something hot, but Diane takes one look at the conditions within the trailer and says, 'NO WAY, JOSÉ!' She may have a point. Despite this, the whiff of burgers and kebabs co-mingled with the oil from the ticking engines of Kamaz trucks is highly addictive.

So, we sit down at the trestle tables provided and dig into packets of Lays chicken flavour crisps, sipping a cup of very sweet coffee (I have no idea what the words for 'diabetic' or 'no sugar please' are in Russian). Despite the three spoonfuls of sugar, it's still a safer option; the navigator has proven the depth of her wisdom more than a few times in the past few days.

The lady who runs the trailer is very friendly, despite the turning up of noses at her sizzling hot sausages. I try to ask her if there is a hotel nearby and am pleasantly surprised when she says 'two fiva kilometer - two fiva', indicating with an upright, flattened hand in our direction of travel. I take this to mean there is a town just fifteen or twenty minutes away. Good news. So, with starvation staved off by Mr Lays' poultry-flavoured potato produce, we remount the Mutt and wave them goodbye. I'm not sure how wise it is to be travelling in the dark, bearing in mind the flag waver experiences of earlier this afternoon, but at least we don't have far to go to safety. And if the hotel is full, then we're stopping right there and kipping next to the bike.

***

Forty-five minutes have passed and we've seen not a single sign of a town or a hotel. The conditions are now pitch black. We are riding in a sea of black where it is impossible to distinguish land from sky.

I don't think we realise in the UK just how much light pollution we suffer in our little island. You can see it in those pictures of Europe taken from space. I've experienced proper darkness in the mid-Atlantic doing lifebuoy ghost duties on the back of a frigate. Standing on the helideck and staring up in awe at the night sky, gob-smacked at its infinite depth. We experienced it, too, in Yellowstone National Park. But this is something else. I can only liken it to wandering through a vast cave with a very puny torch. The lights on the bike are poor at best and, right now, they're struggling to penetrate the darkness before us. Finally, here in the early evening, we can truly appreciate the vastness of Russia. Russia has swallowed up all the light – and us with it.

And then, just as all hope was fading and I've started to think about pulling over, digging out our seven torches, and firing up the Trangia, something catches my eye. It looks like a tiny spot of light. A minute dot of blue light, glimmering in the distance. One minute it's there and then it isn't. Am I imagining it? No. There it is again, like a flickering, dancing blue glow-worm. Gradually, almost imperceptibly, it is growing. Growing until it becomes a permanent feature ahead of us. The minutes tick by. Unwittingly I've accelerated like a moth towards the light, which has now changed from blue to blue and white – and orange. It's got to be a service station!

At the very least, we'll be able to get something else to eat – I hope. I desperately hope. Then, maybe, we can catch some sleep next to the bike on a patch of grass beside the station. Many of the stations we've seen have been quite modern, with well-tended grass verges, so it wouldn't be too much of a hardship to kip down under the stars.

Now we can see it clearly. It *is* a service station, by jingo, and clearly it's open too. As we pull in, you could knock us both off the bike with a feather duster. There, in front of us in all its red, cream and white glory, sits a brand new, big chain, purpose-built motel. The first one we've seen for a thousand miles. With one solitary Lada parked outside the front door. It feels like a mirage in a desert, but it turns out to be completely real. Hallelujah!

⸺◈⸻◈⸺

Chapter 13
Goin' to the Chapel

The motel is rather splendid. It has a fine little café on the ground floor that was thankfully still open when we arrived last night. We had no idea what the menu was going on about apart from managing to decipher the word for 'soup' and the word for 'chicken'. Beyond this, my wee travel companion English-Russian dictionary was as useful as a Cadburys fireguard. We resorted to pointing at a lorry driver who was eating something resembling an omelette and sign signalling, 'that x 2 spasiba', hoping we didn't get pan-fried medallion of lorry driver served up with fava beans.

Armed with the word for soup, I couldn't resist sampling it. It was a delicate and finely flavoured broth with a single poached egg swimming around the generously-proportioned bowl, accompanied by bits of hen and seasoning for added texture and taste; a real case of chicken and egg – the Russians are partial to such puns as we found with the cat and mice sculpture back in St Petersburg. I love a good soup and this one was top-drawer. Diane, I have taken careful note, doesn't like black bread one bit. She also is none too partial about the broth, either. She may have to live solely on Lays crisps at this rate.

The brand-new motel is uber clean, with no sign of the urine-scented disinfectant of yore. The receptionist is almost a facsimile of the one in the previous hotel (severe, but quick to smile when a dose of charm is attempted). Sitting adjacent to the motel, the service station is similarly brand new and, wait a minute, what's that building over there?

It turns out to be a tiny, yet beautifully crafted log cabin in the form of an orthodox church – or, more to the point, chapel – complete with its own miniature golden onion dome. While Diane is doing her hair, I take a wander over to check it out. The elaborate exterior belies the fact that the building is really a very posh shed – and none the worse for that – quite square and functional but lovingly cared for and substantially built, with a simple wooden bookstand-cum-altar flanked by two elaborate, free-standing brass candlesticks and a tea light holder where you can strike a light for your loved ones and leave a small token for the upkeep of the chapel. Behind the altar are three large iconographic paintings, one of Jesus and two of characters unknown (one might be Mary).

Finding a brand-new chapel in a service area on a stretch of newly laid road is a genuine surprise, especially when you consider that religion was more or less banned/repressed for fifty years in this country. It shows that it is very much alive and kicking today. I dash back so that I can share my discovery with my navigator.

***

I have an air of expectant confidence about me today. There's a jaunty stride in my step. It's mostly to do with a feeling that we'll make it to Volgograd before sundown – even though I don't know where we actually are at the moment. I mean the road is excellent. Fair enough, it grinds down a bit when we meet the flag wavers, but beyond those occasional annoyances and the dereliction of the roads in any towns we happen upon, we really did achieve quite a distance yesterday. What could go wrong?

Executing a right turn at the service station entrance we accelerate confidently up to a decent cruising speed, hustling and rustling along under a fabulous, cloudless summer sky. The road is truly excellent, and the view from the saddle is one of expansive farmland and woodland coppices – mile after mile of it. How lucky we were, to happen across the motel last night, only really becomes apparent a few short miles from where it stands – it all starts with a colossal traffic jam.

How really, incredibly lucky we were becomes completely clear after we've sat in the queue for a good half an hour or so: unable to filter, increasingly hot, yet at this point not too bothered. Then it hits me like a jack hammer. On the crest of a gentle hill the road takes a slight sweep to the right. Then, quite simply, it vanishes into thin air and exhaust fumes. No perceptible signs or warnings – just the end of tarmac and the beginning of a very, very large hole. The reason for the traffic jam.

The hole has been scraped out by the tens of thousands of vehicles that have been forced to negotiate from the terminus of the perfectly laid bitumen to a patchwork stretch of Soviet-era concrete-based carriageway some way in the distance, with a huge gap of some few hundred metres in between. As we await our turn to enter the depths of the hole, I find myself in small dilemma. Progress is in tiny fits and starts. The truck in front is moving a few feet at a time, blocking my view ahead and making it almost impossible to plot a course. I'm in danger of not being able to keep my feet on solid ground. Oh well, the worse that could happen is we're going to tip over and fall off at zero miles per hour… we've done it before and the Mutley can absorb that kind of abuse almost without a scratch.

Imagine what would have happened if we arrived here last night, nudging eighty miles an hour… we would have crested the little hill and sailed off into oblivion. It's a sobering wake-up call. We should not, under any circumstances, be travelling these roads at night. This is the reason why the Russian Lada drivers pull up at sunset and light up their stoves. Putting these rather grim thoughts aside though, we have to negotiate our way forward. We can see the line of traffic ahead, snaking its way down the lee of the hill towards a sizeable settlement.

Complete, chaotic logjams provide only modest obstacles to the average Russian driver in his trusty Lada or UAZ-452 'Bread Loaf' van. A steady stream of escapees can be observed to our right, abandoning the traffic queue and heading pell-mell across the steppe. In the distance, we can spy a line of vehicles rolling violently along a minor road or farm track that runs parallel to the main E4, about half a mile away, kicking up a huge cloud of pale, orange dust that hangs wraith-like in the air and, for some reason, reminds me of a Wild West wagon train. The escapees from our traffic jam are heading like lemmings for that road and will simply end up in a new logjam at the terminus with the farm track. The cars, vans and trucks already on the parallel minor road are *not* letting in new arrivals. There is no entry for 'give way' in the Russian phrase book.

UAZ-452 'Bread Loaf' van.

A small group of Honda Gold Wings (Russians seem to like them a lot) filter past us with a toot from the riders and a wave from their pillions. I wonder for a second or two if it's worth following them, but elect to stay put and am eventually duly rewarded as we start to make some progress. In little leaps and bounds we gradually reach the point where the broken-up part of the road becomes a proper road again and the traffic, by now covered in fine dust, begins to crawl steadily forward into the birch-lined entrance to the rural town of Tarasovskiy, population 9,000, a settlement that lies along the meandering path of a small river.

***

At this point in our journey, it comes as something of a surprise to discover how close we are to the Ukrainian border, a fact supported by the numerous signs initially for Xapkib (Kharkiv) and latterly for Луганськ (Luhansk). Western Russia is not as huge as we in the west have come to think, at least not in its east-west axis and not since the fall of the Soviet Union and the resulting loss of the former republics. It dawns on me just how vulnerable Russia is to threats from the west. If Ukraine were allowed to join Nato, for example, it would be very easy to place an army and air power at a point that could seriously threaten Russia strategically, to cut western Russia in half just like the Germans very nearly managed to do once they'd swallowed Poland.

Progress through the town is grindingly slow. We pass down a street lined with the now familiar open markets. We're travelling along an important arterial route to the south and each town we pass through provides sustenance for the weary traveller. The road in the town is much repaired – one fix over-layering the next, occasionally successfully so, but more often than not in the form of a melted blob of folded bitumen. Beyond the town, it improves again. It seems as if the local authorities are responsible for fixing the roads in the town and the state is building the nice modern highway in between.

After half an hour's riding, we hit another town called Kamensk-Shakhtinsky, crossing a bridge over the River Siversky Donets. Arriving at a traffic junction, we spot the unmistakable signs of a Chinese restaurant down a side road and make the quick decision to pull in for chow. It's slightly early to be taking lunch, but the journey is going well and I'm guessing that the leg over to Volgograd will only take a couple of hours tops. Let's eat!

* * *

The inside of the restaurant is, thankfully, fully air-conditioned and rather swanky. It is deserted, apart from two well-dressed businessmen, the occupants of the shiny new BMW car parked just outside the door, who appear to be deep in conversation as we arrive. Having taken our seats in a 'snug', a few rows away from them, we peruse the menu. The truth is that it might as well be in Chinese, because to us it is completely indecipherable. I'm desperately looking for soup options but, even here, my memory has failed me and it's out with the Collins dictionary again.

'Can I help you?'

We look up from our deliberations and come face to face with one of the nice urbane gentlemen who, it turns out, speaks impeccable English.

He explains the menu to us in detail, going through each of the sections: beef dishes, fish, chicken and rice, asking us where we're from and where we're going.

'The turn-off for Volgograd is very close. You won't be able to miss it,' says he, something I take to be slightly presumptuous.

'It's good that you are going to Volgograd. It's safe there, more or less. Very little robbery or violence.'

Ok.....

'Rostov is different. Very dangerous. If you go to Rostov you need to be very careful. It's full of mafia.'

Hmmm.

'It isn't safe here either. Why have you parked your bike away from view? You must never do that! It will be stolen while you eat, and they will shoot you if you try to stop them. Go and move it to this window,' he points to the window opposite. I do exactly what I'm told to do straight away, feeling like a chastised child.

Ten minutes later, after cold drinks are served the two 'men in black' depart, complete with shades now covering their eyes, having come over and said a very polite 'goodbye'. Diane and I look at each other a little awkwardly. I don't really know what to say. My travelling *modus operandi* is to assume everyone is basically a decent human being. Am I being inordinately naive?

Diane poses the question that hangs in the air:

'Do you think they actually *were* the mafia?'

***

It doesn't take long to reach the junction with the M21, the road to Volgograd. There aren't many junctions and this one is a big one. The signpost says 'Волгоград' and the distance is around 380 kilometres. That doesn't sound too bad. What's that? Rough calculation: 250 miles or thereabouts?

Whoa. Hang on a minute. It's around 2:30 in the afternoon and we have at least four and a half hours of travel, maybe more. As we turn off the M4 the road conditions take a swift descent, plummeting instantly from 'excellent' into 'abysmal'. My heart sinks a little. This could be a very long leg indeed. Initially, we make reasonable progress. The suspension is handling the new road conditions reasonably well, floating over the irregularities more often than not, but occasionally being hit with a very heavy jar as we slam into a deep pothole.

We are now riding roughly along the same path as the German 6th army took on its rapid advance from Rostov to Stalingrad, across the great steppe of Southern Russia. The fields on either side of the road are huge and are being cultivated by enormous tractors with caterpillar tracks, reminiscent of the tanks that once fought across these plains. The topography is, typically, long rolling swells of cultivated field or of grassland, scattered with trees, almost like a vast ocean dotted with green patches of flotsam.

Two crops have become increasingly familiar: sunflowers – huge fields of them – and melons. The latter are sold at regular intervals by the roadside and often found crammed to the roof in low-slung Ladas that toil along the highway with bottomed out suspension. The sunflower fields are a source of fascination. They're in full bloom right now – a truly incredible sight as they all point heavenwards, tracking the sun in unison. A vision of bright yellow.

The drivers hereabouts seem to take an almost Italianesque delight in racing. They're mostly driving ancient Rivas and Samaras with the odd GAZ Volga for good measure. Tootling along at sixty or so miles an hour risks finding yourself neck-and-neck with some young Russian blade who will veer out and attempt to overtake you with his foot firmly planted to the floorboard, overtaking straight into the face of a stream of oncoming traffic, swerving back inches in front of you in a last-ditch attempt to avoid catastrophe. In one heart-stopping incident, the driver overtaking a car in front of us doesn't make it in time. A white GAZelle van travelling in the opposite direction flashes their lights furiously before taking to the broad grass verge in a shower of dust and stone chippings.

After a while, I decide that being overtaken in this manner isn't much fun. In fact, it's downright dangerous and it feels like we're living on borrowed time. I decide to switch into overtaking mode myself in a bid to get ahead of the stream of traffic. One by one, we start to pick off the cars in front, causing them to increase speed as we loom in their mirrors. But the Mutt is sufficiently faster than them, even in its overloaded state and despite the paucity of proper time-served RONs in the fuel. We sweep past them with the rider cackling away and the navigator preparing to administer her evil rib-dig, in the event that things don't calm down.

Gradually, we work our way ahead of the traffic and find ourselves on open roads, where it feels just a touch safer. Although some sections of the road are reasonable, there are others that are diabolically poor, featuring melted tarmac that resembles violently folded marzipan, manipulated by a demon baker. The huge trucks have worn seriously deep ruts in the carriageway. The choices we face are to ride along the tips of the ridges or consign ourselves to the depths of the ruts. Once stuck in a rut it's a proper, dangerous wrestle to get back out.

We gain a short respite at a fuel stop. Across the road sits a thoroughly modern Lada emporium, in front of which lie a clutch of derelict, abandoned Rivas. I'm standing in the queue patiently waiting my turn to pay with a little piece of paper on which I've written different litre figures for the dollops of fuel I'm likely to need to top the tank up and the desired quality: 97 RON. In this way no Russian language is necessary. Just a smile and a point of the finger. Well, at least that's the theory.

Unfortunately, in this station the assistant asks a question (which turns out to be, 'which pump?'). Naturally I'm completely flummoxed by this.

After a few quizzical seconds, somewhere at the back of the queue a huge guffaw roars out in the deepest of baritones.

'HA, HA, HA. Ayea can elp. Ayea speyak fairy cood Eyangleesh. Fairy cood.'

Everyone turns around and gawps. The translator to be is a huge – and very young – traffic policeman. He's just expended his whole English vocabulary in that one sentence. But it has brightened up everyone's day and he's now beaming broadly at everyone beaming back and repeats, 'Fairy cood Eyangleesh.'

***

About halfway through this leg to Volgograd, we pass reminders of the cataclysmic events that took place seventy years ago on these very plains. One such memorial is a quite outstanding piece of Soviet art. It stands some distance from the road. Huge hooked gears rise up out of the earth, morphing into a massive, monumental bar of steel which itself transforms into a half formed, stylized tank launching off into the clear blue sky, then it mutates into a second one, recognizable as a T34. Both tanks appear to be life-sized, guns pointing defiantly at the west.

As the afternoon drifts towards the early evening, we spy a small range of hills ahead, a break in the vastness of the steppe. The road gently rises, taking a slight sweep to the right, finally revealing a fine vista. We have arrived at the point where the road crosses the River Don – at the small town of Kalach. We've arrived exactly seventy years since the mid-point of a great battle that took place here when the 6th Army forced a bridgehead, against desperate Russian opposition, crossing the river just to the north and allowing for the final push to Stalingrad. We're just 30 kilometres away from the great city. It's all going very well. All that remains is to negotiate the city and find accommodation. Diane has carried out her usual thorough research and has identified a hotel that gets the thumbs up from *Trip Advisor*. She carefully observed that one hotel needs to be avoided, recognisable for having the smallest, tightest-fitting lifts in Christendom, possibly in the whole world. The recommendation was 'avoid this hotel at all costs and if you can't avoid it be sure to use the staircase'.

As we approach the city, the traffic density increases and the penchant for a race rises in similar coefficient. Everyone from cars full of young men to family men with the wife and two kids seem to want to scalp the foreigners with hair-raising attempts to overtake or not be overtaken. But then the fun is brought to an abrupt halt at a railway crossing at the mid-point of a very run-down, almost derelict area comprising ancient factories and what appears to be a substantial army settlement of some kind.

The queue at the crossing is a long one and there's no sign of a train. Everyone alights from their cars, gathering in the road, lighting smokes, and chatting sociably. We climb off the bike to stretch our legs. A few people wander over: some of the youngsters who were racing us and one of the family men with kids in tow. I honestly felt a few miles back that this lot were trying their very hardest to force us into the ditch, but no! In fact, they're all really interested to look over the bike and to examine it in detail. The father figure points to the roundel on the plastic tank declaring to his son, 'Bey emm Vay' in approving fashion.

'ochen' khorosho machina!'

I know that 'orchin carashore' as it sounds phonetically means 'very good' and I can work the rest out.

'da, ochen' khorosho,' I reply.

Everyone smiles, words are passed around. The western pussy speaks a smidge of Russian. I'm as proud as Larry. My new friend points to me.

'Americkanskiy?'

Damn, I'm stuck now. I really should know the word for British.

'Niet. British,' I try in unconvincing tones.

'Ah nemetskiy,' he responds... 'Deutsche!'

'Nein, Nein, I mean No! Niet'..... 'Englishsky and Scottishsky.' This is turning to a farce.

In desperation I blurt out 'London!'

'Ah <u>LON-DON</u>!' His eyebrows are raised in genuine surprise. We've finally got there... he turns to the others - 'Angliyskiy!'

Well, yes and no. Diane is a Scot, but she doesn't normally take offence. Alex Salmond would be mortified and would be rooting through the bags searching for his tartan trews.

We've learned something here today at this railway crossing. Russians, it would seem are exceptionally keen to meet Americans. There's a genuine desire to do so. After that, they want to meet Germans – something I find a bit surprising. They clearly admire German machinery and seem to have respect for them as a race. Simply by riding a German motorcycle, we appear to have proven ourselves to be reasonably good sorts. Beyond that, I guess we poor Brits are forced to accept that we rank somewhere in the second or third tier of 'interesting people and potential future enemies it would be good to meet' – slumming it with the French, Spanish and Italians. Russians respect size and power. They may not ideologically like the Americans, but they do seem to want to meet one in person.

Note: Some time after the trip I was talking to a Russian friend of mine about this very encounter and she told me that, even nowadays, Russians are taught from a very young age that Americans are poorly educated and can therefore be quite stupid.

'The sheep decided to speak very slowly. For it was a cold fact of nature that wolves were ignorant, and nothing would convince them otherwise.' Babe.

***

It is a cold fact of nature that time is dragging on and we are now into the early evening. Eventually, the train clanks slowly by with a line of screechy wagons, then the barrier rises, and we all head off again. But now there is no racing. The cars snake through the increasingly built-up area and, within a few minutes, a sign for the city seems to indicate that we need to take a left down a road that, quite frankly, resembles a tank driver's training ground. We pull over at a large junction to take stock. It's dark now. The roads are dreadful. Some of the potholes we're encountering are slamming the bike so hard I imagine something will break. We need to find this hotel fast! I start to get a bit narky and Diane responds with a few well-aimed nips.

Parking up at a petrol station, we try to take stock. Is Volgograd on the eastern shore or the western shore of the Volga? Did we cross a bridge back there? – I thought we did, but I can't be sure. We are returning to the pitch-black conditions of last night – have we learned nothing?

The satnav is duly consulted. It flicks through the A-Z of VG and raises its little electronic eyebrow. 'Don't seem to see any hotels hereabouts, chief – should we press on to Beijing?' I flick through the available modes until it kindly produces a five-millimetres-to-the-mile rendition of the city on its tiny little screen, cleverly switching itself to 'nighttime settings', which makes it a lot harder to locate the river... maybe when we get to the river, we'll just ride straight in. This is enough though. I can see that we've ridden back out of the city and then, in a fit of brilliance, managed to bypass it.

'I think we should just find the river,' I declare to my patient passenger. 'The city centre seems to be just off the river, so let's head down there and try our luck.' Diane gives a shrug, along the lines of 'whatever!'

Zooming in a little on the device helps me plot a course and, pretty soon, we find ourselves on one of the main arterial routes. What happens next makes me feel incredibly fortunate that we did get lost and especially lucky to have arrived after dark. As we crest the brow of a hill on our final descent to the river, I happen to glance to my right and find myself genuinely flabbergasted. There, lit up by floodlights, is the most evocative, ethereal sight: a gigantic statue - serenely rising stratospherically above a screen of trees. It's only a brief glimpse, but it is enough to take our breath away. It's a truly stunning sight.

━━◆〉◆━━

Chapter 14
The Mamayev Kurgan

As we ride along the riverbank, we encounter more badly broken road. Every few seconds, we crash into another merciless pothole. Still, we see no sign of any accommodation.

Despite the late hour, the streets are still busy with cars and buses. Crowds of people pack the bus stops. The most common form of public transport seems to be the Volga ESTelle mini-bus, into which people are packed like sardines. Suddenly, Diane shouts out. She's recognised the area we're approaching and believes we are near to our desired destination. Tapping me on the shoulder, she shouts that we should take a right turn. We arrive at a large square, which is bordered by restaurants and a floodlit hotel called the Hotel Volgograd.

My partner is posted on anti-mafioso duty whilst negotiations take place at the reception desk. Initial impressions are of an establishment drenched in faded grandeur. Back out on the pavement, Diane is uncertain whether we've found the correct hotel and is deep in animated conversation with a young lady. It turns out that we've walked slap bang into a wedding party – celebrating outside the hotel with lots of wine, vodka and a rather impressive fireworks display being fired off into the night sky from the square across the road. Our new friend, one of the wedding guests, is an Anglophile. What a pleasant welcome to Volgograd!

We slowly decant the luggage into the smallest shoebox of a lift I have ever seen, confirming our fears that we've landed at the 'wrong' hotel.

***

Saturday 28th July. Last night saw the opening ceremony for the London Olympics.

We've decided to stay three nights here, allowing for a visit to the Stalingrad memorial tomorrow, then a day of slumming around doing some catch-up on clothes washing and carrying out a long-planned and potentially stressful, but essential, servicing task.

One of the important pre-conditions of our trying to ride around the rest of the world together was a clause that says: 'thou shalt ensure my hair is coloured at regular intervals, not exceeding four weeks (28 days) or thou shalt forsake thine pillion passenger at the nearest suitable air or sea port'. At the time of clause insertion, my attitude was 'fairy Nuff'. But now, I'm not so sure. If truth be told, I would much prefer to disassemble the Mutt down to component parts, sans-Haynes Manual, and try to put it back together again, than mess around with my pillion's locks and partings. When Diane explains the procedure for applying said hair colour, I have little doubt that the bike would be less of a challenge. Also, I have little doubt that her scalp is going to end up the same colour as the bike, else it will be green.

Never mind. That is all a day from now and can be consigned to the back of the mind in much the same way a trip to the dentist for a root canal fix would be. A trip down to breakfast allows for a little more consideration regarding the history of the hotel, which I find quite fascinating.

Originally built in 1890 as the Solichnye Nomera, it was a rather grand hotel in its day and was visited by many famous people, notably one J. Stalin, who used it as a base for his work arranging the supply of food and ammunition for the Red Army in 1918 (at a time when the Red Army was engaged in a civil war with the White Army). Stalin was an intelligent nascent dictator and a supreme organiser. He would probably have flourished in many modern organisations by mixing a canny sense of the strategic with the ability to analyse details. Someone who would have had a blast with Excel spreadsheet pivot tables.

Fast forward twenty-five years to 1943, and the whole of Stalingrad was completely destroyed by the German Luftwaffe in preparation for the arrival of Von Paulus' 6th Army. The hotel was leveled to its foundations. Rebuilding work commenced in 1948. The devastated city was gradually resurrected by the efforts of the army, the population –

mostly women – and a large contingent of German prisoners of war. The Hotel Volgograd was completed and opened in 1955, built on the original foundations of its predecessor in a form called *Stalin's Empire Style*, a neo-classical form that bears a surprising number of fancy flourishes.

We have arrived at a crucial tipping point in the fabric of the building because there are signs of significant modernisation. One entire wing is screened off as work commences and the huge inner quadrangle behind the hotel is essentially serving as a builder's yard, with just enough room to squeeze in Mutley. Consequently, these are the last few months where the hotel can be savoured in all its communist-era glory. Most people would probably prefer to stay in a fully functional, modern hotel, but I don't count myself amongst them. Despite the dreadfully tired, threadbare room and the endlessly long corridors with equally threadbare carpet and deep red curtain dividers, I firmly believe we are witnessing a historical treasure.

***

In the morning, over breakfast, we decide to walk the 6.2 kilometres from the hotel to the statue we spotted on our arrival. The site of the statue is called the Mamayev Kurgan. It's a very hot and dry morning. One kilometre into our epic trek (epic for someone with arthritis in the right foot, at least) and we need to take on board liquid. A street kiosk provides relief and we push on past the final few blocks of the city centre and into a stretch of pavement that gradually deteriorates in both standard and upkeep.

The city is a decaying shrine to the battle, with many memorials both large and small. The ones in the city centre are quite splendid, but there are many more in varying states scattered along the road we are taking. Every so often, we're passed by a lovely old tram that looks like a refugee from the 1960's, clicking its way along slightly overgrown tracks. It's quite tempting to wait for the next tram at one of the stops, but I can just imagine the mayhem we would cause trying to buy a ticket for somewhere we can't pronounce. Like Rex in *Toy Story*, I couldn't bear the humiliation and opt to chicken out of that one. As we finally approach our destination, we pass by a derelict football stadium, complete with overgrown car park and faded posters advertising the final game played there – a poignant and slightly sad sight – a reminder of past raucous times, now a passing memory.

***

A *kurgan* is a Tartar burial mound, a tumulus, if you like. This one is quite huge and almost triangular in shape. Before the battle of Stalingrad, it dominated the city and provided a broad green space where young lovers would picnic in the summer. It must have made a wonderful place for tobogganing in the winter. In contrast to the soccer stadium across the road, the entrance to the Mamayev Kurgan is very grand, with well-tended parkland and immaculate steps. Large crowds are gathering there, arriving in their busloads, young and old. An enterprising little group have assembled some old Red Army vehicles – Russian jeeps – with actors in uniform, allowing visitors the opportunity to purchase a photo posing with them in the jeep. We get frowned at for taking an impromptu (free) photo!

Passing into the site, we commence a long and energetic climb up to the memorial, across a railway bridge where we pause to photograph a train clanking past below. Even at this height, far below the summit and not even having set a foot on the tumulus, we get a fine view of the outskirts of the city. And what a strange sight it is too. You see, in some ways Volgograd hasn't changed much at all. Across to the north lies a district of very heavy industry, pumping out the un-mistakable orange cloud that signifies a working steel works. This is the site of the famous tractor works within which the Russians and Germans fought a desperate battle just under seventy years ago, neither side being able to fully capture or retake it. A place where T34 tanks rolled off the production line straight into battle.

And then there's the Kurgan. In 1942, it was a strategic height, so much so that it seemed whoever managed to hold it would win the battle. The Germans repeatedly drove the Russians from the summit only for it to be retaken. Now it lies in peace, but beneath the verdant grass the top layer is comprised of a grim mixture of shrapnel and bone. Nothing would grow on that mound for years after the battle.

The climb up the hill takes us through a series of zones in which the visitor experiences images of the monumental struggle that took place here. One of the most impressive is formed from two vast walls with stark reliefs depicting a city in ruins, the defenders of which appear to grow out of the broken brickwork. The figures who populate this hell-on-earth are portrayed larger than life - muscular, chisel-faced, and grimly determined superheroes. They are subsumed by the city. The value of life, in such a desperate struggle for survival was infinitely small to those commanding the armies. During the course of the battle, the Soviets executed over 13,000 of their own troops for crimes ranging from desertion to merely voicing doubts about how the battle was going.

The humans are portrayed as if they are formed from the bricks of the city. A soviet portrayal of the value of human life where the state subsumes the citizen.

It occurs to me, standing here, that we all owe a huge debt of gratitude to the Red Army soldiers who brought the German Army to a shuddering halt at this spot. The two armies fought with a ferocity unique in the European theatre of war. The abstract depiction of the battle on these walls gives a clue to that ferocity - the soldiers were both victims of the situation they found themselves in and heroes for rising above it and winning what was arguably the most crucial land battle of the whole war.

∗∗∗

A little further on, we come to the entrance of a building built into the hillside. A low relief façade flanks the entrance to the building, which presents another surprising take – this time regarding the circumstances of victory and defeat. Fittingly ,the soldiers of the Red Army appear on the left side of the frieze, jubilant at the German surrender. These soldiers are portrayed in a far more naturalistic style than the previous, heroic ones, in fact almost photographic. This artwork shows the victors to be ordinary human beings, representing the different ethnicities of the Soviet Union – many of the soldiers who took part in the battle were from the Asiatic republics of the USSR, transported vast distances to be thrown into the desperate struggle. On the right, the broken and utterly defeated 6th Army shuffle along in a line. The portrayal shows them, heads bowed, uniforms tattered, wrapped in dirty bandages. Some of their senior officers are well fed whilst the troops are shown to be starving. I can't see any anti-German sentiment in this monument, rather it portrays pride in the victory of communism over fascism. It's an image that captures reality. The Russians flew in American and British journalists to witness the German generals they had captured, most of whom were relatively well-fed, whilst the ordinary soldiers were lice-ridden, frostbitten and starving. Cases of cannibalism were not uncommon in the makeshift prisoner camps out on the steppe.

The entrance leads into a vast and a strangely beautiful, circular *Military Honour Hall*. A huge hole in the roof provides natural lighting and the walls are tiled with golden mosaic. The centerpiece is a large, sculpted hand holding a torch in which the everlasting flame burns. Two soldiers stand on plinths as guards. The path through the hall curves gently up around the perimeter of the building, flanked by long lists of soldiers' names set into panels on the golden walls – many thousands of them, but surely, just a fraction of those who died? Perhaps these are the names of those with no known grave. As we're walking up to the exit, a soldier approaches and physically removes the baseball cap worn by a young man walking in front of us, thrusting it firmly into his hands. The message is clear: here, you show respect.

It strikes me that the hall has a semi-religious feel to it – which is strange, considering it was built by an atheist regime. It has the faint whiff of a modern Catholic church. The central plinth is decorated with wreaths bearing the red star and the ribbon of St George, a black and orange ribbon that symbolises valour in combat. We've been seeing many stickers on cars depicting this ribbon on our way south.

We stroll out into hot afternoon sun, casting its bright glare from a clear blue sky. Above us the view is dominated by *The Motherland Calls*, the amazing statue that towers over two hundred and seventy feet from tip to toe, dominating the whole complex. Once the highest statue in the world, now merely the second highest. It takes the form of a woman wreathed in classical robes that are cast around her by a mighty gale as she thrusts a broadsword skywards with her right hand, beckoning a whole country to resist the invader. It is an extraordinary sight, fashioned from concrete – apart from the mighty stainless steel sword.

***

Here at the top of the hill, we find a splendid view of the river, the steelworks and much of the city beyond. A bridal party have just emerged from a lovely orthodox church, the church of All Saints, that sits a short distance away. Many famous men have been buried here in a long line of graves, each marked with a granite slab – heroes of the Soviet Union. Vasily Zaytsev, the legendary sniper, who was made famous in the west by Jude Law's portrayal of him in the film *Enemy at the Gates*, was finally laid to rest here in 2006. It was his dying wish to be buried here when he passed away in 1991.

After a good couple of hours wandering through the complex, we locate the exit at the back of the hill. We wander past a bus park and café complex, skirting around the barracks, which presumably houses the guards. A small old military bus is parked outside, an austerely equipped, olive green transport for the squaddies, cheered up on the inside, quite bizarrely, by a British Royal Navy sticker. The Senior Service manage to get everywhere, even in this age of endless defence cuts. Nelson would surely be impressed, and Hardy too.

*** *

Day two in the Hotel Volgograd. Various accoutrements associated with ladies' hair emporiums miraculously appear from that part of the baggage train marked 'navigator only'. After breakfast, we wander down to the river for a stroll/stay-of-execution. The Volga is particularly wide at this point. It really is a major super-highway in transportation terms, navigable from the point where it drains into the Caspian Sea right through to a point far north of Moscow – the largest river in Europe.

The walk down to the river follows a broad formal parade that takes you through a fine set of war memorials, neatly laid with flower beds. A pair of triumphal arches stand at the terminus by the river in a state of gentle deterioration. Like so many buildings that were erected here in the 1950's, their construction is cheap, consisting of crumbling red bricks rendered with what appears to be concrete plaster, which is gradually peeling off in places.

We are staring towards a vast steppe beyond the river that extends to the Ural Mountains and beyond that is Asia. The Germans surrounded the city behind us, but never managed to completely take this western bank here in the city. Somehow, the Russians managed to cling on to it, ferrying soldiers and equipment across at this very point and evacuating the wounded back the other way. At the height of the battle, these banks were covered by thousands of wounded and dying soldiers and civilians, many of whom didn't make it to the other side. It's all very quiet now, but, seventy years ago, this place was truly 'hell on earth'.

After a stop-over for coffee in a restaurant, where we have a considerable degree of difficulty explaining, 'no meal – just coffee please,' we head back to the hotel and my destiny with doom.

When we arrive at the hotel, things get off to a bad start. I find myself beset by an urge to check the bike, which is sitting under its lightweight travel cover in the builder's yard at the rear of the hotel. My attempt at entering the courtyard triggers something of an explosion. One of the great things about the hotel and the yard is that it has 24-7 security provided by a man in an office at the arched entrance. Wandering past him, I discover, is not recommended. Much to my travelling companion's mirth, I get delivered the most vocal and (frankly) aggressive bollocking of my travels to date. Then, once he's satisfied that I have been verbally lashed to within an inch of my life, he lets me through to check out my baby.

***

I am to hairdressing what the 1950's Russian bricklayers were to building regulations. I will not be receiving a kite mark any time soon. No. Rather, I manage to find some comfort in the fact that preparations for application of the required consistency of hair colouring goo, resembles something very close to mixing Araldite – and, being the epitome of a 'botcher', a master-botcher no less, I do have some skill mixing Araldite. I once tried to fix a cross-threaded Mobylette moped exhaust flange with Araldite because I had it on good authority that it would 'fix anything'. My mate Steven 'Tush' Usher told me so. It didn't.

Diane is not impressed at all. The 'Araldite fix' method of hair restoration becomes increasingly fraught, with a mixture of quite bad language and the naked scent of fear on the part of the applicator and the victim, but mostly the applicator. The result is a clearly distinguishable black line down the centre of Diane's bonce, the very thing she feared the most – although if I keep my squint going it doesn't look too bad. And, let's face it, her head will be contained within a motorcycle helmet for most of the next three or four months, so really that's alright, I think. Diane isn't having any of that! She's already muttering about a repair job before the current one has set properly (or whatever term they use for 'completion in any colour other than green').

At this point, I feel that we are really getting on famously. My evidence to support this is that an incident like this could descend into the most enormous shouting (possibly shooting) match and eventual separation or burial of one of us. Yet, miraculously, it doesn't do so. Instead, we are weathering the storm with just the odd well-aimed nip. She doesn't humiliate me completely, and I don't retaliate too badly when nipped. Nicky Clarke would be ultra-impressed and would probably offer me an apprenticeship, which I would gracefully decline.

Chapter 15
No one is forgotten

Sometimes, a small event in a bar can lead to serious consequences. Our last night in Volgograd turns out to be one of those situations. Or at least that's how it seems...

It all started out tidily enough. The Hotel Volgograd might be tatty around its frayed edges, but it does boast a very decent, if ever so slightly old-fashioned, dark wood-clad restaurant and bar, in which we decide to spend a relaxing evening, sampling the wine list and the menu. And a mighty fine meal it turns out to be too, attended by a very helpful young waiter who speaks quite fluent English. Sometimes it is best to quit while you're ahead, but, if truth be told, a nice grill and a splash of the old glass of red often leads my eye to the shelf behind the bar where, tonight, I spy a selection of spirits – most notably, one or two bottles of Scottish whisky.

'Do you like whisky?' asks the friendly, English-speaking barman.

'Do little Russian brown bears pap in the woods?' I reply.

'Which one of these is good whisky?' he enquires, ignoring my riposte.

I scan the assembled bottles with the critical eye of a time-served expert, and the wit of a lesser amateur. I've been very fortunate in spending precious hours with a true whisky connoisseur called Dave Reid (senior), Diane's father-in-law, over a period of a few years. I think a smidgen of his encyclopaedic knowledge has rubbed off on me. All the way across Russia, I've been spotting the main export output of the Scottish and Irish Whisk(e)y industry: cheap, blended grain whisky with dubious-sounding names and warlike labels. If truth be told there is only one bottle worth a sniff on the hotel shelf and that's a Macallan 12-year-old. I decide to order a glass of that, explaining to the waiter the bottle's raised status, it being a single malt. He still seems none the wiser. No doubt, if I were giving an opinion on vodka, things would be different.

Before I can enjoy my unexpected snifter, Diane needs to be catered for. She is partial to the odd nip of whisky herself, but my roving eye has spotted something more fitting for her: a bottle of Hennesy XO cognac. Diane likes cognac.

'Is this a good cognac?' asks our waiter.

'Maybe.'

Is this the first time they've ever sold this stuff?

A wedding party has kicked off in earnest in the function room next to the bar. At odd moments, the door is banged open allowing a beating base throb of disco music to chase out the odd guest or two on their way out for a ciggie. While we're tucking into our spirits, we note that a rather domineering gentleman has entered into a vigorous, animated discussion with the barman and waiter. I'm guessing he's the father of the bride. Something is wrong and his protestations have the desired effect for a while, eliciting a scurry of activity.

Then they return to the bar for a further chat.

It turns out that they are both students in their final year of studying, working evenings at the hotel. They're very interested in where we've been, questioning us about our trip to America – somewhere they would dearly love to go themselves. The function room door opens, and a very, very irate father of the bride returns to issue a further bollocking. Where on earth is the hotel wedding organiser?

We decide it is probably a good time to take our leave. The barman prints off the final bill.

I have to admit to a slight feeling of faintness. I do a double take and realise that one nip of Hennesey XO is very nearly equal to three nights stay in a faded and slightly tatty room! Holy shhhayeat!

***

The morning ride in the shoebox lift to the restaurant for breakfast is accompanied by a faint hangover on both of our parts and a greenness around the financial gills on mine. The breakfast here in the Volgograd is actually very good, as was the meal last night – and the wine – and the £175.00 cognac, according to she who downed it.

As we're sipping a dark coffee in recovery mode, we are surprised to see the young waiter and barman arrive in their civvies. They come over to say 'hello' and shake our hands.

'You're in early,' I note.

'We are here to be terminated,' replies the better of the two at speaking English, reminding me of the scene in the film *Downfall* where the German general arrives at the Fuhrer bunker and, when asked why he is there, replies, 'I have been ordered to come here to be shot.'

'Why on earth are you being shot... sorry, 'terminated',' I ask.

'They do not require us anymore.'

I may be a bit muzzy-headed, but I have no doubt what's going on here. They spent a lot of time chatting with us and far less time wheeling drinks through to the wedding last night. I feel certain that we've been bit players in their demise, albeit innocent ones. We both feel exceptionally bad for them. They tell us not to worry. 'It is how things are,' says our friend of last night. What a terrible shame.

***

During our three-night stay here in Volgograd the bike has been sitting quietly in the builder's yard, nestling under its cover, protected from the dust and guarded by a maniac. It's a busy place down there. The various restaurant and hotel staff from the buildings that make up the square regularly take a fag break, sitting on old metal framed chairs, laughing and chatting.

During my check of the bike the other evening, I noted that the pannier frame has been chafing quite severely against the odd rear splash-guard that BMW adorn their products with. It's a strange appendage to the motorcycle, something to do with German regulations. I'm not sure it really serves any effective form or function and many owners seem to just chuck it away. But, having said that, it is part and parcel of the whole bike and, to my mind, it seems to suit it. Having carried out another look at the damage that the frame is causing to it, I notice that the bolt holding it on has come loose from the repeated impacts on the dreadful roads. Out with the tools to give it a quick tighten, checking around the bike to see if anything else is noticeably loose (which it isn't). This isn't really a fix, something will have to be done about it, when and if we get back to Blighty.

Our subsequent departure from Volgograd is not the glittering success one would hope for. After following the road signs for (what I deem to be) the correct direction, we eventually find ourselves out in the steppe next to an airport and, most clearly, heading towards nowhere in particular. The satnav is sitting with its arms crossed in recalcitrant mode. I inform my passenger that the pilot is lost, satnav is non-communicative at worst, speaking Russian at best and that normal service will be resumed ASAP. My passenger is inclined to believe that normal service commenced upon departure.

Much later, we hit a vaguely familiar section of rutted hell, backfilled with rocks, cans, broken glass and the odd dead cat – a road that is thankfully recognizable as one of those we met on arrival in the city two days ago. We are an hour adrift but, after a quick right turn, we are definitely on the road to Rostov-on-Don. It is slightly surreal that a highway travelled in reverse, throws up a whole new series of features that were missed when travelling in the opposite direction – most likely because we were being harried by nice people who seemed to want to kill us. But this is true of every road in the world – I think. Not the harrying, but, rather, the perception that the road feels completely different. The first noteworthy new feature that springs out at us is a railway locomotive.

***

The locomotive in question is a magnificent beast, painted with a thick coat of matt black and adorned with a huge red star on its 'face'. If it featured in *Thomas the Tank Engine* it would undoubtedly be called 'Ivan', although I think that name is already taken. Displayed on a section of track by the roadside, towering above anyone who cares to stop and take a photo, it appears to be quite a complex design, fashioned for hauling carriages across the vast distances of the steppe, with twin bogies and no fewer than ten drive wheels, painted in bright red with white rims – splendid indeed. And yet it bears all the signs of very basic manufacture. It is, upon close inspection, quite incredibly crude in execution and materials. But, no doubt, it did its job and then some.

Back on the bike, we take a much more relaxed approach than on the outbound journey a couple of days ago. The traffic is light, the weather warm and the endless steppe stretches out both northwards and southwards. Having finally managed to get my bearings, I now know that we are travelling through the extended western end of the pocket that the Germans found themselves trapped in when Zhukov's armies crashed through their rear in two massive pincer arms, attacking from the north and the south, breaking their lines of communications with the west and sealing their fate. The successful manoeuver trapped them in the pocket, while they in turn surrounded the defenders of the city in one too. Out here, a desperate attempt was made to lift the siege by German armies attacking from the west, but it petered out and, from that moment, the German 6th Army was doomed. For the Russians, the meeting of the two arms of the pincers was a moment of wild celebration, carefully reconstructed in a famous propaganda film.

We trundle along westwards, glad to be back on the road but, at the same time, a little sad to be leaving Volgograd – an interesting city with a wealth of things to see, perched on the edge of Europe.

***

After an hour or so of riding, we come across one of the many impromptu roadside markets. It's relatively quiet, just a couple of cars and an army tank transporter (*sans* tank), pulled up for a spot of shopping. So, we pull over into the packed dirt of the car parking area and wander over to see what's on sale. The stall holders all try a line in sales patter, to which we nod, smile and shrug. I'd really like to buy fruit, but it seems like we've hit the wrong market. The primary foodstuff on sale here are tomatoes, which makes it very difficult to turn one seller down at the expense of their neighbour. I mean when you've seen one tomato, you've seen all of them really, even if it is actually a fruit. In the end we just take pot luck and buy off a lady who smiles the most. She seems well chuffed.

Having bought our tomatoes, which I have to say are the most gigantic tomatoes I have ever personally seen – literally humungous – I wander back towards the bike and find it being checked out by a couple of gentlemen of indeterminate age, somewhere north of sixty. The older of the two nods appreciatively.

'Bay Em Vay,' he smiles pointing at the badge. His friend nods.

'Lada,' retort I, pointing at the ancient square brick that sits adjacent to the bike, attached to an old trailer.

'Da. Lada.'

This is all very encouraging. I am, in fact, having another conversation in Russian. We wander closer to the Lada and he points through the open window to the trip meter. I have no idea what he says next, but it's clearly something to do with the mileage, and a quick squint inside shows me that this little baby has done plenty of miles.

'Mercedes kaput, Lada gut,' he opines.

He thinks I'm German.

With a little bit of sign language, we manage to communicate that the Lada is very reliable in all weathers and can survive the kind of road conditions that will put paid very quickly to a Mercedes, hence his choice not to purchase a rubbish, luxury German automobile. They are simply no good when jam-packed with melons. Their Tiger tanks suffered a similar problem. Russia broke them very quickly.

He points to the bike.

'Bay em Vay gut?'

'Da, sehr gut.'

Up until that point, I was doing very well. But now, I've managed to mix two languages in three short words and, consequently, I feel like I should quit while I'm ahead. I decide to shake his hand.

'Americkanskiy?' he asks with, a curious smile and an upward intonation in his voice. Sheep, wolves….

As we pull out of the market, back onto the road, waved off by our newly-found friends, it occurs to me that we aren't getting very far, very fast, and I recall that there was a decent-looking motel some way along the road at a junction we passed the other day. After that, there probably isn't anything until we get to Rostov-on-Don and we've already been told by our friends of a couple of days ago – the two gentlemen we decided were 'probably mafia else otherwise maybe the KGB, or whatever it's called nowadays' – that we will probably die a horrible death when we arrive in that fair city. So, balancing all this up, on reaching the motel, we decide to pull over, just so we can live one more day.

***

Today, we will ride the remaining miles to Rostov-on-Don. I'm not sure what we will do when we get there, but if it looks safe to do so, we'll have a look for a hotel and perhaps barricade ourselves in our room, preferably with the bike located inside, chained to the bed. It's a two or three-hour ride (at a guess) and I'm expecting it to be very pleasant; at least, until we arrive at our destination.

We initially pass through the wonderful, endless farmland that is part of the great steppe. It doesn't take too long before we spot somewhere to stop and have a look-see. It's a place we noticed on the way out, but failed to stop, since time wasn't on our side. It appears to be some kind of war memorial, but in fact, once we've parked up and climbed the short hill to the main part of it, turns out to be a cemetery.

On top of the dusty and dry plateau, amongst the rustling grasses of the plains that make up the steppe, lie a series of graves. On each grave rests a Red Army helmet, simple in construction, turned out by the million in factories across the Soviet Union. Each helmet bears the signs of age and the ravages of battle, torn asunder by shrapnel or drilled by a single sniper's shot. One, in particular, attracts special attention. It has been riddled with machine gun fire; so much so that it resembles a grotesque form of colander. A sign in Cyrillic on the grave bears the date 2012. I wonder if these are veterans who have died this year and been buried with their comrades. The following translation of the plate on the grave explains. It was kindly carried out by my friend from Atyrau Kazakhstan, Danara Kalenova:

1942-2012

No one is forgotten, Nothing is forgotten!

Krasnov Vasiliy Ivanovich – Red Army soldier, born: 1922, Gorkov oblast, Pochinkovsky region, Simbukhovsky selSoviet, Simbukhovo village

Shevchenko Petr Afanasievich – born: 1907, technician-intendant 2nd class, conductor, Kiev oblast, Moroligersky region, Mokrov village

Volykov Alexey Ivanovich – born: 1922, sergeant, Penza oblast, Poimsky region, Linevsky selSoviet, Lineika village

Zagvozdin Vasiliy Egorovich – born: 1923, machine gunner, his relative - Ionkina Maria Egorovna

Korobeinikov Mikhail Stepanovich – born: 1923, Omsk oblast

Mordvinov Timofei Spiridonovich – born: 1900, junior sergeant

Remains of the named above soldiers and other 66 unknown Red Army soldiers were unearthed in 2011-2012 and reburied on 17/07/2012

It turns out that the remains of these soldiers were laid in their final resting place just a few days before our visit. I guess it is fitting that they remain near the battlefield and within earshot of the busy road to the city they helped to save. And I have no doubt that the inscription is heartfelt. No one is forgotten!!

Chapter 16
Feels like Madonna

If Rostov-on-Don is, to a pair of western motorcyclists, what Mirkwood was to a band of dwarves and one reluctant burglar hobbit, then I don't quite get it – at least, not initially. On our approach, the traffic starts to increase in density as we ride along a tree-lined motorway, ushering us into a pleasant enough city with plenty of greenery and busy streets. We ride along a decent dual carriageway and poste-haste spot a BMW car-and-motorcycle dealership. This hatches a plan in my head. It's an opportunity to get an oil and filter change, avoiding the inevitable roadside dilemma of 'where do I put the waste oil?'

When we pull into the dealership, we find that the 'meet and greet' person is an armed guard. At the reception desk, I ask if anyone speaks English. Once she gets over her initial surprise, the young receptionist makes a finger-in-the-air sign of 'wait one minute' and rushes off to return with a tall, slim, blonde lady in her early twenties called Anna who might just have wandered in off the front page of Vogue magazine. Anna advises me that the service director must be consulted to see if the workshop can fit us in. She heads off gracefully to consult, returning quite some while later with a big beam on her face declaring with a flourish, 'it can be done!' This is just the start of an amazing level of service. The dealership book us into a hotel – a 'very good' one that is 'reasonable price' and they also book us a taxi to get there. We can come back at eleven tomorrow and the bike will have been treated to a nice oil and filter change and general check-over.

One of the interesting features of the ride down to the hotel, past the airport, is a MIG 15 (might be 17), proudly mounted on a sky-bound plinth high above the road. I like that quite a lot, it reminds me of the Airfix models that I saved my pocket money up for, as a child. In fact,

I'm starting to like Rostov quite a lot, too. It's a bit edgy, but in quite a nice way - green, busy, rough *and* edgy.

***

We arrive back at the dealership in good order in the morning.

Last night, we stayed in the Hotel Valencia, a modern, clean hotel with a very camp waiter who was both entertaining and lackadaisical to the point of annoyance, leaving us wondering if we would ever be served. At breakfast this morning, he proffered his excuse for the previous night's tardiness, declaring proudly, 'yesterday, I was not good waiter. Yesterday was my birthday!'

I thought it would be a good idea to thank everyone at the dealership for helping us out. A trip down the road on foot to a supermarket to purchase a few bottles of beer for the boys in the workshop and choccies for the girls in reception seemed the order of the evening. The reception staff advised us that the supermarket was a short walk down the road, so I decided to risk kidnapping and 'go for it', leaving my navigator back in the room attempting to repair her stripy head.

The walk down to the supermarket was a short, ten-minute hop past rows of nice houses, sitting behind high security walls, topped with razor wire and no doubt guarded by slavering hounds. At the end of the road, I came across a wide square, beset on all sides by reckless traffic, but quickly found myself bewitched by an immaculate and subtly pimped Lada Riva, parked in front of the supermarket, all gleaming chrome and mirror-glass paintwork. I was then taken aback, not a little, by the quality and range of the food within the supermarket. Just like the one in Moscow, this one had shelves crammed with goodies: cheap luxurious goodies. What a surprise this whole country is. The apartment blocks are nightmare creations, fashioned from breezeblocks and concrete with nary a straight line to be seen. The cars are creations of the seventies, loved and cared for in part, else stuffed with pumpkins or melons and running on canvas, and a journey outside your hotel is a venture into the unknown. And yet, I think I like it a lot. I almost feel at home here.

***

Back at the dealership. The lovely Anna advises us that the bike is being checked over by the mechanic and will shortly be run around the front of the dealership. We are invited to enjoy a coffee and biscuits in a lounge area that is an exact replica of the one in Woolaston BMW of Northampton – a kind of home-from-home. What is distinctly different, apart from the armed guard on the door, is the method of payment, which involves handing one's card over to a pretty cashier through the bullet-proof window of an armoured cash office. Not at all like Woolastons, that bit. That done, I find myself chatting with an English-speaking biker who is window-shopping for a GS Adventure just like the Mutt.

'I want one with metal boxes,' he declares pointing to the example on a plinth in the window. 'They are fairy cood.'

'Not that good,' I reply, 'they leakalot.'

'No, no. They are fairy cood.'

I try to explain that they are OK if you don't pack them full to bursting. But if you do abuse them so, which I have been known to in the past, then they really do leak. Mine filled with water more than once and were dispensed with pronto when I got home from the US of A. He sounds less than convinced. Notwithstanding the old farmer yesterday, in Russian eyes the Germans can do no wrong (short of the odd invasion, that is). I'm about to start explaining how my BMW trousers once sought to embarrass me by exploding in a Chinese takeaway, when the sound of a bike drawing up out front distracts us both. The Mutley has arrived. I head off to locate Diane and to dispense beer and chocolate to the wonderful staff of Rostov-on-Don BMW.

When we arrive outside, we find my new friend and the mechanic deep in conversation. In fact, there is a polite argument going on. They're both on their knees underneath the bike speaking in animated fashion, the mechanic pointing out features of the pannier brackets while a small collection of onlookers assemble – ourselves included. The potential customer arises and turns to me.

'The mechanic says he has never seen panniers like this,' he declares.

'I told him these panniers no cood. They are weak. He told me they have brackets like for a tank and they are not weak. Perhaps you are correct. Where do I buy?'

I point to the Metal Mule sticker in reply. The bracket is indeed nuclear explosion proof, and it is gently stroking and caressing the crud catcher to death, mile after bone-shaking mile. But hey, there's no point in grasping defeat from the jaws of victory by revealing that fact. Honour is satisfied. We can depart on a high note.

The first part of negotiating our departure from Rostov is a little nerve wracking. After humming along past the supermarket, we find ourselves riding through a decidedly dodgy looking 'hood, where pauses at traffic lights help recall the nervous memory of a deserted Sunday ride through the Bronx. It doesn't last for long though. Approaching the River Don, we pass through a busy retail section, where the traffic is nose-to-tail and people bustle to and fro along the pavements with nary a violin case in sight. Then, we pass over a long bridge spanning the great river before taking the opportunity to top up with fuel at a filling station, where the woman serving in the kiosk greets me with a huge grin when I pass to her my now customary slip of paper bearing: '25L 97RON'. We have escaped Russia's version of Gotham City with our lives and are now heading safely on our way towards the Black Sea, exact destination to be confirmed.

***

As we pass through the (by now) familiar Russian landscape of long rows of trees flanking flat fields and the odd roadside vegetable seller, a whiff or two of aged industry in the distance, my mind turns to the route plan and the bothersome matter of a forthcoming border crossing. Back in Aberdeen, my Russian colleague had poured water on my plans to cross the Caucasus Mountains into Georgia.

'Crossing here is not allowed, and why would you want to go there? This is where I am from and it is very beautiful. Much better than Georgia! I recommend you go here and forget the crossing,' he said pointing to a point on the map just north of Sochi. I became mildly excited.

'What about the ferry from Sochi to Georgia? I heard there was one. Is it still running?' I asked.

He sighed and shrugged his shoulders. 'I don't know. Perhaps not.' I think he'd formed the conclusion that we were completely barking mad.

Part of me wanted desperately to cross those mountains. Why? Because the first part of my attempt to ride around the world involved crossing the Great Divide, and here was another 'divide' – a mountain range twixt Europe and Asia. It had an alluring symmetry to it.

Sadly though, the crossing seemed one mountain transit too far. War has blighted the route. There is another crossing further over to the east, but that route would bring us perilously close to Grozny and even closer to South Ossetia. I decided that I do not want to unexpectedly take my better-half sightseeing in a rebel breakaway republic. This led to careful, nay, forensic consideration of the alternatives. One of the more promising options on the Internet involved taking a ship from Odessa in Ukraine over to Georgia. The reports on the net were far from confidence-inspiring. Apparently, the vessel was prone to being barred from entering harbour at its destination, regularly running out of food in the process. The second viable alternative? Ride right around the Black Sea in a counter-clockwise direction, racking up thousands of extra miles to make up for the fact that you can't ride a hundred or so miles down through Russia and pass through a border post. Welcome to post-Soviet geo-political meltdown.

We don't have to decide right now. We've started to discuss the options together, but our plan is to spend a couple of days relaxing on the Black Sea, then make a decision at our leisure. In the meantime, we pass through yet more farmland. Vast flat swathes of it.

The sunflowers are starting to suffer. It's extremely hot and they have ripened and withered almost to blackness, their fields appearing desolate and ruined. But it is just part of a transmogrification that will doubtless result in perfectly good cooking oil or parrot fodder. An hour or so into the ride, we approach a line of people selling fruit along the roadside and decide to pull over to make a purchase. We wander over to the nearest couple who are selling various fruits, sitting on fold-up chairs next to a battered old Lada. After a short debate, we opt for a large bag of plums and hand over what we think is sufficient money, receiving change in the process. The couple seem genuinely surprised at our appearance and are full of smiles, especially the lady. I guess they can put 'International' after their company name now. As we walk back to the bike, Diane notices a lorry driver carefully washing his produce with clean water and remarks that we should do the same. My navigator regularly draws from a deep well of caution. Compared to the total lack of any such care on my part, Diane is our voice of reason.

Just as we prepare to tog up and depart, the lady runs over to us waving. She thrusts another bag of plums in our hands with a smile and a wave.

***

A little further into the ride today, and we start to hit a lot of road works. Invariably, they mean traffic queues which, whilst not holding us up particularly badly on each single stop, still add up to a considerable amount of down time. A relatively short hop turns into a long haul.

The road being laid is of snooker table quality, but the original road, where it survives, is a washboard. And it is extremely hot. The lands we are travelling into were once the home of the Black Sea Cossack horde, or, more politely, host. Like their cousins who lived further north on the Don, these time-served warriors of the steppe were not to be taken lightly. For many years, they provided cavalry and infantry for the various Tzars: Ivan the Terrible, Peter the Great and Catherine the Great. The city we are heading towards, Krasnodar, was once called *Yerkaterinodar*: Catherine's gift, the gift of the region to the southern Cossacks for all their hard work being repulsive. Interestingly, the Cossacks, who have a strong connection with Ukraine, from whence many of them came, are thought to have their ethnic origins in Turkey – the Ottoman Empire possessed many outposts on this northern shore of the Black Sea. They and the Russians have been squabbling over the region piecemeal for years and the Cossacks were always there when the going got tough, happily repelling all and sundry.

Krasnodar received its name change in 1920 courtesy of the Bolsheviks. Its name means 'Red Gift' or 'Beautiful Gift'. When we arrive, we discover a hot, dusty and grittily industrial city – a mixture of worn-out roads, semi-derelict housing districts and grinding traffic, belching out fumes. Beauty isn't the first adjective that springs to mind.

Our hotel of choice for tonight is a new one that sits in a district notable for a mixture of modern toy emporiums juxtaposed with an utterly derelict, abandoned factory complex. It's a testament to how badly everything was put together in the world's first socialist utopia. To underscore the point, instead of knocking down the hotel's predecessor when they built this one, they left it standing alongside, just to let us know how lucky we are to be in the new one. Fred Dibnah would have had a field day around here!

We don't care at all about this. The shower works perfectly, the room is comfortable and, down in the restaurant, Diane swears blind that her sea bass is the finest meal she has ever eaten in her life, ever. Entertainment for the night is provided by a little girl sitting at the next table who is determined *not* to eat her sea bass and is spitting out the dummy (and the fish) in all directions. Meanwhile, her mum appears to be chewing wasps.

***

Thursday 2nd July.

The morning dawns spit-roastingly hot.

I commence the now familiar routine of lugging five loads of gear down to the bike, ending up perspiring very freely. A small group of the hotel's staff sit outside having an early morning ciggie, observing the ritual with just a wee smidgen of humour. In between trips in the lift to the room, I ponder upon the fact that I'm getting appreciably fitter. In Sweden this was a hell of a chore, but constant repetition is reaping rewards.

The whole feel of southern Russia is subtly different to the north. Gone are the quaint wooden houses and vegetable patch gardens. We pass settlements of houses topped with corrugated asbestos or tin roofs and increasingly come across a menagerie of livestock grazing by the roadside – mostly chained up on tethers, but occasionally free to roam, oft tended by a human. We also pass increasing scenes of mechanical carnage, in the shape of old broken-down trucks, stripped down for repair by the roadside.

After an hour or so of quite slow progress, we find ourselves climbing into a series of hills: the south-western fringe of the Caucasus Mountains. It is green and very pleasant. We start to encounter roadside shops that specialise in beach paraphernalia – lots of blowy-up rings and animals alongside racks of flip-flops and sun cream. The whole ambience has the feel of a day trip to Cleethorpes. Up the road climbs, higher and higher into the hills – the Cleethorpes impression dissipating like a puff of stage smoke – clinging to the contours with a series of impressive bends until, near the summit of a steady climb, we nearly meet our maker courtesy of a Lada Samara that has gone completely out of control, probably with a failed braking system.

With some luck and very little in the way of judgement I happen to spot the 'out of control situation' at its very inception, the thought passing through my brain to the effect of: 'ooer, that car is going way too fast, and its driver wears a strange grimace upon his fizzog,' just in time to take avoiding action by picking up the bike and heading for the right-hand kerb. As the Lada slides past, just a gnat's whisker away from our left-hand pannier, we heel well over again to make the corner, proceeding back in the queue of vehicles as if nothing has happened. There isn't even a squeak from the pillion. Diane has nerves of steel!

At the summit of the hill, we crest out on a minor peak that boasts a very scenic panorama – albeit just a glimpse – there is no time to stop to appreciate it at the roadside viewing point, the traffic is too heavy, so we press on. In the early afternoon, we arrive in a surprisingly laid-back area of the country that is ever so slightly hip. Bronzed young people in cool clothes and shades drive around in open jeeps (of the Russian variety), for all the world looking like Californian surfer dudes. The hills are lush and green, the houses are decked with heavily laden vines and I would happily pull over right now for a couple of days to explore – if we could just find somewhere to stay.

We fail to spot anything looking remotely like a hotel, so we decide to press on – up hill and down dale until we happen across a relatively large town called Novorissysk, by way of a smaller town called Gelendzhik.

On the face of it Novorissysk is a wee bit scruffy and frayed around the edges – I'm putting it mildly. Initially, we pull over to get our bearings before heading in a north-westerly direction that takes us right past the docks, offering up our first glimpse of the Russian Navy in the shape of a few old corvettes belonging to the Black Sea Fleet that are tied up in the distance – nothing that would worry an American carrier task force here, but nice to see them in their natural habitat.

As we ride a little further into the town, we are greeted by a steady stream of young soldiers packed into and hanging out of the windows of cars. The flags they are waving bear the unmistakeable device of a parachute and wings, part of the 7th Guards Airborne Division, or more precisely the 108th Kuban Cossack Order of the Red Star Parachute Regiment if I'm not mistaken (OK, I admit to adding this after a bit of research), and I think they've just passed out of their training.

We haven't travelled very far today as the crow flies, but we seem to have been travelling for ages. The main reason for this is the weight of holiday traffic and the leisurely way we've progressed through countryside that is often quite captivating in its beauty. Having caught our first glimpse of the Black Sea, we need to find decent accommodation for a couple of days' R&R. Passing by the airborne regiment's barracks doesn't qualify. I've lived the barracks life before and am keen to find something a bit better than that for my partner today. Onwards and upwards.

A few miles out of Novorissysk, we pass into a flat stretch of countryside, past homesteads with the (by now) familiar corrugated roofs. One notable house has a couple of delightful old Russian cars parked up outside it – for all the world they could be American cars from the 1950's, but they aren't, they're Russian and they're stylish in a grand old swoopy-flanked manner all of their own. Eventually, we happen across a junction, where the signpost indicates a town, so we hang a left and head in that direction. The town in question is Anapa, and it turns out to be quite an interesting gem of a place.

∗∗∗

Anapa is to Russia what Blackpool is to England, but bear me out before closing the book, because it's a lot more interesting than first impressions might suggest. But, before we get to the interesting bit, we need to find a hotel. The road into town isn't anything to write home about, flanked as it is by the usual assortment of quite badly built apartment blocks, which then start to look a bit more like possible hotels, but maybe not very nice ones.

Diane and I are peering around as we putt gently into town, craning our necks, trying to spot somewhere appropriate. It quickly becomes apparent that this is a very busy holiday venue. There are lots of people wandering around in various forms of holiday attire, kids licking lollies, old ladies baring more leg than is probably sensible and everyone in pretty much laid-back mode. At the centre of the town, we chance upon what appears to be a very nice hotel, but it's clearly overwhelmed by trade and more than likely bears a Russian 'no vacancy' sign. Added to that, it doesn't appear to have an easily accessible car park. We find ourselves, very quickly, riding along a straight road heading out of town.

Fast forward ten minutes and we finally pull up, after a second pass, outside an impressively large hotel called The Sofia. This is more like it! It's a high tower of a building of indeterminate age – I'm guessing not much more than thirty years, placed conveniently close to the beach, directly opposite a complex that seems to be some sort of theme park (complete with live tiger). The surrounding street is thronged with families, walking back to their hotels, weighed down with beach paraphernalia, including the ubiquitous inflatable animals. As we pull up outside the hotel, we attract their attention and a small group gather around to witness our arrival. We seem to have created a bit of a stir.

***

There is room available at the hotel. In order to check in, we have to leave a cash deposit. I don't have sufficient cash, but the receptionists tell me not to worry. It is *very important*, they stress upon me, that we do not mess around trying to get any money out of the hotel's cash dispenser, because the restaurant is due to open imminently, and we MUST NOT miss our allotted timing for our table. Missing dinner is forbidden.

Having parked the bike up in the underground garage, we are led to our allotted room by a bell boy who insists on us putting down our bags before leading us, almost at a sprint, to the restaurant on the first floor. He insists that we present ourselves to the administrator who will allot us a table, which will be our table for our stay. The room is very large, immaculately clean and comfortable, dressed in rather sombre dark brown and cream. On the way down the stairs, I manage to trip on the final stair and come close to falling, spread-eagled, on the floor.

While we're waiting for the administrator to attend to us, we gaze around in bemused fashion as lines of Russian families maintain a vigorous assault on the buffet bar. I realise this is going to be a challenge. We can't speak the lingo, don't understand the routine, and will definitely struggle with the pace and purpose of everything. We might end up crushed underfoot in one of those queues. But it turns out that there's no need to worry about such things. As soon as the administrator attends to us, we find ourselves being led away from the scrummage and back up the stairs (nearly tripping for a second time on the first step). It turns out that we've been allotted two seats at a large round table in the posh restaurant, safely removed from the organised mayhem and attentively waited upon by a group of young ladies. We are honoured guests.

Chapter 17
Anapa

In the morning, we arrive at breakfast precisely at our allotted time and are served by a new girl who delivers us a light meal and a puzzle in the form of a piece of paper with lots of Russian words on it. A gentleman appears from one of the other tables and introduces himself as Alexander.

'I couldn't help noticing that you speak English. I speak it too and wondered if you need any help?' We nod like Churchill the dog, times two.

'This is the menu for the rest of your stay. You need to let the staff know what you would like to be served for each of your meals.'

He goes through the menu with us, pointing out the various dishes and helping us fill in the form. There's no doubting that everything is extremely well organised at the Hotel Sofia. It is, in fact, a feature of the whole resort. When we arrived last night, having checked in, I returned to the bike to be met by a burly guard who looks after the car parking arrangements. As with some of the other hotels, he looked ex-military and was, shall we say, a tad assertive, but once I'd honourably surrendered and followed his instructions to the letter, he was all smiles and helpfulness personified. You just have to behave yourself and play the game. The upshot is that nobody, no-how and no-way is getting near the bike.

***

The theme of organisation takes another twist on a brisk walk into the town. It is searingly hot. The road into town is tree-lined and bordered by a strip of grass parkland, dotted with attractive flowering plantations, notably rich in bright orange and brown marigolds. The luxuriant nature of the marigolds probably means the snails have shrivelled up in the heat. Every time I plant marigolds back home, they get decimated!

We pass a few families walking in the same direction at a slower pace, past the entrances to a series of Soviet-era holiday camps. Billy Butlins would have been over the moon if he ever visited Anapa.

One or two of the camps have been modernised, but others are overgrown and in a sad state of decay and dereliction, their wrought iron gates locked, barred and peeling paint. Clearly, in the old days people came here in their tens of thousands, to enjoy a week or two on the Black Sea, recovering from their heroic efforts on the land or in the factories. It has a nostalgic 1950's feel that draws you into the warmth of its embrace. It's charming in a way that I think we've mostly lost through commercialisation, a bit like a repeat episode of 'Hi-De-Hi' on TV.

In the midst of this rose-tinted nirvana, I suddenly stumble into a bit of a crisis. Or to be more precise, my ability to walk fades very alarmingly into a jelly-legged failure of energy. I've never experienced anything like it before and it happens so suddenly that it is quite alarming. I manage to blurt out, 'honey, I'm in trouble here!' I feel really odd and quite ill, sufficiently distressed for Diane to be alarmed too. 'Maybe it's some kind of sun stroke, it is very hot, and we haven't had much liquid intake,' she proffers. I'm not so sure – we've barely walked a mile. We stop at a small shop where Diane buys a savoury snack and some diet coke, while I rest up against the wall. I suspect some kind of diabetic episode. I'm guessing I need sugar, maybe a can of 'full fat' coke. Thankfully, a few minutes after scoffing the savoury, I start to make a recovery and we're able to continue our investigation of the town. Suffice to say though, I was a tad worried back there.

***

The centre of town is a curious mix of the familiar and the ever-so-slightly-strange. Various retail outlets along the street vie for trade with a substantial and well-stocked open market. Three things spring out at me as we wander through the market. The stalls selling food display a brilliant, vibrant mix of produce, most of which is coated in sugar products. Surprisingly, the most predominant, iconic symbol on the fashion stalls in the market appears to be the Union flag of Great Britain, whilst toy stalls do a brisk trade in MIGs, Kalashnikovs and T-72 tanks, just like they did in Moscow, and all made in China – as were those sold in Moscow. It occurs to me that they were probably fabricated on a production line next to the one making F-16s and Tomcats for American and European market reasonably-priced, slightly jingoistic toy stalls.

Anapa, quite surprisingly, hasn't been a Russian town for as long as you would imagine. It was eventually handed over to the Russians by the Ottoman Empire in 1829, who then re-occupied it during the Crimean War. In the Second World War, it was occupied by the Germans and Romanians who completely levelled it. The whole town has been reconstructed since, with hotels, a town centre that was bang up to date forty years ago, and numerous sanatoria, where people can find fun, sand, and various forms of health treatment. Despite the sugar crisis, we manage to complete a very pleasant wander through the market to the pleasure beach via a formal square in the town centre and thence back to the hotel, past the camps, in time for lunch, taking note of the empty bars that will surely be buzzing later tonight. With previously jelly-like legs getting stronger by the minute, I end up feeling so good after lunch that I plan to take a dip in the Black Sea this afternoon for good measure.

***

The Black Sea is quite a remarkable body of water. It has an anoxic zone with properties that perfectly preserve ships after they sink – just like the brackish waters of the Baltic. Apparently, it has properties that can perfectly preserve the crew too, so it can't do any harm to have a dip in there, can it? It might even hold the secret for eternal youth. And, God knows, I need a bit of that!

After conducting our own wee dip in the briny, we find ourselves approached on the beach by a young couple who explain to us, in very passable English, that they understand we are British and staying at the hotel. It turns out that we've become quite famous, all in the space of twenty-four hours. When I mention that Diane is from Scotland, they become almost excited.

'We are planning to get married in Scotland!', exclaims the young lady.

I ask Igor, for that is his name, if he intends to wear a kilt? His future beloved one is mortified. 'Oh no, no, he cannot wear one of those,' she says, filled with wide-eyed alarm. It just wouldn't do for a Russian male to be seen dead in one. No. The reason they wish to be married in Scotland rests on the venue.

'We will be married in a castle!'

'And what about bagpipes. Will you be having any of those?'

***

In the evening, we are served with brisk efficiency in the restaurant. We ended our afternoon poolside, out the back of the hotel quaffing a few very passable Russian beers and feted generally by everyone we got to talk to. I've come to the firm conclusion that average, everyday Russians are fine people: friendly, interested in talking to you, if it is at all possible to do so, and keen to know what you think of their country. I'm also very impressed with how they look after their children. They seem to be very happy in family groups and the younger members are most likely to be found attired in inflatable animal rings. It takes me back to Whitby, circa 1963.

We've only had a wee glimpse of Anapa and we leave in the morning. I probably couldn't spend too long here – I mean it is a holiday resort, when all's said and done, and that isn't my thing. But the bit I've seen has fascinated me – especially the Cold War era holiday camps and the Soviet signs that still flank the roads. They're all out of date, clashing with the night clubs, bars and boutiques that are starting to take over the town. And yet they provide a glimpse into the order and the social well-being that went before - at least for some of the people.

Before we set off, we need to make a command decision. Do we search hereabouts for a ferry to Georgia or should we ride anti-clockwise right around the Black Sea? It's a tough decision. Riding right around the Black Sea (minus a few miles) is not a light undertaking. And yet, the number of new countries that are waiting to be experienced is a draw –Ukraine, Romania, and Bulgaria. Perhaps the most enticing thought is the opportunity to visit Crimea. I have a passing interest in visiting the site of the Charge of the Light Brigade. Maps are checked and the navigator is consulted before the decision is taken. Tomorrow we will head northwards and then to the west. Our next planned destination will be Ukraine.

In the morning, we head down for our final Anapa breakfast. Before eating our meal, I pop over to the table occupied by Alexander, his wife and his daughter. I have in my possession my last piece of UK coinage: a two-pound coin. I always think that our two-quid coin is a bit of a design icon, and, whilst being far from numismatic myself, I always have a passing interest in the currency of the countries we ride through. So, with that in mind, I head over and present it to Alexander's young daughter.

I tell them that I would like her to have the coin as a thank-you for their help, explaining that the design of the coin was part of a competition and that the winning designer was a teacher who taught my children back home in the UK, in a village called Martham, in the county of Norfolk. Alexander translates this for his wife and daughter, and they seem very pleased by the gesture. Never in the field of coin-collecting has a two-pound coin gone so far.

* * *

My friend, the security guard, has patrolled (if not prowled) the garages under the hotel very efficiently. Nothing passes by without his noticing. I know this very well. I've snuck down there a couple of times to check the bike and recover things from the top box. On each occasion he's miraculously appeared over my shoulder like a character from the TV series 'League of Gentlemen' ('We didn't burn him'). As I start to pack the bike, he greets me at the entrance and smiles and waves every time I appear with another bag or two for loading.

Out in front of the hotel, a small, inquisitive crowd has gathered. I joke to Diane that she now knows how it feels to be Madonna. This is not the time to cock things up and fall off. The weeks of climbing on and off have improved her goat-like tendencies and she manages to hop on lithely and professionally. Memories of the laughing cyclist in Harwich are thankfully fading. It's now up to me not to stall the bike, or teeter over trying to negotiate the throng of people around us. The pressure to make a grand sweeping exit is almost overwhelming. With a wave to the security guard and a nod to a couple of dads in the crowd we ease past them, pick a space in the traffic, and open the big red baby up. Nice!

I have a simple plan for today's journey: we'll ride back to Krasnodar and overnight at the same hotel as before, in the toy district. Then, tomorrow, we'll head to a point as close as possible to the Ukrainian border. When we cross into Ukraine, there are two places I would like to visit: the first is Yalta, where Churchill and Roosevelt met Stalin during the Second World War – don't know why, but the photos of their meeting seem to show a very plush place – and the other is to go to Sevastopol, home of the Russian Black Sea Fleet and, I believe, quite close to the place where the Light Brigade were told to charge and failed to have the gumption to signal back: 'wtf! Are you being totally serious?'

Surprisingly, we are literally just a few miles from the eastern tip of Crimea. But I don't think there is a ferry across the little gap that exists between it and Russia. In order to break things up, and not simply backtrack our steps of a couple of days ago, we've decided to take a different route up to Krasnodar on the A146. This takes us up into the hills, past a huge depot for the mineral trucks we've seen taking road-building materials northwards throughout the country. Hundreds of trucks are lined up in a vast park, awaiting their loads, from what I guess is a massive quarry, no doubt the mother of all quarries. It has the feel of a quasi-military operation.

Initially, we make good progress. As with the outbound leg, though, it seems a painfully long journey when that isn't really the case, at least not in terms of distance. The early, smooth going eventually grinds down to a halt at a small town around midday. The reason for the traffic jam isn't clear initially, but the effect of it is immediate. We start to overheat very rapidly once we lose the benefit of airflow. Not just rider and pillion either. The bike has a useful temperature gauge, which I think is located near the engine and gives a good indication of the faithful flat twin's suffering down there beneath the fuel tank. Mechanical sympathy prompts me to switch off the engine in between short bunny hops forward.

The impromptu traffic jam serves to reveal the true gulf in Russia between the rich and the poor (or for that matter, the burgeoning middle-class). The hoi polloi stew patiently in their modest carriages, vans and trucks – whereas the posh cats seem to think they have the right to try any outrageous manoeuvre imaginable to get past. The patient masses seem to put up with this with the quiet reservation of those who know their place. We choose to sit with the masses. Over the course of ninety minutes, we find ourselves greeted with a 'hail good fellow' by a mixed community of bikers also heading north – those without wide-assed panniers who are able to filter through the traffic jam.

It happens gradually over time in the queue. A battered motorcycle appears alongside us with the rider bearing one hell of a grin. He salutes us with a nodded greeting and a hi-five then roars off. Five minutes later, another rider appears alongside and sits there with an appreciative smile and a nod, offering a clenched-fist tap before making his own departure into the mass of vehicles ahead. Sadly, we are unable to follow. Our panniers are simply too wide, so we are stuck.

I realise, with the passage of more bikes, that we are meeting the returning throng from the bike rally that our Gold Wing-riding friends, whom we met on the ride south of Moscow, were pondering visiting. I think maybe we've missed a trick. It would have been fantastic to visit a Russian bike rally. What a wasted opportunity! But then, on the other hand, I'm also glad that we stopped in Anapa. It was such an appealingly fresh and different place – and meeting all those friendly, relaxed people taking their annual vacation in surroundings that were faintly reminiscent of Britain in the 1960's was a truly refreshing experience.

***

The gridlock lasts for well over an hour and a half, after which the traffic gradually sorts itself out and begins to move, skirting the edge of the small town and revealing the source of the problem at the far edge of the settlement. It isn't a pretty sight. An articulated lorry lies in a ditch on the right-hand edge of the road, its roof broken open. A crushed car lies beneath. No one is going to get out of that car alive, that's for certain. A crane is being used in an attempt to lift the truck off the car. It's very tempting to stare as we go past, but we just take quick glances to acquaint ourselves with what's going on, as we ease past.

Shortly after the crash scene, we hit a stretch of dual carriageway and, for a while, I think we're going to make up time – thoughts and hopes that are cruelly dashed a few miles further on, when the road reverts to single carriageway and the traffic queues build again remorselessly. Fits and starts, all the way to the outskirts of Krasnodar. In the final few miles to our destination, heading at speed in busy traffic, we arrive at a scene of impending catastrophe. A young dog, most likely wild, has wandered into the dual carriageway in a confused and desperate state, and is now ducking and turning in amongst the traffic. We swerve to avoid it and pass safely by. I desperately want to try to stop and do something, but it's simply too dangerous to even try. Deep down, I know already that the dog is doomed and trying to help would be suicide – there simply isn't any safe place to stop. Feeling dreadful, we press on.

When we finally arrive, in the late afternoon, we enter the town from the south, a different direction from the one we departed on a couple of days ago. What a difference! You may recall that I had quite negative feelings about the place – I mean, it was plain scruffy. But arriving from the south it is quite magnificent, all flashy new buildings including a riverside hotel of substantial proportions, oozing quality and, no doubt, high room prices. It is tempting to hang a right and hammer the credit card, but, fortunately, I manage to resist the urge and proceed through the busy streets, following my errant friend, Garmy, right to the Forum Hotel front door, which I had carefully and unusually sensibly marked on departure, a couple of days ago, with a line of electronic breadcrumbs.

***

On the way out of town in the morning, heading past the myriad toy stores, I notice an impressive Lada dealership. My latent pigeon fancier's admiration for the marque infuses me with a pang to pull over, walk in and go sit in one of the final examples of the Riva to leave the production line, take a deep sniff to savour the aroma and feel the width of the upholstery. But, at the last minute, I bottle it and we ride past. I have visions of initiating some kind of mix-up over intentions and getting shot by the security guard.

The plan today is to head to a point as close to the Ukrainian border as possible; a location that will allow us to arrive at the border control with plenty of daylight remaining. This plan revolves around two nuggets of information that have been bouncing around for the past few weeks. Firstly, we know from our days of trawling the internet that passing through the Ukrainian border can be an insey-winsey bit tricky. Tales of corrupt border officials were aplenty on the web. Secondly, we read that the Russian side of the border can develop into an advanced form of 'operation stack', with trucks laid up for miles. And to reinforce both those two visions, we only need to recall the situation we witnessed ourselves on the Russian side of the border at Narva. So, we've decided to head for the city of Taganrog, which nestles in the Rostov Oblast, a mere 20 kilometres from the border. We've also taken the precaution of arriving at the border with a few days left on our visa. Getting there is a relatively short hop of around 220 miles, most of which are a reversal of our route south, a few days ago.

We plough our little furrow up the vaguely familiar M4, tracking the coast of the Sea of Azov, well inland of its lake-dotted shores. Eventually we pass into the Rostov Oblast, a passage indicated by an impressive roadside marker. An oblast is one of a number of divisions of the Russian Federation that are called 'federal subjects'. There are eighty-three such subjects, the highest level of administrative elements that make up the Russian Federation, including whole regions as well as oblasts and cities.

When we arrive at Rostov itself, I'm pleasantly surprised to find that I can bypass its dangers and hook up to the road to Ukraine without too much drama. Towards the north of the city, we chance upon a true icon of the Soviet Union proudly displayed on a plinth by the roadside. It surprises me that it has taken so long to find a decent specimen, but there it is now: a fabulous example of a T-34 tank.

I believe that there are two machines from the Second World War that prove the adage 'if it looks right, it is right'. One is our own Spitfire and the other is the T-34 tank. Both are timelessly right. But, where the Battle of Britain Spitfire only just shaded it against its main opponent, the Messerschmitt Bf109E, the T-34 completely outclassed anything the Germans could field when they invaded Russia. This fine example is painted with a broad orange and white stripe bearing a laurel leaved badge – perhaps the emblem of one of the guards regiments. The recently placed wreaths at the front of the plinth bearing testament that indeed 'nothing is forgotten'.

A little further on, we arrive at some roadworks just ahead of one of the most impressive war memorials we've seen outside Volgograd, built on top of a man-made hill and formed of two colossal, curved walls carved with figures of soldiers. We pull over into a car park to investigate further. The memorial is in a fine state of preservation. It is clearly some years old, but the gardens around it are well-kept, and the statue looks almost new. The walls have a chiselled appearance, forming bricks that I think symbolise the cities, while the figures of soldiers, male and female, are climbing out of the city, presumably to face the enemy. It appears to be another rendition of the people being part of the city theme – similar to the example we saw in Volgograd.

While I'm closely examining the statue, Diane has made a friend. One of the workmen from the nearby roadworks has wandered over to say hello. He's a huge bear of a man with a very firm handshake and zero English to match my Russian. Thankfully, he turns out to be friendly.

Chapter 18
Ukraine

The Hotel Congress, Taganrog, has an impressive pink and white frontage, built in the style beloved of 1960's high rise developers in the UK, with the added twist of really, really bad build quality. The current owners, whoever they are, have not let that handicap put them off. They've applied a lick of paint and stuck a modern entrance to the reception area. It's enough to make it appear strangely welcoming. Better than that, they've spruced up the interior and parked a couple of smiling receptionists behind the counter who speak fluent English. I already feel at home.

I'm advised by them, that security of the motorcycle is paramount and am directed to park it around the back of the hotel. I nip out to pass the good news to Diane that 'we're in' and then whisk the Mutt round to the rear, past a set of wrought iron security gates, built circa 1955 in the Soviet post-modern 'iron girder painted any colour as long as it's blue, white or pink' style. The rear of the hotel reinforces the true story of building standards in the Soviet Union, circa 1968. The walls are a horror story of bricks laid with casual disdain for straight lines, cemented by lazy dollops of mortar. Nothing of the rear elevation of this building raises itself above the well-known Norfolk phrase: 'bag-o-shite'. But hey! It's still standing.

A couple of kitchen staff are sitting outside, having a relaxed fag, close to where I park up. They nod and smile, getting up to usher me through a back door, past the kitchens and through a bar populated by a smattering of guests who look like businessmen. The whole place has a nice feel to it – apart from the brickwork.

The city of Taganrog has a proud history. It was founded as the very first Russian naval base by Peter the Great, first mentioned in 1698 – a date it proudly boasts on its coat of arms. It has since been the home to an impressive number of famous Russians, perhaps most notably the birthplace of the author Anton Chekov. Notable as an industrial centre, one of the interesting factories still here is the Beriev aircraft factory, which specialises in manufacturing amphibious aircraft. Among its many products of the Cold War was the remarkable Beriev VVA-14, a surface effect craft, designed to hunt nuclear ballistic submarines. It resembled something from the film 'Star Wars'. Physically, it looked the least likely aircraft to lug itself off either the ground or the water, yet it was so well designed (to fly ultra-low) that the test pilots who flew it found it almost impossible to land! Neat! An aircraft that can't crash.

＊＊＊

My ferry trips up and down the stairs to our modest, but very clean room introduce a repeat of the issue I had in Anapa. I keep missing my footing on the very last step of the staircase as it exits into the threshold of reception. Except here, there is one difference: I miss my footing even more emphatically at this hotel. It flails embarrassingly. The only thing worse, about advancing late middle-age, than the flailing leg syndrome, is wearing jeans that don't fit in the ass department. But the flappy leg, it turns out, is not a product of age (just yet). The reason is quite simple. When they built the hotel, they didn't quite get the overall dimensions correct and the staircase turned out a smidgen too short. So, the builders just made the final step shorter than the rest. The easy way is the best way. Catches me out every time...

What the hotel lacks in build quality, though, it makes up for in the quality of its service. The staff are pleasant, the food and beer better than acceptable, and there's a nice lady who has set up shop in the foyer, selling souvenirs. It serves as a reminder that this is our last night in Russia. And do you know what? I'm really quite sad about that. I've come to appreciate Russia, despite the initial shock of the dreadful roads and the drab austerity of the towns we passed through on our way to St Petersburg. Taganrog is a perfect case in point. It is a bit frayed around the edges, but despite that, it's a nice place to spend your last night before crossing the border.

The lady in the foyer must surely only scrape a pittance from her sales to the hotel customers but, regardless of that, she's there and she's a friendly soul – something I can say of many of the people we've met in the course of the last twenty or so days. We buy a couple of key rings from her selection of touristic 1960's era novelties.

**

We're a tiny bit apprehensive about the border crossing. The entry into Russia went exceptionally well, but this is an entirely different border at the other end of the country. Sandra/Victoria's warnings about having the correct paperwork in place resonate in my head and I remember that the bike is registered to my limited company. Why on earth did I not change that detail? On arrival, we approach a uniformed border guard who asks for passports. Diane hands them over. He carries out a quick check and then politely directs us to the first of two booths. Diane dismounts when we arrive at the booth and, paperwork in hand, ready to dispense Scottish charm, approaches the open window. I dismount and wait by the bike.

Contrary to my reservations, it actually goes rather well. Customs papers are checked. The precious form declaring our chattels is accepted with nary a raised eyebrow, and our passports are firmly ink-stamped by the uniformed immigration officials. A border guard checks all is complete at a final barrier and we are ushered politely through into the no-man's-land, twixt Russia and Ukraine. Before you can say 'tiddely pom', we're through. Part one has passed without a single hitch. Now for the Ukrainians.

As I mentioned previously, there have been some very negative comments about this border crossing, varying from huge queues, hassling of foreigners, over-enthusiastic 'searches', and outright extortion. So, when the first border guard approaches, I'm prepared for the worse. And initially his demeanour leans towards an assertiveness that might spell trouble.

'Documents!' he shouts in a boisterously official manner. We pass over our passports and the bike's V5 registration document. He gives them the most cursory of glances, then smiles and says, 'follow me!' We both think we might be heading into trouble here, but he leads us up to the first booth in the line and deposits us at the front of the queue. It occurs to me that what we may have here is a motorcycle enthusiast…. or an Anglophile… or both.

As we were approaching the border between Russia and Ukraine, we noticed that the traffic had thinned out appreciably, and the remaining cars and trucks all bore Russian number plates. Very recently, the Russian football fans at the European Championships had caused trouble in Ukraine by marching to matches chanting, 'This is Russia!' We are entering the country at a time when tensions are high and being ratcheted up by the Russians. I wondered what kind of welcome the Russian travellers will get, or for that matter, what kind of welcome we'll get once we've negotiated customs.

The assistance of the young guard proves to be critical. We find ourselves politely dealt with and more or less ushered through the sequence of procedures, which are by now becoming familiar – passport check – customs check – security check and exit. The whole procedure taking no more than ten minutes. We depart the border station with a sigh of relief and ride along a single carriageway road towards the nearest settlement on the Ukrainian side of the border.

Note: What I was unaware of at the time was that we were entering an area where the majority of the population are ethnic Russians. I only found that out later when events unfolded with the uprisings both in Kiev and in the areas of Eastern Ukraine.

✳✳✳

The road we are travelling along is in a state of modest disrepair compared with the modern highway on the Russian side of the border. After a short distance, we arrive at a long, linear village that straddles the highway. The village boasts a modern store with a cash point conveniently placed near the door. Time to grab some cash and some lunch. The inside of the store strikes us as rather strange. The counter runs right the way around the inside of the building, right up to the door, forcing you to walk around trying to pick out what you want from the groceries arranged behind the counter. Purchasing is done at a counter by trying to elucidate what you want – a bit of a hindrance when you're only able to speak six or seven words! The people in the shop are quite restrained, which is not to say they're unfriendly. There aren't any of the smiles we witnessed from many Russians in recent days. When we leave the shop, victualled with sugar-free Coca Cola and Lays chicken flavour crisps, we encounter a man who is showing his son around the bike. He seems friendly enough, but ushers the boy away and off into the shop as soon as we arrive.

Apart from this slight feeling of unease, the experience on entering Ukraine is of a relative nose-dive in prosperity. The roads are much rougher than those across the border, clearly dating from Soviet times and patched up many, many times since. The comparison is almost startling. Russia felt like it was booming, whereas here it feels like the country is stuck in time. We press on, along a road lined with huge fields. If this country is poor economically, it certainly isn't lacking in agricultural potential, the former 'bread basket' of the USSR. The agriculture is one of mixed crops, not unlike those across the border, especially notable in the sunflower department. But these sunflowers are still busy ripening, while, as we noted a few days ago, those in Russia are black and rapidly shrivelling. Eventually we see a sign for Yalta and head southwards, passing along a rather remote road, in the direction of the Sea of Azov.

Yalta doesn't ever 'heave into view' in the manner a historically famous city should. Rather, it gradually materialises to reveal a small village with one road in, same road out, bordered by diminutive, single storey houses with predominantly tin or asbestos roofs, painted in varying shades of white, grey, cream or blue. The police station lies abandoned and overgrown and the terminus of the road is marked by a couple of shops, one of which sells inflatable animal rings for children. I believe that Churchill was very fond of taking a dip in the briney, and I briefly entertain a whimsical thought of him heading into the surf with a blow-up giraffe around his ample torso – perhaps one presented to him by Stalin. But the humour is tempered by the realisation that I've made a monumental navigational cock-up. It really does put most of my previous ones to shame.

***

Having reacquainted ourselves with the Times Atlas, and discovered that the 'other' Yalta' is situated in Crimea, we return to the main road west, heading towards the city of Mariupol, with our tails between our legs. It appears quite early in the afternoon, revealing itself as a gathering of Soviet-era tower blocks on a horizon that is mostly blotted out by the mother of all steelworks. If ever there was a monumental brown field site, polluted beyond salvation, then this is it. And that is something coming from a lad from South Yorkshire. Mariupol manages to throw a carcinogenic cloud of biblical proportions in our direction and, at the same time manages to make me feel entirely at home. I'm overcome by nostalgia and spend most of the considerable time it takes to ride past the works reminiscing about the Don Valley, South Yorkshire, over my shoulder to my pillion, who I think might be asleep - if she hasn't choked to death. (In truth, it transpires, she is ignoring me - taking lots of photographs).

The plant looks to be very old, a dusty-brown reminder of the heavy industry that somehow has survived the collapse of the USSR. It is now run by a private company and is called the Ilyich Iron and Steel Works, producing rolled structural steel as well as pipes for oil production, water, and gas transmission. I think my instant affection for it is genetic. My maternal great-grandfather started his working life as a purchase ledger clerk at the Parkgate Iron and Steel Works in Rawmarsh, near Rotherham, eventually rising through the ranks to manage it. It was one of the largest steel manufacturers in Europe and my grandfather also worked there as an engineer. The difference between the Ilyich works and Grandad's works is that the latter is now mostly a retail park. Although I think one section of the outer wall remains standing.

What the Parkgate Iron and Steel Works was missing in its day was the fabulous Soviet-era artwork that can be found at the worker's entrance to the Ilyich plant. I'm sure it really cheered the workers up as they clocked in on their way to a daily manifestation of hell on earth. So much so, that the current owners have elected to keep it standing there to cheer up the current crop. I'm tempted to pull over and stare for longer at this wonderful monstrosity of decaying industrial architecture but, seeking to benefit from an early arrival, we press on along the road up a long hill into Mariupol. I feel like I've just smoked twenty Woodbines.

***

Mariupol is a sizeable city with a population of a little under half a million souls. The steel works are the most notable industry and you sure as hell can't miss it, but it also has a sizeable port. Like many of its Russian counterparts, Mariupol's public transport system consists of beaten-up trolley buses and trams. But I think it is fair to say that the trams and trolley buses here are a smidgen more beaten-up than their cousins across the border, which is saying something. The roads into the city betray the general lack of investment in Ukraine. Everything feels worn down and, frankly speaking, slightly depressing. Having said all that, Mariupol has a very vibrant seafront crowded with holidaymakers who head there at this time of year. And it's here on the seafront that we find something of a gem in hotel terms, which is fittingly (considering the location) called the Hotel Poseydon.

The hostelry in question is one of the very few new building projects to have made it into bricks and mortar since the collapse of the Union. It nestles up a slight incline, with a view across the seafront road and the adjacent, tree-lined railway track that you must negotiate if you want to go to the beach. Every so often, a train rattles past, towing long lines of empty mineral wagons, presumably on its way to the steel mill. The hotel is virtually empty, and the receptionist is unable to hide her delight in checking us in, or in showing us proudly to a room that is massive, well-appointed, and virtually brand new. We have softly landed into a luxurious feather bed of a room for something resembling the price of a Colonel Sanders' bargain bucket chicken meal.

On arrival in the city, we initially thought we'd found a hotel in the city centre. We pulled into a long, tree-shaded entrance road to be met by a security post manned by what looked remarkably like a soldier. The barrier across the road remained firmly in the 'down' position. Neither I, nor the soldier, could speak each other's language, but one word in the common tongue managed to convey what was obvious. I pointed to the fine building beyond the barrier and asked, "Otel?'. The soldier smiled and shook his head. 'Niet'. Nuff said.

***

In the late afternoon, we decide to walk over the railway lines to investigate what the resort side of Mariupol has to offer the discerning, hard-up tourist. If truth be told, it isn't much, really. There's a café area and a relatively pleasant beach, not quite as nice as Gorleston, but probably quite similar to Hartlepool. The view up the coast towards the east is one of fume-belching behemoth and the one down the other way is of something resembling Tilbury docks. The section of beach nearest the hotel is cordoned off and reserved for a party of teenage children who are chaperoned by adults; beyond that the general public hold sway. The older Ukrainians look to have dropped in from the early to mid-1950's. Some of them are wearing knotted handkerchiefs on their heads.

The folk heading for the beach disgorge from trolley-buses and climb over the railway lines en-masse to get to the beach. A bloke, sporting a dayglo jacket and carrying a flag, tips a nod to safety. An old man stops halfway across and, with hands on hips, takes in the scenery. There is absolutely zero urgency on getting across the railroad safely; it's a day in the life of the Mariupol holiday experience, so far removed from our politically correct, cotton wool-wrapped western life-experience. It is strangely comforting and downright pleasurable to bask in it, just for an hour or so.

***

Note: Between March and May 2014, fighting broke out in Mariupol between pro-Russian militia and the Ukrainian police and military in the city. The unrest also included many civilians from the city. The police headquarters, which we almost certainly mistook as a hotel, was destroyed by fire. The Ukrainian army eventually evacuated the city. The company who owned the steel works then organised the workers to peacefully take back the city from the militants, after which the army re-entered and drove out any that remained. A number of Ukrainian border guards were killed when their vehicle convoy was ambushed by the pro-Russian militia. I sincerely hope that our motorcycle-admiring friend from the border made it out safely. At the time of writing this book, Mariupol is a city under siege. The Ukrainians have built three rings of defence and bolstered the city defences with armour and heavy artillery. It is regularly bombarded by heavy weaponry.

* * *

We're back on the road again, heading west. The bike is running smoothly and is handling the road conditions very well, mostly. Occasionally, we hit a deep pothole, but this can generally be avoided by keeping away from the kerb, for it is here where the particularly vicious ones lurk. If we do hit one, the bike crashes through it with a sickening crunch, bottoming the suspension and eliciting a wince of mechanical sympathy for the poor old beast of burden. On such occasions, I shout 'sorry' over my shoulder to my pillion, carrying out a quick check to make sure she's still onboard. Shortly after midday, we pull over into a brand-new service area that nestles amongst the most wonderfully colourful sunflower fields you could care to cast your gaze upon. We are entranced. The masses of golden heads march over the gentle hill, faces raised in unison. A symphony of colour that typifies the richness of the earth hereabouts.

The next major city on our unplanned route is called Melitopol. We arrive there in the mid-afternoon of a hot and dusty day. Melitopol carries on where Mariupol left off. As you ride into the city, you form the impression that progress has been slow since the fall of the Union. In truth, this is only partially true.

Melitopol is considered to be the 'gateway to the Crimea'. The main railway line from Moscow to the Crimean Peninsula passes through its main station. As we ride into the city, we pass through tree-lined streets, bordered by the now ubiquitous Soviet-austerity tenement blocks. We are on high hotel alert. The city wants to help us find one. It has signs for hotels scattered everywhere, but we quickly find that the signs lead to many a blind alley. After a lot of riding around, avoiding the odd open manhole cover, we find ourselves heading towards the outskirts of the city, where we spot a rather bijou hostelry sitting some way back from the road.

There is a distinctive Bavarian flavour to the small hotel we have arrived at, which isn't as strange as it might seem, at first glance. Melitopol was once home to a significant population of Germans. They settled here, peacefully, many years before they opted to invade militarily. In modern times, the city has become notable for its broad ethnic mix (as we are about to discover). The ground floor comprises a cheerful, if basic, café and bar, whilst the room upstairs is decidedly threadbare. I'm being generous in describing it thus. I'll avoid describing the shower facilities in too much detail right now.

The lady who runs the establishment is very friendly and welcoming, as is the feel of the downstairs bar/restaurant. Another lady is working extremely diligently in a little room at the end of the upstairs corridor, pressing linen manically, adding it to a growing mountain of neatly folded sheets, pillows, and covers, stacked next to her. She fleetingly reminds me of the girl spinning straw in the story of Rumpelstiltskin. The sight of her imparts confidence that bed bugs won't be an issue. Unfortunately, though, all is not well in other departments – the shower room, in particular, has led to a severe drop in the confidence levels of the navigator. At the end of the day, a lady needs acceptable washing facilities. Attempting to gloss over the patent flaws in their cleanliness does me no favours at all. Diane is not impressed. One thing we are agreed on is that it might be prudent to sling the cover over the bike, so I head off to carry out the task, only to find that two guys have beaten me to it and are having an uncomfortably close look at the Mutley. I approach them and make a point of applying the alarm-cum-lock and cover, thus indicating 'ownership' and 'don't mess with this motorcycle'.

Despite my initial concerns, they both seem friendly and decent individuals. We exchange greetings and handshakes and the smaller of the two indicates that they are both bike riders, themselves. He introduces himself as Sergey. He manages to convey in sign language that his bike is parked in a car workshop that sits adjacent to the hotel, inviting me to take a peek. Inside sits a gleaming Suzuki GSR 600, a model not too far removed from my old Suzuki Bandit, common ground to build upon. On leaving the garage after further motorcycle admiration, he signals that he needs to make a phone call – we pause as he dials. Then, triumphantly, he hands me the phone.

'Hello?'

A voice with a distinct London accent chimes in at the other end.

'Hi mate. My name's Reg. I'm Sergey's friend. I'm English and I live here in Melitopol. Sergey wants me to come over and help translate for you.'

***

In the half hour or so before Reg appears, Sergey and I repair to the hostelry bar to sample a bottle of the local beer, introducing Diane at the same time. I don't know how we manage to achieve such a feat, but we seem to be able to converse with the absolute minimum of words. By the time our would-be translator arrives, I've discovered that Sergey is an ethnic Russian, that he was once an officer in the Ukrainian air force and that he worked on Ilyushin aircraft as an engineer. In return, he now knows that I'm ex-Navy and that his interest in military machinery is mutually shared.

It turns out that Reg has minimal mastery of Russian. The translation is provided via a five-way conversation between myself, Diane, Sergey, Reg and his wife Olga who is Ukrainian but speaks excellent English. Translation is achieved over Reg's phone. Reg asks us what we are doing for dinner. He adds that he knows a good restaurant in the centre of Melitpol and suggests we meet up a bit later and go there for a meal. Sergey is meeting up with some of his biking friends and can't make the meal, but he is very keen for us to see the aircraft that he used to fly on. Events are snowballing, very rapidly. Before we have time to consider the risks and dangers of bundling ourselves into an aged Audi with someone we met only an hour ago, we find ourselves in the said Audi, speeding through the town, dodging potholes and being given a guided tour of the city in Russian, by a Russian. Things start to take an even more bizarre twist when we pull into what looks like – and turns out to be - an old Cold War airbase.

It is abundantly clear, right from the outset, that the airbase fell into a level of immediate and terminal disrepair as soon as the former occupants departed. The roads are part overgrown, wholly (and holey) non-maintained and the former barracks and administrative buildings are in a similar state of decay. The new occupants appear to be civilians, but there are also a few men strolling past in Ukrainian air force uniforms, carrying attaché cases and looking suitably smart. After threading his way to a tree-shaded road bordered by apartment blocks, Sergey pulls over and signals to us to wait in the car. It's all starting to feel a bit James Bond.

We wait for a while, perhaps ten minutes in all. The apartments appear to be irredeemably run-down. We've become accustomed to the state of Communist-era apartment blocks, but the married quarters for servicemen are often built to a pathetically poor standard in western armies, navies and air forces, so it shouldn't be a complete surprise observing the efforts of Soviet military planners. That having been said, this is home for Sergey. And more than that, there is a distinct feeling of community in this bizarre mix of military and civilian occupancy. On the way in, people nodded, waved, and acknowledged our new friend as he drove through, window down, shouting greetings to all and sundry.

He eventually appears with his wife, Elizabeth, a strikingly attractive and friendly Russian lady, whom I would estimate to be in her late twenties, with dark hair and a big, warm smile, clad in motorcycle leathers. Evidently, she is going to accompany her hubby to the meeting, later in the evening. Introductions complete, Sergey starts up the motor and we head off for a surprising, if not totally unexpected, rendezvous.

Chapter 19
Cardigans and Balaclavas

Having driven to the outskirts of the aerodrome, our journey takes an interesting left turn, off the road, and becomes a kind of overland rally – something the aged Audi seems to relish, blessed with the genes of the '80s Quattro. We duck, dive and delve over, around and through various obstacles. By now, I've managed to switch my camera to 'film' mode and am attempting to keep my hand steady enough to capture the moment, enjoying the lunacy of it all so much that I completely forget why we're here in the first place. Then, a sight heaves into view that takes us both by surprise, as Sergey gently eases back the pace and the land flattens out before us.

We've arrived at an open area, bordered in the distance by trees and the odd, derelict airbase building. Lined up before us are a collection of huge, and rather beautiful aircraft. They are all painted in weathered white, broken by a pale blue flash along their flanks, all of them are Ilyushin IL-76 strategic transports. Powered by four turbojet engines and squatting on twenty wheels, with high-mounted wings that droop in a slightly sinister fashion, their multi-glazed cockpits betray their Soviet origin. One of these beasts flew right over our heads, just a couple of days ago when we rode towards Taganrog. And we saw another one flying past, on our way to the border.

There seems to be a lack of security people around. We're able to take photographs of the planes at our leisure. As we do so, Sergey explains in a mixture of very simple English words and sign language that only one of these aircraft is capable of making it into the sky, the remainder are grounded and cannibalised for spares. Despite that, surprisingly, all their tyres are pumped up, so someone must be carrying out the odd bit of tender loving care.

Ilyushin il-76.

Before too long our luck runs out. A gentleman in military fatigues approaches in a determined manner, occasioning our host to declare, 'We go now.' And so we do. Quickly, and by the same route and manner that we arrived. Overland, by Audi.

On the 14th June 2014, the Ukrainians lost one of their few, precious IL-76 aircraft to ground fire from Russian separatists. Forty soldiers and the crew of nine perished.

✳✳✳

Splendid as it was to view those fabulous aeroplanes so close-up, almost close enough to touch, Sergey hasn't finished our tour. His next assignment is some distance across the town and out into the countryside – sweeping gracefully along roads that were no doubt rough, even when they saw better days. The pace of driving is fast, but the quality is excellent. The old Audi drifts over lumps, bumps and potholes with panache. We skim past another relic of the Cold War:

a derelict radar station, replete with a cluster of vast, circular, steel-ribbed dishes, all pointing vaguely in the direction of Turkey and all resembling a prop from Thunderbirds. A little further on, we pass through the remains of a sizeable barracks complex, which, we are told, is now the school and home of the fire service.

Presently, at about five minutes to five, we draw into the car park of a landmark of some prominence and distinction, although it isn't immediately clear to us what it actually is. And it looks like we're not going to find out too quickly either. The gates are being swung shut quite briskly even as we arrive.

Our host is not to be deterred that easily. He negotiates in animated fashion through the gates for quite a few minutes before finally coming back to us and saying, 'We go in, small time.'

The site that we wander over to is called the *Stone Graves*. It doesn't sound particularly enticing or spectacular, but it rivals Stonehenge in both its physical scale and the air of mystery surrounding it. For here, on the vast Ukrainian steppe, sits an incongruous, jumbled mass of rocks, sunk into a beach of sand. Amongst the rocks are dozens of caves with petroglyphs carved into them. Unlike Stonehenge, though, the rocks haven't been transported to the site. They are formed from the sandbank of an ancient sea. A historian dated the petroglyphs from 2000 years BC right through to the 1600s AD, perhaps the longest running timeline of any graffiti in Europe. Even Banksy would be impressed.

Following our whirlwind tour of the highlights of Melitopol, we find ourselves delivered back to our abode. Sergey and Elizabeth tog up and head off to their biker's meeting in town. But, before they go, I search for something to give them, just to say thanks. I don't have much left. My last British coin was given out in Anapa. In the end, I decide to present to him a personal talisman, an Ace Café badge that I wear on my riding jacket. He seems quite made up with it and pins it to his jacket before departing.

***

Reg arrives in his car shortly after, with his wife Olga, interpreter par excellence and a striking lady, with blonde hair and high cheekbones, by my estimation quite a bit younger than Reg. The mix between Ukrainian, English and Russians is very relaxed – they're all good friends, joined together by a common love of motorcycling. This is quite remarkable when you consider that the slightly viral spread of motorcycles in Melitopol is down, in no small part, to this rather remarkable Englishman. It transpires, during our conversation in the car, that Reg arrived in Melitopol with his Yamaha R1 (an early version of the breed) and took the place by storm.

No-one had seen a pure-bred sports bike such as this before. Up until that point in time, the staple fare consisted of Russian-era flat twin four-strokes and smoky Communist Bloc two-strokes, which I actually like, a lot. Over a period of a few years, Reg married Olga and started a family, settling down to life as an immigrant. Young guys like Sergey were drawn to him and, more to the point, his R1. Drawn like moths to a searchlight. And, gradually over time, they started buying their own Japanese pocket rockets. So much so, that, nowadays, you will see quite a few people buzzing around on proper sports bikes. All thanks to this slightly eccentric geezer.

We spend a very pleasant evening with Reg and Olga, eating a meal in a modern, western-style eatery that borders the main city square – a pleasant place, built during Soviet times. On departure, we walk over to the car and are greeted by one of the local sports bike riders, a young lad on a Japanese 600. There really is a sense of brotherhood around here.

***

When we arrived in Melitopol, we found ourselves a tiny bit downcast about the prospects of staying in the hotel. Diane braved the torment of the shower and, quite by coincidence, we met a group of terrific people. We trusted them from the outset, largely because they appeared to be motorcycle enthusiasts of the finest order. It was a quick judgement call. That trust led to a fantastic evening, full of surprises.

In the morning, we're visited by Sergey, who has come in early for a pre-arranged breakfast with us, prior to starting work. He arrives in an animated state, asking me to pop round to the garage. Through a bit of phone translation provided by Olga, he tells me that his friends at the bike club were deeply jealous of the Ace Café badge. A couple of them knew all about the 'caff' and explained to him its significance in the history of motorcycling and sporting road machines in general. Sergey headed to the market early this morning to locate a militaria stall he knew about, picking up a range of badges, buttons, uniform shoulder flashes and belt buckles, which he now hands to me, explaining where each of them came from and their significance. One object is particularly rare. He also gives me a new talisman: a keyring with the name Andrei in Cyrillic emblazoned upon it. I feel this is fortuitous and that it will keep us both safe. I'm a tad OCD with matters such as carrying a range of talismans. I can't do anything about it. Apart from washing around the taps in the bathroom five times in a clockwise figure of eight before exiting, stage left.

***

In a final act of friendship, Reg and Olga pop by in their Rover. They've come to guide us out of the city – to make sure we depart on the correct road for Crimea.

'Be very careful of open manhole covers', he advises – 'that and the maniac drivers who hate motorcycles riding anywhere, other than in the gutter'. He goes on to tell me that Ukrainian drivers haven't really got used to bikes that can reach sixty miles-per-hour, so they try to bully you back into the gutter if you appear to be in their way.

'Can't say I've really noticed that, so far, Reg,' says I. 'We've had a few races with Russians, but it's all been fairly reasonable.' Famous last words.

As we reach the edge of town, they honk the horn and pull over, signalling us to turn right onto the road to Crimea. Destination Yalta. Hopefully the correct Yalta, this time round!

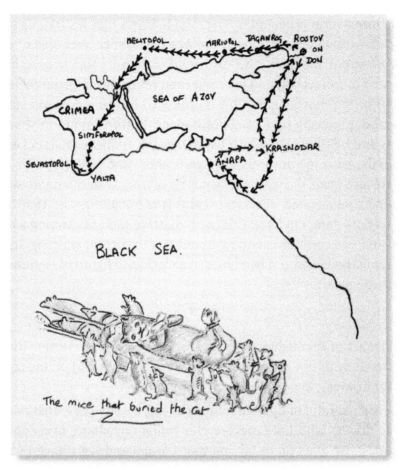

The mice that buried the cat

Southern Russia, Ukraine and Crimea.

We find ourselves trundling through familiar countryside – past small settlements and almost endless fields, along roads flanked by trees and bushes. Our direction is south-westerly on the M105, by-passing the town of Yakymivka and covering the sixty or so kilometres to the thin strip of land that links the Crimean Peninsula to the Ukrainian mainland at its north-eastern tip. This is one of two land bridges onto what otherwise would be an island – the other, the isthmus of Perekop, lies further to the west.

True to Reg's words of warning, I've detected a certain hurriedness about the traffic hereabouts. I glance in my left-hand mirror and spot a large 4X4 SUV looming ominously close to the rear number plate. Then, when they overtake, they do so far too close for my liking, and into oncoming traffic too, swerving alarmingly to avoid a head-on collision, thereby cutting us up quite badly in the process. I am not a happy teddy. Reg's advice, quoting Corporal Jones of 'Dad's Army', rings loudly in my ears, 'Bully 'em back. They don't like it up 'em.' And so it begins...

The first victim is not driving a 4x4. He's in a lowly Lada Samara. He wheezes past and cuts us up, executing a desperate lunge back into our lane, almost clipping off our nose. As soon as he's completed his manoeuvre, I clamp myself on his tail, sitting at the seven o'clock position where his darting eyes can see me fixated in his rear-view mirror, riding the slipstream with the throttle eased back. He then proceeds to try to overtake the lorry in front, swerving in and out to find a space in the traffic, lest the red beast behind scalps him and reduces him to the status of 'wuss'. Too late. I see a gap that he can't make, but we can, and we take him out. There is a howl of admonishment from the navigator, heard faintly in the battering windblast, but I'm on a roll. We swing in and out, using our gathering pace to put four or five vehicles between us and our victim, who seems to have given up and taken his 'pied' off the 'plancher'.

We pass over a wild and remote strip of land, where seabirds wade on the edges of mudflats and blocks of old concrete lean into the sand at funny angles. The isthmus is guarded by a seriously large border post, an incongruous feature that Reg told us about over dinner last night. 'They're a strange lot, those Crimeans. They've got a border post down there and they sometimes man it and close the border. They can be most unwelcoming'. Some distance further on, after a top-up of juice for the bike, we spot a large roadside market and decide to stop and check it out. As we pull off our helmets, I notice a Lada Samara is pulling in and parking next to the bike.

I'm half expecting a bit of an altercation, but the person who steps out of the Lada with his wife is a small balding man who smiles and says 'Zdravstvuyte', a word that is virtually un-pronounceable for the average Brit. Whenever I try to say 'Zdravstvuyte' to my Russian or Kazakh friends they just laugh and tell me to say 'Privet', the informal choice. Either way, it would be nice to follow up with, 'were you trying to kill us both back there,' but, being unable to even start the conversation, I decide just to nod.

The market that we've arrived at is a fascinating one, totally dedicated to the sale of fish. Fish of a multitude of shapes and sizes, all hanging from the racks of individual stalls. Without any ado, we find ourselves accosted by a lady stall-holder who has a razor-sharp sales technique that would be a positive asset to her if she ever decided to move to England and start selling double glazing at the entrances to supermarkets. She doesn't really speak any English, probably thinks we're Americans or Germans, and has honed-in like a wasp to an open jam jar, no doubt considering us to be a pair of curious, dim-witted tourists, ready for the fleecing. Added to that, in a similar vein to the lady selling painted boxes in St Petersburg, she is both adept and charming in equal measure, offering us samples of the various fish on offer. Option one, a small oily fish, similar to a sardine – could, in fact, be a sardine - is truly revolting.

Roadside markets always provide a feast for the eye.

She doesn't bat an eyelid at our impression of cats bringing up fur balls. Instead, she smiles widely and offers me an alternative of dried fish that tastes like a dog chew (you may ask how I know this, and the answer lurks way back in my childhood). The third attempt strikes gold. It's like a tenderly cured salmon fillet and it really is very delicious. Our friendly vendor moves in for the kill, asking what size we would like to buy. At this point, there is a bit of a debate.

I have mentioned before – Diane is a person of considerable caution. Whenever I'm about to dive into the deep end, she will raise a doubt, a question that deflates my enthusiasm with the voice of reason. 'Could this fish give us the shits?' OK, those are not exactly her words...

***

Back on the road, weighed down by a few pounds of fish that is probably already going rancid as we speak, I determine to throw the fish away at the first opportunity. Never mind. The stall holder was nice. It was very pleasant giving her some money. She seemed to appreciate the gesture.

Once we've relaxed into the flow of the traffic, skimming along the long and very straight, flat, tree-lined roads, I notice that the coefficient of 4X4s, many with Russian plates, has risen exponentially along with the level of aggression in the overtaking department. We're repeatedly hounded with incredibly dangerous overtaking manoeuvres – in both directions. On more than one occasion we find ourselves swerving violently to avoid oncoming vehicles that have failed to complete their overtaking manoeuvre and miss us by a hair's breadth – it is quite frightening. At the time, I took Reg's words of warning with a pinch of salt, but now I can see that, far from exaggerating, he was actually putting it rather mildly, so as not to put us off no doubt. If the oncoming traffic isn't bad enough, we end up with a series of bad boys in the mirrors, tracking us, inches behind the number plate, trying to bully us off the road and into the gutter. In the end, I'm sad to say that something has to give.

I'm deeply ashamed to record that I completely lose the plot. Each time someone cuts me up I latch onto them and harry them down in return. Their behaviour, on finding the recently bullied bike on their tails, would be hilarious if it wasn't potentially catastrophic. To a man (for they are all men), they switch to a headless-chicken, panic mode, lest they are overtaken in return. This leads to them executing astonishingly dangerous overtaking moves, into the oncoming traffic. It seems that the average male hereabouts, risks losing his very manhood if he is overtaken by a motorcycle, regardless of whether he's driving a fast, expensive car – or a beaten-up old Lada. I realise that I could be partially responsible for a fatal RTA and decide to back off, not before I receive a well-timed whack from Diane, who has also decided enough is enough. The big red Adventure agrees with her sentiments too. It's wheezing quite noticeably at these speeds. Diane and the Mutt are happier at a lower speed, being bullied, while I'm still quietly fuming.

***

Yalta turns out to be unlike any of the cities we've passed through, recently. It has more in common with the Italian Riviera than somewhere in Russia or Ukraine. Everything about it, from the rugged hills above the city, the modern high-rise towers, the classic older buildings, and the beautiful green trees that line the road, exudes a quality and relative wealth that is both surprising and very welcome, after such a fraught journey. What isn't quite so inviting is the logjam of traffic.

We crawl, very slowly and fitfully, through a thoroughfare packed with holiday traffic, alongside street pavements that are similarly packed with people. It is also incredibly hot. I'm not sure what Diane is thinking on the back of the bike, but my spirits are dipping ever so slightly with the realisation that finding a hotel vacancy is probably going to be a non-starter. Yalta is clearly a very popular holiday resort.

With the bike and Diane parked up under the shade of some trees in a street close to the seafront, I conduct a swift and fruitless search, heading back to report to the boss. Ten minutes later, we ride out of town. Such was our visit to Yalta.

Despite the hasty retreat, I gleaned the impression that Yalta has improved immeasurably since Churchill, Roosevelt, and Stalin met there in February, 1945. At that time, the area hadn't recovered from the devastation laid upon it by the retreating Germans. Churchill considered it to be 'lice-ridden' and asked for his clothes to be de-loused on boarding a British ship, after the conference. The conference itself, which took place at the old Tsar's Livadia Palace on the outskirts of the city, remains controversial. A new world order emerged from it, along with the foundations of the Cold War. The effects still resonate today.

Our departure in the late afternoon takes us along a stunning stretch of coastline, heading in a westerly direction, marvelling at the monumental grey-white cliffs that tower above us. The road traverses a point with cliffs to seaward and more cliffs to landward, a bit like travelling along a huge sofa. We're following the recommendation of the receptionist of the first hotel we tried, back in Yalta. She suggested trying our luck in Sevastopol, which, she said. is quieter and less touristic. In truth, I wasn't too concerned about having to move on. Yalta was too busy for my liking, although I'm quite sure it would have been perfectly acceptable for a couple of days' stay. My fingers are now crossed that we find something decent in Sevastopol.

After a while, we turn inland towards our next destination, but not before the early sunset splashes a fabulous pastel palette of rose pink, blue and greys upon the wonderful cliffs to our right – a reminder that we're running late, but a display worth being late for. The route then twists and turns across an increasingly rugged terrain on a well-made, twisty road – a delight for a motorcyclist. We pass the outskirts of Sevastopol, populated by tower blocks, mildly concerned that we'll have trouble finding a hotel if it gets too dark, but, as we pass across a set of traffic lights, past a petrol station and along a one-way street that drops steeply towards the city centre, we suddenly spot one on the left, just in time to brake and pull into the forecourt. Phew!!

The hotel is protected by a low wall, a small fact that imparts a feeling of potential security for bikes and baggage. So, for the first time in a long while, we leave the bike parked outside the main entrance and Diane follows me into the reception to witness my technique in the receptionist-charming department. To our left, we notice an older man who is glued to a bank of CCTV monitors. Good. The bike, with all its gear, is safe. He eyes us with a hint of suspicion. I enquire if the receptionist speaks English. She does. She confirms that they have plenty of room availability. We progress to pricing and payment terms.

Initially, there's some confusion about the room deposit. The manager is consulted and demands immediate payment in full, in cash. I explain that we don't carry that much cash. He relents' after a brief discussion with the receptionist, and says we can pay a deposit, but it's still more than we have. Further extensive negotiations ensue. After giving them everything we have, including small change, they agree that we can leave our bags in our room, then walk into the city to find a cash machine. We are led up a couple of flights of stairs to a spacious, but very dated room. As we check the state of bathroom sanitation, we decide to christen the place 'The Hotel Strange'.

We head down a steep hill to a large square and quickly find a cash machine and a convenient restaurant. When I ask the waiter if he's from Sevastopol, he replies, 'Oh no! I'm Ukrainian, this place is full of Russians. Very few Ukrainians.' He goes on to explain that he's a teacher from the north west of Ukraine and is spending the summer here working as a waiter.

In hushed tones, he leans down and explains further, 'The Russians don't want us here. They want it back. And they *will* take it back!'

* * *

In the morning, still smarting from being short-changed by the waiter at the end of our evening meal, we decide to try a different eatery for breakfast and head for one across the square called The Patio, which sits in a strip of shaded park. We are greeted warmly by a young waitress with long blonde hair. Over a nice cup of *latte*, we survey the view from our slightly elevated position. The Patio is a strange kind of establishment, built from temporary materials and (presumably) opened for a limited period during the summer. It's a pop-up restaurant.

The far end of the restaurant stands above a considerable drop, partly masked by trees, where the hill falls away, down to an inlet which is part of a huge natural harbour. The buildings on both sides of the inlet are of considerable age and, in many cases, rather grand. Various ships, military auxiliaries if I'm not mistaken, are berthed by the stern, tied to a long series of stone jetties. They are our first glimpse of the much-vaunted Russian Black Sea Fleet, distinguishable from their Ukrainian counterparts by red, white and blue stripes on their funnels. Each of the auxiliary ships is notable for its vintage and apparent decrepitude. Whilst we are sipping our coffee, we find ourselves entertained by the sight of a Russian officer parading a group of sailors past the restaurant, marching smartly by. It occurs to me that this is strange behaviour for a foreign power. I can understand that the Russian navy is based here on a lease, that bit I get, but it seems a bit off that they are the ones marching through a Ukrainian city. But that's not the whole story. As is often the case, the city's history is slightly more complicated than that.

Sevastopol was founded as a naval base in 1783 by a Scot. At the time, there were a few Scots in the Russian navy and one of them, Thomas McKenzie, spotted the potential of the magnificent natural harbour and reasoned that it would be a fine base for the ships that were busy fighting the Ottoman Empire. So, from the outset, Sevastopol was a Russian city. And I think it is fair to say that the Russians have invested a great deal of expense to build what is quite a beautiful city. Interestingly, and coincidentally, the official flag of the Russian navy is a St Andrew's cross, a saltire, the same as the flag of Scotland. It has no connection to McKenzie and is the inverse of the Scottish national flag, being a blue cross on a white background, designed by Peter the Great.

As if to underline this historic naval tradition spanning over two centuries, Sevastopol boasts a fabulous museum dedicated to the history of the Black Sea Fleet. A modest fee gains entry. The museum is housed in a purpose designed, classical building, which was built from the outset to hold a growing collection of nautical artefacts. For me, the wonder of maritime museums are the ship models. I love them and could stare at them for hours. And here there are lots of them, ranging from the sailing ships of yore, through to the rakishly splendid ships that were part of the burgeoning Soviet navy of the Cold War. A considerable section of the museum is dedicated to the Siege of Sevastopol, which took place between 1854 and 1855.

Despite having a long history of Imperial expansion, Russia has repeatedly suffered invasions and conflict with countries from the west. The Black Sea Fleet Museum has two major themes: firstly, the repeated attempts by foreign powers to invade and capture the city, thwarted by brave resistance and the courage of the defenders; secondly, the rise of the fleet and the prestige that came with strength and power.

There are a series of very striking exhibits. One is a large painting of the fall of the German garrison in May, 1944. The central character is a German officer who strikes an abject pose, realising that all is lost. His Luger pistol is held loosely in his hand, pointing at the floor. In a case nearby the painting, hundreds of iron crosses spill down and flow across the base – relics of the invaders who, most likely, never saw their homeland again.

Russian museums have a penchant for displaying countless photographs. Pictures of people, some ordinary and others who became great heroes. I've read in Lonely Planet that people find them a bit boring, not least because the accompanying cards are in Cyrillic, very rarely having any translation or context. But I find them quite fascinating. One that catches my eye is a series of photos of a Russian general in the Second World War (or Great Patriotic War, as the Russians call it). He is photographed amid the paraphernalia of war, accompanied by a very striking soldier with long blond hair, who might just be a woman, dressed in combat smock, trousers and boots and sporting a very large, 'don't mess with me' looking dagger.

Perhaps the most poignant exhibition is housed, separately, in its own case. It contains artefacts recovered from the Kursk, an Oscar-class cruise missile submarine that sank on the 12th August 2000 (almost twelve years ago to this very day) in the Barents Sea, following two explosions in her forward torpedo section. The objects recovered are all personal effects, articles of uniform, badges, pens, a cheap plastic torch. Diane has a connection to these objects. The company she worked for provided submersibles and divers, tasked with reaching and entering the wreck to recover the bodies of the victims.

***

The centre of the city, which sits on a hill above the bay, isn't huge, although the wider city, population of around 340,000, is quite sprawling. The main streets that lead down to the harbour are serviced by old and somewhat battered electric trolley buses, or 'tracklesses' as we used to call them back at home in the '60s. A series of small, tree-shaded parks follow the line of a pathway above the creek where the auxiliary ships are berthed. Some of the ships are busying themselves, moving around and returning from various duties. As we walk along in the sweltering heat, we catch glimpses below a well-ordered naval base and spot a couple of examples of the more serious fighting end of the Russian navy, ships recognisable to me from way back in the late 1970s. The first ones that we see are a Kashin-class destroyer and a Krivak-class frigate, both very old vessels, yet immaculately turned out.

Scattered ignominiously in amongst this array of Russian military firepower lie a few Ukrainian vessels, former Soviet ships that were handed over to the Ukrainians when the Soviet Union split up. We wander around the perimeter of a Ukrainian naval barracks, noting that the sailors appear to be confined to barracks. A strange feeling comes over me and I comment to Diane that these people seem almost imprisoned within their own country, recalling the words of the waiter from last night.

Down by the seafront, we wander into a busy, open market, where the stalls sell a mixture of souvenirs, toys and cheap clothes. Nautical references abound and many of those are dedicated to the Black Sea Fleet. We buy an amusing fridge magnet bearing the cartoon of a bear dressed in an admiral's uniform, the friendly face of the navy. It's worth having a careful look around some of the stalls selling antiques. At one stall, I find a small box of Crimean War memorabilia – notably Victorian era bullets and uniform buttons. The stall holder points out the musket balls of the different warring parties: a large, squat projectile that he says is French – and I think he's correct – it looks identical to the Civil War Minie bullets that I bought in America, and smaller ones that he says are British. He picks up a different example that he says is Russian. After a bit of humming and hawing, I buy a couple of British examples. It seems fitting that they should be repatriated, after all this time.

Eventually we reach the broad sweep of waterfront. And a quite splendid waterfront it is too, lined with elegant white, red-tiled buildings overlooking the distant, outer harbour wall. The sea splashes vigorously against the wall, tossing small pleasure craft around as they strain against their ropes, eager for the next group of passengers to be taken over to view the ships. The pleasure craft are being advertised by salesmen who parade up and down, shouting through megaphones. I stare over at the main body of ships, Russian and Ukrainian, that are berthed in the distance on the far side of the harbour. A man approaches and speaks in Russian. The cruises to see the ships all head up the smaller creek that we have already viewed on our walk along the hill. I point over to the bigger ships in the distance across the bay, 'I want to go and see *those* ones!'

A debate ensues between the salesman and the pleasure craft captain. The salesman returns with a deal. We can go across to the main naval base if we pay more money – it amounts to about twenty pounds, double the price of the trip to see a load of old decrepit harbour auxiliaries and a 1970's Kashin-class destroyer. The deal is struck there and then. We are hastily bundled on to a bouncing white boat, ready for our mission. Jason Bourne could not have improved on this achievement.

*** *

In the evening, over dinner at the Patio Restaurant, we ponder the events of the day. I thought the trip to see the ships was worth every penny. The lively ride across the bay was fun. The centrepiece of the Russian navy was the guided missile cruiser Moskva, an impressive and immaculately painted vessel of twelve and a half thousand tons. Even her anchor cable, which stretched out down to the waterline in front of her, was nicely painted white. The Russian method of tying up ships seems to be a case of backing them in whilst running out anchor cable and tying up at the stern. It seems quite an efficient parking method, allowing lots of ships to take up relatively little room. It also allows would-be spies to hire a vessel and get a surprisingly close look.

The ill-fated cruiser Moskva

The plan for tomorrow is to locate the memorial to the Charge of the Light Brigade. A hotel tourist pamphlet describes it simply as: 'the British memorial'. References to the Anglo/French invasion of the Crimean Peninsula are mostly notable for their absence. The authorities don't appear to make much of a fuss about it. The map in the pamphlet places its position a short distance outside the town, along the road heading back towards Yalta. As well as locating the memorial, we plan to head down the coast to Balaclava, which was the main logistical base for the British invasion fleet. The Royal Navy famously crammed the harbour full of ships and turned it into a festering cesspit. Let's hope it has freshened up somewhat since!

Rightly or wrongly, I've almost ceased to think of Sevastopol as being Ukrainian, the Russian influence is all-pervasive. Crimea was 'gifted' to the Ukraine in 1954 by Nikita Khrushchev, something that is now clearly regretted on the Russian side. Our new waitress at the Patio bar/restaurant is Ukrainian but, in similar fashion to the waiter at the previous restaurant, she describes herself 'not of these parts'. She forms part of the 23% of her countrymen, or women, resident on the peninsula, around 60% are ethnic Russians.

Of the original Tartar population, who once called the Crimea their own, only a few remain – around 12% of the total Crimean population. This Turkic-speaking Muslim race was once dominant across south-eastern Europe. They are now part of a wide diaspora. Their greatest concentration can be found in the republic of Tatarstan, many miles to the north east. I suspect that the lady who sold us fish the other day was probably of Tartar descent. When you consider the racial mixture of the people of the Soviet Union, and the tensions that already existed between them, it is quite astonishing that it held together for so many years.

We manage to complete the steep climb up the hill to our hotel just before a terrific thunderstorm breaks, arriving at the hotel reception as the first bolts of lightning flicker across the night sky. The hotel is considerably busier tonight with, the arrival of a professional football team. The security guard lifts his gaze from his screen to give us a thumbs-up, indicating towards the monitor that the bike is still parked underneath its own personal camera. Security is taken very seriously in this town. We visited a bank earlier today and were assisted at a cashpoint by a gentleman in fatigues, packing a very purposeful sidearm.

✳✳✳

Today is the final day of the London Olympics, with high hopes of a spectacular closing ceremony. Sadly for us, we won't be able to see it so, by way of consolation, we'll take a little tour of the battlefields of the Crimean War. Our first stop: Balaclava. The town nestles in the lee of a pair of very steep, partially fortified hills and boasts a marina stacked with flashy recreational craft of various shapes and sizes. The streets on the eastern side of the port are narrow, lined with shops and cafes and packed with tourists – mostly Russians.

As I mentioned earlier, the Royal Navy managed to turn the port into a proper cesspit. But the memory of that has receded into the distant past, and, nowadays, it is a fair town with attractive white buildings, red roof tiles and a deep azure blue harbour – most photogenic and not entirely different to some coastal towns in Cornwall. Balaclava has one important other claim to fame: it gave its name to the cold-cheating headgear beloved of bank robbers, sex-slave gimps, terrorists, and all-weather motorcyclists. As a motorcyclist, I personally own my fair share of balaclavas. Unfortunately, though, I'm unable to put my hands on a single one of them when I need to. They're very similar to socks in that respect. I would be completely useless as a gimp.

Having parked up the bike in a convenient spot on a shopping street, we head for the harbour and queue at a fast-food trailer to sample a local minced beef wrap that tastes rather fine. It's nice to relax like this, but we are on a mission to find the memorial, so, having taken a few photos and sipped a coffee, we head back to the bike, mount up, and mosey on out of town.

Since we have no idea where our target is, and only a limited clue of what it is, we rapidly find ourselves reduced to scouring the hillsides for likely suspects, something that sounds stupid, but is productive almost immediately. One thing this part of the peninsula isn't lacking in is monuments. It's just a case of finding the proverbial needle. Our first one sits up the road from Balaclava on top of quite a steep hill, accessed by a tricky, steep dirt track. Things get a bit tasty halfway up the hill. The rocks littering the track increase in size and the bike is scrabbling for grip. I think I could make it all the way but, in fairness to Diane, I get her to hop off, park the bike up and we walk up the final hundred feet or so together. Simon Pavey – he of Paris-Dakar fame - would justifiably be totally disgusted at this lack of off-road fortitude and would berate me, mercilessly.

The monument that we spotted turns out to be a relatively modern one, something to do with the siege of Sevastopol in the 1940's. It marks a place where a series of zig-zag trenches were dug to defend the hill, their remains partially filled in, yet very clear to see. Going by the number of empty beer cans and broken bottles scattered around, it is a popular place to light a bonfire, get drunk, and fall over.

Half an hour later, after riding back down the road, we find ourselves trekking up and down the Yalta road, having a bit of fun in the corners. It's a fine road to ride – hot day, warm tyres, and fast, predictable curves, with the added bonus of empty panniers. We spot another memorial and check it out. This one is more like it! At least the dates are correct.

It's a Crimean War memorial erected in memory of the soldiers from Piedmont-Sardinia who fought here. What on earth were they doing here? Whatever it was, there were 15,000 of them and their memorial is quite an impressive one. After a brief stop, we head up and down the road two or three times, gradually despairing of finding anything more. Then, we spot an even larger edifice than that of the Sardinians. Surely, this will be the one.

It looks like the Russians are having the last laugh. This monument is better placed to overlook the battlefield and is rather grand. The battle in question was the Battle of Balaclava. In the minds of most military historians, the battle was a draw, but the Russians generally consider that they won fairly and squarely, not least because they decimated the British Light Cavalry Brigade. I think we British displayed sufficient incompetence to claim that we decimated our own Brigade – all the Russians needed to do was lock, load and fire. Without a shadow of doubt, this monument is victorious in nature and, all things considered, I think that's fair enough. But it isn't the one we're searching for, so we mount up and continue scouring the countryside.

We ride up and down two more times before Diane glimpses a white obelisk and shouts out. It turns out to be a difficult one to pin down and locate – the best we can do is catch brief glimpses as we try to reach it via various roads, including one horrendous, rubble-filled cart track, before realising that the obelisk isn't adjacent to a road. It's stuck in the middle of a vineyard, on the far side of a railway track, for goodness' sake!

We park up at a conveniently situated petrol station, stared at by a pair of bemused attendants as we wander across the road, up the bank, across the railway line and onwards towards the vineyard. Finally, after tramping a short distance up the vineyard access track, we finally reach the obelisk. Of the three monuments, it is by far the least impressive. Sad to say, it is quite badly weathered and suffering from considerable neglect. It bears a plaque commemorating a visit by the Duke of Edinburgh in 2004, which I think was probably the last time it received any upkeep. I'm not sure if HRH took a pot of white paint with him, but that's about all that was done to it: a quick lick of paint and a brass plaque.

The Crimean war was a complicated affair, with numerous combatant nations (including the Sardinians). I don't really have sufficient knowledge to go too far into it. But arriving here has led me to do a quick swat-up on the 'net, and I found myself drawn towards the antics of one of the chief protagonists on the British side. If you tried to make up a character to fit the stereotypical Victorian senior army officer, James Thomas Brudenell, 7th Earl of Cardigan, would fit the bill to perfection. The late, great Trevor Howard played him in the excellent 1968 film covering the events of 1854, a fitting actor for the part, I think.

Cardigan was quite a character. At a young age, he fell from a horse and took a head injury, giving rise to family concerns that he might have been slightly intellectually challenged. His father prevented him from joining the army, despite being a fine horseman (presumably he improved his skills after the fall). Following a spell at university that didn't result in a degree, he headed off to travel on the Grand Tour, including visiting Russia. I'm warming to him already. He eventually used his wealth to buy a commission and raise a regiment at his own expense, which was an admirable act of self-aggrandisement. But he wasn't all sweetness and light. He was notoriously badly mannered towards those of the 'wrong sort', whatever that was. On the day of the Charge of the Light Brigade, he was its commanding officer. He was fifty-seven years old, which I think is quite senior in years for such a vigorous activity.

There is a lot of debate about what happened, especially surrounding the communication to attack, given to Cardigan by his direct superior Lord Lucan, his brother-in-law, whom he detested. He claimed he didn't treat his sister well. Lucan, in turn, had received the order to advance on Russian troops who were removing guns from some Turkish fortifications that they'd managed to over-run. The messenger, a man called Captain Louis Nolan, who was quite a character himself, a distinguished cavalryman who had written books on cavalry history and tactics and even invented a form of saddle, delivered the message to sally forth and recover the guns. Exactly the kind of task the Light Brigade were designed to execute, with flashing lances and a heavy dose of alacrity. Neither Lucan nor Cardigan could see the Russians in question and asked where they were. Nolan gave a big sweep of the arm and said (un)helpfully, 'Over there'. The only guns visible were those in a completely different valley from the one intended – this unintended location holding a very well protected battery of guns, belonging to the Don Cossack formation. From what I've read about Cossacks in general, I don't think the required course of action, namely charging them, was at all advisable and neither did Cardigan. One thing Napoleon had learnt, a few years previously, was not to go messing around with the Don Cossacks. It was a quick way to an early grave.

Nevertheless, Cardigan carried out his duty and charged, by most accounts leading so far in front on his horse Ronald – great name for a horse – that he lost touch with his troopers and became a bit confused when he got to the cannons. One account has him fighting bravely up to a point where he risked being killed by 'common soldiery', then retiring gracefully at nothing much greater than a trot, to avoid such a dreadful outcome, no doubt with Richard III in mind. Other accounts have him heading pell-mell back to the British lines, passing the elements of the Light Horse who were still charging forwards, heading to safety in the opposite direction. Apparently, when he got back, he denied all blame for the failure then headed to his luxury yacht, anchored in the Balaclava cess pool, whereupon he treated himself to a well-earned champagne dinner.

The 'British Memorial'.

Chapter 20
Life without maps

After our initial misgivings, the 'Hotel Strange' has proven to be a comfortable and convenient place to stay. The security guard, who seems to live at his desk, has shown dedication to motorcycle security beyond the call of duty, something I feel is deserving of a tip, so I have a rummage about, wondering what we could give him that would be useful. The answer is obvious: we have seven torches. Tipping a nod to the film *Night in the Museum*, I think a torch would be a fitting gift for such a diligent security guard. He could probably practice and develop some impressive torch twirling tricks and techniques to counter rogue monkeys, were he that way inclined. A smart, red anodised mini-Maglite is forthcoming and handed over in reception just prior to departure, much to the dutiful guard's delight.

Our initial route is in the direction of the city of Simferopol, then it cuts towards the west. I am faintly surprised and comforted by the lack of aggressive traffic during the early part of our journey, so much so that I get lulled into a state of lazy happiness. The result is that we completely miss our turning and ride blissfully back towards Melitopol, without a care in the world. I only realise the error of my ways some hours later, when we arrive at the town of Izumrudne which was definitely not on our route-plan for today! Shit!

A quick reassessment of the situation results in a detour along a minor carriageway of variable quality that cuts a dash across country, following a canal. Occasionally, it feels like it is going to peter out, but then recovers and becomes a little more serious. Every so often, it arrives at a canal sluice gate complex and then wanders off track. There are very few signs of habitation; no petrol stations or eateries. We encounter very little traffic. Then, just as the fuel is starting to run a tad low on the petrol gauge, we spot a small village. No fuel station, but at least a sign of life. A few miles further on, we meet the road we should have taken in the first place and rediscover civilisation. The relief in the air is palpable.

We arrive at a junction, across the road from a very large airbase, which is liberally dotted with old, decrepit military helicopters, including examples of the impressive MIL MI-24 Hind. These are fearsome-looking beasts, a gunship that pre-dated the much-vaunted American Apache by many years, having first flown in 1969. The ones sitting across the fence are well past their sell-by date and look like they haven't flown in years, another example of the parlous state the Ukrainian military finds itself in. Riding on for an hour, we pass into an increasingly populous part of the country, marvelling at the sight of an articulated lorry that has collapsed on the side of the road with a broken back, like a brontosaurus that has suffered an unfortunate altercation with a T-Rex.

On arrival at the city of Kherson, we top up on fuel and grab a light bite to eat before pressing on, in the hope of reaching Odessa. Alas, our day's ride has taken its toll on time. It's very doubtful we will arrive there before nightfall, so we eventually decide to start looking for a hotel when we reach the city of Mykolaiv, which sits on a huge bow in the Pivdennyi Buh river. We pass along the now-familiar environs of a post-Soviet city. The painfully grim apartment blocks, tired pot-holed streets, trees with white paint on their trunks, cigarette kiosks and corner shops, necks craning as we scan the streets for signs of a hotel. This afternoon, our luck is in. We spot one that looks as tatty as the street it resides in.

✳✳✳

The next day, we ride the short distance to Odessa, arriving in the very early afternoon to find another gritty industrial city, dominated by the factories and old warehouses that you would expect to find in a port. For some reason, I've always thought that Odessa is a grand and romantic place. It sounds exotic to my ears. But it's a port city, the site of a set of the most lethally-placed tram lines in the world. Ever.

Shortly after negotiating the tram lines, I wander into the tall reception lobby of a hotel, noting that it has clearly experienced much better days. I imagine that it was once rather grand, where now it is distinctly faded, though not without a certain charm. I make a value judgement that the room facilities will probably echo the reception and press on with negotiations. There are rooms available, and the price of a double room is exceedingly cheap. I'm on the point of handing over the plastic when the nice reception lady drops her bombshell.

'There is no hot water.'

The day is still quite young. I don't want to put either of us through the misery of a cold shower, especially after the incident in Melitopol. I decide to press on. We mount up and leave Odessa in our wake. We are both a tiny bit grumpy with each other at the failure to find accommodation.

$$***$$

We have no idea where we are heading, but I'm reasonably certain that the next country is Romania. I haven't had sight of a decent map for two days and my memory of the last one I saw is fading fast. I do have my pocket Times Atlas, which shows only one road leading to the west. An hour or so later, we arrive at the border and are met by a well-ordered crossing, occupied by Ukrainian guards in smart blue uniforms bearing the yellow and blue flag of their nation, which, incidentally, is supposed to symbolise golden fields of corn under blue skies (or, alternatively, blue streams in the mountains) – isn't that nice? The reception is polite and efficient, allowing us to whistle through into 'no man's land', where a line of Portacabins allow for insurances to be paid and cash exchanged. I peer expectantly over to the next border.

There is something nagging me. This doesn't feel right. Perhaps it's the flag that is flying from the pole over there. It's some kind of green and red thing. And isn't that a hammer and sickle on the top red portion? Wavering ever so very slightly, I potter over to the bank-cum-shack, where a man is standing at the door, nonchalantly smoking a fag.

'Romania?' I ask tentatively, pointing up the road.

He shrugs, then nods, 'Da.'

We pass through the security gate in the tracks of a white Ford

Transit van with Latvian number plates. A border guard in wide-brimmed, Soviet-style hat and fatigues bars our way and asks bluntly for our passports. Diane hops off and hands them over. He inspects them very closely, then tells me to get off the bike and go to the first cabin, walking off with our passports. I am not liking this one bit, and neither is Diane.

There's nothing for it, but to wait for our turn. The Latvians seem to be getting the third-degree. Everyone is told to get out of the van, all five of them, then the driver is told to pull it forward and to one side. In the meantime, we get called to the sliding window.

'Where from?'

'United Kingdom.'

'Why here?'

'Tourist.' This doesn't seem to have had much effect on proceedings.

He gets up and walks out of the office, heading for a larger building, holding our passports. We are left to wait, bemused at the grilling that the Latvians are suffering, followed by what turns out to be the initial preparations for the disassembling of their van and a forensic inspection of their luggage. After a few minutes, the border official returns with a second man, who is clearly of elevated seniority and a bit of a prick. He speaks slightly better English.

'Where you come from?'

'The United Kingdom.'

'Why you are here?'

'We're arriving here on our way to Georgia.'

'Georgia? Why you go to Georgia?' This is asked with a distinct edge to the question.

'We are tourists.'

He smiles in a way that nudges me one step closer to developing a nervous tick.

'You pay me one hundred dollars.'

It's the moment I've been dreading. The first time I meet a corrupt official. It's not bad going. I've ridden over thirty thousand miles to arrive at this low point in my travelling career. My eyes wander over to the van and the preparations being made to tear it down. Back in Melitopol, a few days ago, Reg described his tactics when faced with demands for money such as this one: 'I tell 'em to fuck off. If they don't like it, I tell 'em I'm going to camp in their compound and, while they're at it they can get me the British Embassy.' I did appreciate Reg's bluff directness and liked him a lot. Despite that, I'm not sure this approach will work with the Romanians. At least not with these Romanians.

'Why do I have to pay one hundred dollars to enter Romania?' I enquire, in what I hope to be a reasonably assertive tone.

He shakes his head knowingly, the smile never leaving his face.

'You are not in Romania my friend. You are here...'

He stands up and turns around, removing a well-worn map from a shelf behind him, which he holds up with a triumphant flourish. 'This,' says he, 'is the Peoples' Republic of Transnistria.'

'Can you spell that for me?'

⸺⸰⸙⟨⟩⸙⸰⸺

Chapter 21
Lost in Transnistria

Grudgingly, I hand over the dosh. Not a hundred dollars, thankfully. I manage to convince the thieving wretch that I'm not carrying dollars, so he then insists I pay in Euros, of which we have a few. His exchange rate conversion lets him down when he demands 50 Euros, which disappear straight into a side drawer, no receipt - almost by sleight of hand. Paul Daniels would be very impressed and, no doubt, Debbie McGee would too.

Having paid up, we're instructed to ride the bike past the van, acknowledging the poor Latvians with a sheepish smile, graciously returned. They are accepting their fate without rancour, bless them. Then, after negotiating the next cubicle, we're told to park the bike up alongside one building and to then proceed on foot to a different one. It's quite nerve-wracking. We have no idea what is going on – for a short period, it looks like they want to split us up, and we're not having any of that! We're made to wait outside a small office for a short while. A few minutes later, we are greeted by a pleasant young man who speaks excellent English.

'Hello, welcome to Transnistria. I need to take you through our customs process. It won't take too long. I am sorry, but there is a charge to pay for your motorcycle.' He reminds me a little of the nice, polite centurion in the film *Life of Brian*, the one who reluctantly lines up the people condemned to suffer crucifixion.

I decide not to mention that I've already been fleeced plenty and need no more fleecing. I notice that (fittingly) he has a crucifix mounted on the wall of his office and decide that perhaps he is indeed 'straight'. It turns out to be a good call. The customs charge is just a couple of Euros. There are, however, lots of forms to fill in, so we're going to be here for quite a while. And, during that time, the bike and luggage are unattended. When we complete the customs procedure, we're thanked politely for our patience and told that we need to register in one more office. Here, we join a queue of lorry drivers, one of whom takes interest in where we're from and signals, with slightly more relish than I think is appropriate, that we are likely to be spending more money before we get much further. The Latvians are still being searched.

Eventually, we get to the sliding window and hand over the bike documents. We're required to pay another minor bill before receiving a transit visa and being told we're free to leave. We pass the young driver of the Ford Transit as he heads, flush-faced, into the customs office, his ordeal hopefully close to ending. He's hot and bothered, but visibly relieved. And so are we. One way or another, we've all had a bit of a roasting.

***

Just beyond the border, we get our first view of a country that, frankly, I never knew existed. To be precise, it officially calls itself the Pridnestrovian Moldavian Republic, although it also can be called Trans-Dniestr, or Transdniester, or Pridnestrovie, all of which are fine outside the halls of the United Nations because, according to that organisation, this place (whatever you choose to call it) doesn't exist. At least, it doesn't exist in international law. To put it succinctly, we have somehow managed to get lost in a country that doesn't exist – a fact that I proudly hold as something of a badge of honour. I mean there are different levels of navigational incompetence, and I happen to think I've just managed to achieve gold star (honours).

It is slightly worrying riding into a country that has a border post, a lot of fields and not much else. Are there any towns worthy of the name? I don't know. The roads are worse than those on the Ukrainian border, being entirely of Soviet origin and, I'd warrant, not having seen a repair crew since Yuri Gagarin shot into space, or possibly even the woofer, Laika, that went up before him. On one occasion, we pass a gaggle of people standing by a field and we receive a good, sharp staring at – a kind of 'at the sign of the Slaughtered Lamb' moment. The countryside is one of low, rolling hills. We find ourselves riding in a state of bemused wonderment. Then, roughly ten miles from the border, we spot a ramshackle wee building – a single storey house... could possibly be better described as a shack – with an ancient pair of petrol pumps in front of it. Considering it prudent to top up, we turn right into the establishment and draw up at the nearest pump.

An unshaven, black-haired, wild-eyed, middle-aged man in unkempt clothes approaches us from the house, followed by his family of wife and children, who spill out to observe the alien invasion. Diane climbs off the machine. She does so, nowadays, with the litheness of a panther (the mountain goat has been relegated).

I signal to the pump attendant and, no doubt, owner of this establishment, that I would like a fill up of his finest 92RON fuel, offering him my customary, tatty notepaper. The production of a credit card during this attempted transaction is met by derision and the wagging of a finger. Such an object is a product of the west and hence of Beelzebub himself. Diane and I scour our pockets for banknotes and change, managing to recover a few Russian roubles and slightly more Ukrainian hryvnias (I can spend them but I definitely can't pronounce them). We just scrape enough acceptable folding currency to interest him in removing his nozzle.

Replenishment completed, and now officially destitute, we ride on a little and then spot a road sign to a settlement. We turn off and head in the direction of what turns out to be a reasonably-sized town called Bender (Titter-ye-not), crossing a bridge over a river and passing an impressive medieval fortification, before entering a relatively traffic-free town with a large square and the welcome sight of a modestly sized supermarket.

As usual, our first task, on arrival, is to find some money; second to find a hotel and third, to find food. Parking up outside the supermarket, we venture inside, searching for a cash machine. When we find one, it spits our cards back at us with words (in what could be Russian) to the effect of: 'This is a local cash machine, for local people – there's nothing for you here. We'll have none of that foreign 'Visa' or 'Maestro' malarkey around here! Good-bye.' I must confess at this point that I'm starting to get a tiny bit concerned and I might have uttered the 'F' word at the machine in response.

Back on the bike, riding around the streets, one gets the distinct feeling that Bender doesn't have a hotel. We scour the streets, which are quite pleasant tree-lined affairs, to no avail. Then, we spot a taxi – a Lada taxi to be precise. He's picking up a fare, but kindly takes time out to respond to our question of whether there is a hotel nearby – spoken in one word, 'Otel?' He signals: 'Follow me!'

We race after him, cutting across town in a very determined fashion. After a short drive, we turn right at a semi-derelict sports stadium, heading along another perfectly pleasant, tree-shaded street, pulling up at a building that does indeed look moderately hotelish. In fact, it looks like a hotel with a restaurant attached, and outside the restaurant there is a patio dining area – populated by people who appear cultured; indeed, who are enjoying a spot of proper café culture. I am already praying that there is room at the inn.

We thank the taxi driver and make as-if to pay him with the few coins remaining in our possession, but he very generously refuses to take anything. Parking the bike up, I head into reception to be greeted by a young lady with short hair and trendy clothes. She tells us straight away that we can stay. Indeed, she says we are most welcome. The room rate is reasonable and they insist we inspect the room. We head upstairs. The hotel is most impressive and quite a surprise – the room plush, with plump mattress and crisp, immaculate bedding. It seems we have arrived at a boutique hotel of some standing. Back at reception, I produce my card.

'I'm sorry, I can't take your card. You see we are not allowed to operate any card apart from those issued by our bank here in Transnistria. We can only accept dollars.'

It's like a rug has been pulled from under my feet and I'm about to disappear down a black hole into deep despair. She must have noticed my crestfallen expression...

'But you don't have to pay me now. Take your bags to the room. You can pay me tomorrow.'

I find it hard to go along with this. I don't want to spend a night worrying about whether I'll get any money.

'I'd like to get money for you tonight. We looked for a machine earlier and couldn't find one that would work with our cards. Do you know if there is one?'

One of the guests has overheard our conversation. He introduces himself, saying that he's German and often comes here contracting. He tells us that there is but one cash machine in the whole country that dispenses dollars. The good news is that that it's in Bender, sitting directly across the road from the supermarket. We resolve to go there immediately and get our dollars. Failing that, I assure the receptionist that I will leave Diane as a deposit, ride out of the country, come back and pay to have her back. If, for any reason, I don't return, Diane has experience of waiting on tables, gained from working at the Altens Hotel, Aberdeen. Granted, it was thirty years ago, and the hotel name was different at that time, but I think it's a small detail and she'll be able to hack it for a year or two. She is very adaptable, after all is said and done.

***

The hotel is just a short walk from the town centre. To get there, we stroll through a small park. It's interesting to observe such a fine example of a communistic patch of municipal greenery. In fact, it's fascinating to observe the whole town, because Bender is frozen in time to a period long before the fall of the Berlin wall. The park is constructed from very rudimentary materials: appallingly badly-laid concrete paths with bits of reinforcing steel laid bare, sharp enough to maim the odd bairn, benches made from twisted, misshapen metal and roughly-hewed wood, painted a lurid colour of blue and contrasting white, and beds planted with flowering annuals that struggle to survive in a dry, dusty soil, shaded by trees that have the familiar white paint on their trunks – I believe it's purpose is the repelling of insects. Further up the road from the park, we pass single-storey houses that have been liberally spattered with bullet and shrapnel holes. Bender had a hard time in the civil war that erupted during the breaking-away part of its history, or so it would seem.

Walking into the square, we come across a bunch of young kids sitting on motorcycles and scooters – various incarnations of the 1970's two-stroke motorcycle output of the old Soviet Union mixed with more recent ones of Chinese manufacture. I'm conscious that we're wearing strange motorcycling attire and probably look weird to them. We attract a few whispered comments that are probably ribald in nature. Ignorance is bliss. Spotting the cash machine, we dash over and offer up our first card. It works! Wonderful!

Eastern European cool. The Jawa 350. This one was photographed earlier in Sevastopol.

In greatly relieved spirits, we wander back the way we came. It's a bit embarrassing having to walk past the same group of youngsters for a second time, but, spotting that one of them is sitting on a Jawa, I decide to attempt a spot of biker banter.

'Jawa?'

He nods.

I tell him in Russian that it is undeniably 'very good'. The snickers of amusement have subsided, and we depart the square detecting a sniff of envy from his scooter-riding compadres, measured with an equal amount of puffed-out-chestery from the rider of the Czechoslovakian steed. And I'm not even doing it for effect. Jawas *are* cool. I hanker after one myself. They were cheap as chips and unfairly sneered at when I was a kid, but, nowadays, they have a certain cred all of their own, and values in the UK have been going up accordingly. I wonder if he would sell it to me? And if he did, how would I get it back to Blighty? I imagine it would involve some kind of bribery at the border. But that could be arranged – we've had practice and now we also have dollars!

***

On awakening and partaking of breakfast in the morning, we discover that one final challenge awaits us here in Transnistria. The registration process, common back in Russia, but totally absent in Ukraine, has made an unwelcome return in this little breakaway sliver of socialist utopia. Our host, who has stationed herself this morning on the customer side of reception, seated on a tall bar stool, casually scrolling through an internet site selling high-end designer shoes, tells Diane, our queen of registration processing, that it is essential we register. But unfortunately, the registration process can't be carried out by the hotel reception (unlike in Russia).

'You must present yourself at the registration office in person, they do not speak English,' she tells us cheerfully. 'They will not understand you. I will take you there.'

We were so delighted in the efficacious securing of dollars last night, that we got all carried away with ourselves and checked in for two nights, hence the need to register. There was some method in our madness. The first factor in the decision was that we really like the hotel and the people running it. Then there's a natural inquisitiveness to see more of this mysterious place. And finally, I think it would be a good time to do a spot of servicing on the bike. Whilst finalising the checking-in yesterday, I tentatively asked if it would be possible for me to work on the bike and they replied, 'Of course!'

Back in the room, we both came to the same conclusion. 'I think they're mafia, but maybe nice ones,' said I. Diane is in full agreement. Our opinions should be taken with a pinch of salt. In south Russia, Diane passed the hours by surreptitiously using the reflective screen on her little Panasonic camera as a mirror, monitoring the following vehicles, forming the impression that we were being tailed. She started to reveal her concerns around the time we turned off towards Volgograd. I, on the other hand, was of the opinion they were ordinary people who were just intent on killing us in revenge for having the temerity to overtake them. The big black 4X4, complete with blacked-out windows, parked under a car port in the lush garden at the side of the hotel here in Bender, seemed to reinforce our mildly outrageous stereotyping, but then... how do you get so rich that you can set up a place like this in the final frontier of Stalinism? Even if they are mafia, I don't care, because it's all so comfortable and exotic, and they're so friendly and helpful.

Fast forward to this morning, and we're wafted through the streets in the 4X4, straight to the offices of the 'department for strangers arriving accidentally into our clutches', to be formally registered. I have no doubt that there is some kind of monetary charge for registration, but regardless of her youth, our immaculately and expensively dressed host seems to exude the aura of power and influence, ensuring that we are – embarrassingly – moved straight to the head of the sizeable queue of people waiting to be processed and that the forms are filled in very quickly with minimum fuss, before delivering us back to the hotel ready for me to commence my maintenance task.

***

The purpose of the maintenance in hand is entirely preventative. As far as I'm aware, the bike is performing faultlessly, but there are certain things to do at roughly the correct mileages to keep things ticking over nicely. Changing the oil in Rostov-on-Don was, if anything, slightly early but entirely opportune. That means we have plenty of available miles before the next oil change, which will also need to include a filter change. So now is a good time to clean the air filter. Mileage-wise it's just about perfect timing. We can then ride another few thousand miles before finding somewhere to change the oil and oil filter, change the tyres and also check the valve clearances.

At the Adventure Motorcycle Maintenance course, Mr Pavey, our esteemed Paris-Dakar racer, recommended fitting an aftermarket filter made by the famous filtration wizards and worker elves at K&N. He reasoned that such filters are fully cleanable and can last the life of the motorcycle. So, instead of carrying spare air filters – which are quite bulky – you carry a plastic bottle of cleaning fluid and one of a light red oil, both propriety items with K&N written all over them. Remembering how to prise the filter out proves to be a real exercise in lost memory recovery, but I finally manage to succeed. The clever chaps at BMW have designed a couple of cunning little plastic clips that hold the filter very firmly in place, using a method akin to that seen in old-fashioned wooden clothes pegs. It takes a while to suss out how to remove them, but once that's been achieved the job (as Ed China of 'Wheeler Dealers' fame would say), is a good 'un. Having removed the filter, I carefully use a clean cloth (might be a pair of old merino wool pants in disguise) to cover the hole in the airbox and proceed to spray the solvent on to the filter medium, watching the remains of quite a few hundred bugs slowly soften and dissolve, before washing everything clean under the outside garden tap. I'm hoping I haven't polluted the nice hotel garden. Then it's a matter of letting everything dry very thoroughly in the warm sun that is beating down, perfect conditions for K&N filter cleaning.

While the filter is drying, I busy myself checking over everything I can think of: brake pads, hydraulic fluid level, spokes tinkling nicely when rung with a screwdriver, various nuts and bolts tightened and a drop or two of oil popped into the filler to restore the engine oil level. Wheel bearings are checked front and rear along with the security of the rear suspension and the lack of play and smooth running of the head races. Very importantly, I check the tyres for any sign of damage. The list of things to check is partly from memory and partly from having read the bike's workshop manual on the loo last night. After days of racking up mileage or wandering around the various towns en-route, it's really quite cathartic to spend a bit of time wielding the spanners. It feels like I'm giving something back to my trusty steed and, to be honest, I just like tinkering.

As I've noted before, I clean my bike more-or-less every day. I think it is a great way to spot problems. I also inspect the tyres daily, along with things like the wheel bearings, which are checked every few days.

So, it's true to say that many of the jobs I've just done are regularly carried out. Others I do less frequently. But doing them all together helps to confirm to myself that the integrity of the machine is good. And, over the next few weeks, I'll have a mental note that I did all these tasks at this point on the trip.

The final job is to spray the red oil onto the filter, let it dry and then check it's evenly covered, before fitting everything back together, at which point I can satisfactorily report, there are no left-over nuts and bolts. Phew!

A quick start-up of the engine reveals that it is running nice and quietly, revving fine and is, no doubt, breathing just a little bit more freely than it was with all that dust and all those bugs that were clogging up its air channels. Being methodical, I made sure to remove the protective pants before putting it all back together. Having finished the servicing, we decide to take a wander into town.

Bender shares features similar to other Soviet-era towns that we've previously visited. The centre of the town has a wide square, where people bring their toddlers to play and the local youth bring their mopeds. Generally speaking, the buildings surrounding the square, at least those that are municipal in nature, are better built than the other buildings in the town. They bear the decoration favoured by the party – namely renditions of the red star, sheaves of corn, wheels of industry and sometimes a bit of weaponry thrown in for good measure, just to make the natives feel secure. Lenin often gets an airing and usually looks a bit annoyed and determined. People with chiselled features exhort the populace to greater deeds of production. It's all very interesting and, dare I say it... strangely endearing. I find myself quite liking it, perversely. At least, no-one is trying to get you to buy a time-share. And, if the banks are trying to collectively rob you, like ours do, then they're doing it by stealth and a strange lack of cash machines, rather than singing at you or showing you pictures of horses.

Another common feature in ex-communist countries is the small kiosk. We've seen these everywhere in the old Soviet Union. They sell all sorts of things: ciggies, cans of soft drink, kiddies' toys, newspapers and magazines. The one we stumble across here is populated by a formidable woman of indeterminate age, who bears the unmistakeable demeanour of one who takes absolutely zero prisoners. Especially if the prisoners in question are limp-wristed, reactionary enemies of the revolution. I imagine children begging their parents *not* to buy them a toy at this particular outlet, dragging them by the arm to get safely past. We could just walk by, too, but I'm on the lookout for a map to take home as a souvenir – one that will prove that we managed to get 'properly lost' but, more importantly, one that will allow us to navigate from here to Romania. I try an opening gambit of smiling and saying hello in Russian, attempting the unpronounceable word. She frowns at me, looking me up and down as if weighing up how far I could be thrown and whether the throw should be conducted with a full-bodied spinning action or just straight out from under the chin.

Like a fool, I then resort to English, saying enquiringly, 'Map?' raising my voice in a way that worked yesterday with the taxi driver.

Her brow scrunches up tighter.

I try French: 'Carte?'

I make a sign of a square and then point to the ground, 'Carte? Map?'

She says something very brusquely in Russian, waving me off dismissively. Diane is hovering quietly, slightly behind me – a good tactic when faced with bears in the wilderness, or an angry kiosk owner with a right arm the size of a very large joint of ham who seems to be chewing wasps. Then my luck chimes in.

A lady has approached without me noticing and is listening intently. She says something to my nemesis which does include a word very similar to 'Carte'. The kiosk owner's eyebrows are raised and a smile spreads across her face, 'Ah Karta, da, da!' She rummages around, then triumphantly flourishes the same map as the one used by the scumbag official who nicked our Euros yesterday. I try to ask if she has a bigger map, one with other countries on it, preferably Romania.

'Niet! Eta Transnistria!' she says, forcefully jabbing the map, then flourishing her hands, as if to say, 'you're here, buddy – centre of the universe'. It turns out that the map isn't for sale, but Diane has the presence of mind to ask if she can photograph it and takes a few shots extra for good measure. This is the first in a long line of photographic maps that we will use in our ongoing travels, a method that has never occurred to me before and one that advertises the quality and foresight of my navigator. Diane has elevated herself to the level of 'shit-hot navigator'. If this was 1943, Guy Gibson would immediately recruit her into the 617 Dambusters squadron.

The centre of the universe.

***

I guess there isn't much point in having maps of the world if you live in one tiny part of it and don't travel anywhere else. It's a bit like living your whole life on the Isle of Skye or Jersey. Then again, you won't find a battalion of Russian soldiers on the Isle of Skye or Jersey. At least, not yet anyway. Here, though, they are quite visibly occupying some of the public buildings. After the civil war, they came to keep the peace and they've stayed here ever since – a little pocket of the Russian military, peacekeepers in a strip of land that nearly everyone else considers to be part of Moldova.

But, as with many such things, it seems that the picture is far less clear than just lines on a map. The land that makes up Transnistria has changed demographically through the years – indeed, greatly, during the monumental periods of conflict and revolution in the twentieth century. Various nationalities have settled here. A quarter of a million Jews perished in Transnistria during the Nazi occupation, driven here by Romanian and Moldovan fascists, encouraged by the Germans, then left to starve. A quarter of a million! In a tiny sliver of land. After the Second World War, many Ukrainians and Russians were encouraged to settle in the area and that changed the demographics significantly, to a point where there are nearly as many Russians and Ukrainians resident here as there are Moldovans. In March 1992 it descended into bloodshed. As a result of the short conflict, Transnistria officially became a de-militarised zone, subject to a cease-fire, and in a kind of state of limbo. As far as I can recall, it was a conflict that completely passed by, without the BBC noticing.

In a way, the issues that affect Transnistria also affect many other parts of the former Soviet Union and, indeed, other countries in Europe. The whole continent is a patchwork of varying sizes of land that are disputed in some way or other, some peacefully, others less so. It's a tinderbox, one of many, waiting to flare up. A sleeping, yet active volcano.

Chapter 22
Part of the Union

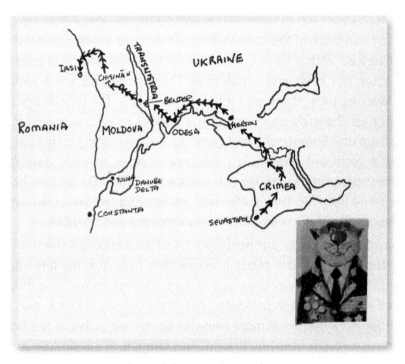

From Crimea to Romania.

The morning of departure, and I'm forced to admit, despite the little niggles, and the feeling that we're completely out of sorts dealing with some of the people we've met here, we've both thoroughly enjoyed getting lost in Transnistria. It's in no small part due to the fabulous staff at the hotel. We've both agreed with each other that we'd like to come back and have a better look around. Not least, I'd like to visit the castle.

On a darker note: when we walked back from the town centre yesterday afternoon, having sampled a very vibrant market with stalls selling all manner of goods, we passed the derelict sports stadium – in truth, I'm not sure if it is derelict or only half built, then abandoned. I'm guessing that it probably was last used before the civil war, possibly by a football team that suddenly found itself in a league of one. But, that aside, what really disturbed me was the sight of a pack of feral dogs that are now the resident team. It's the first time I've come across a pack of wild dogs at such close quarters and it became immediately clear that if you end up being in such a pack, you do not want to be female.

The main bitch of the pack looked vaguely like a thoroughbred corgi when viewed with a squint. It was clear that she had produced litter after litter. Her teats were trailing on the ground and, even while we were walking past, there was a boisterous battle for supremacy going on amongst the male members of the pack as to who was next in line, apart from one Romeo who had given up and was sitting on his backside having a good old scratch. It made me wonder to what degree the wildlife programmes sanitise the nature they film. Do wolves behave in the same way? Do they suffer with mange? I don't know the answer but, faced with the reality of it, it was shocking and horrible.

Saying goodbye to our hosts, we head back through the town and along the road past the castle and over the river, turning left heading towards Moldova. Two days ago, I had absolutely no idea that we needed to ride through Moldova, but there we are, I know that's the case now. It's a matter of mere minutes before we arrive at the border, expecting a rough time. As it turns out though, it's a doddle and we breeze through both crossings. Once over the border, we head in a westerly direction.

When we carried out a check of the countries we might need to pass through, back in the mists of time, we mainly used Google maps and we saw a border between Ukraine and Romania. Even now, if I check my little Times atlas it still looks like there is a border, leading me to think we just took the wrong road. With the minimal degree of information supplied, courtesy of Diane's camera, we're left to guess the best way forward, and it seems to me that the safest bet is to head to the capital city of Chisinau then try to find a road that heads to the west. We press into a country, the landscape of which is a mixture of agriculture and woodland, spread over gently rolling hills. This change in landscape, from the more or less flat and uniform, cultivated (and not so cultivated) steppe of the east was barely perceptible at first, but it's becoming more pronounced the further we head into the west.

Thinking about it, I was never completely sure, in days of yore, whether Moldova actually existed. This gap in my geographical knowledge is entirely the responsibility of the scriptwriters of 'Dynasty', a television programme that I religiously never, ever watched. Honest. Still, despite not watching it, I have a faint recollection, gleaned perhaps from browsing 'Hello' magazine in dentists' surgeries, that a British actor played the part of a prince from Moldova, who nearly married someone. I think they all died horribly, perhaps at the wedding, or something like that. And, unlike Bobby Ewing, they didn't come back to life. Anyway, the point is that I thought that Moldova was invented by a script writer, a bogus land-locked principality that was, without doubt, surrounded by Italy – or possibly Germany – in the eyes of the American TV script writers. The reality is that it did exist and, at the time, was secretively languishing, if that's the polite way of putting it, behind the Iron Curtain.

Moldova is a small country, about one third bigger than Wales in land area, with a population roughly the same size. Where it differs from Wales is that its rugby team is dreadful, it is about sixteen times poorer, and Wales possesses a real, live prince.

The entry into Chisinau turns out to be quite a grand affair. The road runs up a hill, flanked by greenery along its dual carriageway, leading to a portal in the form of the most monumental, cheese-wedge-shaped apartment blocks that seem to part in the middle to allow you through, towering high above you, as you do so. I think the city planners might have been eating hallucinogenic mushrooms during the project design phase. We're arriving after a short ride from the border, around 1 p.m. The city is busy, but relatively easy to navigate through, although we are reduced to using a form of dead reckoning to pass through in a westerly direction. We find ourselves sitting at the front of a queue of cars at one of the major junctions in the centre. A bus passes across in front. A small child peering from one of the windows notices the bike and shouts something then waves to us. We both wave back, before Diane lets out a little exclamation, 'Oh!'

I lean back and ask her what's wrong.

'Well, that little child waved and I waved back, but then an older child next to him saw us, and his face… it had a look of hate, a really vicious look of hate and he shook his fist at us. It looked like he was screaming at us.'

***

A couple of hours later and we find ourselves in something of a quandary. We've successfully negotiated the city and emerged on the far north-western side, an achievement of sorts, I think. Seeing a nice, modern petrol station, we pull onto the concourse and I head indoors to look for a map – to no avail, so we have a brief conflab and try to guess which direction to take. There's not much to do, other than 'zooming out' on the satnav map and dragging out the little red pocket Times atlas, resting it on the tank bag for a forensic inspection.

The truth is that there is very little choice. There's a road back to Chisinau behind us, one that heads south and east – Transnistria being the most likely outcome – and one to our right that heads north. I trace the northward route up to the end of the page, searching for the next page number and…. Oh, poo! It goes straight to north-westernmost Ukraine!

I'm hovering, poised to head south in the hope that the road will change direction and loop back to the west but, in the end, we decide to cut northwards in the vain hope that we'll find a road that crosses west into Romania. It's a vain hope because there are no such roads on either of our maps, electronic or printed copy. Right now, we are heading away from the Black Sea and straight into the east European land mass. Not a good situation at all.

***

Four hours later. We are waiting patiently in a queue of traffic at the border with Romania, having passed through the small unassuming town of Ungheni. It revealed itself to be a nondescript place, with strong overtones of the Soviet era: quiet streets, modest housing, plenty of trees, unpretentious and clean, lots of blue and white paint. You could say 'a bit boring'. Until you discover *the* stand-out feature of Ungheni: the town's railway bridge was designed by none other than Gustave Eiffel. Ungheni can stand proudly alongside Paris and spit in the eye of Florence, Barcelona or New York. The landscape we have passed through almost took our breath away. Incredibly rural and steeply undulating, it almost tempted me to pull over and try to tempt Diane into a spot of wild camping. Then, closer to the border, it changed into something I found breathtaking. A series of long, rolling hills that remind me of a vast ocean swell, clothed in deep greens fading to blues as they march off to the horizon. I've never seen anything like it before. It has a soft, languid, feel to it that makes you want to lie down on the hillside, stuff a straw in your mouth and drink it all in – preferably with a jug of raw Somerset scrumpy.

The border between Moldova and Romania is marked by the river Prut, which wriggles its way down from Ukraine. We arrived at the Moldovan border post after passing through the small settlement of Sculeni, joining a queue of cars parked up in a patch of woodland and killing our engine. We have a short wait before it's our turn to be processed. Compared with the tribulations of entering Transnistria, it all goes smoothly. We ride across the bridge that separates the two countries and arrive at the Romanian side. The document checks are relaxed and friendly. When we arrive at the customs kiosk, we are met by a pleasant, rotund gentleman with the air of a genial professor of history, urbane and polite – a fine English speaker with an impressive head of grey hair. I like him immediately.

'Welcome, welcome. You are returning home to the European Union. I see you are from England. I once lived in England, in London and I have family there. I go there very often, and I love it there.'

And, strangely enough, it does feel like coming home. We are back in the Union and we are no longer lost. He carries out a few perfunctory checks then bids us safe travels, touches his hat and waves us through. Nice.

Chapter 23
Romanian Hospitality

A new, slightly different vista of rolling hills heralds our arrival in Romania, as we wend our way from the border, through a small town, then on towards the city of Iași, a few miles further on. When we arrive, we spend a short while riding around looking for a hotel, initially in an outlying industrial area, typified by ugly buildings and a very poor road, before finding our way in towards the centre, where we very quickly spot a large tower advertising itself as a hotel. It seems quite grand from the outside, is very welcoming on the inside and before you can say 'Jack Robinson', we're ensconced in a large and very comfortable room and the bike is parked up in the large basement garage, quietly cooling down.

The adventures of the past few days of 'lostishness' are gently fading, following a nice hot shower, a change of clothes, and a ride in the lift down to the restaurant. We ask the receptionist if there is a restaurant and she replies, 'yes. It is there,' indicating past a large screen-door to her left. We approach the door, grab the handle and pull. Nothing. It's locked.

Returning to the receptionist, I ask her why the door is locked - are we too early?

'No. Not too early. Door is locked because restaurant is clos-ed. We do not serve food in restaurant now. Only breakfast. Free breakfast. You have paid.'

We are a mite nonplussed.

'Where can we eat?'

'There is no restaurant nearby. It is long walk to restaurant. There is one bar. It is in that way.' She signals in the general direction of the city centre.

I'm really not convinced, but we do get confirmation that there are cash machines in that direction too, so we decide to take pot luck.

Half an hour later. We are sitting in a large bar with a bottle of local and very decent red wine poured into two glasses awaiting a healthy grilled meat dinner. Altogether cushty.

We discuss the mix-up over the restaurant at the hotel.

'Did you notice that there aren't any guests?' asks Diane. She's right too. We haven't seen a single guest and the car park is as empty as the basement garage. She adds, 'I think we're the only ones there.' She could be right.

One of the sights that stood out to us almost as soon as we rode into Romania are the small, low-slung, wooden horse-drawn wagons. They have two metal wheels (with tyres), flared sides, and a pair of long shafts attached to the pony. The sports model has an output of two horsepower, baseline model has one. They clearly serve as a form of general transport for families, old and young but, perhaps more often, for older people. We saw quite a few where the pony had been tied up outside a shop or a house, whilst the owner went about their business, just like in cowboy movies. This, and the generally simple, rustic nature of the houses, many of which are single storey and not a million miles away from those we've seen in Russia, Ukraine and Moldova, seems to underscore the considerable difference in the way people live in the east, when compared to the west. It's something Diane and I have been discussing ever since we left Finland. Simply put, here in 2012, there is a vast chasm between how most of us live in the west, compared to those in the east. We suffer from rampant materialism and they suffer from a lack of the means to 'enjoy' rampant materialism. Those in the east who can enjoy a materialistic existence are part of a tiny minority. I'm sure some in Britain would point to the comparison between the haves and have-nots in our own country, but everything is relative and the differences in the comparison are huge.

It feels like the global financial crisis has hit Romania particularly hard. Of course, we haven't been here before so we can't accurately make such an assertion, but that's how it feels. In Russia, things were different. Buoyed up by the high oil price and wallowing in mineral resources, Russia clearly has a lot of money swilling around, but it's only ending up in a few people's pockets. Despite that, it does feel like Russia is on the up. First impressions of Ukraine, Transnistria, Moldova and Romania appear to tell a different story. We discuss the things we've noted over the past few days and conclude that it was, without doubt, a poor existence for most people living under communism, but I think there were some benefits: full employment, state-provided accommodation and a level of social security. Are these countries better off without that? Right now, the jury is out on that one.

After a few drinks and our meal, we're ready to leave and head back to the hotel. We've been sitting in the warm evening air at a table overlooking the street, dining al-fresco. Just as we are about to leave, a sizeable group of young locals turn up and start to occupy a couple of tables next to ours. They ask us, first in Romanian then in English if we can spare a couple of chairs.

'Of course, but we're about to leave anyway, so you can have all of them if you want.'

'But you don't have to leave. Why don't you join us? We're just here to have a drink.'

It's a nice offer, one we take up without protest. They tell us that they're members of a rock band and are working on a project. They've just finished band practice. Over the course of the next hour, we quaff a few bevvies and talk music. Ed is the lead singer. By profession, he's an actor who has worked in London and was recruited into the band because he has a good voice, but his first love is acting. He reminds me very much of Jack Black. Vlad is an architect who is writing music and plays the guitar and Camelia, Vlad's wife, is a doctor and doesn't play in the band. They have a young son, Victor. Vlad and Ed speak excellent English, Camelia's is more halting and she consequently speaks a little less. They ask where we're staying and we mention the hotel.

'Oh you can't stay there. It's a terrible place,' blurts out Ed.

'You have to stay with Vlad and Camelia.'

I'm not sure this was foremost on Camelia's mind, but Vlad nods in affirmation.

'Yes, come and stay with us for a couple of days. In fact, stay as long as you like.'

Ed adds spice to the proposition. 'They live in a vineyard!'

***

It's a bright and sunny morning. We enjoy a leisurely get-up, heading down for breakfast in the restaurant, which is now open, but nearly deserted. The arrangements that we parted with, leaving the rock stars to finish their drinking last night, were that Ed would arrive with a cab and would lead us to Vlad and Camelia's house – he in the cab, we following it. We were assured that it wasn't too far from the hotel.

At the allotted hour, with the bike nearly loaded, I head to reception to see if he's arrived, half expecting that it's all been forgotten. Wandering out of reception, I spot him immediately. He's sitting on a kerb that surrounds a flower border with his head in his hands bearing the unmistakable demeanour of a badly broken man. I approach him and say, 'good morning!'

He groans loudly, 'I have a terrible headache. I don't do mornings.'

I don't think this would impress Keith Moon at all! At least, not if he were still alive.

During our ride through Iași, it becomes apparent that the city has some wonderful, older buildings, along with a lot of trees and parkland. It's like finding a grand emerald in a well-worn Victorian gold setting. The transport system includes a fleet of trams and the car of choice is the Dacia, which appears to be to the Romanians what the Lada is to the Russians. After negotiating a series of crossroads and junctions, the taxi driver heads purposefully up a long street bordered by mature trees, parks and large buildings. Before too long, we find ourselves on the outskirts of the city. Then, without warning, the taxi veers off along a new road that deteriorates in quality and upkeep by the minute.

Eventually the road peters out more or less completely at a point where the gardens of a series of quite grand houses meet. Vlad is standing there waiting for us.

Vlad and Camelia live in a house that is owned by her parents. It sits in an eclectic mix of other houses, most of which are quite sizeable, built on what I imagine was a mixture of farming land and the vineyard that Ed mentioned last night. We've seen many similar developments of large new houses on the edges of towns and cities in Russia, the only difference being that in Russia the houses were in the process of being built, whereas here they are a few years old. Our immediate problem on arrival is working out how to get the bike to the house. The pathway from the end of the road to the front of the house is very narrow. In the end, I decide to unload the bike, remove the panniers and squeeze it through, naked. The bike that is, not me.

***

Vlad and Camelia have very graciously given up their occupancy of the top floor rooms so that we'll have a comfortable stay. Their room has a balcony that overlooks the rolling ocean of hills sweeping in from the Moldovan border. The nearest hill has a scattering of homesteads on its flanks but, beyond that, the landscape appears to be very sparsely populated. It's an entrancingly beautiful view. Despite the development of houses, the setting is still charmingly semi-rural – a great place to bring up children. Vlad explains to us that they've arranged for some friends to come over and meet us in the afternoon and evening. It's the start of a very relaxing and convivial two day stay. The people we meet are laid back, friendly and downright talented. They feed us, we drink a little wine, Ed talks in depth about his love of progressive rock, I let him sample the '70s music on my iPod and Vlad entertains us with a few songs from the rock opera that the band are working on, which they tell me is 'a bit like Pink Floyd's The Wall'.

In the morning, we are served with a simple breakfast, including grape juice, pressed straight from the vine, my sugar levels probably going stratospheric. A little later, Vlad and Camelia take us for a stroll down the hill to a hidden gem of a place – an old walnut grove. The trees here must be very old and are producing nuts right now. We've hit high season. We all sit down on the grass and cut open the fresh, green shells – revealing the pale nuts within, which have a slightly creamy taste once the skin has been peeled off. The skins are very bitter, being laden with tannins.

I offered Vlad one of my two Swiss army knives as a thank-you gift last night. Having two of everything has gradually started to make sense. I'm never short of something to give away. Unfortunately, he wields it a little too enthusiastically whilst cutting open one of the walnuts and cuts himself quite deeply, putting an early end to our foraging expedition. We head back to the house in preparation for an afternoon ride into the city. Before that, though, with Vlad's hand attended to, we check out our plans on a map for the next stage of our journey.

I mention to him that we would like to travel through Transylvania. It turns out that to do so is feasible, if a little out of our intended direction. He recommends heading to a town called Brasov and then to track along a range of mountains before heading south. 'This is the Transfagarasan!' he says, with emphasis, adding, 'It is a wonderful road. From there, you can ride down to Bucharest, our capital city.' The mountains in question are the Carpathians, shaped like a giant fish hook, with Brasov sitting in the crook of the hook (so to speak). Last night, he spoke about Romanian history, about the country's Dacian roots, the Roman occupation and the history of resistance to the Ottoman Empire. A little later, after being dropped off in town by Camelia's father, we explore together some of the grand old buildings that make up the city centre, initially pestered by young beggars who are unceremoniously shooed away by our hosts.

Iași was once the capital of Moldavia. When Vlad told me this, I initially got confused and thought he was talking about Moldova. But the Principality of Moldavia existed in medieval times and stretched from the Eastern Carpathian Mountains to the river Dniester. It eventually formed a union with Wallachia in 1859 to become the Romanian state. It transpires, therefore, that Romania isn't a particularly old state, but it is formed from smaller states that had a long and rich history – and independent ones at that. The edges of the region have been nibbled at by the Russian Empire over the latter years, for example: after the end of the Russo-Turkish war when Bessarabia, was ceded to the Russians.

After meeting up with Ed, we head through the city centre and its impressive buildings to visit an old church, arriving during an afternoon service. Vlad explains that we won't be allowed in while the service is in progress. Apparently, the bearded orthodox priests carry a fearsome reputation. They all look a bit like Rasputin to me. It leaves me wondering about the nuns; what are they like? Ed appears less than impressed about the religious formalities of his country. He's a different character to his friends. He's blessed with a riotous, non-conformist attitude (and wicked sense of humour). In the early evening, we meet up with a couple of other friends of the group and spend a relaxing and enjoyable meal in a restaurant in the centre of town, situated in a very modern new complex that demonstrates the first signs of economic shoots of recovery, perhaps signalling better times to come for Romania, after joining the European Union. Let's hope so. Vlad explains to me that there haven't been any palpable benefits, so far.

'They seem to be building some new roads,' he says, 'but the general conditions for many people, including ourselves, are very difficult. We can't afford much at all, despite working very hard. For many people, it is terrible. Everything is so expensive – even the basics in life.'

***

Morning arrives bright and clear. A beautiful day. After our short but very enjoyable stay with our newly-found friends, it's time to load the bike and head off towards our next destination. In addition to recommending the Transfagarasan, Vlad also strongly advised us to head for the Danube Delta. We're no longer bound by visa date considerations, so we've decided to take this advice onboard and do just that. It means that we'll be weaving an erratic zig-zag course through Romania, but we're both looking forward to doing so. Once the bike's packed, Vlad, Camelia and Victor come down to see us off. We say our goodbyes. Behind where they're standing, I can see the wonderful hills that stretch back to Moldova. I get a very brief pang to head back in that direction, but that soon fades away into the crisp morning air.

Brasov is quite a major town. The route to it is easy to pick up by following Vlad's instructions and the signposts along the route. It takes us out through the city and along a range of low-lying hills, on a road that has a strange feature in the form of a split carriageway. The right-hand side of the split is a narrow lane and the left one is broader. After passing a few horse and cart combinations heading in the narrow lane,

I'm fairly convinced that its primary purpose is for their convenience, so I avoid using the 'horse lane'. But, when faster cars approach, they seem to want you to give way into the narrow lane. It's one of those conundrums of travelling in a foreign country without fully knowing their driving conventions and rules. Thankfully ,we steer clear of any road rage incidents.

The route we are taking heads in the direction of the Carpathian Mountains and is typified by more of the long, rolling, oceanic hills that we noticed, arriving from Moldova. It is truly very beautiful and unique. We are also both smitten by the almost medieval feeling of the villages and settlements that we pass through, where the horse is a major factor of life. People are out and about in their carts, many of which have been driven to roadside places where they cut grass using a scythe to load the cart up with fodder for the pony. The women wear clothes that seem cast back fifty, sixty or seventy years: patterned dresses, smocks and scarves on their heads. The men wear trilby hats and silk scarves, worn old jackets and workmen's trousers. Love it!

Churches are omnipresent. In a similar vein to the depths of America, each village has its church, some grand, some less so, but they're everywhere, as are religious roadside shrines. It is also common to see a working well at the foot of a garden. When we pass by schools, the children in the playground dash over and wave to us excitedly.

As we ride through this landscape, I find myself contemplating the events of the past few days. We've talked together with some humility about how we were taken in and looked after by Vlad and Camelia and have wondered if such things still happen in the UK. We pondered whether we've lost some of our values of decency and openness as our circumstances have improved and we've become more materialistic. Have we lost our trust of people and, along with it, this kind of common decency?

* * *

There's a section of today's ride that passes through some outstandingly scenic, hilly countryside. The road takes on a satisfying twistiness as it climbs forested hills. Most agreeable. Then it transforms into longer, straighter, flatter sections that are just a mite boring. When we finally arrive at the outskirts of Brasov, the afternoon is on the wane and we elect to stop and find a hotel here. And, in truth, 'tis a nice place to stop – an attractive town, nestling in the lee of the Carpathian Mountains, with a mixture of apartment blocks and some signs of industry on the outer limits, but an older, and more camera-friendly countenance in the centre. After a short spell of 'riding around a bit', we spot a modern tower-block hotel and navigate our way to the car park where we are greeted by a parking attendant and an electric barrier. There's an element of guard-like behaviour in his deportment, but nothing like the brusque and thorough assertiveness of his Russian counterparts.

* * *

Today is Transfagarasan day! We depart our lodgings at the usual hour, close to kicking out time, with the rider in a state of anticipatory excitement. Heading quietly out of town following signs for the road that will take us westwards towards the town of Sibiu. It promises to be an epic ride. I'm in no doubt that we face many miles of switchback corners, with adjacent bottomless drops and am questioning the wisdom of taking such a heavily-loaded monstrosity anywhere near it, but my confidence has grown, now that we've survived the hellish conditions of some of the roads in Russia and Ukraine, and I'm girded with a 'can do, won't fall off' attitude. Perchance the fool.

About fifty kilometres into the ride, we spot a petrol station and are pleasantly surprised to find pumps dispensing proper EU standard fuel. These are quality RONs, nothing like the tat found farther east. The Mutt drinks deeply from the pump. It's like putting spinach into Popeye, straight from the can! We celebrate with a coffee and pastry from the adjacent café, which has an Italian flair to it – complete with an outdoor patio and a scattering of fashionable young things in sunglasses, sipping espresso.

With the bike, pillion and rider suitably refreshed, we head the final few miles to the turnoff for the mountain pass, riding through a couple of sizeable villages and turning off a little too soon. This slight wayward detour leads us through some lovely, sinuous roads that carve through the foothills of the Carpathians, which are drawing ever nearer. They pass through more long villages, where families sit alongside their houses and the parents point us out to wee children, encouraging them to wave. I doubt if you could find a friendlier nation.

After riding a few miles, we turn onto the Transfagarasan proper, an event marked by a series of corners that are properly serious in their intent – a continuous series of 'S' bends that pass through increasingly rocky, forested hills. For a while, we find ourselves tailing a Mercedes car that is happily belching blue smoke, leaving the acrid whiff of unburnt oil in our nostrils. After a few tight corners and short straights, we eventually manage to pick a spot to safely trundle past him, diving into the next few corners and stretching out our lead until it's a comfortable one. The addition of some decent petrol has done no end of good to the bike's peppiness. It's fair sailing up the steeper and steeper inclines, which are surely the precursors to even more challenging switchbacks.

The Transfagarasan is a manifestation of a latent fear of Russia going back many years. It dates back to the time in the early 1970s, shortly after the invasion of Czechoslovakia, when the then President of Romania, Nicolae Ceauşescu, decided that a road was needed so that troops could be moved swiftly from north to south across the mountains, a route that was less easy to attack than some of the other mountain passes. More recently, it was introduced to the wider western world by the BBC 'Top Gear' trio, who drove three supercars (the finest of which was obviously the Aston Martin) over the 6,600 foot summit. At the time of the TV show being recorded, it was rumoured to be the 'best road in the world'. And, in truth, it is pretty amazing, comprising a seemingly endless series of 180-degree switchbacks as it climbs into the heavens, but those are just teasers for the gloriously insane curves that carve up a wide valley a few miles further on. The most famous photographs of the Transfagarasan are taken at the head of this valley and it's while pausing to take a few shots ourselves, that we are joined by a young couple who have a rather serious problem.

They putter to a halt in their faded old Daewoo Nexus a few feet behind us. The driver steps out and lifts the bonnet to free a few wisps of steam. The young guy makes out as if to check the engine, but it looks suspiciously like this is the first time he's ever opened a car bonnet. I wander over and ask him what the problem is. He speaks a smidgen of English.

It turns out that he and his partner are newlyweds, having tied the hitch yesterday. Her father loaned them his car, the wreck now sitting in front of us. He did so as a wedding present – to help them travel to the south on honeymoon. The problem is that the car has seriously overheated, having lost most of its coolant – I'm guessing a warped cylinder head has developed and resulted in water leaking into the combustion chamber. I do have some history with these dreadful cars. My daughter once bought one as a follow-up purchase after she wrecked its predecessor, another old clunker, by firmly pressing her foot to the floorboard at every possible given opportunity. The Daewoo still holds the record for her in terms of vehicle destruction. I think it lasted about two days.

The problem now is that the car won't even start. The young lad cranks it over, but it fails to fire up. Then, suddenly, it kicks and pops erratically before all four cylinders chime in and suddenly it's running.

He leaps out of the driver's seat, sprints around the front and drops the bonnet as his new wife jumps in the passenger seat and, with a big wave, they're off in a suspiciously ominous puther of white smoke. We spend a little longer taking in the view before mounting up and scratching around a few more corners. The weight of the bike means that it drops into corners a little more exuberantly than I would really like; the delicate application of power after the apex of each corner helps to keep us shiny side up. Apart from that tiny concern, the bike is performing amazingly well in the handling department, bearing in mind how much weight it's carrying and how high up that weight is. And I think it is breathing better too after its little service in Transnistria.

I'm expecting to catch the young couple up fairly soon, but, sadly, we do so far too quickly, within not much more than a mile. They've managed to find a layby and have conked out again. This time it looks terminal. I ask them if they need to borrow a phone, although I'm not sure I even have a signal, but they tell me they've already phoned home and that the owner will be coming out to assist. I think assistance with a quick push over the side of the mountain would suffice but refrain from letting my thoughts be known. They tell us they're sure they'll be OK. They are so seriously 'loved up' that nothing is going to get in the way of their honeymoon. We wish them all the luck in the world and leave them with a big wave, hurtling towards the next glorious corner.

***

The first proper hairpin bend that I rode around happens to be quite famous: the Ramsey Hairpin on the Isle of Man TT circuit. The first time I rode around it, my riding companion Neville couldn't hold back his guffaw (he was on the back of the bike, riding pillion), and he's repeated the story of 'Andy's fifty-pence piece method of riding around hairpins' ever since. I think every time we've lapped around the circuit together, since this episode, his shoulders have been shaking in mirthful anticipation that I'm going to cock it up again big time. The only riposte I have to this, is to mention the word 'Gooseneck' to him. It's a private joke, he knows exactly what I mean.

Hairpins galore!

A few miles further along, we start to notice advertising signs for a hotel and for camping. Eventually, the signs point off the asphalt road and up a very badly made, rubble-strewn track that dives over a stream and into a dark forest. This really is pure Bram Stoker. We follow the track for a while as it gradually declines in surface quality, without ever becoming properly perilous. After a while, we're starting to question whether the sign was a bum steer. But then we pass a group of hikers who wave cheerfully and, shortly after that, the trees thin out and we ride around a corner to what is quite a sight.

The hotel is called the Cumpana. It's a large and impressive building, rendered in stone up to about a third of its height, with white render above that, and capped by a broad, snow-bearing roof, altogether alpine in appearance. The setting is spectacular, situated as it is alongside a deep blue lake. A few cabins can be seen in the hotel grounds, adjacent to a pleasant patch of grass, dotted with a few tents. For a minute I consider going for a pitch. But we're only staying one night, and I'm pleasantly surprised to discover that a twin room comes to about £16.

The price becomes a little less enticing once we've seen the room. Frankly, it's pretty awful. Completely worn out and crusty. It also has a very unusual toilet with what can only be described as 'an inspection ledge' in its pan. Anything deposited in the pan hangs around in its full glory until the water flush swirls it around then dumps it down round the 'S' bend. A retentive toilet, no less. We unpack the beast of burden and settle in for the night. A little later, we find ourselves relaxing, post-dinner, with a glass of Romanian wine on the hotel's restaurant terrace, transfixed by a spectacular display of formation flying by hundreds of house martins, whose nests line the eaves of the hotel.

I've never seen this many house martins in one place. They're super little birds, with skill on the wing to rival a swallow. There are hundreds, if not thousands of them swirling around; a maelstrom of tiny bodies, piercing the air with their shrill 'chirrups' and screeches, catching insects on the wing then darting up into the eaves to feed the hungry mouths gaping within the entrance of their neat, mud-pot nests. If you stare up through the lower patrolling squadrons, then peer up as far as your eyes can see - there they are: tiny little dots, swirling around the warm evening sky, thousands of feet above the ground. And, as if that's not enough, just when you think this display is thoroughly disorganized and wouldn't pass muster with the Red Arrows, a whole gang of them will suddenly break away from the mass and fly, pell-mell, in formation across the lake, little white rumps glimmering in the fading light – like tiny missiles locked onto some distant imaginary target. Wonderful. Truly magnificent.

***

The lake that the hotel overlooks is called Lake Vidraru. It's actually a reservoir, something hinted at by a pale line of raised bank running around the shoreline, a giveaway to the fact that the water is slightly depleted. It was formed in 1965 by the building of a dam and underground hydro-electric power station. As is common with such mega-projects, a poor little village was sacrificed and drowned. It remains at the bottom of the lake sleeping with the fishes, like Luca Brasi in *The Godfather*. In the morning, we have enough time to drink in the view of this impressive body of water which reflects the tall peaks of the Fagaras Mountain range – the mountains that lend their name to the legendary road we are about to rejoin.

Today, we will ride the rest of the Transfagarasan and then take a dog-leg route southwards. After that, we'll head back towards the east, hopefully arriving in Bucharest in time for high tea. Although we have a proper map, purchased in Iași, I'm hoping that we'll pick up road signs for the capital, once we're free of the mountains. Bucharest, being the capital city of Romania, shouldn't be too hard to miss, even by my standards of navigation. The initial stage of the journey involves backtracking along the rough, broken road, dodging puddles of indeterminate depth that testify to a heavy rainfall having been deposited during the night, eventually arriving back on the glorious, snaking strip of tarmac.

The road remains outstanding for a few more miles, culminating in the splendiferous sight of a dam holding all those millions of litres of water in check and ensuring that the lost village remains that way. There's no denying that the best of the road across the Fagaras Mountains lies behind us and it peters out into a series of small towns. We manage to spot signs for Bucharest and make our way through quite heavy, late morning traffic.

Once we've negotiated the traffic, we find ourselves on a route called the A1, heading purposefully across a wide plain under a clear blue sky. It's a brand-new section of motorway, which has almost certainly been paid for by the European Union. I say this because I've read that funds are quite quickly fed into major infrastructure projects, once a country gains accession. In the blurb from Brussels on the internet, it considers the beneficiaries of this financial largesse to be 'regional road users and international travellers'. So, there we are. We're benefitting right now by barreling along at a considerable rate of knots on a carriageway of exemplary standard, better than anything I can think of in the UK, estimating arrival in Bucharest in about forty minutes – as long as the road doesn't run out of steam like some of its Russian counterparts do, from time to time.

The outskirts of Bucharest are marked, initially, by an increase in advertising hoardings and outlying areas of retail and storage units.

The A1, that has borne us so efficiently across country, transforms into an altogether more urban beast and we join lines of traffic heading into the city through an area called 'Sector 6'.

At 228 square kilometres, Bucharest is a medium-sized city. It's a bit smaller than Birmingham in area but it has a considerably larger population at around 1.9 million, which is a bit of a surprise to me. I've read snippets in the past about the vast follies built in Bucharest by Ceausescu, including the Palace of the Parliament, and I'd like to see at least one of them. As it happens, we pass by an example on our route, but it is being torn down and all that remains are vast blocks of concrete with twisted steel rods sprouting from them. I have no idea what it once was – it resembles a submarine pen. A little further on, we run into the older city centre, which is graced by a series of rather grand buildings. They are amongst those that survived the razing of significant parts of the city by the dictator as he tried to re-model it in the image of his monstrous palace.

Nicolae Ceausescu was a divisive character in history, to put it mildly, and, for that reason, it's easy to forget that he was hugely popular when he first rose to power. He was also popular in the west, in part due to his habit of cocking a snook at the Soviets. But eventually, his excesses and policies regarding paying off foreign debt led to extreme hardship in Romania, resulting in his being overthrown and subjected to a summary trial in December, 1989. He was found guilty, taken around the back of the building with his wife and shot, without managing to get much of a word in edgeways. Getting rid of him was over in a flash. Getting rid of his legacy has taken a lot longer. But there are clear signs of recovery, despite the current dire state of international finances.

***

In the morning, after breakfast, we head out to try to find a post office to post some of our travelling souvenirs home. Taking instructions from our hotel receptionist, we locate one a few streets away. I join a long queue of remarkably patient individuals while the lady at the counter takes her time serving each person. I'm really not too sure how this is going to go. Will she understand English? As the queue shortens in front of me, it lengthens at the back with new arrivals. It takes ages for me to approach the front. By the time I arrive at the counter, I feel like I'm standing out like a sore thumb. I might as well have a neon sign planted on top of my head – 'Danger, Foreigner! No speako de lingo!'. There is a confused pause, and with it a look bordering on panic across Mrs Posties face when I try to explain that I want to send my package to England.

The lady behind me chips in, 'Excuse me, I can help. I was language teacher. I speak German much better than English, but I can try translate for you.'

It really is quite amazing how pervasive the English language is nowadays and how often this situation has been repeated. I gratefully receive translated instructions to fill out a customs declaration form. In order to do so, I have to leave my precious place in the queue, no doubt resulting in another twenty-minute wait, once I've filled everything in. My translator doesn't have time to hang around, but she checks that I'm doing OK before leaving, which is a nice gesture. Once I've filled in the forms, I do the British thing and take my place at the back of the queue, only to be waved through to the front by the post mistress. It's all a bit un-English to be queue jumping, but the other customers don't seem to mind and they wave me through with smiles. It all adds to the impression that Romanians, whilst being potentially quite deadly to the average dictator, are, in general, polite and courteous to foreigners; as well as being talented, professional queuers.

* * *

Bucharest was always going to be a stopping off point – somewhere we could rest up for a day in a hotel, do a bit of washing, post our chattels back home and buy a few new clothes. The temptation to adjust our route to take in the Transfagarasan, as recommended by Vlad, meant that we have wandered far from the Black Sea and now we need to reacquaint ourselves with it. The plan is to ride to a town called Constanta, which lies about 260 kilometres to the south east of the capital, an easy ride's distance from the Danube Delta and similarly also from the Bulgarian border to the south.

Having negotiated our exit from the capital city without significant drama, we find ourselves travelling along the road to Constanta, following a railway line. We ride alongside a multi-coloured train, each carriage painted in a different livery. The track and the road pass over the mighty Danube as it winds its lazy way northwards towards the sea. The rail crossing is an impressive old suspension bridge. This road was originally laid down in communist times, but it was never close to being finished properly. I guess the money just ran out. Then, the good old EU stepped in to hurry the party along a bit, and the result is that it is due to be completed later this year. The final stretch of the road is very nearly finished. It carves through long, low-lying hills, presenting a fine view far into the distance.

Constanta greets us with an unusual city sign in the form of a large and very impressive patrol boat, raised above the road on a plinth, with the name of the city emblazoned on its after flanks. We initially get a bit lost in our eagerness to find accommodation, eventually ending up on a road that runs parallel to the seafront, where we find a hotel with spare rooms. After checking in, the staff open a side door and beckon me into the depths of a seriously challenging garage, with a perilously steep ramp. Getting in safely requires the skills of trials riding supremo Dougie Lampkin; getting the behemoth out from the deep would probably challenge even him.

The town we've arrived in is a holiday venue, a major port and an industrial centre too, feeling ever so slightly like Mariupol in Ukraine. It is a very ancient city, with a Scythian history going back way before Roman times and has many beautiful buildings, probably the most notable being the casino. The Roman poet Ovid is reputed to have spent his final years in Constanta (then called Tomis), banished by the Emperor Augustus, his crime never revealed by either party. The works of Ovid were on the curriculum when I studied my history degree. I recall that his poems were quite risqué by Roman standards and he pushed the boundaries at a time when doing so risked censure. Luckily for him, he appears to have had a run-in with an older and more mellow Augustus and was merely banished to a violent, midge-infested town surrounded by a swamp, on the very edge of the empire – a town not entirely unlike Hull.

***

We wake up to a slightly cloudier day. After breakfast, we pack the cameras and our wet gear before negotiating the bike up the near-vertical ramp. To complete the extraction, we have to attract the attention of the receptionist who promises to open the door, but it all goes a bit pear-shaped and I'm left frying the clutch and mildly disgruntled. Eventually though, it's all sorted out and, with Diane loaded aboard, we can head off to find the road out of town and onwards to discover the Danube Delta.

Our destination is the town of Tulcea, which sits at the inland edge of the delta, about 110 kilometres north of Constanta. After shaking off the outer fringes of the town, the road deteriorates a smidge and strikes out across an increasingly wild and remote area, dotted by small settlements. Like much of this part of the world, it is typified by long, low rolling hills, but here they are more like long, long folds in the land, mostly tilled into large fields that are unfettered by enclosures of any kind, just ploughed into strips and occasionally planted with a wind farm or two.

We pass through a series of roadworks, of varying lengths and stages of tarmac re-laying, scrabbling in some sections on a very rough top surface of gravel. It takes us a good two and a half hours to reach Tulcea, arriving in the early afternoon.

The town presents itself as a rather higgledy-piggledy place – a mixture of low-rise buildings of uncertain vintage, Soviet era apartment blocks and areas of docks and light industry, all dominated by an impressive hill bearing an obelisk on its summit. After a brief ride around town, we pass through a series of cobbled streets, bordered by older properties, and pitch up outside the park that encloses the hill and its monument. It certainly looks like a good place to view the Delta. Without further ado, we clamber up the broad steps, perspiring outrageously, reaching the top flushed and breathless to discover that the view is outstanding. The Danube performs a mighty loop around which the town drapes itself. The river passes from left to right to a point where the town peters out and only river and woodland can be discerned, heading right out into the distance as far as the eye can see, onwards to the Black Sea.

The delta is one of Europe's truly wild places. If you are travelling from the north-east along the Black Sea coast, it provides an effective block to your progress and is one of the reasons we found ourselves lost in Transnistria and Moldova. The only way to navigate this wilderness is by boat, by horse or by foot – although Dougie would do quite well on his trials bike.

Chapter 24
Asia Minor

After departing the monument, we negotiate the streets of the town, eventually pitching up near the banks of the mighty river, parking the bike in the lee of a modern hotel, housed in a tower overlooking the river. Our plan to stroll along the riverside is interrupted within a few yards when we spot a set of advertising hoardings, promoting river trips that are clearly a 'twitcher's' delight. It's an opportunity to witness the rich and diverse bird life of the delta. Having wavered no more than a couple of seconds, we're pounced upon by a very proficient salesperson.

About twenty minutes ago, from the vantage point of the monument, we watched the pleasure boats head off up the river and discussed whether we had time to take a trip. We thought that it would probably take a few hours and decided, not without regret, that we probably didn't have time. But our good fortune quickly becomes clear. This river trip on offer is in a speedboat and will take just two hours – tops. The price is extraordinarily reasonable. If we make a decision right now, we can go – the boat is ready to depart. It's a no-brainer. In the blink of an eye, we find ourselves negotiating a collection of ramps and miscellaneous vessels and clambering aboard a very nifty-looking sports boat with a humungous American Johnson outboard motor strapped to its nether regions. Once onboard, we are introduced to our fellow passengers, three guys who are merely taking a taxi ride up the river to be dropped off at a party. They come armed with a LOT of beer.

Having slipped the fore and aft lines, our pilot eases the throttle forward and fair skips his vessel over the water for a short distance before stopping at a fuel station on a pontoon for a quick top-up of juice. Well, that was quite enjoyable! It doesn't take long to refuel. That done, he eases her round to point downstream and rams the ...

HOLY SHIT… rams the throttles to 'all ahead full, lash me to the wheel Cap'n and don't spare the cat'. In an instant, we find ourselves hanging on for dear life as the boat hoists itself right out of the water and flies. Slamming down violently on the crest of each wave, a huge rooster tail is thrown into our wake as we hammer our way down the delta. What an experience!

We fly past the outer fringes of the town, skirting an interesting array of semi-derelict boats and ships, including what must be the remains of the Communist era Romanian navy, and then on into the wilder, more remote parts of the delta. After about twenty minutes we've covered perhaps the same number of miles – I don't know how fast this thing goes, but I'm thinking around fifty knots, at least. The skipper slows down as we approach a settlement of neat chalets. The other passengers are disembarked along with their beer and greeted by partygoers who clearly have been warming up already. I suspect that hangovers are absolutely guaranteed.

If we were expecting any mercy, once the bad boys have been discarded, we would have been sorely disappointed. We're invited to move forward and sit in business class, which we do with thanks, and then the throttle is pushed forward to the breaking point of the wire and off we go again. But this time, we depart the main river and head off up a series of back waters, ploughing a massive furrow through the center of the waterway and depositing a veritable tidal wave onto the banks. If the delta has any endangered water voles or coypus, then they've just been liquidated. When another vessel is encountered, both boats slow down for a few seconds as they pass, before revving up and hurtling into the widening wake with gusto.

It isn't all high-speed jinks though. The pilot regularly kills the action and slows at points of particular interest. He doesn't tell us what the object of interest is, but he doesn't really need to. The places he slows down are mostly gaps in the waterway where it opens onto a flooded wetland attracting the incredibly varied bird life with feeding opportunities. Divers, grebes, pelicans, egrets and many types of ducks and geese are included – more than three hundred species of birds inhabit the delta. But the one that takes my breath away is the sight of a white-tailed eagle, skimming the treetops that populate the banks of the river as it hunts for its fish supper.

Apart from the abundance of wildlife, the delta is also supremely beautiful, a space comprised of deep blue-black waters, towering reed beds, abundant water lilies, secret, secluded meadows and wide wetlands, all bordered by trees that dip their roots and branches in the water, a landscape painted in shades of green and grey. I imagine it to be the perfect place to try wild camping – I tell Diane that it must be so, and she agrees with me too. As long as the equipment includes the 'bog in a bag' portable loo (which we left back at home).

***

I will freely admit that Romania has been a huge surprise to me. It's not that I've harboured any particular preconceptions about the country before we experienced it. But our short journey through the parts we've visited have really wowed me. I love the variety of countryside that we've traversed, the warmth of the people, the rustic, almost medieval nature of the backroad villages and the majestic beauty of the Carpathian Mountains. I loved the experience of waving to the children as we passed through villages and easing off the throttle as we pass a horse and cart. But to cap it all off, the Danube Delta, the second largest and most pristine river delta in Europe, has been one of *the* experiences of the trip so far.

***

Today, we will be heading down the coast and across the border into Bulgaria, where we will hopefully spend just one night before crossing into Turkey.

The road to Bulgaria, the E87, is coastal in nature and relatively short in distance, passing through the town of Mangalia, where we decide to stop for a coffee and panini at a pleasant café with a few outdoor tables arranged tightly on a patio, of sorts. After our meal, Diane pops to the till to settle the tab. The café is situated at a bus terminus and this makes it a target area for intensive begging. The first attempts to get us to part with cash come in the form of a very well-organised family, comprising: mum (director) and three incredibly savvy wee children who work the tables for all its worth, initially looking very poor and sickly. When this is unsuccessful, they change miraculously into happy scamps, joking around with the regulars. I was taken in very easily by the initial tactic and would've felt quite badly suckered if I'd parted with any cash.

In amongst those begging from the people in the bus queue outside the restaurant, is one young man who stands out the moment you spot him. The children from the family appear to be clearly healthy and probably not in any immediate danger of abject poverty (though, honestly, who can tell?) Unlike them, this person is really struggling. His clothes are threadbare and dirty, his shoes are too small and have split right open, revealing weathered feet with no socks. His face is swollen, as if he's literally taken a physical beating from poverty in its worst extreme. He shuffles along the queue of people, offering out his hand for the briefest of moments before moving on, either rejected or just ignored. At a guess, I would say he's in his late teens.

In an instant, before he's even seen me, I decide to give the boy my remaining Romanian money and start searching all my pockets for every last note and coin. Diane arrives back at the table to find me in a frantic search for dosh. But, when I try to explain the reason and look over to where he was, he's gone! Without properly explaining to her why, I grab the remaining change in her possession and leave her to look after our gear, exiting the café and looking up and down the street, to no avail. Then, rounding the corner of the café, I spot him. He's moved into a crowd of people who are queuing to buy a drink from a window in the side of the café. I ease my way through them to a point where I can tap him on his shoulder. He half turns around and I press the money into his hand. He's shocked and surprised. As I stroll back round to meet Diane, I do a quick calculation; we've given him about forty pounds – a lot of money here in Romania. A few minutes later, togged up, with Diane sat on the pillion, we look over into the café. He's returned there and has approached an older man, a kind-faced gentleman, himself dressed in poorer clothes – maybe a relative. The young man holds the money up, beaming and the older man smiles and pats him on the shoulder. They don't see us as we ease out into the traffic, heading for the border.

***

It's the early afternoon as we cross the border, passing through the frontier post without incident. I didn't expect border controls within the EU, but here they have them. The road passes over a wide expanse of farmland, skirting the small towns of Shabla, Kavarna and Balchik. Then it turns towards the coast and starts to climb into hillier country. We've arrived at one of the increasingly popular holiday destinations for westerners seeking a budget get-away. We spend the night at the resort town of Golden Sands, where we are introduced to the epitome of Teutonic efficiency. We are the sole Brits in a hotel crammed with Germans who are very polite and very regimented, much like the Russians in Anapa; a strange comparison, but true nonetheless.

Departure in the morning finds us easing through the town of Varna, before climbing along a series of ridges, overlooking a splendid landscape of long, forested hills drifting dreamily away into the distance, with variations of greens giving way to blues, very reminiscent of our early experiences in Romania. Our experience of the wilder side of the country doesn't last for too long. The road settles back down to lower elevations as we pass through the resort of Sunny Beach – the town planning authorities clearly had a minor lobotomy in the naming department after the fall of communism, hereabouts. My pillion passenger isn't overly impressed. We've been chatting as we ride. One of the towns that we passed through a while ago had a really pleasant, relaxed feel to it, with an agreeable street of cafes and the odd souvenir shop, frequented by bronzed people in faded shorts and flip-flops. It fired up a modest level of enthusiasm on my part.

'I wonder how much you can buy an apartment for hereabouts?'

It was just a thought in passing... I didn't mean too much about it really.

'I wouldn't bother,' replied Diane, 'I don't think I would like to live here.' The happy thoughts of early retirement, popping down the shop for a day-old British newspaper and sipping a coffee while reading it, are snuffed out as quickly as a wet-finger-nipped candle. Perhaps she's right. We don't really do holiday resort vacations, so why would I even think of buying an apartment in a town like Golden Sands?

We pass along a road that heads into an increasingly built-up area and arrive in the mid-afternoon at the sizeable town of Burgas, passing a lake, one of two that flank the town. It's very busy, with a flow of traffic heading into the town centre. After a considerable degree of faffing around on the hotel search, we eventually opt to head back out of town to one we spotted earlier.

In the evening, we take a stroll around the local area, which we find to be mostly comprised of older apartments and a football ground. As we wander past, we find ourselves greeted by the rising and falling racket of a rowdy crowd – a game is in mid-flow. The road passes by various emergency exits allowing us to peek on tiptoe into the ground. We find ourselves at the same elevation as the top tier of seats in the stands. The stadium is built into the hillside, much like a Greek amphitheatre. We savour the edgy, tribal atmosphere of the crowd for a few minutes. The home team, PSFC Chernomorets Burgas, play in blue and white and have a neat badge consisting of an anchor flanked by a shark and a football. I'm not sure what the significance of the shark is, other than that is their nickname: 'The Sharks'. Perhaps that is sufficient.

Burgas has a rich history dating back over 3,000 years. Like many cities along the north of the Black Sea, it has been occupied by various powers, including the Roman and the Ottoman Empire and was influenced by the Greeks before that. A quick spot of research on the internet confirms that the citizens of Burgas didn't conform too readily to the wants and wishes of Mr Stalin and his subsequent heirs, although Bulgaria itself certainly embraced those Cold War years with poisoned umbrellas and a heavy dose of enthusiasm. When communism arrived, Burgas was an economically vibrant city, something it seems to have seized back in recent years. It is the largest port in Bulgaria, has the second busiest airport and a thriving industrial sector. So, it comes as a bit of a surprise to also find out that it also has an excellent spread of biodiversity in the avian and reptilian areas of fauna, mainly due to the large lakes that both surround and are part of the city. The locals seem very pleasant, too. There isn't much not to like.

***

At first glance of the map, I thought that the border with Turkey looked quite close to Burgas, but in reality, it turns out to be a fair old haul. My mind did its usual trick and translated fifty kilometres or so into ten, and those fifty kilometres are taken at a very sedate pace, not least because the view from the saddle becomes increasingly alluring and... well... wilder. The road is very poor, full of old repairs and potholes. We pass through sections where workers are busy trying to improve things – ripping up the old tarmac to lay new. A little further along, we spot an innocuous road sign at a deserted junction, optimistically advising that a left turn will take us to Istanbul. The road starts to climb into a region of remote hills with steep, rocky outcrops, cool forests and a strip of old tarmac that throws up a series of fun corners. This is just terrific.

The first and last town in Bulgaria – Malko Tarnovo – is a throwback to a completely different era. The houses are shabby chic, the livestock roams nonchalantly around its edges, with cows congregating in a bus stop, and the people stare as you ride past. Thankfully, we don't spot any banjos. In fairness, I'm being somewhat disrespectful. We're only clipping the edges of the town and are probably missing some of its charms. I imagine it to be a place of ancient intrigue, perhaps like Haparanda in Sweden – a place where spies, smugglers and cut-throats conversed in dark corners of bars; probably they still do... something akin to Chalmun's Cantina in *Star Wars*.

As we approach the border, we pass through another stretch of altogether more purposeful road works, where the hillside is being blasted and the tarmac is being laid with a quality that would rival the Danes. No doubt another EU effort. It fits with their pattern – Bulgaria joined up in 2007 at the same time as Romania, so one would expect a spot of road building to have been a priority and where better than one of the borders to a neighbouring country? Not that there are any signs of a flow of trade between the two countries. Far from it. All we've spotted are road builders and the free-range cows of Malko Tarnovo.

The Bulgarian border post with Turkey is very remote. It has a slight feel of the wild west about it, but passage through is both orderly and relatively quick. Confidence-inspiring, one might say.

All of which is blown into the long grass when we arrive at the Turkish side. On the face of it, things initially seem to bode well. We ride down a slight hill and are told to park up outside an office block and take our papers inside for processing. This border is different from anything we've experienced so far. A wee peek through one of the office doors adjoining the reception area reveals a senior officer, asleep, with his head tilted back and his feet up on his desk. But, just when we think everything is well relaxed, and that we might be about to sail through the rubber-stamping of officialdom with ease, we're delivered a rude awakening. We approach an office with a glass window and document aperture, coming face to face with two young girls, one of whom, it turns out, is training the other in the subtle art of officialdom. Today's lesson concerns the practice of offensive techniques when dealing with western riff-raff.

'Passports', demands she, very rudely, almost prompting a response of, 'if you keep that attitude up, young lady, I'll be having a word with your parents.' Diane hands them over. The trainee has noticed the look of shock and awe on my face and has developed a teenage smirk on hers.

'You go pay money over there, then come here', the leader orders abruptly, signaling dismissively to another office. I'm not liking this.

We head over and make a payment. It transpires that we could have done this online, but that nugget of knowledge escaped us, a lame excuse if truth be told, and I think Diane pressed me to do it way back in the mists of time. I think my reply was something like, 'let's leave it 'til we get there. No rush.' With a pristine new visa, gum-licked into our passports we head back over to the offensive juveniles – sorry, to the two officers of the law, at the first window.

'Motorcycle papers,' demands she who must be obeyed. The minutes tick by. By now, it feels as though we're squirming a bit. She's putting us through the wringer and enjoying it immensely, to the delight of her accomplice. I feel like snatching our papers back and saying, 'I can't be bothered with this, we're off back to Bulgaria....' But keeping one's head when dealing with border officials is (generally speaking) most advisable. They can make your life a misery.

'This no good. Go and give papers over there', she points to the office with the comatose officer. Thankfully, he's woken up from his nap and has now taken to saying a prayer on a small prayer mat, laid out on the floor in front of his desk. He completes that and approaches us with a smile, handing us a form to fill in for customs. After that, we're directed back to the dreaded portal. More waiting – stretching it out just to make us squirm like worms on a hook, pointing things out to her trainee, before casually flicking to the page with the visa and stamping it.

'You can go now.' Begone. Charming!

***

An experience such as that can ruin your impression of a country from the very off. I compare it with the fabulous treatment we received entering Russia and wonder if the Turkish authorities care in the slightest how foreigners perceive them. But the negative feelings gradually subside as we sweep down an immaculate stretch of road, marveling at the difference in landscape from that just across the border. The hills ease us gently down towards a broad, dry plain covered in parched, straw-coloured grass, thorny-looking bushes and the odd larger tree. As the land flattens out, we approach the town of Kirklareli. The sensation is akin to a smooth landing in an aeroplane.

As we enter the outer fringes of the town, everything is quiet; it feels as if this is a day of rest. The town is completely different from anything we've seen before. For the most part, it looks to be a modern place, with apartment blocks that are coloured part salmon pink, part cream. They appear to be very well constructed, far better than the old communist ones to the north and east. We also glimpse our first mosque, with its central dome and pointed minarets, underlining the cultural divide we've just crossed, abruptly passing from Christendom to Islam. We pull up to stop at a red light.

While we're sitting there, a car pulls up alongside. The occupants are older gentlemen. They peer over at us, then one of them winds his window down. His hand is extended bearing a long, thin red and white object. It unfolds to reveal a Turkish flag, a bold white crescent and star on a rich red background, attached to a white plastic flagpole. He shouts 'Welcome!' to us. The light turns to green, the window is wound up and we pull off, parting company as they turn off to the right, waving to us as we head on our way.

***

Our plan is to ride to Istanbul and to search for lodgings when we arrive there. It's over two hundred kilometres from Kirklareli to Istanbul and the afternoon is wearing on. Thankfully, the navigation is simple, at least until we arrive at our destination, and it's well signposted too. The excellent condition of the road also assists our progress. We follow the E87, a major route from Sofia in Bulgaria that goes all the way to Tehran, if you wish to continue to that destination. Our plan is to follow it to Ankara via Istanbul, then part company and head northwards to rejoin the Black Sea coast.

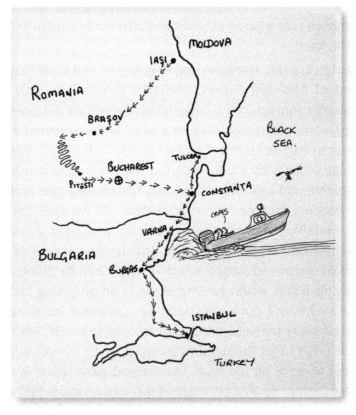

Caption: The route to Istanbul, through Romania and Bulgaria.

After a brief stop at a deserted service area for a quick snack, we press on towards our destination. The traffic is light and the weather warm. The past week or so of riding rough roads, broken only occasionally by decent blacktop in Romania, has given way to a long ribbon of dual carriageway heading eastwards in a determined fashion, allowing us to count down the kilometres at a satisfying rate. This progress continues until we hit the outskirts of Istanbul, at which point we hit the mother of all traffic snarl-ups. Istanbul is suffering from the twice-daily strangulation of crawling rush-hour traffic. It doesn't take long to work out that Turkish motorcyclists use the hard shoulder to negotiate the stationary queue of traffic. I don't know if this is legal and decide that it's not worth the risk, opting to stick to the traffic queue. Gradually, the reason for the immediate queue becomes apparent with the sighting of a line of pay stations ranged across the lanes of the motorway. When we arrive at the barrier, we hit a major problem. The light is red, but I can't detect a way to pay the fee. We sit there, a tad flummoxed, get pipped at and decide the only course of action is to jump the light.

I'm fairly sure this transgression is going to end badly, possibly in some kind of *Midnight Express* scenario, arrested, forcibly split up and summarily thrown into a Turkish jail. Once past the barriers, the traffic progresses reasonably well for a while and we presently arrive at another set of barrier stations, with a slip road off to the right leading to a real pay office with a real person sitting behind the window. Once the nice gentleman can understand me, I'm advised that motorcycles pass the barriers for free, normally at pace. As we walk back to the bike, considerably relieved, a couple of men approach us and ask us where we're from. On learning we're British, the younger of the two welcomes us warmly to Turkey, which is nice. Then he points to Diane and clasps his hands whilst looking at me in an enquiring fashion. I'm flummoxed – haven't got a clue what he's on about but suspect that he's asking if we're married. I nod and say, 'yes, married'. We're not, of course but I don't feel the need to complicate the conversation. I just want to get us back on the bike. The clasped hand query is repeated twice more during the dying embers of the conversation, just so he can make absolutely sure.

Back at the bike, Diane comes to a fairly obvious conclusion, 'I think it's you he liked,' she says, with a wry smile.

Istanbul is an impressive city to ride through, even on a major motorway. The sights from the saddle are often outstanding. It takes us a couple of hours to crawl along our way, perspiring in a heat exacerbated by the tens of thousands of engines idling away in the queues. Arriving at the Sultan Mehmet Bridge, we are transported across the wide channel of the Bosphorus, the waterway that links the Sea of Marmara to the Black Sea. It's also the crossing point from Europe to Asia. We peel off the motorway to search for accommodation, fail, and return to the gridlock. I shout back to Diane, 'I think we'll head out to the airport, there's got to be a hotel there!' And for once I'm right.

***

I am fortunate indeed to have a very good friend in Istanbul, a lady called Gamze. I worked in Denmark with her back in 2003. She and her husband were very kind to both myself and my wife of the time and I have fond memories of socialising with them both. Before our departure, I contacted her on Facebook and she insisted that we let her know when we arrive here. But now we've arrived, we're a bit pushed for time. I've decided to press on to Ankara. There seem to be more opportunities to get the bike booked in there for a tyre change than here in Istanbul. After a conflab, we decide to ride back through Istanbul on the way back west and spend a couple of days here so we can see the city and also meet up with Gamze and Tayfun, her husband.

***

Tuesday 28th August

Things are not so sunny today. Last night's hotel sits on the fringe of the Sabiha Gokcen Airport, a short and easy ride from the E80 where we hang a right and head east, following signs for Ankara, which are helpfully maintained in both Turkish and English languages. By the time we arrive at the coast some ten kilometres further on, the heavens have opened with a monumental downpour of almost biblical proportions. Within seconds, the road is awash.

Despite the conditions, we find ourselves overtaken by cars travelling at breakneck speed. Two BMW saloons hurtle past, their drivers no doubt believing all the hype about ABS brakes and traction control. It doesn't take long to catch the second one up. The car lays in the fast lane, smashed to smithereens, the young driver climbing out dazed, surrounded by police, wreckage scattered across the three lanes of the motorway. Having picked our way through that, a little further on we meet the leader – he's suffered the same fate, but this time with far worse results. I'm not sure he's made it.

Since leaving Finland we've hardly felt the need to don our two-piece rainsuits. Sitting behind the big screen on the Mutley, basking in the warmth of the heated grips that are gently toasting my pinkies, everything is pretty much well with the world. It's a wee bit chilly, but survivable. The suits are holding out. The acid test is all about the integrity of the seams in the vital crotch region. Experience has taught me that even the most expensive suits tend to leak eventually, and the crotch is where they go. Cold, wet gonads are then guaranteed. I learned the hard way when I was a daily commuter into London and followed the example of a lot of dispatch riders, buying cheap, waterproof trousers from the Army and Navy store and replacing them at regular intervals. Fashioned thus, I managed to keep a dry crotch for five of six years and only rediscovered wet crotch syndrome when I went and bought an extortionately expensive suit from BMW. These Finnish suits are unfashionable and relatively cheap. I think the omens are good. They won't last forever, but they will hopefully keep the rain out for the duration of the trip. We press on for an hour or two until a sign comes up for a service area and we pull off for some grub and a fill up for the bike.

When we dismount at the petrol pumps, there is the very slight feeling of general dampness that is pretty much inevitable, considering the downpour we've ridden through but, thankfully, there is absolutely no reason to walk like John Wayne, so I don't bother to do so and merely paddle round to the pump to start filling our big red buddy.

278

Wet, wet, wet.

Fast forward forty minutes. Diane has returned from the loo and sits opposite me at a table strewn with the remnants of our meal – the saucy meatballs were exceptionally nice.

'What were the men's toilets like?' she asks.

'Okay I suppose, I wasn't in a hurry to use the hole in the ground, I've never quite got the hang of those', I reply.

'I've just been told-off for not wearing head dress!' she exclaims indignantly. 'By the woman taking money.'

'Really?'

'And then I went into the western-style toilet.'

'Lucky you! We blokes don't get one.'

'And do you know what? It's completely vandalized. The walls were covered in sh...'

'Excrement?'

'Yes. Covered in poo. It was disgusting.' She shivers at the very thought of it.

We tramp out, back to the bike. The rain has eased, just slightly. When I think back to the toilets we encountered south of Moscow, I can't help but draw a comparison. Those were just un-be-lievable, but at least they hadn't been vandalised and left so. As we pull off into the plume of spray billowing in the wake of a truck that just flashed by, I can only hope that things will improve when we get to tonight's destination. There's a lot resting on the shoulders of poor old Ankara. If that doesn't come up trumps, at least one of us is not going to want to stay in Turkey much longer.

Chapter 25
Green Cross Pork

We haven't seen much scenery today, mainly on account of the torrential rain. We did get a glimpse of the ocean, far below us, at a point where the motorway met the Sea of Marmara, but the accidents on the road kept us occupied. Gradually the rain subsides and the clouds gently give way to a few patches of blue. This coincides with our entering an area blessed with high hills that could almost trick you into thinking you were riding through parts of America. A pervasive feeling of being back in a proper wilderness washes over me. The effect is transformational. Where I found myself beset by negative thoughts, shocked, I think, by Diane's revelations, I now find positive ones sneaking in and giving the negative ones a sharp shove.

We part company with the E80, following signs for the capital, heading along another well-maintained stretch of dual carriageway that sweeps magnificently around the shoulders of countless hard, rocky hills. Hopefully, the landscape is having the same effect on my fair pillion too. We can't converse to find out, we're travelling at speed, and the wind noise buffets our helmets seeking out all the little crevices that conspire to add turbulent shrieks to the cacophony of sound. I can see ahead for considerable distances, allowing plenty of notice of speed traps, so we crack on a bit. An hour later, we find ourselves meeting the Ankara ring road, catching glimpses of what appears to be a thoroughly modern city.

After a short period of faffing around seeking out dead ends, we eventually strike double lucky, something akin to winning the lottery, in my world. We decide to head in towards the city, turning off the ring road at a nondescript junction. The road winds through a pleasant district, flanked by attractive houses, then past a large building that looks faintly academic in nature. The city starts to thicken up with intent.

Entering a busy thoroughfare, we immediately spot a motorcycle shop on the right, sitting at the top of a steep hill that plunges down into the district of Cankaya. Now that's just great! A minute is all it takes to find a hotel. Bingo!

The hotel we've landed at is called the City Hotel. It's a modern tower, clad in buff-coloured stone across its broad frontage. I scoot inside and enquire on room availability, saying that we'd like a room for two nights. It turns out that the hotel is full, apart from one 'high quality' room that comes at an eye-watering price.

'I can assure you sir, that this is a top boutique hotel. You will not be disappointed with the room.'

Walking back out to Diane, who is waiting by the front door bearing a hopeful expression, I decide to give the credit card a hefty whack. What price comfort, nay, possibly even luxury? Diane surprises me.

'I'll pick this one up Hun.'

Horse dentures are not examined. We repair to the reception.

'We'll take it thanks. Diane will pay you,' I declare, happy as Larry and heading gleefully for the ritual unpacking of the bike.

The receptionist, a smart-suited gentleman, is thrown completely by this and suffers somewhat by being forced to take payment from a woman, one bearing a different passport name than the male of the species, no less. It's an important lesson. We've been judging Turkey by European standards and haven't acclimatised to reality, forgetting (some might say rudely) that we are in a completely different, largely alien culture – at least it's alien to us. A little later, we discuss this in a restaurant just down the road, whilst savouring a stonkingly good shish kebab, washed down with diet Coke.

There are things to like about Turkey. It seems to be very clean – mostly – and quite beautiful in parts too. We've found the roads to be modern and well-maintained so far, and the people are polite, teenage border officials notwithstanding. But we've started to realise that the experience is different, depending on whether you are a man or a woman. This wasn't the case in the airport hotel, but it is, without doubt, the case out beyond the tourist trail and, since that's where we will be spending most of the rest of our time here, we just need to cast aside our western sensibilities and, perhaps, even tone down some of our behaviour. Sadly, this is more a problem for my travelling companion because women are treated differently and, right now, her jury is well and truly out on the matter.

＊＊

Despite our wee troubles on checking-in, we can't deny that the City Hotel is the bees-knees when it comes to the quality of both accommodation and service. It is rich in quirky, modern décor and comfort. We spend a very relaxing night, surrounded by our grubby luggage.

Being checked in for two nights allows time for a wider search for an alternative tyre supplier, should one be required, but I'm hoping that won't be necessary and tog up in my riding gear for the short hop up the hill, once the rush hour has subsided. It's a gloriously hot day, with blue skies and temperatures rapidly rising. I'm immediately impressed with the surroundings. The city is modern, with a progressive feel to it. People are well-dressed and busily going about their lives; in short, it has a bit of a buzz to it and I particularly like the twee little powder blue and cream micro buses that pass by at regular intervals. When a gap appears, I pull into the traffic and head towards the shop, passing it by and using a roundabout further up the road as a turning point, avoiding cutting across the dense flow of traffic.

A lady in the shop is busy serving a customer. She makes sure they are happy in their quest to find a helmet and comes over to greet me. After confirming that she speaks 'a little' English, I explain the situation: that I'm looking to fit a pair of tyres, to be fitted on our way back in a few days' time, and perhaps also have a service and filter change. The bike doesn't really need oil, but I think it would be good to change the filter. This would mean the new filter has enough life in it to last through to when we get home. A cup of tea is served up and I'm shepherded to a seat to await the boss of the shop, who, I'm assured, speaks better English.

Nihat, the manager, turns out to be a friendly person, exuding the kind of knowledge that puts you immediately into the comfort zone;

he is indeed fluent in English, telling me that he's visited England many times, including one educational trip. He invites me into his office where we can discuss things in more detail. We sit there, me sipping my Turkish tea, he explaining that Endo Motors is shortly to become Ankara's first and only official Harley-Davidson dealership and already has an excellent workshop, staffed with very professional mechanics, not least because it runs a successful racing team in a series that is the Turkish equivalent of British Superbikes. They would be happy to carry out any work I require.

'Have you worked on BMW's before?' I venture to ask.

'Of course, all of the time. There is no BMW dealership here in Ankara, so we see lots of them. Come my friend, let me show you our workshop and we can have a look at the Harley-Davidson shop too. It's just down the road.'

Nestled in the impressive workshop are three race bikes, the nearest one an MV Agusta.

'Oh! You've got an MV!' I exclaim enthusiastically.

'Yeah, yeah. They're really useless. Way too complicated and a nightmare to maintain, just like Ducatis.' I refrain from mentioning my Monster 900 to him.

'Have you seen that new Panigale? Heap of rubbish! The engine is right in the middle of everything, you can't get to anything to service it. Takes hours to strip it down. But these… these are perfect,' he says pointing to the other two race bikes – Suzuki GSXR 600s. Yeah, but the MV looks a million dollars…

We head down the road to a shop that already has its stock lined up in the showroom but is still in the final throes of being set up. There's a good spread of the 2012 Harley models within. On introduction to the shop manager, I ask him when he'll be opening.

'These Harleys are truly awful,' opines Nihat.

'I know, I have one at home,' I reply with a smile. 'It's like riding a tractor. I love it.'

'We're going to sell lots of them,' he admits. The shop manager smiles and chips in, 'Harleys are great!' Honour satisfied, we head back to the shop to make the final arrangements.

When I arrive back at the hotel to update the navigator on my successful tyre-sourcing mission, it transpires that I'm not the only one who's been busy. Diane has reconnoitered Cankaya and located a hair stylist shop a short distance from the hotel. She is mindful to let them carry out very urgent repair work on the inverse-badger-stripe disaster that was visited upon her locks back in Volgograd. We agree that this might be a good plan, with a bit of local shopping thrown in for good measure. In short, a predominantly girlie afternoon. The first one of the trip.

***

In the evening, we dine out at the restaurant we frequented last night, greeted by the same tall, rangy waiter, who treats us very cordially. Earlier in the afternoon, we walked into the hair stylists, run by a young couple. They gave Diane a booking, leaving us time to wander around the shops and, in my case, to buy a pair of sheer silky socks from a street vendor, so thin that they almost look like cut-off black ladies stockings, clearly designed for comfort in hot weather and not at all feminine. Honest. Then, with Diane safely ensconced in a comfortable chair, the hair stylist went to work, expertly removing any trace of the debacle that went before. The couple were genuinely pleasant, questioning about our journey so far, and informing us that it was a new business and how hopeful they were to make a success of it.

Over dinner, it becomes obvious that Diane's initial doubts about Turkey are softening.

'I read a post today on the internet about a western woman who lives and works here,' she tells me. 'She said that there are downsides, but there are also many upsides too – she finds she's treated with respect and says the streets are entirely safe to walk through alone, even at night.'

I can believe that. Today, we've only been met by genuine kindness, not least by the waiter here in the restaurant. It's taken a couple of days, and we've had the odd bad experience, but I think we're warming to Turkey – there's a lot of things that feel good about the place, especially here in Ankara. Diane is very impressive in her openness. She's devoid of preconceptions on just about anything you care to mention. I think her upbringing as a child in Africa has a lot to do with it. It seems to have equipped her to take on the world as she finds it and to be neither surprised, or too offended, when things aren't what you'd expect them to be. Filthy showers and poo-daubed toilets notwithstanding.

In this respect, she's a perfect travelling companion. I feel safe with her around. I know she'll stick up for herself if the need arises and I know she'll stick up for me. Despite our differences, of which there are many, we work well as a team out on the road, supporting each other, often annoyed by each other, but always there for each other. She puts up with my grumpiness when I get lost, or things aren't going to plan, I put up with our late departures and her minute attention to detail, which make me grumpy. It has a certain symbiotic balance to it.

***

One interesting event – at least, it was interesting to me – occurred just before I left the Endo motorcycle shop yesterday. A fair-haired Scandinavian visitor arrived for a meeting with Nihat. It turned out that he was the European Sales Director for Öhlins suspension. He'd taken a studious peek around the Mutt, parked up outside the shop. Nihat informed him that we'd ridden north to south through Russia.

'I see you're running the original BMW suspension on the bike. How did that fare in Russia?' he asked.

I replied that, in the words of the Norwegian football pundit Bjorge Lillelien, my suspension had taken 'one hell of a beating' and was now feeling decidedly second-hand. At well over 40,000 miles, it seems that the suspension has reached the end of its useful life.

'They normally need to be changed around the 40,000 mile mark,' he commented, adding that a replacement set of Öhlins wouldn't cost that much more than the original equipment BMW shocks – a well-placed sales pitch from a seasoned professional, although, in fairness, I'd already started thinking that the suspension must be upgraded if we go any further east, after this trip. I left the shop dreaming of nice, shiny yellow-and-gold Öhlins.

We're heading northwards then eastwards today, riding up to the Black Sea and then hanging a right – to avoid getting wet – and following the coastline all the way to Georgia. I'm expecting to take two days to get there. We should arrive back in Ankara in about ten days. Nihat has asked for a few days' notice so he can order in the tyres. Having wended our way back to the ring road, we take a left and ride the near-deserted motorway under a clear blue sky, past modern, attractive suburbs that nestle in the hills that surround the city. When we return here, we'll spend a bit of time getting to know the city centre, but today we can bask in some seriously attractive views as the road snakes its way through the dry hills north of Ankara.

The road we're travelling along is thoroughly modern and the route very well signposted, passing over semi-arid plains, then carving through low hills. Higher ranges of hills follow our route, slate grey and blue on the horizon. We flash past roadside markets at regular intervals, each selling bright yellow melons and earthenware pottery, proudly flying the Turkish flag. We occasionally pass through towns, without stopping. At one point, we pass what is probably the largest flag I've ever seen, gently straining the enormous flagpole that bears it aloft, gracefully billowing in furls and folds in perpetual slow motion. The Turks rival the Danes in the flag-waving department. They might not quite rival them in quantity, but they certainly make up for it in size.

We pull into a petrol station early into the afternoon, seeking a quick top-up for the bike and a light bite of food for rider and pillion. Our chosen stopping point is a small, nondescript town that looks like most of the others we've passed by today: salmon and buff apartment blocks, houses with deep pantile roofs and the odd retail outlet on the high street. A common sight, on the outskirts of such towns here in the rural heartlands, is a machinery vendor selling either tractors or vans. Being a van man myself, I'm very pleased to see that the Turks like their white vans – proud members of the brotherhood of vans.

We top up the bike and then look around to see if we can find somewhere to eat. Apart from the young guy in the petrol station, the whole town seems deserted, much like our experience a couple of days ago in Kirklareli. An older gent appears and wanders over to us. He asks us if we would like refreshments. We tell him that we're looking for somewhere to buy a coffee and perhaps something to eat.

'You don't need to buy coffee, please take one with me – as guests visiting our country.'

He disappears off and presently returns with tea, coffee and biscuits, asking us to sit down at a table and chairs in the shade.

'I used to be a teacher in this town for many years, teaching history. But now that I'm retired, I work here at the gas station.'

He asks us what we think of Turkey. We tell him that we've only recently arrived, and that we find it to be very beautiful.

He asks me if we have a map. We hand him our paper map, purchased at our first stop in Turkey on the road to Istanbul. He spreads it out on the table and studies it closely. Eventually he points to a spot on the map and says, 'we are here, this is our town.' He then traces his finger to a point some miles to the south east of where we are.

'This is a very famous place, a shrine on a hill. I can recommend it to you if you have time to go there.' It's difficult. We don't have time to make such a diversion, but I tell him we may get a chance to visit it when we pass back this way. And then, almost as soon as the conversation started, he says that unfortunately he must return to work.

'There is no hurry. Enjoy your tea and coffee and welcome to Turkey. We have a tradition of welcoming strangers.'

$$***$$

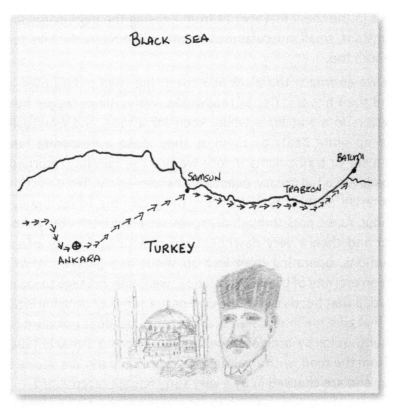

The northern coast of Turkey.

Our road-riding routine has now become almost second nature. A typical day involves travelling around 250 miles or so, often along roads that permit an average of 40 or 50 miles per hour. The only stops we take are for petrol or food and we only eat a proper meal if we can find a roadside café at the right time, which has been quite a rare event. The rest of the time is taken riding and enjoying the views. Diane enjoys shooting photos from the back of the bike, resulting in the gradual building of a pictorial library detailing the experience of long-distance motorcycle travel – something I was unable to achieve riding solo in America back in 2009. One of the big differences from that trip is the effect of averaging around 250 miles a day, day-in, day-out. In America, I found that I suffered from an increasingly painful back, the result of having strained my back muscles in the run-up to departure. All my aches and pains have disappeared on this trip, apart from the arthritis in the toe. I feel very fit from heaving the bags every day, and the constant, small muscular movements when riding the bike seem to contribute too.

As we approach the Black Sea coast, the road passes over a high hill and then hits a series of roadworks. We've been tagged by some youngsters in a Fiat for a while, keen for a race, and eventually get carved up quite badly by them as they make a desperate lunge to reach a set of traffic lights before we do. The rain has returned, and the roads are a tad greasy, eventually becoming snarled up with traffic as we arrive at the city of Samsun, bang on time to hit the evening rush hour. As we pass through the town, we encounter a busy shopping district and then a very downbeat street with businesses of varying descriptions, operating from lock-up shops and garages. After what seems an eternity of traffic negotiation, we finally manage to locate the coast road that heads out of the city, past a series of outlying industrial areas that give the impression that the town just does *not* want to end. And here, quite by accident, we happen across a sizeable hotel, set back from the road, with an almost deserted car park. We decide to call it a day and are checked in by a very surly female receptionist.

The city of Samsun, which sits a few hundred miles along the Black Sea coast, has a population of around half a million and a history going back to the Bronze Age. The original settlement had a role in the spread of Christianity, having a sizeable population of the Jewish diaspora that were important in the very early transmission of the religion. A careful study of the map reveals that we are well on the way to Georgia, yet have quite a long haul before we reach the border at the Georgian town of Batumi. I'm hopeful that we can cover the distance tomorrow, but it will be a long day's ride. A slightly less optimistic target would be to find somewhere to stay near the border and cross over the day after tomorrow. As we sip a beer with our meal next to the rather luxurious pool, nibbled occasionally by the odd mosquito, we can allow ourselves a wee pat on the back that we've made it this far. Our trip objective, the border of Azerbaijan, is starting to appear tantalizingly close.

***

The morning ushers in ominously dark clouds on the horizon and the whiff of precipitation flavours the air. Our initial departure is dry. We ride along the coast road, which is mainly built up with a long, thin line of buildings interspersed with greenery. Small towns appear at regular intervals, then the occasional larger one as the coastline becomes increasingly hilly, the foothills of a more mountainous region just a few miles inland. The towns are heavily built-up with a mixture of low-rise apartment blocks, shops, offices and the occasional Mosque and football stadium. These are seaside towns, with beaches and pleasant blocks of park alongside the road. The morning traffic is heavy. The rain soon arrives and gradually becomes more persistent.

It quickly becomes apparent that this area is more religiously traditional than the big cities of Istanbul and Ankara. We see a lot of minibuses bearing the words 'Allah Korusun', which I wistfully imagine to mean: 'God's Taxi', but which really means 'May God protect you'. The mosques that we pass are often very simple, sometimes grafted onto other buildings. Others sit in splendid isolation, with bright blue-tiled domes, nestling in the green hillsides. Progress would be good, despite the rain, if it wasn't adversely affected by the regular crawl through the towns. We stop at a local shop to buy a snack for lunch and are greeted very warmly by the occupants.

As morning passes into the early afternoon, the effect of riding through the rain becomes tiring and arduous. A regular check on the map confirms that we are crawling along the coast like an asthmatic snail, eventually reaching the sizeable city of Trabzon as the persistent rain turns into a bucketing downpour, the sky darkening almost completely. We ride through the city, scanning for accommodation and finally spot a hotel far below us as we ride along an elevated overpass, prompting us into a quick exit at a convenient slip-road.

Our prospective host is delighted to be booking in bearers of a foreign passport. 'This is a fine boutique hotel, very comfy, you will be delighted to stay here, my friend,' he declares, almost echoing the words of the receptionist in Ankara.

Neither of us are particularly convinced, the reception area doesn't inspire a gush of confidence. The hotel sits below the overpass and borders the busy junction, which is becoming increasingly blocked by the early rush hour, signaled by the constant use of vehicle horns blaring out in the downpour. We're booking in at the same time as an Iranian family who are unceremoniously told to move their car so that I can park the bike under one of the front reception office windows; the friction created is palpable between the hotel owner and the Iranian father. The hotel has a very small footprint, made up for by stacking its cramped rooms over a number of floors. We share the lift with the disgruntled Iranians, arriving at our floor near the top of the hotel. Our room is a reminder of childhood times when we would visit older relatives or friends of the family and be ushered into the front 'posh' room. Often, these were furnished with sofas, chairs and china cabinets from circa 1930. I remember the hard, gravelly feel of the (not so) soft furniture and the slightly musty smell of those rooms. This one feels exactly like that. On the plus side, the view from the open window is terrific, peering down on the rain-sodden streets that sharply reflect the myriad neon signs and vibrant frontages of the shops and offices that sit directly opposite the hotel. We have arrived safely, and we are dry.

Trabzon. A city at the terminus of the Silk Road.

A little later, having settled into our faded room, we grab our brollies, don our Finnish wetsuit jackets, and wander the short distance into the town centre. The shops are still open and the city is busy. We do a round of window shopping, particularly admiring the bright gold on offer in the jewellery shops, then seek out a restaurant, settling for one in the Meydan – the city square – where we are served a delicious lamb shish kebab with salad. Riding in continuous rain is a pain, but the sparkle of reflected light in Trabzon after dark is a photographer's delight, a reminder that there truly is a silver lining in every cloud and a fitting end to what has been a difficult day's riding to this great old town, once a terminus of the ancient Silk Road and now a bustling and interesting place to visit, albeit for such a short window of time.

***

I'm confident that we will make the border today. It's still a considerable haul to get there, bearing in mind the interruption of more small towns along our route. On the plus side, the weather has improved. There's still the whiff of rain about, but things improve as we get under way, departing the hotel around 9am, passing under the elevated roadway that arches on its concrete pillars high above and turning left to join it, heading out of town. We've departed a little earlier than usual to allow us to reach the border at a reasonable hour, perhaps around midday, allowing plenty of time for the crossing, the hassles of a few days ago at the Bulgarian/Turkish border fresh in our minds.

The vista we pass through becomes increasingly hillier, with stately mountains visible close inland. While we were travelling yesterday, we started noticing long sheets of plastic and tarpaulins covering something on the roadside. Now that the rain has dispersed, the covers are being removed, revealing what look suspiciously like hazelnuts, spread out to dry in the sun – millions and millions of them in huge swathes laid out on protective sheets. Hazelnuts are produced from a small tree that prospers in favourable latitudes and climatic conditions, those grown along and inland from the Turkish Black Sea coast are amongst the finest in the world – so much so that Turkey produces 75% of the total global crop. The natural drying contributes to the rich taste of the nut.

I'm a big fan of hazelnuts and consume more than my own fair share of the global annual production.

Gradually, the towns with their hazelnuts and seafronts thin out as we approach the border. The road starts to gently snake 'twixt sea and towering pale cliffs and the unmistakable signs of an approaching border appear in the form of lorries that are backed up, waiting to cross. To our left, the occasional beaches have given way to a rocky shoreline. We pass through a tunnel bathed in orange electric light, closely followed by a large truck, arriving at the Turkish border to discover a hive of activity around the low white buildings. Queues of traffic wait patiently in lines, directed by men in uniforms. Diane climbs off the bike with considerable élan, a veritable Paula Radcliffe is she. The immaculately prepared document file is recovered from the top box as we prepare for our usual routine, only for it to be rudely interrupted by a short, rotund gentleman demanding our 'paperwork'. From this point, things start to go quite badly out of control. Mistaking him for an official, we hand over our passports.

Initially, we experience no problems. The passports are accepted along with the bike documents, I get the signal to pull up to the first cubicle and data is entered into a computer. The small, rotund one retrieves the paperwork and signals to me to drive to the next queue, indicating to Diane that she can walk over too. It's around this point that I have an inkling that this guy isn't entirely pukka. We head over, regardless, and remain stuck in a queue for a while. When we eventually reach the next cubicle, there is a great deal of confusion. Our 'guide' ends up engaged in something of a fracas with the official in the box and mutters 'is problem' to me, before heading back to the first box, leaving us in limbo, wondering what the hell is going on and more than a smidgen nervous.

It transpires that the man in the initial box failed to correctly type the bike's registration into the computer, which was read to him by the little guy. Once that minor data entry issue is sorted out, we're able to progress and eventually, after stopping at a third station for a spot of document stamping, we get waved through. The little fella appears, perspiring and a little agitated, demanding payment. I shrug and tell him we have no money. There's a short contretemps where I make plain to him that if he volunteered his services then, as far as I'm concerned, he did it for free. A heavy discount is offered in response and, after a bit of eyebrow raising along with the odd huff 'n puff, the much lower fee is miraculously located, hiding in my jacket pocket. Honour satisfied we part company reasonably amicably. Everyone has a living to make. Some need to feed families. But a lesson has also been absorbed. Only hand paperwork over to a proper official, or bona-fide hotel receptionists.

By contrast with Turkey, the border with Georgia is a haven of peace and serenity, staffed by smart people in uniforms who process us through in record time. We spill out of that border into a terminus that is fair thronged with people, some heading for Turkey, others arriving (like us) in Georgia and the rest waiting for people, or perhaps waiting to rip-off unsuspecting victims. There's a lot of milling around, especially around the shops which are carrying out a brisk trade selling, among other things, alcohol. We have landed back in Christendom, with just a small amount of Turkish money at our disposal. We need to find an ATM ASAP.

***

After a brief stop, pondering whether to try and locate an ATM right here, right now, we decide to press on into Batumi, thumbing the bike into life and heading down a badly broken road into town.

The rains that plagued us yesterday in Turkey clearly held no respect for borders. The road is liberally cratered with potholes, some very sizeable and all full to brimming with rainwater. The problem is that, in this state, it isn't possible to determine the depth of the potholes. Cars, vans, trucks and buses are all wisely lurching around their periphery to avoid any broken axles; we follow likewise. To our left lies the Black Sea, bordered by a varying jumble of properties, some of which are quite presentable, but the initial impression is one of serious under-investment and a decline in living standards, compared with those across the border in Turkey. The rough nature of the outlying areas of town are in stark juxtaposition to the massive building works ongoing in the centre of the city. Efforts are ongoing to make Batumi the 'Dubai' of the Caucasus region with huge high-rise developments going up left, right and centre. It is this part of the city that is widely advertised online, with barely a mention of the surrounding decrepitude.

Whilst cruising through this incongruous collection of misfit luxury, we spot a Radisson Blu hotel and decide to chance our luck there, reasoning that the price for a room back in Moscow was bordering reasonable, so one would expect to pay a little less here in Georgia and perhaps get a nice room, to boot. I wander into the cool, air-conditioned atrium at reception, for all the world looking like I've been lolling around in a light mud bath with a few bison for company over the past few days. Less than a minute later, I've surprised the receptionist with my reaction to the room price. A few people have joined the queue behind me, dressed in top-end designer wear, shades pulling back their hair and Gucci luggage at their sides, appearing vaguely Italian, most likely Russian.

'But that's three times what we paid for a room at the Radisson in Moscow just a few weeks ago.' I splutter. 'Why is it so expensive here in Batumi?'

'That is the price, sir.'

'Is there any room for negotiating a discount?' I reply, clutching at straws.

'I will consult with the day manager, sir,' the polite receptionist responds, heading off to an office and leaving me at the head of a mildly irritated queue.

He returns demurely, without any sign of looking down his nose at me, which I think is quite commendable.

'The manager says that we can show you a room and then if you would like to tell us what you think it is worth, we may consider your offer.'

Back at the bike, I realise that I've missed a golden opportunity. I was completely flummoxed by their offer and embarrassingly declined, withdrawing defeated, knowing that whatever I offered wouldn't come close to the asking price of the room. If I could just replay the tape, I would go up to inspect the room, tell them that it comes nowhere close to the luxury of our friends back in Transnistria and offer them Premier Inn prices (with breakfast), just for a laugh. We would get kicked out, but Lenny Henry would be very proud of us. Meantime, I have struck Radisson Blu from my recommendation list.

The next hotel we try looks far more promising, but we end up in the same position, having been quoted a ridiculous price. Fearing the worst, we plunge further into the older part of town which is appreciably rough and decidedly edgy. We pull over, having spotted an ATM sign, whereupon an old man sitting with his friends outside a line of shops points up the road and mouths the words, 'Tiblis, go now!' Despite what appears to be a dire warning, that has affected my passenger quite considerably – 'did you hear what he said to us?' – we can see another hotel, set back from the road. After grabbing some money from the ATM, we head back to the bike.

'I said: did you hear what that man said to us? I don't think it's safe here,' repeats Diane with some urgency in her voice.

'The thing is, it's getting quite late. Maybe it's best to find somewhere here, lock up the bike and hope for the best,' I reply, not fully convinced myself, if truth be told.

We pull the bike into the hotel car park. It's quite a modern building, built in the style and quality of a modern British house, perhaps cobbled together Barratt but, despite this, it does look clean inside. The price turns out to be extremely cheap and the room is ok, despite the flimsy and cheap furniture. The hotel owner, a portly, slightly balding man, who reminds me of Rene in the TV programme 'Allo Allo!', seems very keen to sign us in. After a brief debate, we decide to risk it and we unload the bike as quickly as possible, lock the steering, set the inbuilt alarm and attach the alarm disc lock before popping the cover over for good measure. I'm sure it will all be OK. There is a bonus: the hotel sits next to a large tin barn that, according to the hotel owner, houses a very good restaurant serving authentic Georgian cuisine.

After a wash and brush-up we wander over to the restaurant, to be met by a wall of noise as we walk through the door. A waitress shows us to one of the few available tables, serves us a litre carafe of the local red wine and takes our order. We then spend a bemused hour watching the antics of Georgian men under the influence of alcohol. It slowly dawns on me that the scraps of information I've picked up concerning the male of the species around here might hold some veracity. And then some. They're loaded to the gunwhales with testosterone, boisterous, loud and most likely aggressive when drunk, which this lot most certainly already are. It is also apparent that everything we've heard so far about Georgian wine is also true, it really is excellent. Georgians have been making wine much longer than anyone else – they invented it, so it shouldn't be a surprise.

Back at the hotel, we quickly realise that the night is not going to go well. Some of our fellow inmates are reeling around the place, worse for wear, in the company of loose women. We head for our room hoping to get some kip but, as the night progresses, the shenanigans increase, along with the volume, and we are kept awake until the later small hours of the morning.

Sunday 3rd September.

We arise early and head down for breakfast to be told by Rene, 'breakfast cancelled. No breakfast.'

I've not had much sleep and I'm not in a very good mood. I let him have one barrel.

'We've paid for breakfast and we expect to have one!'

This doesn't have the desired effect. He stares in despair across reception at a young guy who has collapsed on one of the settees, completely inebriated and dribbling from the side of his mouth. We head off upstairs in a huff to commence packing, meeting a drunken couple at the top of the stairs. The man is middle-aged and appears to be Turkish and the girl is, well, the girl is in her approximate mid-teens and presumably Georgian. The man looks away, but the girl meets our eyes and giggles. Her friend, roughly the same age, appears from a room, staggering drunkenly. It occurs to me that the hotel owner downstairs isn't being an arse. Rather he's justifiably distraught. He's probably put all his money into the place and just wants to run a normal two-star hotel attracting decent clientele, not a knocking-shop. And, to give him his due, it is nicely decorated and clean. Breakfast is cancelled because he wants to clear this lot out.

We commence departure procedure, to be met in reception once more by the hotel owner.

'We serve you breakfast. Eggs, now,' he blurts out apologetically. We're grateful for the gesture.

As we pull out of the car park an hour later, we both take a final glance at the hotel. The lady who served us the eggs was painfully embarrassed by the situation and fussed over us throughout our brief meal. Now she has taken a position at the tall window of the breakfast room, vacuum cleaner tube in one hand, watching us leave with a devastated expression on her face. As we look back, she raises her free arm and sadly, slowly, waves us goodbye. We return a sad wave in solidarity.

***

If I cast my mind back to the planning period before the trip, I recall hazily that Georgia is supposed to be covered in dense, primordial forest, clinging to the monumental slopes of the Caucasus Mountains. A BBC Radio 4 programme said so. So it must be true. Informed thus by Aunty Beeb, I'm fully expecting to plunge into the cool interior of just such a forest very soon. For the time being, we ride along the bay in a steamy heat, past railroad marshalling yards packed with long lines of aged petroleum wagons, then under a banner proclaiming to all and sundry that: 'In five years Batumi will be the best city in the world. Donald Trump.' Hope springs eternal.

The road starts to climb in a most entertaining fashion, a series of curves follow the contours of a steep hill rising high above the Black Sea through what appears to be a verdant, semi-tropical mixture of wooded hillsides, dotted with fine houses with rich green gardens. Is this the BBC's forest? We find ourselves leading a long snake of cars, meeting an articulated truck halfway up, grinding its gears and struggling to maintain momentum, belching clouds of black diesel soot. There's no way past, the roads are too busy and the corners too tight. We sit behind, slipping the clutch and wincing with mechanical sympathy at its heroic efforts to get us to the top before it sets itself on fire.

The tropical feel of the place proves to be just the merest tease, wafted in front of us and then rudely snatched away once the road has plunged from upon high, down to the lower altitudes below. Here, we discover fields and a scattering of small villages and towns with a slightly more 'normal' appearance. Post-Soviet driving normality is also resumed with an increase in the tempo of lunacy from the drivers of accompanying cars, displaying a determination to overtake us only rivalled by the Russians driving through Crimea to Yalta, a couple of weeks ago. As with their Russian ex-rulers, Georgians drive like Italians, though with much higher testosterone levels. After a while, we arrive at an important road junction, a surprisingly well signposted right turn that must not be missed if you wish to avoid more troubled areas further north. In something close to a miracle, we avoid getting lost and, with confidence rising, we plunge into Georgia proper, running headlong into a rather fascinating country.

***

The initial impression is one of pleasant, low-lying countryside dotted with towns and villages, all of which appear to be modest in wealth and well-being. The roads are quite poor, especially in the towns, where they descend to the level of a series of water-filled potholes, attesting to the fact that it rained quite heavily again last night. In one of the larger settlements, the road signs for Tblisi become less prevalent and we manage to take a few wrong turns, only realising our mistake when the road peters out to nothing. All of which makes progress a fraught affair.

Once out of town, we approach a rural railway crossing and join a short queue of cars and vans preparing to make their way across. Clearly there is a rule to be followed. Only one vehicle is permitted to cross at any one time. Presumably this limits the death rate at such crossings, which does have potential to be high because the road has all but disintegrated in the section through which the track crosses, increasing the possibility of getting stuck at a critical moment. The resulting monumental ruts cause the vehicles to lurch drunkenly on their way across. I really should have attended the off-road riding course!

We notice a small café-cum-corner-shop on the far side of the tracks and decide to grab a lunchtime snack, then sit at a table outside to witness proceedings at the crossing, in the hope that a train might pass by, whilst being entertained by a feral pig as he grubs his way around the bike, searching for tasty morsels. Before long, a train does arrive, and we manage to wander over to the railway line and take photos of the big green monster that clanks its way past. By the time the crossing has re-opened, we're togging up in our riding gear and preparing to leave.

Then a motorcycle suddenly appears, deftly negotiating the ruts on the crossing before sweeping over next to us, braking to a halt in a cloud of dust. The rider kicks down his side stand and deftly leaps from the machine, a brand-spanking-new Yamaha XT1200 Super Tenere. In a brief whirlwind of a conversation, he explains to us (in English) that he is Russian and has just spent a few days on the beach at Batumi. He lives in Grozny. Would we like to visit Grozny? We would be welcome there. Grozny is now a very fine, modern city and very safe. We could – and indeed should – take the road to the north through the mountains and then visit him there. The road is very beautiful, the city is really very, very safe.

Thankfully, I'm able to explain that we have used up all our visa days for Russia, indeed that we only had single entry visas and that, whilst we would love to visit Chechnya, and would particularly like to visit Grozny, we are simply unable to do so this time around and sadly have to press on to Tblisi. At which point he shrugs, wishes us well with a warm, vigorous handshake, leaps on his bike and is off in a cloud of dust to the tuneful thrum of a well-silenced parallel twin-cylinder Japanese machine. If I blink, it's almost as if it never happened at all. It feels like we've just met Rik Mayall's character Lord Flashheart in the TV comedy series 'Blackadder'. The only difference being that he didn't sweep my partner off her feet, throw her on the back of the bike and roar off to Chechnya with her. And her name isn't Bob.

***

The encounter with the foraging pig was just the start of an increasingly bizarre menagerie found on the roadsides of Georgia, as we pass into increasingly remote areas that exist in the vast, broad valley that makes up a significant part of the country. The topography has become hilly, the road snaking around in quite an entertaining fashion, the villages having a more rural feel. The post-medieval concept of containing animals in fields or pens hasn't quite caught on in this part of Georgia. What appears to be the entire farmyard stock lives right on the edge of the main road to Tblisi. It's a high-risk existence, no doubt with an element of Darwinian selection involved, with the added bonus of occasionally avoiding slaughterhouse costs.

The cattle seem to have honed their roadside common-sense to an impressively fine degree. In one incident, whilst following a truck on the approach to a village, we catch a glimpse of a cow that has turned roadside living to its advantage, with an astonishingly risky strategy. As we flash past at fifty miles per hour, we notice it standing there, with its neck outstretched so far that the lorry in front passes inches from its nose (and so do we, much to our alarm). It's so bizarre that it takes me a few hundred yards to work out that it's a strategy for avoiding pesky flies. Even the reindeer of Finland haven't worked that one out yet, or perhaps they're just more safety conscious. After all, they are Scandinavians.

The goats have gone one stage further than the cows and upped the game. A little further on from the air-blown cow, in the same village, a line of Billy-Boy-Gruffs make full use of a pedestrian crossing to relocate to pastures new, all without the assistance of a herdsman or woman. By the evidence of animal remains left on the road, two species have failed to develop the necessary skills for survival: chickens and, surprisingly, pigs. I think we all knew that chickens are pretty stupid and fodder for any major trunk road if left to their own devices, having a well-known tendency to cross the road at any opportunity, but it comes as a surprise that pigs are equally daft. It's a worry when you're riding a motorcycle. An altercation with a fully-grown porker (average weight anything between 300 and 600lbs) is guaranteed to *really* ruin your day. Even in a car. Does this sobering thought slow the average Georgian driver down? No! Not a bit of it. Pigs be damned.

***

To the mid-point in the trip.

If you observe a topographical map of Georgia, you'll no doubt recognise a few key features very quickly. Firstly, it isn't very big. The distance from the Black Sea to the border with Azerbaijan is just over 450 Kilometres. Depending on the traffic, you could probably ride it in a day. It sits at 120th in the world table of countries by size at 69,000 square kilometres and 133rd in terms of population with around 3.9 million souls present. What is very apparent from the seat of the bike is that: a) it's a very beautiful country and b) it does indeed mostly comprise of a huge valley in the middle, on an east-west axis, with mountains to the north and the south. As we make our way towards Tblisi, we find that we've arrived at a third feature: the hills kind of meet in the middle the

303

further east you go. We have witnessed no forests of any significance at all, but it is all very green and rather beautiful. Nevertheless, I'm now convinced that the aforementioned BBC 'foreign' correspondent posted their article from the comfort of a front room in a house in Epping. Either that, or they were habitually taking recreational drugs. Possibly both. I'm starting to realise that the BBC view of the world is wrapped up in a faintly xenophobic dressing and often lazily reported.

The frequency of roadside livestock reduces drastically when we arrive at one of the major towns, home to a fabulous, ancient steel mill that has fallen into disrepair in a most photogenic fashion. Riding further into the town, it appears that, following the decline of the steelworks, the main product of manufacture became the humble deckchair – they're lined up in colourful rows along the roadside, pending sale.

We also start to come across groups of people attending political rallies, 2012 being an election year. There's a festival feeling to the whole event. The incumbent president and party moved the country significantly towards the west, courting NATO and the EU, much to the consternation of the Russians. Rebellion erupted in two areas that wished to remain pro-Russian and, on the pretext that violence had broken out, the Russians invaded in 2008. A brief, very one-sided war ensued, with more-or-less inevitable results. The lands of South Ossetia and Abkahazia became separatist states under Russian protection. Abkahazia sits by the Black Sea, on the north-eastern tip of Georgia and South Ossetia is located in the centre of Georgia, extending from the mountains down to very near the central city of Gori. Suddenly, things that back home seemed vague, such as: why couldn't we follow the Black Sea coast into Georgia from Russia (?), are now starting to make sense.

As we approach the town of Gori, famous for being the birthplace of one Joseph Stalin, we manage to spend a pleasant few minutes riding along a stretch of exceptional, brand-new motorway. It triggers a thought that the rest of the journey might speed up, and we could even be in Tblisi in time for an early evening meal. Such thoughts are rudely cast aside when the traffic grinds to a sudden halt and is diverted off the new blacktop and onto more rustic by-ways heading right through the middle of the town, which is largely made up of older buildings, ones the young Joseph must have known very well. Stalin, real name Iosif Vissarionovich Dzhugashvili didn't spend too long here, leaving around the age of fifteen to attend Seminary in Tblisi, already equipped with a reputation as a street fighter. Stalin means 'of steel', one of the hard-edged noms de guerre favoured by the Bolsheviks at a time when it paid to be secretive. Strange then, that he was originally destined for the priesthood and was an accomplished traditional Georgian poet before he found his true path in life.

It takes a while to negotiate the streets of Gori but we eventually manage to shake free of it and hit the final quarter of our journey to the capital, the last part of which is covered on a very modern four lane road that whistles us at speed through the valley, with the Caucasus Mountains rising across the horizon to our left. We pass a huge settlement built in the lee of the mountains for refugees displaced from nearby South Ossetia during the war, housed in long lines of semi-permanent prefabricated cabins, a stark reminder of the human cost of ethnic cleansing. A strange thought occurs to me that this must be one of the most scenic refugee camps in the whole wide world. At a brief roadside pause, we are passed by a Suzuki GSXR sports motorcycle travelling flat out, throttle pinned and the engine no doubt nudging the rev limiter, the rider huddled behind the fairing, taking full advantage of one of the few decent stretches of road this side of Turkey or Japan. Estimated speed 160mph. He'll easily make it to Tblisi by tea time. Free range cows permitting.

Gradually, the road eases round to the right as the traffic increases and slowly starts to clump together. We pass over a wild and dramatic river 'twixt tall dry hills, beneath the gaze of a lonely monastery, high above. And then the outer limits of Tblisi appear and we find ourselves negotiating the thick end of an evening rush hour, following the river on our left as we pass through a commercial district and then into the city proper.

Quite by chance, a hotel crops up on our right, optimistically called the 'Golden Palace'. It looks a modern place, with a sharp-edged style involving plenty of glass frontage. We pull in to check it out.

The young lady on reception speaks very good English. After the shambles in Batumi, I'm half expecting to require smelling salts when the price is declared and almost do a double-take when we are offered an entirely reasonable rate. Perhaps there's a catch. We could ask to inspect the rooms, but we take the plunge and check ourselves in for three nights. Following already well-laid plans, this should allow us to execute a spot of tourism over the next couple of days, along with motorcycle servicing on day two, hotel permissions withstanding. The receptionist directs me to park around the rear of the hotel in a sizeable walled back yard, guarded by a tough-looking man with a little hut in the corner. The room is large, well-furnished and immaculate.

The Golden Palace echoes the administrative experience we enjoyed in the Hotel Volgograd. Before we departed reception to head for our room, the receptionist picked up a walkie-talkie and radioed ahead that we were on our way, directing us to the large lifts along the end of the hall beyond the reception desk. We then found ourselves being greeted on the second floor by a short-haired young lady behind a counter of impressive length who, it transpired, was the 'Floor Administrator'. She is there to ensure that everything runs like clockwork. After settling in the room, I pop out to her desk and ask if it will be possible for me to service my motorcycle tomorrow morning, promising not to tarnish the yard with oil spills. After a couple of radio conversations, she confirms that permission has been granted. The guard will be informed. Most likely by walkie-talkie.

This officialdom is an echo of past Soviet days, something that I find quite endearing. It's rarely overbearing, and it adds to a sense of security and order. That, and the spacious, comfortable room help to apply balm to tired, frayed nerves. We are in desperate need of a nice, long sleep in a comfortable bed, followed by a decent morning lie-in; and the Palace offers both.

The next morning dawns fine and bright. After leaving it to the last minute before partaking of breakfast, we order a taxi to take us into town. The receptionist asks if it would be possible to take a lift into town with us, something we readily agree to. The taxi arrives very promptly – it turns out he was parked up around the corner. The driver is a brusque man in his late forties, but that changes once the girl from reception strikes up a conversation with him and he turns into quite a jovial soul. On the way into town, she explains that she has just finished a twenty-four hour stint at the hotel and is now on her way to her second job as a teacher. I'm gobsmacked – I think we both are.

'So, when are you back on duty at the hotel?' I ask.

'I arrive back at work in the hotel on Wednesday,' she replies. 'I will have a rest tomorrow, then I work twenty-four hours up to Thursday, when I will go back to work teaching.' Good grief!

The traffic in town is heavy. The road has multiple lanes that merge into each other with a thronging mass of vehicles, all jostling for a place, horns pipping, the odd hand signal being gesticulated. It reminds me of the roundabout in St Petersburg, with the exception that there are no officers of the law to be seen. Mindful that we will need to negotiate our way through this in a couple of days' time, I pay particular attention to the road conditions and the route, which follows the river all the way into town. Once there, the driver deposits us at a convenient place in a large square, surrounded by grand old buildings. From there, it's a short walk into the old city along a series of narrow streets, passing by an eclectic mix of different styles of buildings, many of which betray signs of significant age and minimal maintenance.

The reason for the heady amalgam of architectural styles is due to Tblisi's geographic position, situated at the western end of the Silk Road, whilst also having being closely tied to Russia over the years. The result is exotic. Down near the old centre, the river carves its way into town in a most dramatic fashion, cutting through the hills to form a deep gorge. The buildings, clinging to the top of the gorge, appear mysterious and alien to European eyes. A large castle, with a broad mantle of curtain wall dominates the towering hill to the south of the river, high above the old part of the city.

The district across the river is relatively modern. A new park complex is being built there with futuristic structures and attractive open spaces. The park is the terminus for a thoroughly modern cable car that ascends the heights all the way up to the castle, crossing the river on its journey. We take a ride up. Here, the brave can wander around and climb up onto the precipice-like walls via impossibly steep steps, with a total disregard for safety, peering over the abyss with churning stomachs, no doubt feeling quite sick and probably experiencing the faintest of desires to jump.

Sightseeing, Georgian style. The lady caught me taking the photo and flashed this lovely smile.

***

Today is a fine day for motorcycle maintenance. Before commencing work, I make sure that I've laid out plenty of paper to catch any errant oil drips. I'm not planning to change the oil, just to check and adjust the valve clearances, to balance the fuel injection throttle bodies, and to change the spark plugs. In addition to this, I'll check the tyres and bearings, the brake pads and the fluids, just to give everything a thorough look over.

I've practiced doing these jobs quite a few times, using the tools in the toolkit. There are a couple of special tools to be used for the throttle bodies: a vacuum gauge and a diagnostic tool called a 'GS 911'. I think it will take an hour and a half at my pace. A skilled mechanic would complete it in a fraction of that time. There's a possibility that the valve cover gaskets will need replacing, once they've been removed. I have a spare set ready if this becomes the case. I also have some spare engine oil in case that needs topping up too.

Before getting into the meat of the job, I do a thorough clean of the bike and check the state of the spare gaskets, then, after setting the throttle bodies using a combination of the diagnostic tool and my laptop, it's off with the valve cover. The trickiest part of the job is safely removing the spark plugs, which are difficult to get to, being very deep inside the cover. A special tool is required to remove the spark plug lead, which incorporates the coil. Failing that, you can use a common-or-garden flat-bladed screwdriver, but it isn't recommended. Following the instructions in the oil stained and dog-eared maintenance manual, I carefully find the correct piston position and check the valve clearances, using a trick found on YouTube to adjust both inlet and exhaust valve clearances at the same time, thereby ensuring that they are exactly correct. I always spend a lot of time checking and re-checking everything.

Once everything is back together, I flick on the ignition, hearing the fuel pump prime a fresh slug of juice along the fuel lines. Thumbing the starter button leads to the welcome sound of the trademark Mutley chuckle, and the engine bursts instantly into life. There's a modest rattle from the general area of the clutch that has been around for quite a few miles; I can't quite remember when it started. It disappears when the clutch is pulled in, so I reason that it might be to do with some kind of clutch wear. It isn't particularly pronounced and my BMW R1150 'hack' back home does it far more loudly, so I'm fairly relaxed about it, but take a mental note all the same to mention it to Woolastons when I get back home. I bought the R1150 as my general runaround and to use as a maintenance practice mule. I've had to repair quite a few things on it and, since many of the parts are more or less the same as those on the Mutley, I've learned a lot of valuable lessons in the process. The job seems to have gone well and I think the bike is ready for the ride to the Azerbaijan border, then back to Ankara where it will get new tyres and an oil change. Then it should be in fine fettle for the ride back home.

Back at the hotel room, I report to the boss that all is fine and dandy. We have plenty of time for a taxi ride (same driver, now very chatty) into the city centre to grab a bite to eat and do a bit of souvenir shopping. We explore the shops in the old quarter and settle for a different restaurant from the one we ate at yesterday, settling for a steak sandwich with salad trimmings, flushed down by local red wine.

Half an hour later, on the walk back to the taxi rank in the square, I realise that all is not well in the plumbing department. We just about make it back to the hotel, whereupon the dash to the toilet becomes a desperate race against time, barging through reception, responding to the cheerful 'hello' from the receptionist by squeaking over my shoulder and praying in the lift for the second floor to make an appearance RIGHT NOW! The floor administrator gets the briefest sight of me as I whistle past towards our room, Diane labouring breathlessly in tow, buttocks clenched tightly (mine, not hers). In days of old, we had a fitting slang description in the oil industry for what happens next: I suffer a major, catastrophic 'mud out'.

⋯⋯◆⟨▷⟩◆⋯⋯

Chapter 26
The Furthest Point East

As surely as Socrates was administered hemlock, I too have been poisoned. Suspicion rests with the limp lettuce leaves that caressed a slightly overcooked sliver of steak nestling between two slices of bread. I almost regret the tip left on the table but, in fairness, the waitress probably wasn't at fault. More likely, the blow was delivered by the scruffy herb in chef's attire who leaned on the door of the kitchen having a fag. I distinctly recall him having a smirk on his face and I'm paranoid enough to ponder whether the whole thing was personal. On all my travels to date, I've been operating under the apprehension that I'm blessed with an iron constitution. No more the fool.

Diane has, thankfully, avoided the same fate. Quite why is a mystery because we both ate the same meal. We always eat the same meal. Diane has a habit of always picking the same thing that I do. Sometimes I try to trick her, but it rarely works. When you think about it, it would be far more sensible for us to never eat the same meal. We head down for a late meal at the hotel restaurant, but it takes only a few minutes for me to need to head back to the sanctuary of the bathroom.

What follows confirms my worst fears. I've contracted a very severe dose of food poisoning and spend the whole night to-ing and fro-ing to the loo, wracked with bouts of dysentery and vomiting. As the cold light of dawn gradually filters into our room, it becomes apparent that recovery won't happen today, and probably no time soon, so I decide not to eat any more and only to take fluids onboard. To make matters even worse, we realise that we've failed to pack any Imodium or salts, a glaring failure in the pre-departure stocking of our first aid kit (which, in other respects is commendably complete). Make note to oneself: pack Imodium for the next trip. Three 50kg-sized sacks of it.

The lack of eating does have some effect and, thankfully, I think we might be able to make it to our planned destination today. We're not exactly sure where that is, except that it is 'somewhere near the border'. The border with Azerbaijan, to be a bit more precise. We'll ride out there and see what can be found in the way of accommodation. If emergencies crop up, we have plenty of loo roll and I'm comforted in the knowledge that there will be bushes aplenty (in a country as green and beautiful as this). Other than that, the basic plan is to just drink diet Coke all day (Diane has the feeling that it is beneficial, especially if it is consumed flat – meaning no bubbles, not flat on your back). By the time I've packed the bike, paid a few final visits to the loo and paid the bill, I feel as though things are under control. But I do feel a bit wobbly.

This decision may, on the face of it, seem a bit stupid. Why not sit it out at the Golden Palace? I have no answer to that question. I seem to be possessed with an obsessive determination to keep moving – bordering on the insane. We've planned three days over by the border and have reserved a room back in Tblisi for one night after that. I hope to recover long before then.

Having said goodbye to the nice receptionist and administrator ladies, who are both back for another twenty-four-hour stint, we pull out of the hotel into the busy stream of traffic, heading towards the city centre. The traffic is manic. We progress carefully, picking our way through the lanes, trying to look obvious in our intent. It's quite similar to Russian traffic. The drivers do make allowances if you're clear where you want to go. Having located the bridge over the river, we start to make our way to our first objective: the airport, our initial waypoint on the route out to the east of the country. God seems to have decided to take mercy on me in my current state of debilitation, ensuring we don't get lost and go around in circles for a few hours. Before long, we've shaken off the city and the airport and have passed into pleasant, rolling countryside that tracks the mountains heading eastwards. At the same time, the traffic has thinned out and we're able to relax a little and enjoy the journey, in company with the occasional roaming herd of cows. The distance to be covered is less than sixty miles, but road conditions, which are best described as 'variable, occasionally farmyard', mean that it takes us a couple of hours to arrive in the general locale of our destination, the small town of Sighnaghi.

We took advice from the ladies back at the hotel about where best to spend a few days in deepest Georgia. One strong recommendation, the name of which I never quite managed to understand, is apparently situated in the high hills to the south. When I asked about the east, Sighnaghi was very highly recommended. Apparently, it is very popular with westerners, mainly walkers and, hopefully, not too many of them. They were certain that we would find accommodation there. We've followed the main road from Tblisi to a village called Chalaubani, which is notable for having a very smart, modern police station, conveniently situated at the turn-off to Sighnaghi.

A right turn at the police station takes us up into the hills. The road is sinuous, occasionally rutted, and quite delightful. When we arrive in Sighnaghi, we find it to be a hidden treasure – a small town, too sizeable to be considered a village. The centre consists of a long street that climbs up a hill with an elongated, attractive square sitting three-quarters of the way up. The buildings are predominantly built of stone, capped by red-tiled roofs. Some houses have ornate wooden balconies clinging to them in a Shakespearian fashion. In fact, you could almost imagine you've arrived at an Italian town, high on a hill, somewhere in the Apennine Mountains. It is a truly wonderful place.

In no time at all we find a hotel. It's situated on the steep street, right in the centre of town. Having parked up on the cobbled street outside, I pop in to see if they have a room, climbing a few steps into a room that is part reception, part office and part living room. The owner of the hotel is sitting at a computer towards the back of the room, a man in his forties with a friendly personality who speaks excellent English. He confirms that they have plenty of room and we can have one of their best rooms. The general feel and décor of the place is so good that we decamp there and then, without any further ado. Needing the loo also has some bearing on the indecent haste taken to close the transaction.

I feel decidedly wretched. I hope to be able to finish the ride to the border tomorrow but, failing that, I'll have to confine myself to the room. The symptoms have become slightly worse and I'm suffering from severe cramps. We've booked up for two nights and have studied the maps. The final town before the border is called Lagodekhi. From there, it looks like we can ride a circular route, heading back into Georgia to the mountains, then back to Sighnaghi. There's a small town up there called Kvareli, so I think we'll make that our first stop after we've visited the border. Depending on timings, we could then ride a bit further along the mountains or just return to Sighnaghi. But that's all for tomorrow. In the here and now, one of us needs to eat. Time is getting on, so we decide to stick to the hotel restaurant, which is situated a couple of floors down from our room.

The layout of the hotel is quite unusual. From the street, it looks like a single storey building but, once inside, you find that there are rooms upstairs from the elevated reception, and a restaurant on a ground floor that must exist below street level. Basically, it only makes sense once you realise that it is built into the hillside. It has to be said that our room is fab. It has wooden floors, bare brick walls and a very trendy eclectic mix of furniture.

For some reason, that frankly defies explanation, I decide to order something to eat. I think I want to believe that my constitution will save me, so I order a Caesar salad, which, when it arrives, turns out to be quite an odd variation on the theme. Is everyone out to kill me? Why am I aiding and abetting them? I suffer for my idiocy by spending an even worse night, flitting twixt bed and toilette, disturbing my partner with moans, wailing and woe. When I look in the mirror around 4:30 a.m., I notice that I resemble Yoda. I struggle back to the bed in typical Yoda manner, albeit without the staff, then, shortly after, find myself having to leap up and bound to the loo with the speed and dexterity he displays when called upon to flash his light sabre in the general direction of a Sith. I don't suffer illness very well. I'm a bloke.

***

Diane awakes in the sultry heat of the early morning, feeling extremely tired, following a long night of disturbance. I don't wake up – on account of not having ever been asleep. We struggle down to breakfast where I manage to consume a cup of coffee. The salad last night was a huge mistake. It has led to a cast iron resolve not to eat anything at all today. The good news is that I think I can manage the ride out to the border. I don't want food poisoning to ruin a crucial part of the trip.

Once out on the bike, riding in the heat of a very beautiful day, it feels great, despite the trots. Reasons to be cheerful: well, firstly the bike isn't carrying its normal load of baggage or major tools, so riding it is an effortless joy. Secondly, we are enjoying very pleasant, late summer weather. And finally, the area around Sighnaghi, and indeed the town itself – well, both of those are amazing. To the east, below the heights upon which the town is built, lies a vast and mysterious plain, shimmering in the late morning haze. And to the north lie the mountains proper – a steeply impressive wall, beyond which lies the troubled Russian republic of Dagestan. We've travelled over ten thousand miles to reach this point and it would be silly to let anything prevent us from reaching out to almost touch Azerbaijan.

We work our way down to the junction and the police station, hanging a right back on to the road to the border, riding gently down to the lower land that marks the nether regions of the vast plain. Before we head further into the countryside, we pass through a town with the unlikely name of Snori, the site of a bustling, sizeable market, with lots of traffic coming and going. The market appears to be the main source of essential victuals and is very busy.

After exiting the town, we settle comfortably behind four guys in a Lada. I'm taking in the surroundings – the long tree-lined road we're riding along, with the expanse of the plain to our right. The Lada arrives at a property on the left. Bizarrely, he signals to the right. There isn't any road on the right, just a field, with no apparent opening or gate. I could brake, but I decide to overtake instead. Suddenly, he veers right, then cuts to the left and sails straight across our path to head into the property! SHIT! I switch direction at the last available moment, passing to the right of the car at speed as he blithely drives into his destination, completely oblivious. I apologise to Diane. It was a bad bit of riding, mainly because I was daydreaming but, in truth, I'm not sure she realised the danger and is far calmer about it than I am.

We pass through a few small settlements, typical of others hereabouts in their simplicity. After a few kilometres, we arrrive at the small town of Lagodekhi, just a short distance from the border. We park the bike and wander over to the local convenience store to buy crisps (for Diane) and diet Coke, sitting on the wall of what looks like a municipal building, admiring a pale blue Dnepr motorcycle combination that is showing all the signs of having had a hard life, being visually (if not mechanically) knackered. I love old working bikes like this. They remind me of the ones we saw in the early 1970's – refugees from the 'forties, 'fifties and early 'sixties. They even smell nice – a lovely mixture of stale petrol and black, glutinous spilt oil, gently heated on ancient engine cases. I can't say that about the Mutt. It doesn't smell of much at all, apart from the sheepskin seat covers, which do smell very slightly of sheep that are overdue an acquaintance with the dip.

I decide to take a photo of the bike and, in doing so, become aware, through the miracle of peripheral vision, of a rangy, middle-aged man with scruffy farm clothes, weathered skin and longish black hair, marching determinedly in our direction. He looks a bit like Roger Lloyd-Pack's Owen character in the TV sitcom *Vicar of Dibley*. Realising that he's the owner of this fine machine, and no doubt proud of that fact, I attempt to strike up a conversation by remarking in my finest Pidgin Russian, 'Hello. Fine machine' – which probably comes out in Russian as 'Hilltop, funkoff miscreant'. He glares at me, leaps astride the saddle, kicks it into life and roars off in an apparent huff. Well, to be honest, he chugs off quite slowly, leaving a trace of blue smoke behind him, leaving me quizzically nonplussed that the world of biker brotherhood has at least one confirmed heretic.

Well, you can't win 'em all. We don our jackets and helmets and head out of town. I consider the small altercation that has just taken place. He was obviously a local farmer type who just happened to ride a motorcycle as a means of transport – something that happened up to the 1950's in the UK, until the advent of the Mini. He was probably pissed at me for photographing his trusty mule, whilst secretly wishing it was a Lada. He was possessed, no doubt, by a heavy dose of Dnepr inferiority complex. It's a certifiable condition and he really should be placed in protective custody for riding a motorcycle whilst not being a biker.

On leaving the main part of Lagodekhi, we cross a bridge that spans a trickle of a river which treads its way through a flood-plain of tumbled boulders. And there we are. Full stop at the border in a tiny village called Matsimi. There before us, stands a sign across the road, borne aloft by a substantial metal gantry, declaring that this is indeed the Azerbaijan border and emblazoned with two words for anyone passing beyond: 'Good Luck'. With the current state of my plumbing, we certainly need some of that.

***

A young boy rides past us on a scooter. He rides up to the border then turns around and rides slowly past for a second look, peering at us while we take pictures of our arrival at this, the furthest point from home. As the crow flies, it's just over 2,700 miles to London, slightly less than the distance from New York to San Francisco. Despite that, we've actually ridden over 10,000 miles to get here. We pull off our helmets and our jackets to stave off the effects of the sweltering heat and take a few photos, including a rare one of us together, using our tiny portable tripod. The young lad approaches us and I signal appreciation of his rather flashy new scooter. It seems to go down well. I give him a badge of a London bus, which goes down even better. He waves 'goodbye'. My good turn for the day is complete.

A few minutes later, just as we're preparing to head off in the general direction of home, we hear the two-stroke buzz as he rides up to us again at speed, brakes very professionally and hops off, popping his scooter on its centre stand and raising the seat, almost in one move. The seats on scooters tend to hide a very handy space, big enough to hold a full-face helmet. On this occasion, though, it's holding a full-size water melon, which is presented with a broad smile by our newly-found friend. I have to admit that this simple act of returned kindness is all the more touching when you are many miles from home.

At the Azeri border, plagued by rampant squits and rewarded with a melon.
A day in the life of a road tramp.

***

Our next stop is Kvareli. We haven't ridden far from the border before we happen upon an interesting set of road works. The carriageway appears to have been completely washed away and urgent works are taking place. We are forced to resort to a spot of reasonably serious off-road riding under the watchful gaze of a digger driver who, I suspect, would like to see an embarrassing spill, just to enliven his day. Kvareli turns out to be quite a nice town to get lost in. The centre for Kakheti wine production, it has pleasant buildings and plenty of mature trees. The northern fringes of the town nestle in the mountains that rise steeply in a hazy blue and grey curtain. In her online investigations, Diane has taken note that the town boasts a very attractive lake somewhere in its environs, so we decide to try to locate it, only to find that the road to the lake gradually diminishes in stature and then rapidly turns into a meeting place for feral cattle.

When I was riding in America, I happened across quite a few wild herds of cattle, none of which attacked me, but some did appear to be on the very cusp of doing so. You can never tell with cows. Since then, I've read on very good authority (the author and mega rambler Bill Bryson, no less) that cattle kill a lot more people than we would expect. Last year, a farmer in the UK was fined £30,000 after his herd repeatedly went on the rampage, attacking ramblers willy-nilly and eventually managing to trample one to death. We pass through one group who grudgingly give up the road. Within half a kilometre, we come across a larger group that look quite brave. The lake seems a bit shy of revealing itself – I'm not sure if we're even on the correct road. So, after a short pause, we decide to head back and run the first cow gauntlet for a second time. They certainly look a tad stroppy and not at all keen to give way to oncoming traffic.

Arriving safely back in civilization, I spot an opportunity to take another photograph of a Dnepr motorcycle, no doubt risking a second encounter with a disgruntled owner. This one is of similar patina to the previous one, but has the added allure of having been converted into a trike, with the addition of a substantial metal-framed box sitting on what appears to be a car axle, turning it into a rather nifty pick-up truck.

Dnepr motorcycles are manufactured in Kiev, Ukraine and are copies of the German BMW R71 flat twin design. The Russians obtained a licence to build them as part of the German/Soviet non-aggression pact (prior to the German invasion in 1941). But in the end, presumably because the Germans failed to deliver the drawings, they obtained a few examples of the R71 from Sweden and then reverse engineered them, adding a special ingredient of fundamental crudity for good measure. There is a second brand of Russian motorcycle, the Ural, which originated from the same licence and was built in various factories in Soviet Russia. It's taken a few thousand miles of travel in the former Soviet Union to reach a place where these motorcycles are still commonplace. And long may that continue. They share a healthy dose of DNA with our own steed of choice.

One of the most striking features of Kvareli is the football ground, sited as it is in the middle of an ancient and perfectly-preserved fort, slap bang in the centre of the castle walls. This is very handy if someone lamps the ball over the sidelines. It just bounces off the walls back onto the pitch. The area across from the castle appears to be the modern administrative centre of the town, currently undergoing a facelift, with a large crane blocking most of the road, lifting heavy steelwork onto a new building that appears strikingly modern in design and somewhat at odds with those that surround it.

The next stage of today's ride takes us southwards across country, riding with our backs to the mountains along a scenic back road through rich, flat farmland, dawdling along without a care in the world, other than having the trots. Then, out of nowhere, we happen upon a strange sight to our right: an ancient car sitting on top of a slightly younger shipping container. Leaping off the bike and scrabbling around for our cameras, we attract the attention of the owner of the lonesome property on which the car and container are sat. I ask in sign language if it's OK to take a photo. He replies likewise, using the language of the Georgian plains, 'Yes, yes, but please do come on inside to smoke the pipe of peace and take photos at your leisure, Ke-mo sah-bee.'

As we walk inside our jaws hit the floor. The place is a veritable treasure trove!

On the face of it, what we've chanced upon is a scrap yard, full of all manner of clapped-out machinery: trucks, tractors, vans, and lots of cars of varying vintage; every single one a product of the Soviet Union. The owner, a pleasant chap who is leading us proudly to a series of open-fronted sheds and lean-tos, is an ardent fan of classic cars. He's pulled himself away from a group of like-minded individuals (who are busily involved in carrying out an engine change on an old Russian sedan) to greet us and to show us around his treasured collection of old cars in the sheds.

I'm reminded again how closely these graceful relics resemble American cars, and how well-built they appear to be. Only the quality of paintwork lets them down, or to be more precise the limited range of colours available. It seems that the Russians had only three or four basic colour options for their vehicles (and anything else made of steel): pale blue, pale green, black or grey (not forgetting orange for Kamaz trucks). He names each manufacturer and model name as we merrily click away: Volga, Gaz, Moskvich, then signals to us that we can wander around taking as many pictures as we like before he heads back to the task of changing the engine.

Despite having been poisoned, I do think we've found a version of paradise in Georgia. The landscape is uniformly beautiful, it's the birthplace of wine and it is full of practical vintage machinery, yet some of the modern building work is surprisingly 'of the moment'. It's also got an edge to it. The people are a curious mixture of wild, wacky and often downright hospitable. And they have a half decent rugby team. What's not to like? Apart from the steak sandwiches.

Elegant leftovers from a bygone age. Russian sedans in the roadside scrapyard.

***

The rest of the journey back to the hotel goes slightly awry when we arrive at a village that is vaguely familiar. Despite this, we can't find the road to Sighnaghi. We ride up and down a few times under the watchful gaze of a collection of villagers, sitting at the end of their gardens in the late afternoon sun. On the third attempt, it gets a bit embarrassing. Eventually, we find the correct road. I'm being generous in classifying it as a road. The surface is very badly broken up and layered liberally with haphazardly-laid dollops of black bitumen. The road winds tightly up a steep hillside, around a series of tight bends. It's quite enjoyable to negotiate these roads, taking care to track around the corners with caution in case a car, or perhaps something bigger, comes hurtling round.

At the top of the hill, we chance upon a more aggressive hazard in the shape of a bouncy wee bundle of fur that hurtles, arrow-straight, from a set of low-lying buildings, heading with murderous intent in our direction, yapping furiously. We swerve out of the trajectory of our assailant, just in time to realise that we are the subject of a very cunning two-pronged attack. A second beastie, no bigger than the first, streams out on a different trajectory, no doubt aiming to deliver a nasty nip to my right leg whilst his accomplice latches onto the left one.

I've discovered, over time, that the natural reaction to combat a dangerous dog attack, such as this one, seems to be to stick out your leg on the side of the attack, shout something pathetic, like, 'Whoa! Shoo! Efff OFF!', then, at the crucial moment, do the sensible thing and try to accelerate out of danger. But, when the attack is as well practiced as this, indeed lupine-like in its efficiency, you're really at the mercy of the courage and tenacity of the little gits doing the attacking. It's at times like this that you make a quick memory check that you did indeed get a rabies shot, and that you're wearing your stout riding trousers and semi-armoured boots with nice shiny metal caps on them, usefully placed to deliver a sharp kick to the ribs of the assailant, which, in this case, would probably result in the said assailant sailing over the nearest hedge.

Thankfully, the yappy little scrotes in question are badly lacking in the tenacity department. The chief protagonist seems to realise that the bike is getting a lot bigger than he originally anticipated. As quickly as he was heading for my outstretched leg, he suddenly changes course and runs behind the bike, then turns in an arc and chases us bravely from behind as we accelerate away. The second terrier bottles it, big time, and just stands there confused, waiting for a tractor to come around the corner and squish him (or her).

It's sobering to think that we may have had recourse to rely on our rabies jab, a few moments ago. And here's a thing. If the lady in Superdrug hadn't pressed this gem of information on me quite forcefully, after equally forcefully ramming the needle home, I wouldn't have known: the jab only protects you for a short while, hopefully sufficient time to get you to a hospital. You get bitten, you go to hospital immediately, or you will die – something that would really make my day after suffering 50 hours of debilitating food poisoning.

***

Diane's mobile phone goes off at some ungodly hour. Strange.

Fumbling around, she passes it to me. I notice that it is indeed the very early hours of the morning, and can see that the caller is my daughter, Suzannah.

'Hello.'

She manages a couple of words before bursting into tears. She phoned me in a similar way to break the news that my brother-in-law, Ed, had died two years ago, perhaps the worst telephone call I have ever taken. Eventually, she manages to compose herself enough to break the news that a family member has died, just an hour or so ago, suddenly, in his sleep. He's still young. It's difficult to take in the enormity of it, but it has happened. We both sit up in bed, stunned by the news.

***

Breakfast in the morning is very sombre. The enormity of what has happened hasn't quite sunk in yet, but we realise that we need to get home. Thankfully, we had planned to return to the Golden Palace for one night to allow secure internet access to pay a tax bill, so we can stick to our plan and ride back to Tblisi today. Then we can phone home to decide what we should do.

Whilst I'm packing the bike in the morning, I notice an old dog hanging around. He's a soft old thing. If I look at him, he wags his tail dolefully. The sad fact is that he's a stray and is riddled with the mange, walking very stiffly to avoid unnecessary discomfort. What can you do in this situation? It's not like you can call the RSPCA, or even find a vet. If I gave some money to reception, would they help him? Perhaps £100 would be sufficient to cover some bills to get him treated. Diane spots him on one of her visits down. In the end, we decide that we probably can't do anything and, once loaded and paid up, we ride off, passing him as he lays down on the roadside, watching the world go by, no doubt in deep discomfort. Can today get any worse?

Chapter 27
Gallipoli

The highlight of our journey back to Tblisi is the sight of a long line of cows, strolling calmly straight towards us along the fast lane of a stretch of dual carriageway. We catch sight of them whilst travelling at motorway speeds, managing to slow down a little by the time we skim past them, but by no means slow enough. I can't criticise them. They're observing the highway code to the letter. Proceeding calmly along in the direction of oncoming traffic.

Back in the safe-haven of the Golden Palace, we're ushered into the same room we occupied a couple of days ago, presumably on the basis that I managed to stink it out the first time and there's no point in my being allowed to stink out a second (different) one, this time around. It turns out that nothing much can be gained by flying home immediately, so we decide to stick to our immediate plan which was to ride back to Ankara to get new tyres fitted and the oil changed. Things should be a lot clearer by then. My own little woes have paled to insignificance. I don't have an appetite at all, so I'm not even missing food.

***

An important milestone was achieved two days ago, almost without us noticing. We have measured ourselves against ex-Soviet road conditions and are now ready to complete our journey around the world. All that stands in our way is lack of funds and a bike in sore need of a few upgrades. E-mail conversations with Nihat, the manager at Endos Motorcycles, have confirmed our service booking in Ankara in four days' time, just enough time for us to get back to the shop in one piece. We depart the Golden Palace with a few regrets. They've looked after us exceptionally well. We bought them two large boxes of chocolates prior to heading to Sighnaghi and I think that went down quite well. I hope so, because I had a bit of an accident and papped the bed last night. Diane and I spent most of the early hours desperately washing and attempting to dry the bed sheet, hoping they wouldn't notice. I think, perhaps, it was all in vain.

We manage to navigate our way out of Tblisi in good time and make every effort to crack on, hoping against hope that we can avoid spending a second night in Batumi. The weather is pleasantly dry and the roads reasonably clear. We make good progress. When we reach the stretch of hills that we enjoyed riding through on the way out, we really stretch the bike's legs before spotting a fuel station and deciding to pull over for a fill-up.

Georgia is so compact that the last time we put a petrol nozzle in the tank was in Batumi, during our ill-fated search for a hotel. This second stop confirms that it is common here for the petrol stations to have pump attendants. We sweep up to the pumps in good order, Diane climbs lithely off the pillion. The conversation with the attendant is carried out using sign language –pointing at the highest RON possible on the fuel pump and signaling with a rising flat of my hand that I would like the tank to be filled to the brim. A small group of locals gather round to check out the bike. It's all very friendly and all filmed on my helmet cam, which I've forgotten to switch off.

There aren't so many animals around today. Maybe it's market day. The roads remain clear all the way across the country. Even the pig at the little café has departed to pastures new. We approach the coast in the late afternoon, riding through the same small villages and towns that we are now very slightly familiar with. A few young car drivers want to race. It's very tempting, but there's always the risk that a cow or goat will pull out on you at a junction, so I try to temper the urge to twist the throttle to the stops and politely ride in the gutter to let a couple of them pass by. Reg in Melitopol would be totally disgusted.

When we arrive at the seafront of the coastal town of Kobuleti, it comes as a bit of a surprise because I didn't register travelling through it on the way out. I vaguely recall the Russian rider saying he'd been staying here for his short break. As we ride through, we spot a pleasant-looking hotel over to the right next to the sea and pull in to chance our luck. Five minutes later, I return to the bike a little crestfallen. I think they took in my ragged, emaciated appearance and thought the better of it, politely declining our patronage on the basis of being full, which I personally considered to be a bare-faced lie.

We ride a little further along the seafront and spot a second hotel called the Chiveni. The entrance is on the roadway, but the hotel is more akin to an American motel, sitting in tree-shaded grounds with an access road passing down the side of the joint and the rooms facing the road. The owner looks me up and down, eyes the bike and the navigator, then nods that we are 'in'. What a relief! I don't feel up to searching again and more or less collapse onto the bed on entering the room. The lack of food is starting to take effect.

An hour later. We're in a very slightly dodgy looking café and I'm jealously observing Diane as she tucks into a chicken dish. We came upon an apothecary on the way to discovering the café and ventured inside. The sales assistant spoke not a word of English and looked suitably confused when I tried to mime 'I have got the heaving jib-jabs big time and need DRUGS.' The assistant called the chemist and she observed a repetition of the mime with a similarly perplexed expression. Diane realised that I was getting nowhere and spoke to them calmly, and slowly, in plain Scottish so that they would better understand. Then, after a brief conflab, they agreed between themselves that indeed they did understand and produced a remedy, conveniently plastered in Russian on both the packaging and the instruction leaflet.

Back at the room, Diane has her sensible hat on.

'I don't think you should take that. We need to check it out.' Good job too. It turns out to be Russian laxative.

***

Today is the sixth day of non-digestion of food. Today, we will pass through the border back into Turkey. I feel that, in doing so, we'll turn a corner and I'll start to recover. We pay the hotel owner, with a degree of gratitude for letting us in last night, and rumble out of town, riding back up the tropical hill and down the other side into Batumi, which Donald still thinks will be the greatest city on the planet in four-and-a-bit years. The strange thing is that it feels completely different when you enter the bay from the south, riding around its broad sweep, with the modern high-rise towers in the distance. It really looks quite impressive, especially if a squint is employed.

We park up at the border behind a couple of German riders on tricked-up adventure bikes, packed with minimal gear – I doubt I could pack all my merino pants in those bags. I wonder how they get away with travelling so light. I suspect their skiddies have emulated the ones worn by the shop assistants back in Aberdeen. The gods of border crossing are smiling down upon us and we pass into Turkey smoothly. We manage a rather pathetic sixty kilometres along the Black Sea coast before we spot a rather nice hotel at a town called Cayeli and decide to stop for the night. In the gentle warmth of the evening, we head up to the top floor restaurant where I sample the menu. Later, in the room, I sleep soundly with nary a single visit to the loo. The nightmare has finally subsided.

***

Fast forward two days. The receptionist in the City Hotel reveals to us that there are no rooms available to tramps such as we, especially ones that occasionally force a woman to pay the bill. We get the sneaking impression that the hotel isn't full, but there isn't much we can do. 'You could try down the road at the Park Hotel,' he offers. It turns out to be a short hop.

The Park hotel is quite grand and has one room remaining on the top floor, room 1005, tucked away from everyone else. We're quite lucky. The Malaysian Embassy have all but taken over the place for a conference, so it's packed with polite, well-dressed individuals wearing identification badges, speaking in hushed tones in the lifts.

Arriving here from Cayeli was not without incident. We rode along the coast for two days, stopping off at the odd photo opportunity. Further into the journey, we passed blithely by a policeman pointing a speed camera in a very targeted fashion. Diane signaled me with a squeeze of her legs. I waved my left hand back at her to reassure her that we were well within the limit, or at least sufficiently near it. A mile further down the road, a second policeman stepped out from the shelter of some trees and waved us in. We both climbed off the bike as he walked over and checked out the number plate, pen and notebook in hand. I felt a bit gutted and decidedly green around the gills.

'Where are you from?' he asked in passable English.

'United Kingdom.'

'You were seen by camera speeding.'

'I think I was inside the limit, I was travelling the same speed as the cars,' I feebly attempted.

'No, you were fast.'

'Is there tolerance, for speedometer difference?' I chanced, leaving my indefinite and definite articles out, for some reason.

'Please come to car.'

See, he left them out too.

A second officer of the law was sitting quietly in the car. He offered his hand and I shook it thinking, 'maybe I'll get off. They both seem nice chaps: good cop, good cop so to speak.'

'This is speed on camera, we have film,' said the nice officer in the car. The slip of paper read 75 kilometres per hour.

For some reason, I looked down and came face-to-face with the first officer's pistol, which was clipped by a leather strap in the white holster on his belt with the checked-plastic pistol butt pointing straight up at me as he reached into the car for something. It occurred to me that it would be a doddle to just reach down, unclip the pop-stud and pull out the gun. I found myself almost transfixed by both the sight and by a strange temptation to just grab it. At that moment, he stood upright, turned around and presented me with a white card printed with a very complicated chart.

'Here is motorcycle. Your motorcycle is large engine'.

He pointed to a very small symbol of a motorcycle that was appreciably bigger than the minute one adjacent to it and continued, 'this line – your speed limit: 55 kilometres per hour on 70 kilometres per hour road.'

'So, er, motorcycles have to drive slower than cars?' I asked, with a hint of incredulity.

'Yes.'

I was bang to rights, done up like a kipper, guv. I asked what would happen next, fearing the worst.

'Do I have to pay you the fine or go to the station?'

'No. You pay at border.'

He told me the fine. It worked out to around £70. He then handed me a carefully prepared speeding ticket, made out by his colleague, which I duly handed over to Diane to go in our nice border-crossing file.

'Many people do not bother to pay,' he said with a smile. 'But they may not easily get back into Turkey next time. You are free to go now.'

'And get a license for your seeing-eye monkey over there,' he said, nodding at Diane.

OK he didn't say that.

I smiled back at him and thanked him for nicking me so politely and even giving me liberal payment terms. I'm glad I didn't try to grab his gun and shoot him and his partner in a gruesome remake of *Fort Apache, the Bronx*. We shook hands and they both waved us off on our way. Thus began my long-standing admiration for Turkish policemen. Some may hate them, but I don't. I honestly and genuinely believe them to be the salt of the earth. You will meet some more in the next book, if either of us manage to make it that far.

That evening we stayed for a second time at the Samsun airport hotel, where I managed, again, to eat without incident. We met a pleasant German couple riding a BMW R1150 GS Adventure, the forerunner to the Mutt. They'd also journeyed through Georgia and, like us, were heading back into Europe. Robert, the rider with a most un-German sounding forename, explained to me that his partner had 'had enough'. He was taking her to the airport in the morning and was patently relishing ridding himself of her. It made me ponder how I would feel in the same situation. Robert seemed quite cheerful about the prospect and was more interested in showing me a wonderful satnav application on his I-phone, which just rubbed in how badly let down we'd been in the Garmin department. I came to the conclusion that, if Diane had had enough and wanted to take the next flight home, I would abandon the rest of the trip and follow her. Riding alone, an experience I relished when I started long distance travelling, has lost its attraction. Bugger the freedom thing. Companionship wins every time.

**

I've arrived back at Endo Motors and am sitting opposite Nihat in front of a large desk in his office. We discuss the forthcoming service in detail. The bike will get a fresh pair of Tourance tyres and a glug or ten of 20/50 oil, along with a new oil filter. Nihat struggles to comprehend that 'tractor oil' is the correct engine lubricant for a modern machine. Even the Ducati Panigale uses decent, modern oil. But I insist that this is the correct grade to be put in my worthy companion (motorcycle, not pillion – she likes wine). I supply him with a spare oil filter.

Our conversation turns to what we're going to do for the rest of the day.

'You could visit the Ataturk Mausoleum,' he proffers.

It's no coincidence that he has a photograph of Kemal Ataturk on his desk, a quite severe-looking man who bears a passing resemblance to my paternal grandfather. I'm a little dubious, something that, I think, shows in a slight hesitation. Sensing this, he says, 'It's the most important place in Ankara; it shouldn't be missed. You must go there my friend. But, of course, it is your time and you must decide.' Well, that was reasonably put. I don't feel under any pressure at all.

Back at the hotel, I explain to Diane that we should really go and see the Ataturk Mausoleum and am pleasantly surprised at how quickly she agrees – especially since it replaces the off-chance of a bit of shopping. Maybe she's read all about him and already knows it to be a gem. We've had a damn fine breakfast in a restaurant full of Malaysians, leaving us akin to a pair of finely coiled tourist springs.

The taxi ride takes us through the centre of Ankara. It's an interesting, attractive city and quite green too, despite much of it being very modern. The common perception casts Ankara as the modern capital of Turkey. In comparison, Istanbul is the ancient and wonderful older sibling, but in fact, at least in terms of age, it's the other way around. Ankara is one of the oldest surviving cities in the world and has a rich history going back to the Bronze Age. Our drive takes us through many of the newer sections of the city, quite a few of which are large military complexes, sitting in green surroundings and appearing quite innocuous. But it does remind me a little of the military district of Moscow and helps underline the importance of the Turkish military in these increasingly troubled times.

The approach to the mausoleum complex passes through a beautifully maintained park, along the paved *Road of Lions*, which is lined with rose beds and clipped shrubs. When you arrive at the site, it's impossible not to be impressed by the scale and stark symmetry of the buildings. Despite the sweltering heat, there's a coolness and simplicity in the design, the building of which commenced in 1944 and finished in 1953. Ataturk died in 1938. I'm not sure where they kept him in between times.

Although it was built in concrete, the facades are completed with beautiful blocks of stone of varying colours. The design is angular. A series of colonnade walkways surrounding a huge square, dominated by the building that contains the tomb. It makes Lenin's tomb seem like a matchbox on the M1. It imparts a feeling of respect and magnitude. The complex is guarded by soldiers in immaculate uniforms who stand at ease in the sweltering sun, matching the statues on the Road of Lions. Their helmets seem a size too small for their heads. It's a minor issue, but one worth noting.

If the mausoleum was simply a tomb, then it would be impressive, but it also houses a fascinating museum showing the life and achievements of Mustafa Kemal Ataturk. He rose to prominence during the Battle of Gallipoli, becoming the leader of the independence movement after the First World War, then Turkey's first president. Many of his possessions are kept in display cases and in halls around the colonnades, including his favourite car and his rowing machine, which is beautifully crafted from wood. He clearly enjoyed smoking, because there are many examples of smoking paraphernalia sitting in the display cases. All the photos of him portray a very dapper man, a little stern in appearance perhaps, but also someone with a liberal dose of humanity, which might come as something of a surprise considering (what are perhaps) his most famous words – an order that he gave to his troops during the battle against the allies on the Gallipoli Peninsula:

"Men, I am not ordering you to attack. I am ordering you to die. In the time that it takes us to die, other forces and commanders can come and take our place."

He was a champion of a secular form of government and eschewed religion. He understood the need to embrace potential enemies and turn them into friends, knowing that, one day, their existing regimes would, most likely, wither away. By the time we've wandered through the halls and walkways, I'm hooked and want to learn more about him.

Trumps Lenin's tomb by a measured mile. The Ataturk Mausoleum, Ankara.

***

Today is my birthday. Normally, back home, it coincides with the weather changing for the worst. I was born to be a portent of colder, wetter climes. But here, the temperatures are holding up nicely and we depart the Park Hotel under clear, blue skies. The bike is running nicely, circulating the new oil and, I swear, running a little sweeter since I adjusted the valve clearances in Tblisi. It takes a few miles to break in the tyres, but once out of the clutches of the city, heading north, we run into a series of familiar, sweeping curves, enabling us to get a bit of a lean on. There is a difference in my riding since we last took this route though. I'm now slightly more wary of police radar traps and only open up the throttle when I can see far into the distance. I'm still quite flummoxed that motorcycles have to travel slower than cars – frankly, it's a bit galling.

I've made contact through Facebook with my friend Gamze and arranged to give her a call tomorrow to arrange a bite to eat. She seems a bit surprised that we've chosen a repeat stay at the airport hotel, but we liked it there the first-time around and want to keep things simple. We're planning a trip into Istanbul in the morning then to meet up with her and her husband in the early evening. We settle back into the ride, enjoying the sweep of high hills and the excellence of the road we are riding along all the way to the outskirts of Istanbul. Happy Birthday to me!

***

One of the good points about staying so close to the airport is the access to transport links into the city. We had a very comfortable room again last night and poshed it up a bit, with a decent meal, a bottle of Turkish red wine (which was very passable) and a room of near five-star standard.

The bus takes a long, long time to traverse the few miles from the airport to the city centre, negotiating the grindingly slow traffic we endured a week or so ago. Once it arrives there, it negotiates its way to a large square that is the main terminus – a place teeming with a mixture of locals and tourists, surrounded by the splendid decay of the old shops and tenements that crowd in on the surrounding streets. We have a whole day of discovery awaiting us, visiting the tourist hot spots of what promises much, and doesn't disappoint.

The Blue Mosque is an obvious 'must see', so we head there. Completed in 1616, It resides high on a hill above the Bosphorus Straits on the European side of the city, sat opposite its older brethren, the Hagia Sophia. Both of these religious buildings are situated in an open space, richly planted with shrubs, trees and flower beds – a honey pot for tourists. Neither of us have ever visited a mosque before, at least not the interior of one, so this is quite an exciting new experience. The only rules to follow are that shoes must be removed, women must wear some form of headscarf and you aren't allowed to walk into the cordoned-off prayer area. The outside of the mosque is fronted by a large courtyard surrounded by a continuous arcade, where you can shelter from the sun. The mosque has six minarets and numerous domes. Diane is given a plain blue scarf, loaned to her on a 'return after use' basis.

The mosque is formally called the Sultan Ahmed Mosque, named after the Sultan who commissioned it. Informally, it is widely known as the Blue Mosque, due to the predominantly blue tiling that decorates the interior. The tiles are a mixture of colours: blues, blue/black, red, yellows and golds, arranged in the most stunning geometric patterns. It is incredibly beautiful and perfectly symmetrical. The reds that are picked out in the walls and ceilings are reflected in the salmon pink and gold carpet on which people kneel to pray. Above them hangs a vast, circular array of lighting strung from high above to a point quite low above the carpet. It is whisper-quiet.

I think we've seen some amazing man-made sights on our journey, so far. If I had to pick out two that have most impressed me, I think I would pick the Vasa in Stockholm and the Mamayev Kurgan in Volgograd. The Sultan Ahmed Mosque in Istanbul has to be added to that pair. It is just so incredibly beautiful that you could marvel at it for hours. The fact that I've left out the Winter Palace in St Petersburg, the Kremlin buildings and St Basil's in Red Square (not to mention the Church of Our Saviour on Spilled Blood, also in St Petersburg), shows just how breathtaking I've found this building to be. And there's one other interesting little fact about it that I think is very cool. It's location is 49 degrees 0 minutes and 19 seconds North, geographically. If they could just have tweaked it to zero seconds it would just be perfect. But it might have found itself in the Bosphorus.

***

Since we're enjoying a touristic day today, we might as well have a mosey around the famous Grand Bazaar, which is situated quite close to the Blue Mosque in an area of the old city called Faith. Built between 1455 and 1460, it is one of the largest under-cover markets in the world, comparing quite favourably with Rotherham indoor market, where I used to shop for records in the 1970's. The Grand Bazaar has over 4,000 outlets to Rotherham's eighty-one, despite which, search as I may, I fail to spot anywhere selling vinyl. It's an obvious gap in the market.

The Grand Bazaar is charming. I'm back in Istanbul, by the way. It has over sixty streets, all of which are covered, and has many vaulted ceilings and archways, with vividly decorated shops spilling their wares onto the 'street'. It is rightly famous for jewelry shops and the sale of gold, but there are countless other products being sold (I love the lamp shops), and the sales technique is typically one of trying to get you talking then get you inside the shop, where tea is normally served as part of the 'closing down' procedure. We're lucky to escape without buying a rug.

We're a little tired when we arrive back at the hotel and could probably do with a quiet night. But we have an arrangement to meet up with Gamze and Tayfun. Very kindly, they've offered to pick us up and take us to a nearby restaurant. It's really nice to meet up with my old friends again and share a mixed grill dinner with them both, and to introduce them to Diane. A great end to a pleasurable day off the bike.

***

We intend to spend two or three days more in Turkey, then to ride through Greece to Athens where we will probably need to leave the bike and head home for a couple of days for the funeral. One of the few positively-planned elements of our trip was a visit to the Gallipoli peninsula. It is one of two destinations on our agenda that have family connections. My grandfather, he who had a passing resemblance to Kemal Ataturk, served in the First World War and was sent to Gallipoli. I could say he fought at Gallipoli, but I'm not sure that he did any actual fighting, but more of that when we get there. The second place on the agenda is Assisi, where my uncle is buried. He served in the Second

World War and most definitely did see combat, but, again, we'll leave that for a little bit later.

In the meantime, with the bike packed to the rafters as usual, we head away from the airport and off towards the nightmarish traffic heading westward-ho. I make a futile attempt to avoid the traffic by taking an alternative route – one that sticks more to the coast of the Sea of Marmara. How futile only becomes clear as the day wears on and we crawl in considerable discomfort under a cloudless sky, in sweltering heat. The traffic is too heavy to filter through, so we remain stuck in a long queue of other vehicles, mostly small trucks, vans and cars. In a whole day of riding, we barely cover forty kilometres.

We finally manage to shrug ourselves free of Istanbul in the middle of the afternoon and ride along the coast for a while before spotting what appears to be a reasonable hotel, to our right. We decide to call it a day and see if they have a room for the night. It's fairly basic, cheap accommodation and they do have a room. There's a convenient supermarket right next to the hotel – seems like a good place to stop.

A little later in the evening, shortly after turning in, we're brought rudely to attention by the unmistakable sound of the Mutley's disc lock alarm going off, followed very quickly by the bike's main alarm. I pull open the window and peer below…. Gathered around in the gloom are a bunch of teenagers, some pulled up on their scooters, others standing around and one of the little scallies caught bang to rights sitting on the bike holding the handlebars. They're all frozen in the moment. Then, just as I manage to shout, 'OY!', they come to their senses. Scooters are kicked into life and zoom away, those not lucky enough to have wheels scurry off pronto and the last one to leave is the main culprit, the receptionist shouting at him and shaking his fist.

They weren't doing any real harm, if truth be told. They were just admiring the bike and the bravest of the bunch had decided to have a sit on it. Still, it was fun seeing the panic instilled by a relatively cheap security device. In Rostov, they would have shot both me and the receptionist.

***

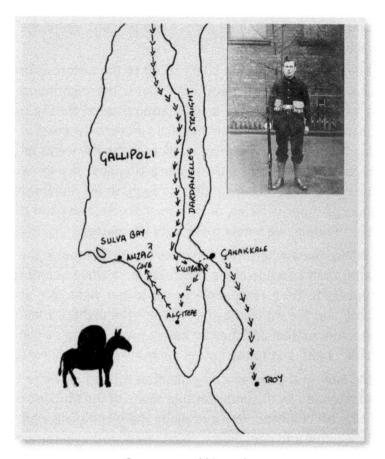

One man and his mule.

After the traffic carnage of the day before, the ride down towards Gallipoli is a far more relaxed and pleasant affair. The density of human habitation thins out and the panorama before us takes on a more wild and rugged appearance. Our route edges around to the southwest. We're still following the Sea of Marmara, an inland sea that has two narrow straights: the Bosphorus Straits passing through to the Black Sea to the north, and the Dardanelles that pass through to the Aegean Sea, which, in turn, reaches out to the Mediterranean Sea. We ride over high hills along sweeping roads, pulling over for lunch in the early afternoon at a deserted café, picking our meal from what appears to be a rather optimistic, fully-laden buffet.

I've read up about Gallipoli sufficiently to recall how incredibly difficult the terrain was for both sides. It is certainly rocky and rugged, with steep hillsides (called Tepe by the Turks). It was these hills that held the key to victory for the Ottoman forces during the battle. To the north of the Peninsula they are long and sweeping, to the south where the battle was fought, they're more closely linked, steep and wooded, rising sharply up from the coastline, especially so on the western side. Perfect terrain for defence.

I was quite optimistic about our progress before lunch but, as the afternoon wears on, we realise that the peninsula is longer than we thought. It's also surprisingly sparse in hotels for somewhere visited repeatedly by Antipodeans. It feels like an opportunity is being missed. The final part of our day's ride passes along a very charming road that snakes along the azure blue Dardanelles Straight – right down at sea level and terminating at the wee town of Eceabat. Here, it becomes rapidly apparent that the best chance of a hotel is to take the regular car ferry over to the much larger town of Çanakkale, which sits on the Asian shore, a mile or so away.

The bustling ferry to Çanakkale

Before we go any further, though, I need to mention a sight that has transfixed me for at least an hour. The Dardanelles is one of the world's great seaways, despite being quite narrow. A continuous parade of wonderful, huge merchant ships pass majestically by, travelling in both directions. You could spend hours watching them churn serenely on their way. Well, I could anyway.

After paying at the entrance to the slipway, there's a considerable wait for the ferry to arrive, then a ride down onto the decks and another wait for departure, a great opportunity to take a few photos. The bike isn't tied down, so we take the precaution of staying close by, just in case.

The waters of the Dardanelles are truly a beautiful colour of deep blue. The vessel judders its way across the straight, passing in between two of the massive ships that are on transit, giving a great view of them both. They're travelling light, Black Sea-bound, riding high in the water, their propellers just visible as they lazily pound the sea to foam. Our destination, Çanakkale (pronounced 'Chanakali'), is an attractive town of 186,000 people (or thereabouts). The ferry disgorges its human and vehicular cargo at a busy terminal in the small port, beyond which is one of the main thoroughfares through the town, lined with shops. On our stop-start ride in the traffic, we quickly spot a hotel that has a vacant room for a three-night stay. The room is tiny, that's the downside. On the plus side, there's a covered parking space accessed by a street that runs behind the hotel, parallel to the main street. An evening stroll into town reveals a very pleasant atmosphere. Çanakkale has clearly thrived on tourism and is a honey-pot destination for Australians and New Zealanders who make the pilgrimage to the battlefield and particularly the site of the ANZAC landings, which is situated across the straight and around the peninsula on the western shoreline at a location called ANZAC Cove.

I too would like to visit ANZAC Cove. But my main purpose is to visit Sulva Bay, because that is where my grandad launched his own personal invasion of the Ottoman Empire, accompanied by his trusty mule (the name of which has been sadly lost in time). When I was working in Australia, the fact that a Pom even set foot on Gallipoli was met by a high degree of incredulity, bordering on snorting derision, largely because the Aussies at the time considered the invasion of Gallipoli to be an entirely ANZAC affair (the ANZACs being the Australian and New Zealand Army Corps). The historical fact is that there were far more British and French troops employed in the campaign than those from 'Down Under' and, even then, many of the ANZAC troops were first generation émigrés (i.e. of British or Irish birth).

I have another connection to Gallipoli, over and above grandad. The ship I served on in the navy had a predecessor that was involved in the main landing at Helles, being directly involved in one of the most famous episodes from the British side of the battle, namely the landing of the Lancashire Fusiliers. The ship's boats from HMS Euryalus, a cruiser, landed the Fusiliers into a hail of Ottoman fire. The Fusiliers famously went on to win six Victoria Crosses 'before breakfast'. Since then, there has always been an affiliation between any ship named Euryalus and the Royal Regiment of Fusiliers. Right now, the ship's silverware resides in the cases of the regimental museum in Bury, Lancashire, held in safe keeping for the day when the next HMS Euryalus is commissioned. One of the finest articles of silverware is an exact scale replica of one of the ship's boats used in the landing, a cutter, presented to her by the regiment.

So, tomorrow is something of a personal pilgrimage. We'll take the ferry back across the Dardanelles and hopefully ride over to Sulva Bay via Helles and ANZAC Cove. I've read that access to Sulva Bay is extremely difficult, due to its remoteness, and am not sure how close we'll be able to get; but that's for tomorrow. For today, we chance upon a quite extraordinary artefact from the battle: a heavy artillery piece, proudly displayed in the town. It was hit by a shell that pierced the side of the gun leaving a huge tear in its heavy steel carriage. There's also a fine statue of a Turkish soldier carrying a wounded Australian soldier, indicative of a close emotional bond that has developed between the two former combatant nations; at least it has in this town.

***

One of the great pleasures of touring by motorcycle is the ability to access areas that a tour bus won't necessarily take you. We found this on our journey through Crimea. It was a simple task to pack a few things in the panniers and head off for the day's sightseeing. I don't think any of my family have visited the place where my paternal grandfather had his own adventure, a place that must have seemed very far from home to a young, conscripted colliery carpenter from South Yorkshire.

The background to the landings on Gallipoli and the Dardanelles naval campaign that preceded it are complex. The strategic aim, championed by Winston Churchill, was to put pressure on Germany by knocking its ally out of the war, and to relieve the pressure on the Russians. There is an excellent book 'Gallipoli' by Peter Hart that has been the source of most of my information regarding the battle. In virtually all accounts, the strategy is seen, at best, to be deeply flawed. That it was mismanaged at both strategic and tactical level caused fissures to open within the British side. In short, the increasing list of casualties were the cause of great scandal between the British and the Australians, New Zealanders and the Irish, all of whom were involved in a great deal of the fighting. Gallipoli is seen as a pivotal moment in the birth of national identity for the ANZACs, but it was also very influential in the outcome of the independence movement in Ireland.

It is also very important to remember the defenders. The Ottoman troops were fighting a desperate battle for survival. Nowadays, it is easy to forget this and to consider the landings to be an abject failure. In part, this does a disservice to the brave and skillful Turkish soldiers, who fought with great tenacity and were very well-led by both their own officers and the German staff officers who commanded them. Gallipoli was equally pivotal for the Ottoman Turks, laying the seeds of an eventual revolution and the last gasp of an Empire. It was here that Mustafa Kemal, who's mausoleum we visited a few days ago, came to prominence as a commander of increasing stature.

My grandfather's role in all this is obscure because he apparently said very little about it. He landed in the great push, up at Sulva Bay, as a sapper in the Royal Engineers. I'd like to think he impressed himself on Ataturk in some way, but I doubt that to be the case. My aunt told me that he returned from Gallipoli on a mission to produce as many children as possible in the shortest possible time – something that turned into quite a success story. He managed to father seven in total – with the assistance of grandma – and, since I'm the son of the youngest, I have reason to thank him for his persistence.

***

On arrival across the water, we first ride southwards from Eceabat on a road that hugs the low-lying coast in a very scenic manner, sweeping past tiny beaches and rocky coves before cutting west, inland towards Behramli. After that, it heads back southwards to a village called Alçitepe, where the road passes through the village, passing bars and cafes that are already thronged with visitors (some wearing strange hats with corks hanging from them). This inland area is predominantly a very scenic mix of fields and trees amongst rugged, rolling hills. Alçitepe (known to the allies as Krithia) was one of the key objectives of the allies and, as such, was subject to a series of desperate battles, culminating in the third battle involving the French and the British forces. As we ride down towards the tip of the peninsula, we arrive at Sedd El Bahr, the location for 'V' beach, where a steamer called the *SS River Clyde* was beached to land troops against a murderous enfilading fire from the defenders. The activities further north at ANZAC Cove were meant as a diversionary attack to support the landings here and on the French beaches. Over time, the fighting at ANZAC Cove developed into its own fierce battle.

As we start to head northwards along the west coast, we begin to see signposts for the Australian and New Zealand Corps landing site, so that's where we head. And what a beautiful spot it is. We find a large, deserted car park a short distance from the cove and park the bike up there. Whilst sorting our gear out, we're approached by two distinguished-looking gentlemen who ask us where we're from. The tallest of the two, a well-spoken Englishman, introduces himself as the chairman of the Gallipoli Association. He tells us that they have an excellent website that we can visit if we want to know more about the campaign. He's very interested to hear about grandad and suggests that I should add any details I have on to the website. I'm not sure they would find our sole snippet of information altogether publishable!

The view from above Anzac Cove. The actual Cove is around to the right of the photograph.

I read in Peter Hart's book that the ANZAC landings on the 25th April 1915 were, initially, virtually unopposed. They started to move inland up the steep cliffs and, increasingly, came under heavy fire as the Ottoman troops were rushed into defensive positions in the hills around the cove. We decide to climb the same route they took, on a pathway up the hills, towards a place called 'Shrapnel Valley', one of the very poignant sites because so many casualties occurred here. It's a very steep and breathtaking climb. Remarkably, it is very easy to pick up small pieces of scorched stone lying in amongst today's scrub bushes. The valley is now a war cemetery. As we climb higher up the slope, the view of the cove and the coast that runs along from it, north and south, is stunning. Far below, we can make out the outline of a sunken vessel. The navy used a kind of landing craft called a 'beetle', perhaps it's one of those. Over to the north lies Sulva Bay.

This idyllic scene is in sharp contrast to the conditions the ANZAC troops found themselves in very quickly after the landings, trapped in a tiny beachhead, with supplies brought in by sea and manhandled up the steep slopes. Water shortages were particularly critical. The hillsides quickly became makeshift encampments as the ANZACs were exhorted to dig, dig, dig. Getting as far underground as possible was essential, yet almost impossible on such stony ground. Much of the supply line from the cove to the front lines came under observation of the enemy, who could rain down direct artillery and rifle fire. It was a very perilous place to be.

Having taken in the superb view from the hills above the cove, we descend back down and ride the bike round to the beach where the landings took place. The sea wall here forms a memorial, alongside which we spot a motorcycle that's been ridden all the way over from Australia – quite an impressive achievement. The battleground in the hills above the cove was deserted, we were the only two people up there, but the beach area is fair packed with Aussies; all that's missing is a lady's volleyball team. A guide has just finished giving them an overview of the landing. And, here it pains me to reflect on the vagaries brought about by myth and legend. We mingle with the crowd on the beach and overhear the reflections of an older man and his younger friend (most likely his grandson) on what they've just been told.

'Think about it mate, the landing craft are coming in, the Turks have got all those bloody machine guns set up right here pointing at yer, and yer bein' mowed down in the boats. Can't do nothing mate. Pure bloody murder.'

In the end, it probably doesn't matter that the facts being described to tourists by tour guides are often incorrect, perchance lifted directly from the film *Saving Private Ryan* to maximise the drama, and much closer on the day in question to the experience of the Lancashire Fusiliers down the coast at W Beach – although even there it is disputed that the Turks manned any machine guns. Many men lost their lives on the 25th of April but, if what I've read is true, the main fighting for the ANZACs happened behind us, up in the hills days later, where inexperienced and often badly-led soldiers were cut down by the withering rifle fire of a well-trained enemy in a bitter, see-sawing fight that then played out over many months. In that time, the Australians and New Zealanders transformed into the tough, battle-hardened force that went down in legend, and new nations were born.

***

Not forgetting that our main mission is to get a sight of Sulva Bay, we re-mount and ride off in search of a road that will take us to the north. This leads us up into the hills and the territory held by the Ottoman forces ninety-seven years ago. The line of hills formed the primary objective of the invasion force, but only a very few were ever captured and then, only briefly. During the early stages of the invasion, especially where the initial landing was unopposed, the tendency was to pull up and consolidate a position rather than push on against the increasing resistance to take the high ground. This gave the Ottoman forces time to march their reinforcements to the hills. Once they had occupied the tepes, it was almost impossible to dislodge them. The campaign was effectively lost. It just needed someone in command to realise the fact and be brave enough to get the troops out.

We follow signs for one of the Turkish war memorials, locating it after riding a short distance in the increasing afternoon heat. It's quite a busy place, with a café and small market selling souvenirs to the throngs of (Turkish) visitors. Across the road lies the cemetery with its line of graves, not too dissimilar to the Commonwealth cemeteries scattered around the coast. A line of trenches arc around a second memorial on top of a hill, recording the moment when Kemal Ataturk was struck by shrapnel above his heart, his life being saved by a watch (which had been presented to him by the Germans). The hill is simply called *Hill 971*, the highest point in the range of hills overlooking the coast. The view of Sulva Bay from here is excellent, if a little hazy, now that clouds have drifted in. This is the nearest we will get to it anyway.

The bay stretches in the distance, a curved indenture on the coast, with a lagoon stretching further inland. A low-lying line of hills can be seen to the east of the long stretch of flat land. The British forces landed there on the 15th of August, 1915 and, from the outset, were beset by a lack of inertia brought about (not least) by the performance of the senior officers, which was singularly woeful. It was a trademark for the whole campaign. In the middle of this, somewhere over there, my grandad, John Earnshaw, and his mule were busy re-laying telephone cables to the front line, following a bout of shelling. Apparently, it was common for the gunners to target the sappers who were carrying out this unenviable task. The mules had large circular canisters on their backs and must have made a tempting target.

On one of these forays, an artillery shell whistled over and landed slap-bang between the mule's legs.

'T' mule shitten hissel, an ah shitten ma'sel,' was grandad's description of the aftermath.

I wanted to be able to cast my eyes over Sulva Bay, knowing that somewhere out there, most likely on that flat bit between the bay and the little range of hills, lies the spot where a dud Turkish shell plopped between John's mule's legs – it might even still be there, laying unexploded. Just like his more famous enemy up here on the hill, he survived the scare. And, unlike Kemal, he went on to father clan Earnshaw, including my dad, David. It's a bit like the circle of life. Minus the lions and plus one very lucky mule.

***

Well, we've looked over the battle sites on the peninsula and I've managed to see Sulva Bay, if not actually place a foot on it. We've booked a further night in the hotel to allow us to visit another place of considerable historical interest, situated down to the south west of Çanakkale, a distance of about 36 kilometres. Its modern name is Hisarlik, but rumour has it that, back in the mists of time, it went by the name of Troy.

Before that though, there's another place nearer home that is of interest – a naval museum that has, amongst its exhibits, the remains of a German submarine. After depositing the bike back at the hotel, we wander down through the town and into the grounds of the museum. It's a bit of a surprise when we come across the remains of the UB-46, preserved in the condition she was when raised from the seabed. The submarine is of the UB-11 class of vessels, built in 1916. These were small boats, weighing in at 300 tons submerged, but they weren't that much different in appearance from the later vessels of the Second World War.

UB-46 had an interesting start to its relatively brief operational career, having been transported in sections by rail down to the Austro-Hungarian (now Croatian) port of Pola. Here, they were assembled and sent to the Black Sea. She ended up being based at Varna in Bulgaria, the city we passed through a few weeks ago. She was sunk after hitting a mine on the 7th December 1916 north-east of the entrance to the Bosphorus Straits. Her entire crew of 20 perished. The remains of the submarine – two forward sections of the hull – were located in 1993 and subsequently salvaged by the Turkish Navy. They make a poignant and quite eerie sight, mounted on a plinth in the gardens of the museum.

The museum also features a replica of the minelayer *Nusret*, which ventured out one night in February, 1915 to lay 26 mines in the projected path of the British and French battleships that sailed daily, and predictably, into the Dardanelles to pound the Ottoman forts, retiring in the same manner each day. Three battleships were sunk: the British *HMS Irresistible* and *HMS Ocean* and the French *Bouvet*. All three were old and obsolete Pre-Dreadnought battleships, but they were hardly dispensable, and their crews shouldn't have been. Their loss sent shockwaves through the British and French establishments.

***

The morning dawns bright and hot. We head off out of town in an easterly direction, passing through the clean and modern outskirts then taking a right down a very modern highway that climbs above the town, giving fine views of the surrounding hills and the sea. The ride down to Troy takes about forty minutes, by which time the sun has climbed high into the sky and temperature has rocketed with it. We spot a sign for the site of the ancient city and hang a right, arriving at an expansive and largely deserted car park radiating heat from its pale, crushed-core surface in a fashion that would cook a pizza far faster than your local Dominos, which isn't that great an achievement really, because our local Dominos are experts in very, very slowly-cooked pizzas.

I have a vague recollection about the finding of Troy, reading about it in a magazine. I recall that they were 'fairly sure' they'd found it, but that very little remained to be seen. It turns out that the location of the ancient and mythical city has been the subject of speculation for many years. A Scottish journalist called Charles Maclaren first pinpointed where the city lay. An American, Frank Calvert, bought fields in the area and started excavating in 1866, which I think shows a certain degree of either conviction, or (possibly) madness. A German archaeologist Heinrich Schliemann progressed the excavations between 1871 and 1879, uncovering a series of ruins of a city that had gone through many incarnations. It is widely accepted that the ruins cover a period from 3000 BC right through to the Byzantine period of 500 AD, nowadays named Troy I to Troy IX. It was probably called something other than 'Troy' for most of its existence. Put simply, it is an ancient city that has been rebuilt many times, all on the same spot. It might once have been called Troy, and it certainly is now.

The Troy of legend is famous through its portrayal in Homer's Iliad, and I guess most people associate it with Helen and the Wooden Horse. But the ruins do include a few fragments that are thought to date from the time of Homeric legend, imparting an element of romance when you pay the fee and wander into the site.

The entrance takes you past a set of impressive angular walls, fashioned from very large stones, which flatter to deceive because very little else is on such a grand scale. Reconstructions of how it would have looked show a fine city with a citadel on the hill and a walled town below. The landscape surrounding the site has changed considerably over the past few thousand years, with the river that once wound past here changing its route and the land to seawards drying out. Historians think that the city eventually lost its strategic and trading importance and it was eventually abandoned in favour of other cities that rose and took precedence. Standing on the hill viewing the broad plain below, reminds me of another ancient ruin called Burgh Castle in Norfolk, which suffered a similar fate when the great sea inlet that once lapped its walls silted up, leaving it stranded, the walls part-robbed to build later buildings.

⸺⸺◆⸺⸺

Chapter 28
Riot Van

Wednesday 19th September, 2012. We depart the hotel at our usual time in the mid-morning, taking the short ride down to the ferry, where we bid farewell to the fine town of Çanakkale – a great place to be on such a beautiful blue morning, fair bustling with daily life. Our route today takes us back to the north, retracing our journey of a few days ago for a few miles until we reach the top of the Gallipoli isthmus. It then forks to the west, heading us into unfamiliar territory, tracking in a purposeful curve around the huge bay that forms the northern shoulder of the peninsula. The views from the heights are glorious, stretching out for miles in front of us. From here, the road heads towards the town of Keşan, where it meets the highway to Greece. We grab a quick bite to eat and top-up of fuel at Keşan, then make the hop to the border. The last settlement in Turkey is Ipsala, a small town of little more than 8,000 people that might pass without comment, but for two points of interest.

The first is that Ipsala is formally identified by the Catholic Church as a Titular See – a title given to former dioceses, once run by a bishop, that have subsequently been conquered by Islam (or any other religion, for that matter) and aren't expected to return to the fold any time soon. As if to underscore the importance of keeping things that way, the second point of note is that there is a lot of shooting going on around the eastern outskirts of the town, just a few hundred yards from the border. The Turkish Army appears to have placed a firing range right under the noses of the Greek border guards. You can almost taste the febrile tension in relations between the two countries as you ride through.

The border post on the Turkish side is large and modern. We are one of only two vehicles passing through, the other being a German 'plated car. Relations between Germany and Greece are at an all-time low – well, perhaps the lowest they've been since 1945 – with the Germans insisting punitive terms for the latest proposed Greek bailout, following their economic collapse in 2009. I wonder how the solitary occupant of the car will fare on the other side of the border. He'll probably get strung up.

Lest we forget, there is a small financial debt of our own making hanging over our heads so, with that in mind, once we've traversed the formalities of passport stamping, we head into a long building and, quite voluntarily, search out the desk where fines can be paid, should you wish to pay one. On locating the correct window, we are met by a very pleasant gentleman who looks sufficiently like Heinrich Himmler to be a little unnerving. In other ways he's not at all like Himmler because he's a very sun-tanned Reichsführer-lookalike and has probably never kept chickens. Diane produces the speeding ticket from the administrative red pouch and passes it to him, while I attempt to appear appropriately contrite, without being too obsequious. It's a difficult balancing act under the circumstances. Heinrich inspects it for a few seconds and then thanks me for bothering to offer to pay, advising me that it will cost me a fraction of the £70 quoted by the very nice policeman, a week or so ago, and asking if we would be interested in buying any free-range eggs. I don't think I've ever been so happy to be fined. So much so, that I'm forced to restrain myself from dancing all the way back to the bike, smiling like a wide-mouthed frog.

And so, with that final act of official kindness, we bid farewell to Turkey, a country that has made quite an impression on us both. There have been a few ups-and-downs, especially in the motorway toilet department (female section) but, taken in the round, I can honestly say that I've developed a soft spot for this large and splendidly diverse country. Turkey rocks.

***

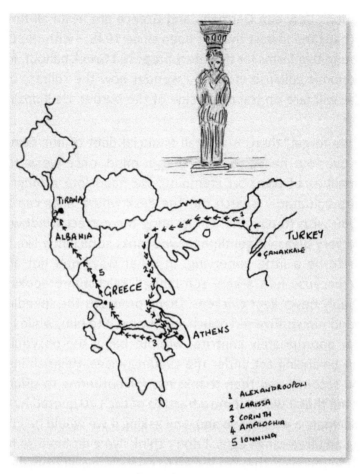

Watch out for dynamite!

In contrast to the smart and well-run border station in Turkey, arrival back in the European Union comes as a minor shock on the Greek side. The border guards are slovenly beyond belief, giving a less than cursory inspection of our passports and waving us off on our way in an 'am I bovvered?' manner. The German gentleman gets through without even the slightest sniff of aggravation which, I have to say, on the potential entertainment front, is faintly disappointing. What's the world coming to?

The road from the border is superb. However which way the Greeks have managed to blow the bank balance, at least they've got a decent road network to and from the Turkish border, I'll give them that.

Once we've overtaken the person driving the German car, it strikes us that the roads are unusually quiet. In fact, they're completely deserted, as if we're extras in a zombie move, which a few of my acquaintances might find appropriate. It continues for a few kilometres until we reach a turnoff to the small city of Alexandroupolis, which sits at the western edge of the delta of the river Maritsa (or Evros, in Greek), an important river that winds in and out of a series of countries forming the natural border between some of them, notably between Bulgaria and Turkey and between Turkey and Greece. It's quite a complicated river.

The city of Alexandroupolis is a garrison town, situated close to the border. Apart from military installations, it has an airport and an important seaport with strong trading links to Turkey. We ride through the quiet streets, wending our way towards a reasonably pleasant sea front, where we execute a smart right turn and head west, pitching up shortly afterwards at a small hotel, warmly greeted by the Anglophile owner who assigns us to a room with half a view. From the balcony we can see the bike.

Once we've unpacked the bike and settled into the room, we set off on a brief walk into the town centre to look for somewhere to eat. It is pleasantly warm and ideal for strolling around in 'T' shirt and shorts, revealing my disturbingly white legs. The heat bounces off the predominantly leg-matching white buildings and hovers just below the threshold of 'oven-like'. The number of shops increases gradually as we arrive at the centre. All of them are open, but their efforts appear to be in vain. Put simply, there are no shoppers in this town whatsoever. Alexandroupolis is a commercial desert. The juxtaposition with the vibrancy of Turkey across yonder to the east couldn't be more pronounced. This is what a financial meltdown looks like.

***

We continue our journey westwards in the morning. Again, the roads are completely deserted. It's uncanny and disquieting to be the sole pair of travellers, passing along a modern, virtually brand-new motorway, unhindered by any form of traffic. A perfect place for Georgian cows to stretch their legs. We pass a series of hills that march along the northern horizon to our right. It is quite a lovely place, if very slightly tatty around the edges.

In the late morning, we pull into a motorway rest area that is surprisingly busy, considering the desolation of the highway. Perhaps the occupants have been stranded here for the past three years... We have a few mobile eateries to choose from. Trade is less than brisk – most of the customers are just sitting around. We're travelling on a trajectory that will take us towards the country's second largest city, Thessaloniki, which we will bypass before swinging southwards towards Athens. A population of around eleven million people live here, which adds up to a lot of glasses thrown into fires. The one's we've met at this stop seem friendly enough, as far as natives go, but I feel we should tread with caution. I consider myself fortunate to have a few friends of Greek origin whom I've always found to be good fun and, occasionally, very slightly nutty in a similar manner to Norwegians. My friend and ex-colleague Constantine springs to mind, or at least a story he once told me does.

He hails from one of the Greek islands, I can't remember which one. Despite being a computer programmer, and therefore a *de facto* Star Wars-loving geek extraordinaire, and a man who managed to bowl himself and his ball down the ten-pin alley quite regularly when we all went bowling in Aberdeen, pause for breath... despite all this, he can be quite a level-headed person. On this occasion, we were chatting about nothing much in particular, when he told me (with a perfectly straight face) about a tradition on his island involving people throwing lighted dynamite sticks off the top of the cliffs overlooking his town, the dynamite being thrown with sufficiently short a fuse to ensure a mid-descent detonation, which in Greek terms is considered a solid safety measure, bordering on over-cautious. He countered my incredulity by showing me the spectacle on an internet site.

A few weeks later, he returned from vacation and told me that a terrible accident had happened whilst he was at home. There'd been some kind of celebration and one of the youths throwing dynamite in a perfectly normal and traditional fashion had managed to kill himself quite badly. After the funeral, the boy's friends went back to the place of his demise with a LOT of dynamite to throw in honour of their fallen chum. Constantine was down in the town having a haircut at the time. A massive explosion rocked the whole town when one of the mourners went to throw a stick, only for it to slip out of his hand, outstretched behind him. The dynamite sailed backwards in a graceful arc and landed in the stockpile of remaining explosives. The resulting detonation removed a sizeable portion from the top of the hill. Constantine went on to say how sad it was that a further batch of mourners were killed, but I couldn't hear him properly. I was overcome by a horribly painful, side-splitting fit of hysterics and was reduced to tears. I continue to carry the guilt of my reaction to this day.

I think this tale demonstrates admirably that it's probably best to avoid messing around with Greeks too much. You never know what they might throw at you. So, having consumed a light snack, we'll be on our way.

***

We are wafted along in a bubble of warmth, past distant high hills, before arriving at a point where the road sweeps over a ridge down to a broad plain that lies below. The compass on the Garmin then swings towards the south-south-east as the road hugs the coast for around forty kilometres after shaking itself clear of Thessaloniki, skirting attractive towns that overlook the Aegean Sea, which sparkles with a fabulous aquamarine blue. We pass through a few of these towns. They appear devoid of human activity. This marks the high point of the day's ride, because a veil of high cloud gradually draws over the sky and the view from the saddle deteriorates noticeably when we swing inland.

We could ride into the early evening to arrive triumphantly in Athens, but there's a town up ahead called Larissa, so, after a brief confab, we decide to pull off when the junction arrives and try our luck with accommodation. We pass into an outlying commercial district that is moderately frayed around the edges. Larissa appears to be a workmanlike, semi-industrial town. We ride across a river with the aid of a bridge and find ourselves in what looks like the centre of town. Over to our left, we spot the sign for a hotel. Bingo!

***

I have to admit that first impressions leave me less than enamoured with Larissa. It takes an hour or so for a gentle warming to develop. The hotel Acropol is located in a street with a mixture of shops and offices and has very little charm to it at all, but it has supplied a cheap and reasonable room for the night. It doesn't have a restaurant, so, after a wash and brush-up, we decide to go hunt one down. We wander through the streets, which are reasonably busy with traffic. Those people still with jobs are leaving for the day and there are plenty of them about. We walk around a couple of corners and up a hill, arriving at a section of street overlooking a very impressive ruin. We have accidentally stumbled upon ancient Larissa.

The ruin in question is the ancient city's theatre, a semicircle of stepped seats built into the hillside below us and the remains of the buildings that formed the *skene* – the wall that provided a backdrop for plays and a changing room for the actors. The seating area was called the *theatron* which means 'seeing area'. Our words 'scene' and 'theatre' come respectively from those two Greek words. The area around the ancient theatre is quite characterful and we quickly locate a restaurant there. Surprisingly, it turns out to be a Greek restaurant.

One of my favourite towns, Great Yarmouth in Norfolk, the armpit of England, is blessed with a sizeable Greek community. They do lots of strange things – like throwing the Greek Orthodox church cross in the sea then plunging in after it, which might not seem strange or stupid, but they do it on New Year's Day, so I think it qualifies. It's a notch or two down in the 'looney department' from chucking dynamite, but it's still damn silly.

In the 1980's, when I lived there, the Greek restaurants were always considered a quality night out. If we were 'going posh', we would head for the Columbia restaurant, a converted public house with a totem pole at its entrance, known to all and sundry as 'Toniponis'. It served the finest lamb kleftiko you could ever wish to slap your chops on. A slightly cheaper night out involved dining at the Metropole on the seafront, which had a charmingly tacky décor, but served a mean fried steak dinner. I'm not sure if that's particularly Greek, but never mind, they did do tinned octopus as a starter, and I think that counts. Both restaurants are still going strong, as I write this tale.

The restaurant we enter, here in Larissa, has a lot more in common with the Metropole than it has with Toniponis. We commence with a starter of Greek salad, which arrives with a monolithic slab of feta cheese drenched in olive oil, slapped on top of the greenery. The restaurant owner seems genuinely delighted to have paying customers and makes us feel extremely welcome, as did the hotel when we checked in. The main course kebab is outstanding and the red wine hits the spot too.

***

Friday the 21st of September. The big hand on my wristwatch is sweeping purposefully towards 11 a.m. and that means we're late departing. But, before we head off on our way, I think I should do a bit of outrageous name-dropping on behalf of Larissa. It has many claims to fame and one is that it is the mythological birthplace of none other than Achilles himself and, furthermore, it was the place where Hippocrates departed this mortal coil, having done quite a lot for medical propriety. It can also justly claim to be one of the birthplaces of democracy, having embraced it in the 5th Century BC and, in the process, allied itself with Athens – a bit of a cock-up, since it turned out to be the losing side in the Peloponnesian War. These events happened a few years before the Metropole opened its doors in Great Yarmouth, but judging by the wallpaper that decorates its walls, not that many.

The slightly grey skies of yesterday have given way, back to blue. We navigate our way to the main road, then hang a right to continue the journey down to Athens, a jaunt that takes up most of the day. The bike is running smoothly, ticking over the kilometres at a one hundred and twenty per hour. Our solitary stop is for fuel and a nibble. Over the space of an hour or so, we pass the peaks of hills that might qualify for mountain status, but they're a touch too far away to be sure. We passed Mount Olympus yesterday and never even noticed it, ignoring the Gods completely. At just over 2,900 metres it is the highest mountain in Greece.

Riding through this beautiful country, you get an impression that huge geological forces have been at work on the landscape, creating a place of monumental glory. Greece was built by a series of tectonic collisions as fragments of Africa crashed into Eurasia, like giant slabs of polystyrene, borne by an ocean, crashing onto a shore, each tectonic plate fragment forced under the previous one, building the mountains we have seen everywhere in a heady mixture of pale limestone and grey conglomerate rocks that are draped in woodland and forest. Sometimes visible way over on the horizon, at other times closer.

Very gradually, as we approach the great city of Athens, the traffic makes an appearance and starts to thicken up, and, by the time we arrive on the outskirts, we find ourselves queuing in a traffic jam, which, surprisingly, almost feels like a relief. Riding unnaturally empty roads was, as I've mentioned, just a little bit spooky.

We've ridden down the main artery into the city from the north, the E75, which follows a gently winding route all the way from Larissa, heading south to the coast then tracking around the Malian Gulf, scene of the famous battle of Thermopylae, between the combined Greek armies and a vastly larger army of Persians. King Leonidas of Sparta fought a legendary rearguard action to the last man with a mixed force of Spartans, Thebans and Thespians. Quite why a bunch of actors got caught up in fighting to the death is a bit of a mystery, but there we are, it's a fact of history.

***

Fast forward a couple of hours or so. We have checked into the Hotel Dorian Inn, a strange, triangular tower situated on a busy street a few blocks south-west of Omonia Square, which, according to Trip Advisor dot NZ is: "Dangerous, STAY AWAY." Crikey! I didn't think Kiwis were a bunch of wusses, but never mind. We'll start whupping their asses at rugby in the not-too-distant future if they keep that up.

Ignoring the dire antipodean warnings, we take an evening stroll up to the square, turning right, then working our way down a hill in the direction of the Acropolis. The streets are indeed quite filthy and increasingly smelly as we walk past a market that is packing up. Rotten things are being swilled down the road, making it pong like an over-ripe trolley-bin. Things improve quite dramatically when we arrive at a shopping precinct for tourists, an attractive and vibrant area where shopkeepers patrol the front of their premises in a vain attempt to drum up business.

As the sun goes down and the Parthenon illuminations are switched on, lighting up in gentle relief what is probably the finest lamp in the whole world, we settle into a meal at a pleasant, open-air restaurant. A three-piece ensemble of guitarist-vocalist, keyboard player and bouzouki plucker extraordinaire strike up the night's entertainment, with the singer sounding a bit like Demis Roussos in his later career. I make this distinction because Demis was originally a progressive rock artist, singing with the band *Aphrodite's Child* alongside Vangelis – creating some very interesting work. His music then went progressively downhill (pun possibly intended), and he ended up releasing a string of mushy solo songs, some of which are now being covered by the house band, including the 1973 anthem 'Forever and Ever'. If, like me, you are fond of progressive rock, then Aphrodite's Child are worth a listen. If not, don't bother, you'll hate it. But the chaps back in Romania won't.

I saw Demis many times on Top of the Pops, but I never saw him do what the singer/guitarist does next. He sidles around the room in a worryingly purposeful manner, singing and playing whilst heading sideways like a glossy crab towards our table, possibly mistaking us for wealthy Americans or Germans. On arrival, he blatantly ignores Diane and starts serenading me, something I find disturbing and ever so slightly gay. And then, just as I'm about to arm myself with a heavy chunk of feta cheese, he places his guitar right next to my ear and picks a series of natural, harmonic notes that are barely audible to the rest of the diners, but which are a secret delight to my ears, reserved - as they are - especially for me. After that, he sidles over to Diane and repeats the trick. Her face lights up in delight. It's a very special moment that earns him a well-deserved, hefty tip.

***

In the morning, I take a trip down the lift after breakfast to visit Mutley the motorcycle – to check if it still has any wheels. I'm surprised to be met outside by a pleasant enough guy who is giving it the once-over. He could conceivably be a thief, but It turns out (if he's to be believed) that he's a fellow BMW GS Adventure owner. OK, he could still be a 'tea-leaf'. He explains to me, in decent English, that he owns an identical BMW that he purchased brand-new a couple of years ago.

'Would you like to buy it?', he asks. 'It is newer than your bike and has less miles. It is in much better condition, like still brand-new. I can sell it to you for 4,500 Euros.'

He asks me how much my trusty GS is worth. Because of the mileage, I'm not really that sure, but guess around £7,000. He says that his bike is worthless and can't be sold.

'You see, we have no money at all. My BMW is worth nothing to me, nothing at all. If you offered me 2,500 Euros I would be forced to sell it to you. I can't even afford to put gas into it.' On that sad note, he wishes us well on our travels and shakes my hand, heading off towards the very dangerous square, possibly in search of hapless New Zealanders.

Having checked the bike out and tidied up our room for the cleaner, we head off in the general direction of the Acropolis, retracing our steps from the night before, walking down past the market, with all its earthy smells, and passing the arcade of touristic shops. Eventually we come across an area scattered with magnificent, fragmentary ruins. Notable amongst these ruins, that sit on this, the northern side of the Acropolis hill, is Hadrian's Library, built in AD132 by the Roman Emperor, shortly after he finished the final course of bricks on his eponymous wall, ensuring continued Pictish independence.

***

And so, on to the miracle that is the Acropolis. On its northern side, it is ringed by an attractive park, planted with mature trees. It's quite a steep climb to tread the pathway that millions have trodden through the millennia, but one that is well worth the effort. Having paid the entrance fee, we turn a corner and walk up the steps into the sacred site, something I've been dying to do for over twenty years.

The citadel of the Acropolis dates back long before its most famous buildings. These were built in what was considered the 'Golden Age', the 5th century BC, under the direction of Pericles. I read, a long time ago, that the alignment and detail design of the complex of buildings was executed in such a way that the view was perfect when you walked up the steps and entered the complex. The columns of the Parthenon are not straight, but rather they narrow at both ends. From some angles they look quite odd. But, viewed from the steps, there is a trick of the eye: they look perfectly straight. The attention to detail goes much deeper too. Each segment of each column has a wooden peg arrangement, designed to twist during earthquakes, providing a degree of flex, preventing collapse. The square slabs making up the main building are bound together by iron straps that were set in molten lead. Protected thus from water, the straps also provided structural integrity during earthquakes.

It's hard to imagine that the Parthenon was once vividly painted, using wax to help the paint adhere to the white marble. It looks so stunning in its 'naked' form – and that's without its famous full-length frieze – a sizeable portion of which resides in the British Museum in London. We can only imagine the splendour of the statue of Athena Parthenos that once dwelt within. Standing around 40 feet high and made of ivory and gold, it cost more to create than the building in which it was housed and acted as the city's gold reserve (in times of crisis, the gold could be removed). Unfortunately, the site is subject to major restoration work and is covered in scaffold. Bugger! In fact, the whole expanse of the Acropolis is one vast building site.

The finest lamp in the whole wide world.

The view of the city from the citadel is spectacular. Above the din of traffic and the grime of the streets, Athens is a particularly beautiful city, draped as it is over various hills, with the highest ones rising above it. The predominant colour of the buildings is a mixture of white and grey. Under a clear blue sky, it feasts the eye with a complex series of layers that are dazzlingly photogenic. I really love it.

The other building that I have been very keen to see is the Erechtheum, a much smaller building that sits on the northern side of the site, facing the Parthenon. The building work might have commenced with gusto back in the days of Pericles but, sadly for Athens, the ongoing Peloponnesian War meant that funds quickly ran down and, as a result, the Erechtheum ended up being much smaller than it should have been. In fact, it is quite a confusing structure to view, but it has an iconic (nay, Ionic) feature, in the shape of a small porch that sprouts from the side facing the Parthenon, with six female figures holding up the roof. The draped ladies give the porch its name: Porch of the Caryatids – a Caryatid being a female sculpture used as a column. Many examples of these columns can be found nowadays in various museums. They are incredibly beautiful and intricate, their elaborate hairstyles giving a fascinating glimpse of the fashions of the day.

The Porch of the Caryatids is apparently a little 'flourish of the brush' to hide a structural support that was necessary when the building plans altered and everything was down-sized; not entirely unlike covering an RSJ with a bit of plaster and three flying ducks. It looks nice, but it is a reminder that all empires end up declining and falling. The great Athenian maritime empire suffered a similar fate to the Erechtheum, reduced in stature, and then suffering total defeat, two years after the building was completed.

✳✳✳

Diane has been eyeing up the city bus excursions with a view to taking one tomorrow. Over dinner in the evening, we decide to have a day apart, she taking in the city scenery from the top floor of a double-decker and me doing a bit of writing and generally relaxing back at the hotel. It seems like a good plan.

We enjoy a lazy get-up. In the late morning, Diane heads off up to the square to catch her bus. I busy myself composing the foreword for *Far Horizons.* For a while, everything seems well with the world. Then, in the early afternoon, my attention is caught by a racket emanating from far below the balcony. Sounds of chanting and shouting. I wander out onto the balcony and peer up the street, immediately spotting the source of the brouhaha. A large body of people carrying banners stream around a corner and up the street towards the very dangerous square. I can see a police cordon blocking off the square – policemen in riot gear, festooned with large, clear shields, looking a bit like modern-day Hoplites. Blow me down, the Kiwis were correct all along!

It dawns on me that Diane's heading off alone around the city was a really bad idea. As I peer up the street a few bangs go off as CS gas is fired and the crowd erupts.

This isn't the first riot that I've witnessed. I was unlucky enough to get caught up in the May Day riots in London in 1999. It coincided with my first ride to work on my brand-new Honda Hornet. On the way into London, a scooterist had run into the back of my new pride and joy and cracked the rear mudguard. Then, when I left work, I found that my usual route down the Embankment was blocked off by police barriers and I was forced to ride a circuitous route slightly north of the river towards St Pauls. Eventually, the traffic became impenetrable and I came to a halt, stuck behind an old lady in a small car.

As I was looking for a gap to slip through, I suddenly saw things flying into the air. It was very slightly reminiscent of those films on Youtube of the Japanese Tsunami. Some form of destruction was heading my way, but I couldn't properly make out what it was. A group of people beckoned me to seek shelter with them behind an open doorway. I looked down the road again and could now clearly make out a howling mob rioting in the street, throwing things through shop windows, climbing on cars, and wrecking them with their occupants inside. A police van was trashed – the occupants wisely remaining locked inside as the crowd tried to tip it over.

It went through my mind that this wasn't my new bike's day. It seemed it was just destined to be trashed. I looked back over to the doorway and was again beckoned inside. But then I thought, 'sod it and sod them, I'm not leaving the bike!' I turned around to see if there was any way of escaping and was quite surprised to be greeted by a phalanx of fellow motorcyclists, mostly dispatch riders, who nodded encouragement and grinned in a 'bring it on' fashion. It appeared that I was 'man on point duty.' Suddenly, I was overcome by a feeling that all would be well. I decided to sit it out and try to protect the wee red Honda. The rioters trashed the poor old lady in front's car, leaping on the roof and bashing it in. Then, they neatly parted and washed around the tight wedge of bikers. One plucky chap did try to snatch the key from my ignition, but I got there first. Two young brightly-painted girls then bizarrely offered me an imitation flower, saying, 'save the earth, stop using petrol,' which I considered slightly ironic, considering that the flower appeared to be made from a byproduct of hydrocarbons. The Hornet survived to live another day and we rode home through a scene of devastation, once the rioters had headed in search of somewhere with television cameras. All-in-all, it was a strange day. On the plus side, the scooter rider had given me £25 to fix the mudguard. I decided to pocket the money and just cut it a bit shorter with a hacksaw – ready for the next riot.

Back in Athens. The police have successfully resisted the rioters and are now on the offensive. The crowd breaks and starts streaming down the street towards the hotel. And towards the Mutt! Sheeyat! I've forgotten that my bike is sitting six floors below, chained to the railings! I've been blithely watching and photographing the events and have completely overlooked the safety of the trusty mule!

Chapter 29
Bad days for Wild Hogs

It's a few hours after the riot. Prior to this, I spent a very worrying time, wondering if Diane was OK, and was deeply relieved when she returned to base with reports of a slightly stressful day on the buses. We exchange our tales of civil disorder. Mine goes as follows:

When the crowd broke, they scattered in all directions, trying to avoid the advancing policemen. Across from the hotel sits a small kiosk, selling newspapers and tobacco. The kiosk owner had wisely locked up the joint and scooted off to safety, leaving a black dog on guard duty and his old car parked in an adjacent lot. In between glancing down to see if the bike was OK, I watched the dog, fearful for its safety. The rioters ran straight past him and turned the kiosk owner's car into a terminally exterminated one. The dog completely ignored them and decided to have a lie down to watch events unfold in comfort. I looked back at the bike, far below, and was relieved to see that it, too, was completely intact, still chained to the railings. Rioters appear to have a blind spot for mutts of all varieties. I headed down in the lift to capture a few images on my little Panasonic camera.

The police were quickly there in force, a couple of them riding up on a white Honda Transalp with blue lights flashing away, looking like a pair of extras from the film *Terminator*. The moment they stopped, a few feet away from the kiosk, violence was unleashed with great, furious anger. The dog leapt up and attached itself to the riot police pillion passenger's right leg. I shook my head in disbelief. The kiosk owner must have trained the dog to only bite rozzers! The pair rode off pronto, with the dog still temporarily attached. Oh, what wonderful chaos!

Taken one-point-five seconds before the bravest dog in Athens became temporarily attached. I do hope the policeman pillion has had his rabies jab.

Diane files her report, describing a tense trip on the sightseeing tour: She headed off to the Olympic Stadium Spyros Louis, a building completed in 1982 and extensively renovated for the 2004 Summer Olympics with the addition of a splendid new roof. The bus to the stadium was a good hour late and she had a similar wait for transport back to the city centre. When it eventually turned up, it proceeded to take a circuitous route home, the driver explaining that some of the roads were blocked off by the police.

Eventually, the bus pulled up some distance from its intended destination. The driver, who seems to have been a decent and responsible chap, advised Diane to walk directly back 'that way', indicating straight up the street (to the very dangerous square). In her quietly resolute, Aberdonian fashion, she continued as instructed, finding it strange that a bus stop she encountered on the way had been completely mangled. Arriving at the square, she also found it 'a bit odd' that the local Subway outlet no longer possessed a front window. Apparently, this kind of thing happens a lot in Portlethen.

'There were plenty of people around. It seemed safe,' says she.

As she rounded the square and headed the final hundred yards or so to the hotel entrance, she passed the groups of riot officers, then spotted me 'inspecting the bike'. The dog, meanwhile, had returned to his position guarding the kiosk against the unwelcome attentions of anyone wearing a uniform.

A bit later in the evening, we discovered that the protest was nothing to do with the current financial crisis. It was a reaction to the release in California of a YouTube film mocking the Prophet Muhammad. Everything seems to have calmed down, so we decide to wander up to the very dangerous square to try to find an undamaged restaurant. Most of the premises have been smashed up and are closed, but one pleasant little restaurant, located up a side street is still doing business. The owner ushers us in, saying that, 'outside not safe.' He makes us very welcome and serves up a fine meal and a decent bottle of wine. Things could be worse.

* * *

Thursday 27th September. We have taken a little jump in time in our travelogue. On Monday the 24th, we flew back to the UK, leaving our gear at the hotel and the bike locked up securely and double alarmed, sitting under a tall lamp in the long stay car park at Athens airport. We flew home to attend the funeral, returning to Greece today. In the evening, we headed back to the restaurant near the square and found the owner to be a lot more relaxed than he was a few days ago.

I didn't mention it previously, but when we returned from our visit to the Acropolis a few days ago, we wandered through a very pleasant neighbourhood of tightly packed streets, overlooked by impressive houses and apartments – a very green and attractive, upper middle-class part of the city. Then we passed down through a small square, where there was a gathering of people who appeared to be public service workers. The banners were out, and speakers were addressing the crowd through a PA system. It was a very reasonable and civilized revolt. We hovered around the edges of the crowd, just taking in the scene. The feeling of stress and despondency was palpable but, despite that, it occurred to me that we were seeing something quite similar to the very early democracy that flourished here two and a half thousand years ago. Slaves with ropes would gather the citizens to a meeting point where speeches were made and decisions taken. The birthplace of political sophistry.

Having witnessed these events, we are leaving Athens today. Ideally, I'd like to stay a little longer, but we are starting to feel the pressure to put some miles under the wheels. The next stage of our journey promises to be interesting. There are multiple routes we could take, but the one we've chosen is to head northwards to Albania and thence through to the countries that were once Yugoslavia. I think Albania will be an interesting country.

We bid the hotel staff goodbye. They've been very helpful, letting us store bags while we travelled back to the UK and reserving us a room for our return. They also kept an eye on the bike when it was parked outside the front and generally made us feel welcome. The view of the Acropolis from the roof terrace bar will be one of my abiding memories of the city and another high point of this trip.

We have a few route options departing the city. After due deliberation, I've plumped for the simplest one: retracing the route of our arrival to a point where it intersects with the E94 – a motorway that heads west towards the ancient city of Corinth. It's a short hop that will take us little over an hour, tracking along the coast towards the Peloponnesian Peninsula.

In my imagination, Corinth is a spectacular example of an ancient Greek city but, sadly, it suffered two devastating earthquakes in the past (1858 and 1928), followed by a great fire in 1933. The modern motorway deposits us in an area that is every bit as shabby as the outskirts of Athens. The local road that we're spat out on passes through a graffiti-decorated tourist spot that has seen much better days, then leaps straight over the famous Corinth Canal. Without even a 'by your leave', we've passed over an iconic heritage site and would have missed it if we blinked. There's no missing the first available accommodation in Corinth though, because we immediately spot a huge hotel on our right, prompting us to turn in and enquire upon room availability. We appear to have caught the hotel manager by surprise and are advised that the establishment is under new management and is 'sort of open, in a closed kind of way – you might be the only guests staying tonight, or even this week'. A short while later, we are checked in and our bags have been deposited in our room.

It turns out that the establishment was once a resort hotel of some renown, with a large swimming pool, a tennis court, and a five-a-side football pitch – perfect for groups of like-minded chaps with an activity-based disposition. I imagine it to have been built in the 1960's. It has a striking, shark-tooth feature down one side, providing full-length windows and private balconies to the rooms. Our luck in securing a room doesn't extend to finding the restaurant open, so we take a wander along to the bridge to view the canal, grabbing a coffee and a bite to eat at a bus station café that sits across the road from the hotel.

The bridge over the canal is a fine place to capture a few photos and marvel at the scale of its construction. I had the impression that it was a very ancient structure, and it could have been so if the original planners had followed their Gantt chart with due diligence and managed their project properly in the 7th century BC. They didn't. As a result, they switched to building a road across the isthmus instead of the failed canal – a 'Plan B', otherwise known as an unavoidable, face-saving gesture. The road allowed them to physically drag their ships 4 km across the isthmus, something they did for a while before giving up altogether. I might personally have given up a bit sooner.

Fast forward a couple of millennia and, in 1882, a new project was formally kicked-off to complete what was started 2,500 years previously. The technology was available to complete the task (although we've already seen that mixing Greeks and dynamite can lead to unforeseen consequences). The result is ranged before us: a canal that is too narrow (and shallow) to permit ships of a meaningful size to navigate the passage. Heads have rolled on much smaller projects for less.

The canal is 21.3 metres wide and 8 metres in draught – obsolete on the day it was completed. Which is a shame, because it is truly a magnificent sight and a glorious achievement, excavated at sea level and thus sitting anything up to 300 feet below the level of the land.

After conducting a spot of light shopping at the nearby souvenir shop, we wander back to the bridge to watch the (very slowly) developing spectacle of a modestly-sized tanker being towed up the canal by a similarly modest tugboat. It's one of the best free shows on earth. And Corinth has one more free show to deliver before we depart.

Dug at great expense for very little gain. But a marvel of engineering, nevertheless.

In the evening, we repair to the hotel lounge, a large room on the ground floor with comfy lounge sofas and a well-stocked bar at the far end. For a while, we are the only guests present, then a man turns up. He introduces himself and tells us that he does odd jobs around the hotel and for that he is provided with a room over his head and meals into the bargain. It's a similar arrangement to the one we found in parts of the United States, where people did various part-time tasks in return for a free room. But this man isn't alone.

He tells us he wants to introduce us to a friend and signals us to follow him outside, leading us to the poolside outside the sliding glass doors of the bar, telling us to wait by the pool. It's a beautiful, balmy night. The temperature is perfect, with just a hint of a passing breath of air, and the chirruping of crickets in the foliage adds to the atmosphere. After a short while, the man appears from the shadows, leading a sleek, black thoroughbred horse called George, to whom we are introduced. Then he leads the way down to the five-a-side football pitch, slipping the halter and releasing the magnificent animal. The horse races away, charging up and down the pitch, tossing its head and shaking itself down. He calls it over to us. It runs pell-mell towards the three of us then slows and walks the final few paces, allowing us to stroke it. The owner tells us that the hotel manager allows him to keep the horse in the outbuildings at the back of the hotel complex. He considers himself very lucky that he's been allowed to keep it there. Having no home for man or beast could be an impossible situation to resolve in these hard times, but the generosity of the hotel owner has saved the day, at least for the time being.

Note: I've kept track of the hotel and, at the time of writing the book, it looks like the manager managed to realise his dream of refurbishing it. It is called the Isthmia Prime Hotel. I don't know if George still lives there.

***

Saturday 29th September. This morning, on switching on the ignition to start the bike, I was greeted by a warning sign on the instrument binnacle with the word 'LAMPF' helpfully explaining the situation in full. The last time this happened was in 2009 on our departure from Yellowstone National Park, and at that time, it completely flummoxed me. But that experience has left me fully prepared for a repeat performance and I know for sure that this is German for, 'your light bulb is completely kaput, Englander. Vot are you looking at me like that for? Change it. NOW!'.

Finding the replacement bulb involves unloading the freshly loaded bike and rummaging around in the panniers. Fitting it is fiddly, especially for fingers that resemble a five-pack of Lincolnshire sausages, but it only takes five or ten minutes. Then we can repack the bike and head off, which is quite good going for a person of my limited technical capabilities. The Araldite spotlight repair that was skillfully executed in Tallinn is still holding out too.

Our first priority is to top up with fuel. We ride down into Corinth and chance upon an EKO petrol station that appears to be about twenty years out of date. It is patrolled by a little white and tortoiseshell kitten that looks a little too frayed around the edges for my liking. While I'm filling up, Diane strikes up a conversation with the old gentleman who is running the station and accosts the kitten for a cuddle, risking flea bites at best and distemper at worst, in my honest opinion, but she's a big girl and can make her own decisions on animal petting. My elder sister was once savaged by a tame squirrel – perhaps I lean towards being over-cautious. The squirrel didn't.

***

I would really like to explore Corinth further. It's such an influential place, one that lends its name not only to the canal, but to an entire architectural order – one of only three in ancient Greece, no less, the others being the Ionic and the Doric. And then there's the biblical references to the Corinthian Christians, who caused a few sleepless nights for Saint Paul, largely due to them living in a rather 'lively' city with persistently low moral standards – a kind of classical version of Portland and Weymouth, circa 1975. Sadly, though, we must press on. So, bidding farewell to the kitten and garage attendant, we mosey on out of town, locating route 8A, the Olympia Odos, a road that dips inland for a while, carving a route 'twixt glorious blue sea and a range of hills, hugging the coast of the Peloponnese Peninsula, heading purposefully towards the northwest and the town of Patras.

We are travelling beneath the arching splendour of a pale blue sky, peppered with a scattering of high clouds. The colour of the sea is uplifting, an impossibly beautiful deep colour of blue. The distance to Patras is just over 130 kilometres (85 miles), taking about an hour and a half to ride. To our right lies the Gulf of Corinth and, beyond that, the coastline of mainland Greece to the north. The whole area is geologically active with a series of major fault lines in situ and a complex set of forces causing the gulf to widen by a heady 15mm, on a bad year. Towards the end of this leg of our journey today, we catch glimpses of a splendid suspension bridge that spans the depths of the gulf, linking the Peloponnese Peninsula with the mainland at a place called Rio. Hanging a right at Rio, we head over the crossing high above the gulf.

The Charilaos Trikoupis Bridge, for that is its name, is the longest fully suspended bridge in the world, according to Wikipedia. What intrigues me is how it manages to stretch itself by 15mm per annum, thus keeping up with the widening gulf? Unfortunately, Wikipedia doesn't explain that small technicality, but it does say that it is one of the design considerations, so we'll just have to assume that it can cope for the next five minutes as we hot-foot across its span.

Once we've set wheels firmly on mainland Greece, we follow the coast for a short while before cutting inland and riding northwards on a circuitous route, along a strip of level ground flanked by low lying hills, modest towns, and the odd lake or two. Our route carries us some distance east of the Ionian Sea. Our target is a town called Ionnina. It lies maybe a hundred and twenty kilometres to the north of our current position, by road. It would be much nearer if the Greeks had completed the shortcut they are currently building, unceremoniously named 'motorway 5' but, sadly, it isn't ready so, pitching up at a town called Amfilochia, we decide to call it a day.

***

The hotel we stayed in last night possessed a lift that was almost as small as the one in the Hotel Volgograd. Its interior was lined with mirrors, giving the impression that guests' reflections were cast back to infinity and (possibly) beyond. It was a nicely decorated hotel, furnished with elegant, well-constructed furniture, in the style of the late '60s/early '70s, not unlike the one we stayed at in Bender, Transnistria.

I should mention an incident that occurred in the early evening, yesterday. We were wandering into town seeking out sustenance of a solid and liquid nature, watching the gentle waves rock the brightly-painted inshore fishing boats. Out of the corner of my eye, I spotted a leathery, mottled, scaly old head as it appeared above the water right in front of me, a dark eye carefully observing the two of us. And before you ask: it wasn't Simon Cowell. Diane had turned her back to the water and was chatting to me, oblivious of events behind her (this isn't a Pantomime by the way). She spied my look of utter astonishment as I pointed and blurted out, 'there's a.. there's a t.. a tur.. TURTLE!!' My astonishment was partly due to not ever having seen a live turtle before, and, in equal part, being oblivious to the fact that turtles (Ninja, teenage or otherwise) grace the waters of the Mediterranean Sea. As Diane started to turn around, the enigmatic amphibian quietly slipped back beneath the waves, leaving nary a ripple. Next stop Loch Ness!

Back to today. We find ourselves winding our way along a twisty road that carves through hills covered with pale, rocky outcrops and hoary-barked stands of trees. As with most of our travels in Greece, we encounter very little traffic. Every mile takes us closer to the mysterious land of Albania – a country that I know very little about – apart from its recent past as a closed-off, Stalinist enclave. In the early hours of the afternoon, whilst sweeping around a series of nadgery bends, we notice what appears to be a tumbledown, deserted café, nestling back from the road to our right. We pull over to investigate, parking up the bike and trying our luck with the door. It creaks open, prompting the instant appearance of an old man, as if from thin air. He might be the owner. Having been served up with some fresh coffee and a packet of crisps, we take up a seat at one of the tables on the patio out front.

Taking our first sips of coffee, we observe the arrival of two young men in an old pick-up truck bearing guns – rifles, to be precise. They drive past us to an area around the back of the café, shaded by low trees, where they proceed to offload their cargo: two wild boars that have only just met their maker. The young men bind the hind legs of the boars, swinging the ropes over the low-lying branches of two of the trees, hoisting the piggies to a suitable height for butchery. While this is taking place, more vehicles arrive, turning off from the road and driving past us to the grove behind the café, leaving clouds of fine dust behind them.

The wild boars are left to hang for a while, allowing blood to drain while a couple of trellis tables are juggled out of elderly cars and erected in the afternoon shade of the trees. Bottles of drink appear from various cars and a bit of a party ensues. Most of the visitors are older, middle-aged men, only the two hunters-turned-butchers are young, perhaps in their late teens or early twenties. Their skill with paring knives and cleavers is impressive. In the time it takes for us to sip down to the grains in the bottom of our coffee cups, the boars have been gutted, beheaded, skinned, and rendered into chops and joints. A few larger cuts are wrapped into paper and distributed, and a barbeque has been fired up to cook the rest.

This rustic theatre serves to remind us that we are heading into a remoter, wilder area of Europe, a part that is alien to those of us who suckle at the teat of urban domesticity. The populous centres of Greece have been left behind us as we head into the hills to the north, a mountainous region typified by the pale rocks that built the mountains and by the trees that clothe their lower flanks. Our destination for today lies towards the end of a wide valley that runs between these hills, on the edge of lake Pamvotis – the modestly-sized city of Ionnina, which, for many of its years, was a commercially successful Ottoman city, flourishing at a time when Greece was ruled by the Turkish empire.

With Diane in hotel meerkat mode, we commence our search for nightly accommodation, unusually failing to find anything on the outskirts of the town, gradually drawing us into the shaded streets of the city centre. Eventually, we spot a large hotel situated in opulent grounds, with clipped lawns, dappled by the shade of tall, mature trees of considerable girth in the trunk department. With the bike parked up outside the impressive main gate, we have a quick discussion about the merits of enquiring within. I imagine the price of a night here will be way beyond the resources of our dwindling budget. I'm minded of my shambolic failure to secure a posh room in Batumi and determine this time to persevere, regardless of the ignominy of failure, wandering into reception like a lost vagrant. Five minutes later and I'm returning with a decided bounce in my gait to notify the navigating officer that the price is less than that of a modestly-priced UK B&B. The hotel, starved of customers, is welcoming two tramps with open arms, if not garlands of gladioli.

We dine in the evening in an opulent restaurant, served by discreet waiters, chinking our wine glasses in the company of a large family gathering, here to celebrate the birthday of a very, very old lady. The party have obligingly provided our entertainment for the night in the shape of a traditional Greek band. It all adds up to a lot of bang for your bucks and a fine final evening in Greece, a country in real crisis that has managed amongst it all to retain the warmth of its heart and its welcome.

***

The border between Greece and Albania is situated in a truly wild part of Europe, a mountainous region, criss-crossed by serpentine roads and the occasional goat track. I imagine the winters here to be particularly tough, even for genus Capra, tough as they are, but we are passing through in mid-autumn under a pale, slightly hazy blue sky, with temperatures that remain pleasantly moderate. Our passage through the two border posts passes without incident. We've slipped out of the EU again, almost without noticing. After riding a few miles into Albania we're forced to stop, just to take in the landscape, which is stratospherically beautiful.

The road winds through a valley, following the meandering sweeps of the River Drino as it drifts its languid way across the border from Greece, depositing a vast, bleached expanse of pebbles across the wide valley that it has carved for itself. It arcs below the road, reflecting the blue of the sky above. A series of hills run parallel to the road on either side, dark green in the foreground fading to paler green, browns and greys where they rise higher, exposing bare peaks where the vegetation peters out. These glorious alpine views only last for a while though. As we plunge deeper into the south of Albania, the hills recede and the landscape becomes slightly less hilly. We pass a series of small settlements where a few notable features take shape.

The first feature is the welcome return of horse-drawn transport. Our first glimpse comes with the exhilarating sight of a group of teenagers spotted in the far distance, driving a carriage at breakneck speed on a dirt track that runs parallel to the main road. We spot further horse and cart combinations along our route, a pleasant reminder of Romania. At a roadside break, Diane reports an altogether darker and, one would imagine, sinister series of sightings.

'Have you seen the hanging teddy bears?'

I admit that, beyond appreciating the welcome return of horses and carts, and the gentle immersion into a world that appears less materialistic, I've been mainly concentrating on riding. I have, however, noticed the third feature, which is the welcome sighting of a smattering of new-build hotels. Of hanging teddy bears, I have seen not one. Shortly after, as we pass through a small town, Diane taps me on the shoulder and points to a half-built house. Right there, in the gaping hole of a breezeblock gap that's waiting for window insertion, dangle a line of horribly murdered cuddly toys. To delicate British sensibilities, this may appear to be seriously wrong. I'm sure the Albanians would consider us immensely stupid. Cuddly toys, or 'monkeys', as they call them, are there for a very serious purpose: to ward off the evil eye, the cursed eye of jealousy that will beset you whenever you build a nice new house, or hotel, or restaurant. Or ride past on a BMW motorcycle. It turns out that we're safely covered because we have our own 'Reindeer Rat' fluffy toy companion, purchased in Finland, dangling from our screen bar.

Despite this safety measure, our own encounter with resident evil isn't long in coming. An hour or so later, we find ourselves in a more remote area, climbing steadily up a road that is trying to emulate a farm track, marveling at the remoteness of it all, when we happen to pass a small mob of juveniles. They all turn and crane their necks to get a view of us as we pass by. I raise my arm to wave to them but am brought up short at the sight of one of them reaching down, picking up a stone and lobbing it at us with a speed and spin that would put Darren Gough to shame.

Having avoided being bowled out, we ride around the outskirts of a small town – in truth, it could be described as a large village. I'm surprised to spot a few cars bearing British number plates, old Fords and Vauxhalls, and a disturbing prevalence of semi-derelict Rovers. Is this where the world population of Rover 214s (Diane's favourite car) have ended up? While I'm pondering this, the road exits stage left.

Chapter 30
The Balkans

The signs are that Albania is making some effort to rectify the lack of decent roads between the Greek border and its capital city, Tirana. Where the road was once a track, they're busy laying something more substantial, but I think I would have settled for the track rather than the horrible nightmare presented before us now. The builders are busy laying the foundations for the new road. We find ourselves sandwiched in the flow of traffic lurching across a treacherous surface of badly-crushed rubble, scrabbling for grip. It's a scene destined to repeat itself many times over the next few hours, as we head higher into a range of hills, passing through scenery of extraordinary beauty and exquisite variation. The towns we pass through are busy places, full of half-built houses, streets lined with litter, the odd broken water main and occasional glimpses of older hilltop fortifications.

The distance from Ionnina to Tirana by road is around 200 miles. According to Google, it should take around five hours to cover those miles but, five hours after leaving, we're still negotiating the wilds, travelling on what appears to be a very circuitous route. Occasionally, I despair of ever reaching the mysterious capital. On one occasion, we ride into a built-up area and I think 'thank goodness, we've arrived', only to find ourselves in a seaside resort. Obviously, this isn't Tirana. I spot a sign for the capital and hang a right. Big mistake. A few minutes later and we're back in the countryside, and the capital seems as far away as ever.

I wonder if a modern infrastructure and a rich economy are prerequisites for happiness in the population? Most of the surveys I've seen indicate that they are, placing countries like Sweden, Denmark and Finland at the top of the satisfaction league. But is 'satisfaction' the same as 'happiness'? Satisfaction can be smug. In an index of happiness based on a sense of well-being, equality of outcomes, life expectancy, and ecological footprint, Albania ranks 13th out of 140. The United Kingdom ranks 34th, Denmark 32nd and Sweden 61st. Wealthy Luxembourg ranks second last. Only Norway ranks higher than Albania amongst the happy countries of Europe.

If this is the case – and I think there might be something in it – then, in truth, you don't need good road maps, or decent bitumen to find happiness. You just need to be riding a big trail bike. A machine that allows you to arrive safely in the capital city of the second happiest country in Europe, feeling fresh and ready for a gleeful beer. We eventually make our way into the outskirts of the city, past a military museum and then into the wide streets that run in a grid pattern towards a square at the centre of the city. There we find accommodation in the shape of a huge, towering communist-era hotel – a busy place, full of earnest-looking businessmen and women in nice suits, carrying laptop bags. The price of a room is quite exorbitant, and the room in question is the size of a shoebox, a sure sign that the hotel was built under a red star. There's just enough space to stow our cases and bags around the bed, strategically placed for a bout of nocturnal toe-stubbing on the way to the loo. Oh, how I will curse.

I've found a spot near the main reception door to park the bike. After offloading all the bags and having heaved them up to the room, I head down to give my big, red travelling companion a proper check over. It doesn't take long to discover that the plastic crud-catcher has finally given up the ghost. The few thousand miles of constant hammering against the diagonal strengthening bar on the Metal Mule pannier rack has finally taken its toll, resulting in a mudguard that now hangs off to one side, flapping in the breeze in a very non-Germanic 'Bobby Charlton' manner.

The motorcycle mud-catching arrangement isn't the only technical failure today either. A few months ago, I purchased a tough-looking Swatch watch for Diane, one that allowed battery changing without opening the watch case. It seemed like the perfect traveller's watch, tough enough to see her into retirement. Sadly, though, as I've noted before, very few items of modern manufacture are built to last. The strap pins of the watch just weren't up to the daily rigours of life on the road and the result is a Swatch that hangs off the wrist in similar fashion to our recently expired crud-catcher.

***

The fifteen-floor International Hotel dominates one corner of the Skanderbeg square, adjacent to the Opera House and across the road from the National Museum of History, a splendid, cubic building, dating from 1981. Once we've sorted out our baggage and changed from bike gear into more casual clothing, we wander over to the Opera House to take a few photos, entertained by a lady who is carefully cleaning the long steps in front with a water hose. She scowls at us when we take photos and, for a few seconds, I wonder whether we're going to have the hose turned on us.

The front of the museum is emblazoned with a massive mosaic, featuring a variety of characters waving guns, bows and arrows and spears around, in a similar manner to the lady with the hose. The central character on the mosaic is a dark-haired female, dressed in a flowing, white, embroidered dress, holding a rifle above her head, whilst exhorting the masses with her left hand held aloft. It bears a striking resemblance to the statue in Volgograd, 'The Motherland Calls'. I think she looks quite attractive, in an authoritarian, totalitarian manner.

After wandering the streets for a short while, we spot a jewellery shop and enquire within about repairs to Diane's watch. The lady who owns the shop is surprisingly young and dressed in very high-end western fashion, heavy on the bling. She speaks perfect English with a slight American accent. She hands us a receipt for the watch and asks if we can return to the shop in an hour or so, advising us that there are plenty of restaurants just down the street. We spend a very pleasant hour or so in a lively bistro, quaffing a few glasses of local beer and polishing off a humungous beefburger meal, heavy on chips and pickles – all for very few pounds of the Queen's realm. Having enjoyed the atmosphere of the restaurant, we return to the watch shop to be told that they don't have the spares necessary to fix the watch. In a fit of financial over-enthusiasm, I decide to purchase a new 'trip watch' for my loved one, much to the delight of the shop owner and surprise of my navigator.

The shop owner explains to me, during the purchase of the watch, that she is an entrepreneur and has built this business up very quickly. She is now planning an investment in a new holiday resort that will be built on the Adriatic near Durres, the seaside town we rode through earlier this afternoon. Apparently, Albania is a red-hot location for inward investment right now, being rich in the potential of its people and in the beauty of the country. She describes a place some distance from the capital that is a jealously guarded secret – a place of incredible beauty, tucked away in the mountains.

'If you come back here, drop by to see me and I'll tell you how to find it,' she says.

It reminds me of the very similar conversation we had with the lady selling the painted boxes and Matryoshka dolls in St Petersburg, who told us of the magical place full of wooden buildings somewhere to the north-east of St Petersburg and the receptionists in Georgia, who knew of a hidden gem, nestling in the high hills to the south of Tblisi. One of the downsides of trying to cover thousands of miles in a mere five months, is the nagging feeling that we might be foregoing a rich seam of opportunities.

Apart from poor roads, aggressive juveniles, hanging teddy bears, and the slightly dodgy appearance of a few too many British-'plated cars – leading to the suspicion that some or all of them may have been nicked (but then who would nick a Rover?). Apart from all that, I find myself warming to the opinion that Albania is well worth a longer trip than the day and a half we're going to be here. I don't think Diane shares my nascent enthusiasm. I think the bears have spooked her.

I particularly like the national flag, resplendent in a shade of the deepest red, with a double-headed black eagle rampant – well, it looks pretty rampant to me. The eagle has shared its place with a few other devices during the flag's history, including a communist star between 1946 and 1982 and the fascist symbology of Mussolini's Italy, when his forces occupied the country in April 1939, but the eagle has always managed to remain, which I think is significant because it represents Albanian nationalism and independence. Albania might have been independent after the Second World War, but it remained a Marxist-Leninist state through to the collapse of communism. For many of these years it was led by Enver Hoxha, an ex-partisan who was an ardent fan of Joseph Stalin (and later Chairman Mao). He managed to sour relations with both Russia and China, whilst remaining resolutely opposed to liberal democracy, which he obviously considered to be a full-to-brim 'bag-o-shite'. On the plus side, he championed the rights of women, removing centuries of paternalist tradition, and opening all jobs to them – apart from his own. And the country had virtually no debt, mainly because it did very little trade. As a result, by the time he expired in 1982, his country was even more isolated than North Korea, and Albania was the poorest country in Europe. Unlike many of his contemporaries in charge of isolated countries though, Hoxha managed to die in his bed. Quite an achievement.

The recovery from the dire economic position of the 1980s to the one where the country seems to be starting to prosper, has been a chequered one. Albania was badly hit by the Balkan war – with a huge number of ethnic Albanians being persecuted and displaced, especially from Kosovo. But right now, it seems to be on the up. The country has applied to join the European Union and has already joined NATO. Tirana has a population of around one million people, about a third of the country's population. It's a busy city with quite a nice vibe about it. Sadly, we are spending just one night here – we need to press on, leaving the legacy of a broken crud-catcher behind, in a bin.

**

It's a cruel twist of fate that, just when you're basking in your most successful city departure, you suddenly discover that you've gone and got lost again.

Navigating out of Tirana is a doddle. The road exits directly out of the main square and just keeps going. It is so simple that it lulls you into a false sense of security and you start to pay too much attention to appreciating the city, with its clean, tree-lined streets, surrounding hills and pleasant apartment blocks. The road wafts you to the outskirts of the city and you notice all the nice retail outlets and signs of commercial well-being, prompting you to contemplate the words of the lady in the jewellers, last night, concerning the general buoyancy of the economy and the positive signs of growth. Then you notice, with a smidgen of foreboding, that the road has shaken itself free of the city and is transporting you, helter-skelter, to somewhere other than where you wanted to go. Somewhere to the east called Durres. The exact somewhere you got lost in yesterday.

In about the time it takes to lose a bet on a greyhound race (mine always seem to lose grip on the final corner), we find ourselves trapped in a loop. We've managed to make a 'U' turn and have pulled over, adjacent to a patch of urban wasteland, overlooked by scattered retail outlets. After a bit of head-scratching, we manage to locate a road that heads north on the map. All we need to do is to ride through a little section of town, turn left to a nearby roundabout and take the second exit onto a route that heads to the north; which is exactly what we do. The only problem is that the road to the north isn't there – it's gone AWOL. We ride around the block, pull over and study the map again. All we need to do is take a left, ride up to the roundabout and take the road to the north, which is exactly what we do, except the road is still not there. It has upped-sticks and deserted.

We've ridden past the same café twice now. The old men sipping coffee outside the café have observed us with amusement on our second pass, befuddlement on the third. We pull up once more to apply an intense, forensic scrutiny to the map. Whilst we are in mid-pore, a posse of three motorcyclists, mounted on similar BMW GS motorcycles to ours, ride up alongside and nod. Their plates point to their being Turkish. The lead rider is wearing the exact same video cam on his helmet to the one on mine, a fact that I find quite remarkable – it's a virtually unknown brand. I point excitedly at his camera, then at mine, but he looks at me blankly, as if I'm a gibbering lunatic. The three of them study their maps then ride off around the roundabout to nowhere, returning the other way, lost in their own little loop. I think we've discovered Europe's answer to the Bermuda Triangle. In time, we'll probably all run out of fuel, just like the ill-fated squadron of American Avenger aircraft pilots did. At least there's a café and we won't starve to death.

On the fourth circuit of the groundhog loop, it occurs to me that the problem might just be the map (I can be quite bright sometimes, normally at the third or fourth pass of something in particular). There *is* an exit from the roundabout, but it heads in a completely different direction from the one shown on the map, parallel to the motorway and back in the direction of Tirana. We chance our luck and discover that the road that will take us north lies a short distance further, just far enough to be out of sight. Bingo! Following a quick swig of fuel at a conveniently placed petrol station we head northwards along a wide, flat plain, a patchwork quilt of farmland that separates the coast from a long range of hills that run parallel to the sea. Compared with the mountainous terrain of yesterday, the landscape is surprisingly similar to that of northern Italy. And by that, I mean flat as a pancake.

We pass many small settlements and businesses along our route, including new hotels that appear to be quite impressive. It certainly wouldn't be a problem to find an overnight stop here. At one such settlement, we spot a sign for the town of Puke, which joins the modest pantheon of amusing place names that we've passed (or visited) during our travels: Puke, Pugwash, Snori and Sleepy Hollow, to name but four.

***

A few hours later, we find ourselves riding up a tree-lined road, entering the Montenegrin capital city of Podgorica, approaching an intersection on the left where we receive the unwelcome attention of a police officer, who steps out and signals for us to pull over. A minor wash of adrenaline and dread briefly floods through my veins – more so than when we were pulled over in Turkey – I'm not sure why, but I'll discuss in full later, 'cos there's no time for it right now. We signal and turn into the intersection, pulling up short of the police car. The policeman blusters over bristling with officialdom and shouting quite brusquely something that sounds like 'Papers!', before he spots the yellow British number plate and promptly waves us to 'go away', which we do, ever so promptly.

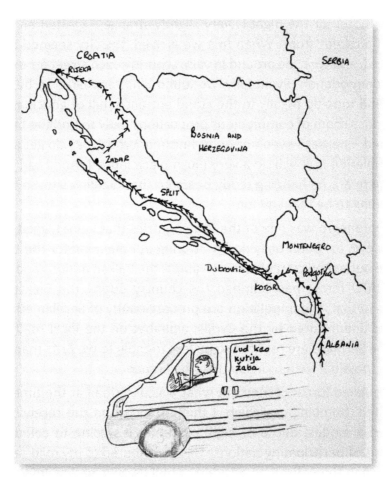

Slightly edgy, brilliantly photogenic, some of the best corners of the trip: the Balkans.

The border between Montenegro and Albania was one of the more scenic ones we've passed through, situated on the shore of Lake Skadar. Podgorica lies just a few miles to the north, a modestly sized city with around 180,000 inhabitants, the capital of a country that is slightly bigger than Yorkshire, with about 1/9th the population of god's own county. Its name literally does mean 'Black Mountain'. The initial impression of the capital is that it retains all the classic features of a recent communist past: cheaply built apartment blocks, roads of a dubious standard and a certain degree of gritty drabness that's strangely compelling, not least because it's disappearing from the world, almost as we speak.

Our hotel for the night is very slightly strange – grafted on to the side of a carpet store. When first we arrived, the city seemed almost deserted, and we rode around in vain, scouring each street for any sign of accommodation. Eventually, we found what appeared to be a fine hotel and rode up regally to the grand entrance, full of anticipation of a luxurious room of commodious proportions, only to find the building deserted – perhaps even not-quite-finished. When they do get around to completing it, it will be a very plush place indeed. And I can report that there are no hanging teddy bears on that building site, so there's something to be thankful for.

Montenegro was one of the few countries that were tagged, in my mind's eye, as 'potentially dodgy'. During our planning for the trip, I'd carried out a modicum of research about the Balkan nations and noted that NATO forces had bombed the country during the Balkan War. Added to that, the population are predominantly of Serbian ethnicity, a point underscored by the Cyrillic alphabet on the local road signs. And the Serbians are reputed to be less friendly to we Brits than some others, possibly even more so than the French.

The Allied forces carried out what was described at the time to be a 'limited' bombing campaign. I think if you're on the receiving end of even a modest quota of high explosives it's going to colour your opinions of participating nations. This contributed to my mild sense of panic when the policeman decided to pull us over, earlier. Imagine my surprise, then, when we find ourselves greeted with gay abandon by the hotel-cum-carpet emporium manager. He seems genuinely delighted to offer us a room that turns out to be quite a fine and commodious one. No stubbing of toes tonight!

***

Some time ago, back in the swinging '80s, when it was fashionable to wear one half of your hair long, and one half short – well, at least it did if you were Phil Oakey… way back then, Norwich Airport was called *Norwich Airport*. Then something startling occurred. Yugoslavia opened itself up, just enough to allow tourists to enjoy the pleasures of places like Dubrovnik. A flight commenced from Norwich to somewhere in

Yugoslavia and the management at Norwich Airport seized on their accidental good fortune and put up a new sign elevating its status to: *Norwich International Airport*, proving just how influential the Balkans have been in recent history, at least in central Norfolk. Alan Partridge would revel in this fact.

Our outline navigational plan for today is to head over towards the coast, where we hope to pick up a road that heads all the way up the Adriatic to the Italian border. The road out of Podgorica is a fine one that climbs over a range of beautiful, gnarly hills. We arrive in a small town and find ourselves temporarily lost, riding around the back streets of a housing estate that has clearly seen better days, we eventually locate a small road that climbs in a very entertaining fashion up into a new range of hills, through dappled woods. At the top of the hills, we break out into a landscape that could almost be from another planet.

Above us, the sky is a brilliant colour of graduated blue, broken by a line of white-capped clouds, pale grey on their undersides, hovering just above the tops of the hills. These are hard and unforgiving lands. The hills are built of grey limestone, covered in rocks, and populated by hardy trees and shrubs of variegated colours and form. The pale road wends its serpentine path through the rocky outcrops, the only obvious sign of human intervention in another scene of true European wilderness. My first impression is that this is a classic Karst landscape – it bears a passing resemblance to Malham in Yorkshire, where we were taken on a school geology field trip (way back in the mists of time). There, we were introduced by our teacher, Mr Oates, to the marvels of clints and grykes – naturally formed fissures in the rocks created by thousands of years' worth of water erosion on (and in) the limestone. I imagine this part of Montenegro is both a geologist's, and a potholer's, delight. And the tight, switchback road is a trail motorcycle rider's dream come true too.

We climb higher into the hills, sweeping around a series of bends. Suddenly, quite out of the blue, we spot a concrete pillbox sitting on the summit of a rocky outcrop, just above the road. We (I should really say I) decide to park the bike up and take a quick look, clambering up the rocks to the top of the wee summit. The ground at the back of the pillbox is littered with broken rubble and a closer look reveals an almost perfectly circular bore hole, right through the roof. This fortification is perfectly situated to guard the road below, but I think it's been taken out by a smart bomb or a missile, and I mean 'taken out with surgical precision'. I realise, far too late, that we shouldn't have come up here.

We decide to make our way down very carefully, using only the rocks to stand on. On the way down, just before reaching the road, we come across a small natural alcove, littered with empty rifle shell cases, which are scattered around next to a couple of empty beer bottles. It's sobering to realise that the last person to stand here probably swigged a few beers in a period of boredom, then fired off ten or twenty rounds at someone approaching from the direction we've just ridden.

Following that revelation, we ride on, eventually meeting signs of civilisation at the tiny settlement of Cevo. A little further along, the road seems to tie itself into ever tighter knots as it tries to hug the contours of the slopes. Then, almost disappointingly, it calms down, just in time to enter the village of Njeguši where everything becomes slightly touristic. And for good reason too.

✳✳✳

Njeguši has more than one claim to fame. It's the birthplace of many famous Montenegrins, not least the ruling dynasty who held sway for hundreds of years, up until 1918. A charming place, noted for its traditional architecture, it remains largely unspoilt. I'm not sure how long that will last though, because it is a prime visitor attraction for hundreds of tourists who've disgorged from the cruise ships that visit the nearby port of Kotor. All of this becomes apparent to us after we park the bike alongside a thriving roadside market, wandering over to a nearby café having had a quick look at the goodies for sale on the market stalls. The café is initially quite empty, but it quickly fills after a coachload of Germans pull up seeking refreshment. Luckily, we got there first, which might be an Anglo-German record.

Two men, who I would guess to be of similar age to me, in their early fifties, walk in through the door, dressed in dark suits and sunglasses. The suits are faded – the shades less so. They walk over and speak with the waiting staff, then take a seat at the back of the café to be served coffee. Their demeanour doesn't feel quite right to me. Never mind, we've finished our coffee, so we get up and make room for a couple more Germans. We head outside into the bright sunlight and wander over to the market, which is now thronged with even more tourists. The bike, which was previously parked on its own, is now almost hemmed in by coaches and by a slightly beaten-up old black Mercedes car, sitting behind it.

The market comprises a line of stalls skirting the roadside, selling various souvenirs and suchlike, but the most interesting stalls are purveying the two other things that the village is famous for: ham and cheese. Not any old ham, but top-quality dried and smoked ham, which apparently takes at least a year to produce, rivalling the finest Prosciutto that Parma can rustle up. The cheese is similarly noted for its excellence and is reportedly famous from the French Riviera to Venice and beyond, yet almost unheard of in Milton Keynes and even less so in Northampton.

Whilst we're availing ourselves of the delicacies provided as samples, I note that our 'friends' from the café have headed to a nearby shop. Rightly or wrongly, the hairs on the back of my neck are sounding the alarm and, perhaps unfairly, I conclude that they're in the 'insurance' business. I imagine them to be ex-militia who've recently turned to a nice profitable life collecting for the boss, not entirely unlike Vincent and Jules in Pulp Fiction. Despite this, I don't feel threatened or unduly concerned. We're just two tourists in a town full to brimming with other tourists and we're not eating Kahuna Burgers. There's safety in being a member of a large flock. Five minutes later, though, things take a slightly more sinister twist.

The two gangster-types return to the old Mercedes and prepare to leave. Spotting that there isn't really room for them to get past the bike, I head over to it, at pace, to move it out of the way. Too late! They start to edge through the throng of tourists, straight towards the Mutt! I quicken my step and head them off, arriving alongside the bike in time to virtually get run-down, getting the evil eye from the driver. Having barged past me, they roar off, heading in the same direction that we're travelling. Time to discuss options with Diane.

'I don't like the look of those two,' I declare. 'I think we should hang back and let them get further up the road. I don't want to meet up with them out in the middle of nowhere. I think they've clocked our plate on the bike and I read somewhere that the British Army sorted out some of the militias at the end of the war hereabouts – maybe they don't like Brits. They damn-near knocked the bike over just then.'

We hang around for a while, hoping to follow one of the coaches on their way back towards Kotor, but there isn't any sign of movement on that score, so, eventually we mount up and head out. On any other day, the ride would be amazing, on such a twisty road with fabulous views. Over to the left is the towering mass of mount Lovcen, sitting astride its very own national park.

After riding for a short distance, we sweep around a tight corner and pass a small roadside café on our left. There, on the veranda, sit our two friends, still wearing their suit jackets and sunglasses, sipping another coffee. Their heads swivel and track us as we skim past them, just like the agents in the film *The Matrix*. I almost feel like waving, but I think that would be pushing our luck too far, a bit too Keanu, perchance, so we press on at a reasonable pace to put some distance between us and them. The scenery to our right gradually opens to reveal a sight that is nothing short of astonishing. We catch glimpses of the sea, far below. Then, with some relief, we spot a tourist bus parked at one of the vantage points and we pull over to take in the sight – cameras at the ready. We're standing above a precipice on the shoulder of the mountain, with a steep, rocky cliff behind us, and the most wonderful sight of the sea inlet of Kotor way, way below, where tiny cruise liners are berthed, huge behemoths in reality, but smaller than the tiniest toy from this distance and height. It's a sight to rival the grandeur of Yosemite – staggeringly, dramatically beautiful. I can't say fairer than that really. Montenegro is one of the wildest, most beautiful countries we have ever visited.

The German tourists are a happy-go-lucky bunch of retirees. I could imagine them flaunting a bit of flesh in lederhosen on a different day, in a different setting – perhaps in a *bierkeller* with an Oompah band in tow, but, hereabouts, they're just normal tourists who are very happy to greet a pair of Englanders on a BMW motorcycle. Well, at least one

Englander. A nice old gent offers to take our picture for us. I think this could be the very pinnacle of Anglo-German relations this century. Our mutual politeness showeth no bounds.

After a while, our newly-found friends drift back to the coach, to continue the precipitous climb over the mountain heading for Njeguši. We, in turn, climb aboard our trusty steed and head in the opposite direction, down towards Kotor, meeting a series of hairpins that would rival any in the Swiss Alps as they plummet from the vertiginous heights to sea level in a most satisfying fashion. The traffic thickens up as we arrive in the outskirts of the town, signalling the end of our safety concerns. The contrast between the wilderness of the hills and the cultured ambience of this plush, Adriatic version of the Cote d'Azur is pronounced. We've returned to civilisation.

***

One could easily be forgiven for thinking that the bay of Kotor is a fjord – in some quarters, it's described exactly so, but, in truth, it's a ria, a submerged river valley not entirely dissimilar to Plymouth Sound. Kotor is an ancient, fortified town, nestling at the end of the bay, surrounded by precipitous hills. It's a fabulously photogenic place. The luxury yachts tied up in the harbour are a source of fascination, as is a modern cruise ship, in the shape of a sailing clipper, anchored out in the bay. Once we've sated our photography thirst, we climb back on the bike and ride out of town, heading out on a road that winds its way right around the bay. It might just be the most scenic road in Europe. There's even a tiny island complete with its own solitary church, sitting out in the bay waiting for its parishioners to arrive by boat. The area clearly attracts a knowledgeable, wealthy elite who can keep a well-kept secret. There's no shortage of very special waterside retreats, basking under bright blue skies, and plenty of high-end cars wafting around. We snick in behind a shiny new BMW bearing German number plates, heading towards the border with Croatia. He puts a spurt on as he notices us looming in his mirror and we spend an enjoyable twenty minutes tailing in his slipstream. He's no boy racer though. He slows down as we pass through the small settlements that are scattered along the coast and only speeds up when there's a decent bend to enjoy, of which there are plenty.

After passing through the small town of Herceg Novi, the road heads inland through a long valley, losing none of the scenic beauty we've become accustomed to over the past few hours of riding. We arrive at the border crossing well behind the German driver. He nipped deftly past a few slower cars on the short straights between corners and managed to embarrass me quite badly. Not my finest hour. I put the tardy performance down to the lack of crud catcher, which was obviously designed to be a kind of DRS system, such as is found on Formula 1 racing cars.

I wasn't sure what to expect of today's ride, but we've made good progress and we find ourselves just a few miles short of the famous coastal city of Dubrovnik. After a smooth passage through the Montenegrin border we head into Croatia, our papers processed by smartly uniformed officials who, for some reason, look a bit Swedish to me (as did the Ukrainians).

＊＊＊

The city of Dubrovnik lies in a small enclave of land, cut off from the rest of Croatia, thereby allowing Bosnia and Herzegovina access to the Adriatic Sea. A UNESCO World Heritage Site, Dubrovnik came to the attention of the world when it was besieged by a combined Serbian and Montenegrin army during the Balkan War in 1991. Without ignoring the human tragedy that was widely reported in the western press at the time, the siege was also a cultural disaster because the city was so rich in classical architecture. It suffered from a heavy bombardment. I'm pleased to say that the structural damage seems to have been completely repaired in the twenty-one years that have passed since those dark days and, nowadays, it looks simply stunning.

Rescued from destruction: the fine city of Dubrovnik.

We almost immediately find ourselves locked in a circular route around the newer part of the city, searching for a hotel. In doing so, we notice people sitting on the streets with boards held in front of them advertising private rooms to passing motorists. We cease looking for a proper hotel and start scanning the boards. After three circuits of the route, I spot a sign for a room posted in the garden of a rather elegant old house – one might even describe it as a town villa – with crucial access to a tree-shaded driveway for parking. On the third circuit we pull in to investigate.

The owner of the house is an elderly gentleman, dressed in slightly threadbare clothes. Apart from that, he appears quite urbane, reminding me of a retired headteacher. He's sitting on an old metal chair enjoying a smoke, waiting for trade to drop in; a bit like a spider anticipating the arrival of a nice, fat bluebottle. He introduces himself as Andrei. I reply ditto. He quotes a ludicrously low figure for a two-night rental and the fly lands neatly into the web. We're led down a flight of steps and introduced to a basement room that bears the now familiar whiff of dusty decrepitude. The cardboard towels and flattened pillows are a given. We've stayed in worse rooms on the trip so far, but not by a very great margin. In the warm glow brought about by budgetary restraint, I fail to notice my navigator's distinct air of disappointment. After a quick shower and change, we take a leisurely stroll down the road for our first glimpse of Dubrovnik old town.

The oldest part of the city is famously surrounded by ancient walls, which originally date from the 11th century, thereafter being improved and strengthened over the next three hundred years. We don't have time to explore the city tonight, so we settle instead for a meal in a restaurant close to one of the entrances called Pile Gate – an area where tourists disgorge from buses and are instantly drawn by a variety of souvenir shops. We've been suffering from souvenir deprivation lately, and have great difficulty avoiding staring through the brightly lit windows, like Victorian street urchins peering at the contents of Mrs Miggins' pie shop window.

Over the meal, we discuss the state of the room, or to be more precise, the bathroom. I opine that the state of cleanliness 'isn't too bad'. Diane reserves the right to disagree; quite forcefully. I'm not aware that Diane has been on her hands and knees giving it a thorough scrub. The disagreement abates during the walk back to the house. It's a beautiful night – one of those nights where the darkness of the sky and the clarity of the air seem to enhance the sharpness of the lights, making the city glitter.

Just down the street from our accommodation lies a bar-cum-nightclub, outside which is parked a rather lovely Laverda RGS. For the non-motorcycling reader, I'll just explain that this is an early 1980's three-cylinder Italian machine, nominally of 1000cc's. A highly desirable classic motorcycle, if a little less so than its more famous earlier sibling, the Laverda Jota. It is notable for its 'unbreakable' Bayflex plastic mudguard and fairing. My friend Neville is an expert on this very model of machine. He takes great delight in grabbing hold and bending the mudguard of any Laverda RGS he comes across, just to prove the degree of 'unbreakableness', at great risk of being accosted by an irate owner. I'm instantly besotted and forget our wee contretemps while I lust over the lovely build quality and chunky lines of a machine I know I'll never own. If I had the money, I would revert to ownership of a Ducati 900 GTS, an altogether humbler yet worthy machine. Just as we're about to leave, the owner appears from the club with a small gaggle of drinkers. After a short explanation to the ensemble, describing the bike and basking in the glow of admiration, he swings his leg over, thumbs the starter button, disturbing the night's silence with the deepest of rumbles, and thunders off up the street in a substantially cool fashion. I don't think I've ever looked that cool on a motorcycle. Even when we swept out of Anapa, I don't think I looked half as cool as that.

An hour later, the night is rent asunder by a cataclysmic explosion of an altogether different kind when our argument spills over into a monumental bollocking. Diane has had enough! Her spleen is well and truly vented, on all fronts. The lackadaisical dismissal of the bathroom as 'not that bad' appears to have been the proverbial tip of the iceberg, or surely more accurately: the straw that broke the camel's back, although references to dromedaries might not help my cause right now. My misdemeanours of the previous three months are laid bare. Grumpiness when leaving hotels, bad manners when searching for hotels, unreasonable lack of attention, the willing acceptance of atrocious hotel conditions and an offhandness brought about (probably) by the frustration of losing the freedom that can only be found whilst travelling solo. These are but a few of the charges laid before me. And to be honest, she does have a point. Or ten. Strangely though, she omits to mention the hair colouring debacle in Volgograd.

***

I recall Robert, the rider of the R1150 GS Adventure back in Samsun. His partner had 'had enough' and was being escorted to the airport to fly home to Germany. Robert appeared quite sanguine about her departure, whereas I remember how I felt about it – deciding that I'd probably abandon the trip if Diane decided to do the same. We skirted around that possibility last night and it just served to reinforce my view that travelling without my doughty partner and pillion would be a decidedly lonely and altogether less engaging experience. I realise that the amazing feeling of freedom that I experienced on large parts of the trip around North America, riding solo, couldn't balance the sense of loss I felt when Diane flew home from Seattle. Secretly, I admire the tempestuous ferocity with which she pressed her point and feel properly humbled. Anyone reading who mutters 'about time' will be studiously ignored.

Thankfully, we've managed to patch up our differences and fashion some kind of peace from the wreckage, so we can enjoy what looks like being a fabulous day wandering around the glory of one of the finest medieval cities you could hope to discover this side of Wymondham. We walk down the hill towards the Pile Gate, hand in hand. Perhaps it's fitting that we've found peace in a country and region that was so recently riven by war, but I shouldn't get too far ahead of myself; overconfidence might just kill the cat.

The history of Dubrovnik is multi-layered. At different times, it was aligned to the Byzantine Empire, Venice, and (for a large part of its existence) was a vassal city to the Ottoman Empire. Much of its wealth came from merchant shipping and trade. A fleet of merchant ships sallied far and wide, setting up trade in countries as far flung as America and India. The result of that wealth can be found in the beautiful Renaissance buildings that survive – although many were destroyed by an earthquake in 1667. Despite the strong Italian influence on culture here, reminders that we are in the Balkans abound. There are no hanging teddy bears to be seen. In their place, the people of Dubrovnik have refined the process by hanging dolls and fairies instead, swinging ever so slightly in the gentle early morning breath of wind. Almost as creepy as clown dolls.

The hanging dolls of Dubrovnik.

Having passed through the impressive, yet modestly-proportioned Pile Gate, we make our way along Placa Street, the main thoroughfare. This follows the path of an old watercourse that separated what was an islet and the mainland. It was more than a physical barrier. It also marked the division between elements of Romano-Greek residents and those of Croatian Slavs. About eight hundred years ago, the two communities decided to fill the divide in with earth, and, after mulling over it for another two or three hundred years, they went the whole hog and paved over the road with limestone. In the intervening years, the limestone has been worn by the footfall of countless people to the point where it now presents an illusion of being made of glass, reflecting the buildings that border the street and the people who wander along it. It's a photographer's dream.

The walls that surround the city are just under two kilometres long. It isn't huge. But what it loses in scale, it more than makes up for in the wealth of architecture and the variety of photographic opportunities – from grand Renaissance edifices, to narrow streets crowded in by the shops and houses that line them, climbing up away from you as you try to frame a shot. Surrounded on three sides by the sea, there are tiny secret beaches to be found outside the walls and, at the far end of the city, there's a sizeable harbour, the departure point for pleasure boats that head out for a mini voyage of discovery, providing a magnificent view of the imposing walls from seaward. From this perspective, it's easy to see how the opposing armies managed to surround the city and mercilessly bombard it. The hills above it are towering indeed. In one of the grand buildings close to the harbour, we find a museum describing the siege and its horrific effects. It's a dreadful recent history, but it seems that Dubrovnik and Croatia are managing to put the horrors of war behind them.

The most talked about subject of the moment is the imminent entry of Croatia into the European Union. The tricolour flag of the country, with its red and white chequered coat of arms, flies everywhere, and alongside it flies the blue flag of the EU with its golden stars. Having applied to join in 2003, the country has been hard at work aligning itself for entry next year in 2013.

***

The following morning. If the short ride from Kotor to Dubrovnik provides any measure, then our journey today promises to be spectacular. One glance at a map reveals that the road we intend to take, the D8, is going to be hugely entertaining – possibly one of the finest of the whole trip. It snakes from Dubrovnik here in the south all the way to the border with Italy – at least I think it does. It seems to get a bit lost up near the border, but I'm sure we'll find a way through to Venice, which is our next major destination. I don't think we'll make it there in one hit. We'll need to search for a hotel somewhere in the north of Croatia. And I guess it's going to have to be a good hotel too, or at the very least, one with a clean bathroom.

We're planning to spend a couple of days in Venice before heading down into Italy towards Assisi, spending a couple of days at a camp site that I've stayed at before. From Assisi, the plan is to ride down to Rome and then further down the Italian boot to the Sorrento peninsula, where we hope to visit Pompeii and Herculaneum, avoiding Naples at all costs. Before that, though, we need to depart Dubrovnik.

The bike is packed, and the room is left dirty and tidy just as we found it, although the bathroom is, perhaps, quite considerably cleaner. Our final act is to post the old set of keys through Andrei's front door. We haven't seen him at all during our stay. I suspect he was seriously disturbed by the sounds emanating from our room the night before last and has decided to stay out of harm's way. I imagine he's waiting patiently behind the door, with bucket and disinfectant in hand ready to give that bathroom a damn good scrub. Then again, he might have gone to stay with his sister, just to keep out of our way.

Departing Andrei's gaff. Having had a bit of a ticking-off.

The first leg of today's journey will take us the twenty or so kilometres to the border of Bosnia and Herzegovina. It's an outstanding strip of road, hugging the coast high above the sea, with a road surface that is imperfect but great for scratching. We're passing through semi-arid scenery, with hills inland and the sun glinting off the sea to our left as we flit between villages, gradually descending to a lower altitude as we approach the first of two borders that take us through the small sliver of land that provides access to the sea for the newly-formed country of Bosnia and Herzegovina. After a reasonably quick and painless border passage, we arrive at the second smallest geographic coastline in the world – just twelve miles long – given to the Ottoman Empire by Dubrovnik in the late 17th century, thereby gaining protection from the marauding intent of the Venetians. It might only be twelve miles long, but it is an attractive twelve miles that pass by very quickly, presenting us with the second border of the day as we cross back into Croatia. After a short excursion inland for a few miles, the road returns to hug the coast in a series of spectacular bends and the occasional tree-shaded straight.

At the port of Split, we pull over to marvel at the sight of a line of gigantic cruise ships berthed below us, the scale provided by the tiny coaches waiting to load up and drive their charges down to Dubrovnik, resembling 'N' gauge models alongside the towering white steel and glass monsters.

Shortly after departing Split, I become aware of a white Ford Transit van, looming persistently in the mirrors, clamped to the back of the bike, swerving dangerously around the corners in a (not altogether vain) attempt to keep up with us and, no doubt, to scalp us in an outrageous overtaking manoeuvre. It might be easier to just pull over, but the rhythm of one corner after another allows me to gain a little distance and things improve further when a couple of nice straights allow me to overtake some of the traffic in front, putting a few vehicles between us. Lulled into a false sense of security, I make the mistake of relaxing a little. A mile or so later, passing through a sun-dappled, tree-lined patch of road, I catch a glimpse of him in the mirrors, making an almost suicidal overtaking manoeuvre, placing himself just one car away from us. Fortunately, there are no signs of any straights for miles, so I remain composed and endeavour to press on a little. The next time I check the mirrors, he's swerving back into line, right on our tail. It feels faintly reminiscent of the cult 1971 film *Duel*, Steven Spielberg's first attempt at directing a film, with an acting *tour de force* by Dennis Weaver – a hombre perfectly cast for the role of the hunted one. But I digress.

For the next thirty minutes, we engage in a game of cat-and-mouse. Each corner offers an opportunity for us to gain a hard-won stretch of road on our lardy-ass mule; each straight a chance to overtake traffic and get our noses further in front. But, when we become stuck behind a queue of traffic, a quick glance in the mirror is all that's needed to spot another example of psychotic overtaking allowing our nemesis to get right back on our tail. Our little race eats up the kilometres. Eventually, we manage to negotiate a line of traffic that proves impassable to the 'enemy', to the extent that we manage to find a place to pull over at a small restaurant and coffee shop, breathing a secret sigh of relief. Shortly after we've dismounted, he zooms past and disappears round the next bend. I don't think he even saw us. Maybe he just drives everywhere like that.

The restaurant turns out to be both open and closed. The door is off the latch, but the three youngsters inside inform us that there isn't any food being served, not even a cup of coffee, declaring 'owner is out,' so we head back to the bike to continue on our way, eventually arriving at a fork in the road where a navigational error rears its ugly head. We find ourselves to be moderately lost. My initial feeling is one of 'not to worry'. The fabulous coast road had gradually unwound itself on the approach to Zadar, shedding its switchback nature and morphing into something a little more mundane, so I think a detour away from the coast will provide a welcome contrast. A quick check of the Times pocket atlas reveals a route that shadows the Bosnian border, passing over quite hilly terrain before offering a westbound turn back towards Italy, so we decide to press on and sample its delights.

The route along the border is more remote than the coastal strip, with long dark hills and scattered settlements that surprise us with an unwelcome reminder of a recent past. Every fifth or sixth house we pass is abandoned, with shuttered windows and, in many cases, daubed with graffiti. The conclusion of our suspicious minds is that these gutted dwellings, many of which were once fine, large houses, bear silent witness to the terrible persecution and ethnic cleansing that took place across the region a few years ago. I imagine the original occupants to have been Muslims or Serbs who have either been forced out or have decided to leave; or worse. Perhaps a little more un-nerving is the way the local population seem to stare at us as we ride past. If truth be told, it doesn't feel entirely friendly. It is, however, very beautiful, with an alpine feeling to the architecture and fine roads presenting plenty of opportunities to wear the edges off the tyre treads.

A couple of hours later. We've passed through a small town, finding diddly-squat in the accommodation stakes and have ridden into the late afternoon, eventually coasting out of the hills and into the town of Rijeka, where we are promptly rejected by the receptionist at a hotel that is clearly only half-full. It isn't even a decent hotel. I ask if there is anywhere else we could try? He shrugs nonchalantly, saying that he doubts it. 'All hotels full,' says he.

The Hotel Continental, situated just around the corner, begs to differ. After a careful look through their booking system, they inform me that there is a room available, although it's at a seriously expensive rate. On the plus side, they say we can bring our bike into a secure parking spot, which is a bonus because a sizeable segment of the town's population appears to be enjoying a spot of binge drinking in the parkland and a quayside area opposite the hotel, lending the area a slightly edgy feel. The bike is locked, alarmed, and hastily covered up. After a quick shower and change of clothing, we head into town towards a restaurant recommended by the hotel, picking our way around the knots of drunken residents and discarded beer cans. It sounds a bit intimidating but, in truth, there isn't any trouble; just the faint concern that there could be. We're failing to follow our own self-imposed travel-safety rule: avoid places where people get drunk (unless we're determined to get blootered ourselves, in which case it's totally ok).

Croatia is not without a few claims to fame. The ball-point pen was invented by a Croat, as was the tungsten light bulb that keeps blowing in the Mutt's headlamp. The first torpedo was made in this very town. The only man with the capacity to both defy and scare Stalin in the post-war years was Croatian. His name was Josip Broz, but he was better known as Tito. I love the story about the letter found in Stalin's desk drawer, shortly after he'd expired. In the letter, Tito admonished Stalin for repeatedly sending assassins to kill him. If he didn't stop sending them, then Tito said he would send one in return to Moscow, and that would be the only one necessary. It seems that Stalin took him seriously and not only kept the letter, but also decided to desist in his murderous intent.

But, for me, the best thing about Croatia, apart from the very pleasant red wine we're sampling tonight, is the outstanding coastal road to the stunningly beautiful town of Dubrovnik. It's a motorcyclist's dream. A few white van drivers are partial to it too, but they seem to be solitary hunters, so that's OK. Tomorrow, we will take the relatively short hop to Venice.

***

Saturday, 6th of October. The weather feels a bit changeable today.

I haven't bothered to study the route to Italy in much detail. A quick inspection of the atlas this morning confirmed that we've reached the top of the Adriatic. We need to execute a left turn somewhere north of Rijeka, such that the pointy thing on the compass indicates west. The route out of town climbs quite purposefully into the surrounding hills and, before we know what's going on, we find ourselves at a neat and impressive border crossing into a place called Slovenia, having fruitlessly searched for the fabled left turn.

Riding a short distance into Slovenia, I find myself ruminating that this is something of an inconvenience, but that all changes as the sun arcs into the sky and this new and unexpected country reveals itself to be one of outstanding natural beauty. It is a tad hilly, with an average height of just under five hundred metres, and fifty-eight percent of it is covered by forest, which is a greater percentage than Russia, Canada, Brazil or (for that matter) Georgia. It shares the slightly Alpine feel that we experienced yesterday in the Croatian hinterlands, with well-kept, shallow-roofed houses situated in smart, prim villages. A few kilometres up from the border, we pass through the neat town of Ilirska Bistrica, population 4,539. We then follow the signs for Postojna (population 9,189) where I hope to pick up the E61 on its purposeful lunge westwards to Italy (population 59.54 million). The demographics might be flawless, but the navigation is less so. We're riding on route number 6, a twisty little serpent's tail of a road that whiplashes its way through the forests, up-hill and down-dale. In fact, I'm enjoying it so much that I completely miss the road to Trieste, which I think might be a city in Italy. Thankfully, as is often the case, one door closes allowing a new and unexpected opportunity to present itself. An opportunity in the shape of a Russian T-55 tank, the owner of which seems to have carelessly parked it by the side of the road, in a fit of gay abandon. When we pull over to examine it, we realise that a few other mechanical machines of war appear to have been parked up in a similar fashion. We've arrived, quite by accident, at the Park Vojaske Zgodovine Pikva, which, despite being unpronounceable, is probably the best military museum that no one has ever heard of.

Chapter 31
Went the Day well?

When the Yugoslavian army evacuated itself from Slovenia, it quite carelessly left behind a substantial barracks and lots of abandoned equipment – things like tanks, helicopters, aeroplanes, trucks, and a submarine. It was almost a velvet revolution, with very few casualties. Slovenia was spared the horrors that beset those in the south and east of the former republic. The Slovenians were quick to spot a touristic opportunity in the windfall of abandoned military hardware and gathered everything together, neatly labelled it, stashing a fair proportion indoors in the barracks whilst leaving a few of the larger exhibits out in the grounds and, Bob's your mother's brother, here it all is.

We spend a good hour and a half, wandering around the museum, surprised to discover that nearly all the early post-Second World War military vehicles are of American origin, rather than Russian. Apparently, the Americans were very keen to support Tito, early in his leadership, but that changed over time, and the later equipment is mostly Soviet by design, if not always by origin. One of the most fascinating machines is a huge trenching device comprising the weird fusion of a truck upper-half and a tank lower called a BTM-3, capable of digging trenches and holes at a phenomenal rate of knots, apparently. In a modern context, something like this might speed up the laying of fibre optic cable, a task that seems to take companies like BT years to accomplish. With one of these babies, they'd have the job done by Christmas.Did I mention a submarine? Yes, I did. It sits out in the yard, for all the world looking like a beached whale. It's a miniature submarine, but a remarkably modern-looking one, for all that. It looks like a scaled-down model of a modern nuclear submarine. The pennant number 913 is painted on the conning tower, identifying it as the Zeta, built in 1987 for the purpose of either laying mines or delivering special forces onto foreign shores; it was decommissioned as recently as 2005. The main flaw in the design was the lack of battery charging facilities, which meant that the impressive range of around 250 miles (better than a 2012 Tesla) stood for nothing if it couldn't find somewhere to plug in for some juice. A small diesel or petrol generator from Machine Mart coupled to a long length of hose would have made all the difference.

I could rattle on endlessly about this museum and the exhibits within because it is quite fascinating to me, but we are pressed for time and need to hit the road. So, I'll just mention one final thing that caught my eye, in the shape of a sectioned Russian tank. I imagine it was built to train engineers on the workings of the type (another T-55). Normally, when you see a tank, it's hard to imagine what they're like inside. And, when you get a glimpse of the interior, they're so crammed full of equipment such as gun breeches, radio equipment and suchlike that it's hard to understand how they're constructed. But here, it is all revealed, like the desiccated skeleton of a large animal lying in the desert.

***

For a substantial part of our journey through the Balkans, we've been travelling through hills and mountains fashioned by the effects of water on limestone, typified by the pale white outcrops of rock. Now, as we head helter-skelter for Italy, we skirt to the south of the very hills that gave the geological term 'Karst' its name. It's the German name for the plateau that lies to the north and east of the bay of Trieste, called 'Kras' in Slovenian. Slovenia is the home to over 8,000 caves – and counting. They haven't managed to find them all yet. And with that thought, we arrive at the Italian border, passing through the defunct border crossing at Gorizia, a town of unflattering plainness, at least as far as the view from the road goes. As with many Italian towns, this is illusory – apparently the old town of Gorizia is very fine indeed, it's just that we can't see it.

This is my third visit to Italy and Diane's second. On both previous occasions I found riding into Italy a disappointment, ranging from mild to quite severe. Diane and I's first arrival here together was only mildly disappointing. We crossed the border between Switzerland and Italy, climbing over one of the stunning passes above Lake Como at Montespluga, back in 2008. As we passed into Italy, the road deteriorated almost catastrophically, and the verges turned into a rubbish tip. It was in sharp contrast to the Germanic cleanliness of Switzerland. Italians are *the* supreme litter louts of Europe, even worse than the Brits and Belgians. Strange then, that, despite me detesting litter, I think that Italy might be my favourite country to visit, for reasons that I hope will become clear in due course.

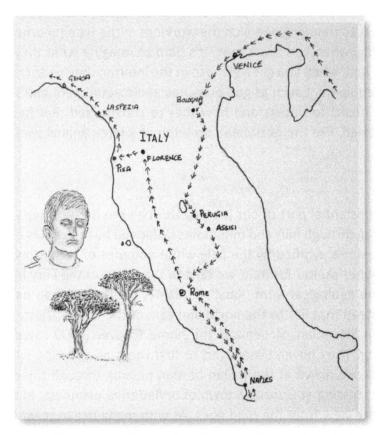

Lots of litter, but still one of my favourite destinations: Italy.

Our route takes us in a south-westerly direction along the A34, crossing the river Isonzo – which defies my stereotyping of Italians by being one of the cleanest in Europe – before hanging a right near a town called Villesse and joining the A4. This is one of the major arteries in Italy, passing right across the north of the country, linking the city of Trieste in the east with Turin in the west, passing by fair Verona and navigating the insane rush hour of Milan on its way out west. The road passes over a rich agricultural landscape that is as flat as a pancake and then some. Away over to the north lie the foothills of the Alps. We can't see them, although we can see a line of clouds that might be a sign of higher elevations beyond. It's a rich area for the growing of grapes. There are lots of fields of vines, giving it an orderly, green countenance. As the road arches towards the south, we spot a sizeable service area and decide to pull over for a well-deserved break.

***

Italian service stations rock. I find them to be bright and cheery places, with excellent coffee facilities, good food, and clean toilets. They kind of feel a bit like home from home, except they don't really, because our service stations back home are quite dreadful. Italian ones are good for people watching too. They invariably have a high quotient of alpha male business representatives, who all sport sunglasses, perched upon their slick black hair and sharp suits, talking endlessly into mobile phones before climbing into their Alfa-Romeos or Lancias.

After a bite to eat and a cup of unfathomably strong coffee, we depart the service area with our eyes bulging out of the front of our helmets, heading into the motorway traffic, which is actually quite light. Here it occurs to me, with a bit of a shock, that something is seriously wrong. And it's taken me quite a few miles to realise it. The Italians are driving like normal people! It's extremely disconcerting. If I wind the clock back five years, to my first two-wheeled foray into the boot of Italy, I recall a deep sensory overload that beset me as I witnessed the apparent total lunacy of Italian drivers and motorcycle/scooter riders. Whether it's the exposure to Georgian, Russian, and Ukrainian driving standards, or whether the Italians have genuinely slowed down a notch or two, I'm not sure. But it all feels decidedly weird. I need to investigate this further. Meantime, a slight thickening of urban architecture signals that we are arriving at the outskirts of our destination. We've arrived at the ring of outlying towns that surround the lagoon upon which the fair city of Venice resides.

**

Our initial attempts to find accommodation take a worryingly familiar turn. Using previously applied logic, we head in the direction of the airport where our first stop is a hotel with no vacancies. The next place we find appears to be deserted, so we press on into the nearest town centre and locate a likely candidate in the form of quite a plush establishment with a long, glass frontage and a trendy reception area. The last time I came upon a hotel with this large a glass frontage was in Dundee.

It wasn't one of my finest hours, as far as hotels go. I went out for a drink with friends and got a bit tipsy. When I got back to the hotel, I couldn't locate the door and nearly froze to death in my attempts (the season being winter), pressing my face against the glass and mouthing, 'help me' in the direction of the reception desk. Eventually, once icicles had formed beneath my nostrils, the night porter took pity on me and opened the (previously invisible) door to let me in. On the way to my room in the lift, shivering violently, I came face to face with the darts legend Jockey Wilson, who nodded and smiled knowingly at me. You meet the nicest people at 2 a.m. in hotel lifts in Dundee.

With Diane on bike guardian duties, I pop into reception to be given the thumbs-down. The explanation seems to be both genuinely regretful and quite worrying at the same time. Metropolitan Venice is fully booked this whole week for some unfathomable reason. The guy informing me of this thinks we will struggle to find anywhere with a vacancy. He asks me to hold for a minute while he speaks with his colleagues.

When he comes back, he informs me that there is one hotel that might have a vacancy – if we hurry. Without explaining any further, he gives me details of how to get there. It's a short distance away and he tells me that it's in a good spot, on the bus route to Venice. So, armed with the instructions, we leap aboard the red express, fire him into life and hot foot it to the hotel in question. Which at first glance seems quite nice. From the outside.

Pulling up in the car park around the rear of the hotel, we pop into reception, which seems quite a homely place, a gathering spot for student types who wish to use the public computer. I tell the receptionist that the other hotel recommended them. She frowns and says that the hotel is full. It seems as if our luck is out and we will need to resort to finding a campsite, or possibly a park bench or railway arch. Then she adds a glimmer of hope.

'There is a room that we don't normally let out to visitors.'

***

In the morning, we arise at a reasonable hour, squeezed into the windowless shoebox of a room. We wander over to the bus stop after breakfast and catch a bus that is absolutely bang on time. The route into Venice passes over a long bridge that spans the famous lagoon to one of the 118 islands on which the city is built. The road terminates at the bus station on the Piazzale Roma. It's a Piazzale and not a Piazza because it is surrounded on only three sides by buildings. The fourth side is a slightly run-down park.

All it takes is a short stroll around a few corners from the bus station to become immersed in this wonderful, water-bound Renaissance city. I first visited it in 2007 and I fell for it immediately. Initially, the natural flow of foot traffic leads you into a series of commercial streets, with shops that are mostly typical of other Italian cities, although there are some interesting variations on the theme. Particularly interesting, is a highly-camp fashion shop for catholic priests and nuns seeking street cred. Cutting a dash in Italy is mandatory, whatever your occupation (or calling).

We've arrived on a very beautiful day. The sun gleams in a pale blue sky and the canal is a beautiful, turquoise blue, framed by and reflecting the riotous variety of pastel colours of the buildings. It really is like looking at a Canalleto painting. The Grand Canal is extraordinarily photogenic with its historic mercantile palaces and iconic gondolas. The classic Italian motor boats that taxi people up and down are works of art of their own, dripping with sumptuously polished teak decking. It's all here, and it's all fabulous. But there's something missing – Venice appears to be somewhat devoid of Venetians.

As a living city, Venice is dying. The population, at just over 50,000, is a third of what it once was, and property prices mean that only the very wealthy can hope to live here. Venice is on the cusp of becoming a theme park; albeit a glorious one; a very sad state of affairs.

The flow of footfall naturally progresses to what is probably the most famous place in the city: St Mark's Square, situated diagonally opposite to the bus station and the bridge to the mainland. Signposts located at regular intervals ensure that you stay on the straight and narrow. But the temptation to sneak around a corner and explore some back alley is all too compelling. Before very long we're hopelessly lost, discovering a different photographic opportunity around every twist and turn, in what feels like a very large, historic maze. Dark ginnels lead to sharp corners hiding secretive canals, bathed in dazzling sunlight. The buildings seem to grow out of the water, it makes you wonder how on earth they built them, and why here?

Venice is largely built on top of wooden piles, driven through the silt and then further into the hard clay beneath. The builders then laid horizontal wood on top of the piles to form a platform upon which they laid stone, often marble, which is impermeable. The piles are mostly sourced from oak and larch, both of which are very resistant to water, driven closely together with rubble dropped between the spaces. What on earth were they thinking of, building a city on a foundation of wood sunk into water? Either by accident, or by design, the builders had plumped for a very effective method and one that has stood the test of time. The lack of oxygen meant that the piles didn't rot. They behaved in much the same way as the timbers of the Vasa back in Stockholm. Then, over time, the timbers became petrified by the minerals in the silt, turning into a material that was more like stone than wood. I recall, as a child, visiting Old Mother Shipton's cave in Knaresborough, North Yorkshire, and being fascinated by the artefacts that had been turned to stone in the same manner, by hanging them in the dropping well.

Despite the fact that Venice is sinking a bit, due to more recent attempts to dig wells into the clay beneath the city, and not helped at all by the effects of rising sea levels, it is a very well-built city. And a strategically placed one, too, if you were looking for a safe place to domicile back in the early medieval period. Even better if you aspired to building a maritime empire. All you needed was lots of trees. Millions and millions of them.

It just so happened that Slovenia, Croatia, and Montenegro were covered with huge forests, which were denuded in short order, leaving the open Karst lands that we've passed through over the last few days. The ancient forests of the countries to the east are standing beneath our feet. It is thought to have taken over a million piles to support just one church here in Venice, so we are talking about quite a lot of chopping and an awful lot of shipping.

Eventually, after spending time at the famous Rialto Bridge, marvelling at the tackiness of some of the souvenir shops thereabouts, we arrive at the famous Piazza. The huge bell tower of St. Mark's Basilica strikes me as looking like it belongs in Red Square in Moscow. This shouldn't come as a huge surprise, since we've already discovered that the Italians designed a significant part of the Kremlin, including its towers. This particular tower is a lot younger than most of the other buildings hereabouts. The original building collapsed in 1902. When I first found out about this, I thought that there was obviously a serious design fault, and perhaps that's true. The pilings beneath the tower were sourced from poplar trees, clearly a mistake. They should've been made of larch. Everyone knows that. But the reason it collapsed was probably more to do with it being one of the unluckiest buildings in history.

Apparently, no one knows when the original tower was built, but some people have plumped for around the 9th century AD. Throughout its life, it suffered a series of calamities, not least being repeatedly struck by lightning and getting burnt once or twice quite badly, at a time when fire brigades hadn't been properly invented. Then it developed a crack and just fell down (conveniently, in a neat pile of rubble, stacked into a small area). It had the good grace to make a lot of 'I don't feel at all well and think I might be about to fall down' noises before giving up the ghost. Reportedly, no lives were lost when it did so. But that's not quite true, because one cat was recorded as getting squished quite fatally and, personally I would count that as a worthwhile life, even if, and I'm not saying it was the case, but even if it wasn't a particularly nice cat.

I won't go on too long about St Mark's Square because it's one of the most famous landmarks anywhere in Europe. It does have some very nice shops selling Venetian glass and we do end up buying a few silicon dioxide trinkets, but I quickly grow bored with that and am lured into buying a tiny German monocular from a camera shop, which instantly comes in handy to peer, along with a few thousand other ordinary souls, at the arrival of the largest, swishest luxury yacht I've personally ever seen, complete with helideck and helicopter. However rich you are, someone richer will eventually swan past you, though doing so won't necessarily make them happier than you. I'm happy as Larry. I've got a new micro-monocular.

After wandering up to the Arsenale and finding a fab little eatery there, we then go and get properly lost, back in the maze of side streets and, before we know it, we're desperately trying to find our way back to the bus station. We're cutting it very fine for catching the last bus back to the hotel! We arrive, slightly ruffled and with sore feet, passing through the park, past a few beer cans and vagrants, before finding that we've made it in time and the bus hasn't even arrived yet.

* * *

Today's ride will take us approximately 400 kilometres, executing a zig-zag route down to the ancient town of Assisi, which is situated in the region of Perugia – roughly in the centre of Italy. The exact centre is reputed to be about thirty kilometres to the south, at Monteluco. We follow signs for the A4 and follow that for a short distance, turning off to the south at the city of Padua, following signs for Bologna.

I imagine most people would make the connection between our first waypoint and the saucy ragu that bears its name. But, for most motorcyclists, Bologna is associated primarily with the iconic Ducati brand. In fact, I have two motorcycles back home that were produced in Bologna and one of them isn't a Ducati, it's a Moto Morini. For the second time in my life, I arrive at Bologna, skirt around it on the motorway and pull up at the same service station for a coffee. On both occasions I purposefully haven't factored in a Ducati factory visit. I secretly think that I'd be disappointed to find that it's just a modern factory, populated by ordinary working people, rather than mystical worker elves. Apparently, the old Moto Morini factory is now a housing development, much like the Triumph factory at Meriden.

Following our coffee break and having negotiated the correct turn towards the south-west, we find ourselves sweeping over numerous viaducts, bouncing the flat twin exhaust note through lofty tunnels carved into the hillsides and glimpsing the odd town perched precariously on the tops of modest, silvan summits. I think riding sections of this road five years ago cemented my relationship with Italy as a whole. I'd been smitten. What lay at the end of it was merely the icing on the Pandoro.

After riding through the hills for thirty or so kilometres, we execute a little detour to check out Lake Trasimeno, a sizeable body of water – an endorheic lake, no less – which is to say that water from two sources flows into it, but none flows out. A bit like leaving the bath water running, very slowly. Surprising then, that Lake Trasimeno is a shallow lake, not much more than forty feet deep on average and coloured a pale greenish tinge of blue. The excess water dissipates by a combination of flooding into marshland and subsequent evaporation. I expected it to be very beautiful, first time around, which it is if you squint, but the area around the northern fringe of the lake feels a mite tatty. The road around the lake is a major dual carriageway with few opportunities to stop, so we press on the final short miles, riding past the town of Perugia and turning off the main road to our destination, which lies just shy of Assisi but bears its name: Camping Assisi.

The last time we knocked a tent peg into the ground was in Finland, three months ago. So, it's with a small measure of glee that the camping gear is broken out, not least because the weather is just about perfect for camping. The camp site is a large, well-run affair, equipped with excellent facilities – including a truly fantabadozi restaurant. We're only going to stay two nights and I'm very keen for Diane to see Assisi so, having pitched the tent, we head the short distance to the town, which provides a spectacular sight as you approach it from the broad valley floor.

Assisi, population 28,200 plus no less than seven, repeat seven (dead) saints, is situated a few hundred feet up the flank of Mount Subasio, one of the mountains in the range of the Appenine hills. It rises a further 3,000 feet above the town, dark and slightly forbidding. Approaching from the direction of the campsite, the walls appear to bear aloft Assisi's most famous building – the Basilica of St Francis. It's not unlike the towering prow of a great ocean liner, gleaming in the throes of a beautiful, serene sunset. By the time we've parked up the Mutt and made our way on foot along the Via Borgo Aretino towards the centre of the old town, dusk has settled. The town lights are springing to life. All across the plain below, the scattered lights of small villages and farms are shimmering in the warm evening air. Lovely.

In the warmth of the early autumn evening, we stroll through the town, checking out the windows of souvenir shops, many of which are selling wares to satisfy the unique, touristic taste of your common-or-garden Catholic pilgrim. The buildings are mainly constructed from the pale stone, mined from the surrounding hills, feeling almost Roman in nature, with wide, shallow-pitched roofs clad in wavy rustic tiles. The first major church you happen upon when walking down the Via Borgo Arentino is the Basilica of Saint Chiara – Saint Clare – a building that is almost overpowered by a series of massive, supporting, arched buttresses, the purpose of which is a bit of a mystery because it looks as if would support its own weight, were it allowed to do so.

St Clare, one of St Francis' followers, founded the Order of Poor Ladies and lived her life in poverty and prayer, passing at the age of 59 from ailments attributed to the rigours of following such a life. She died in August, 1253. The Basilica, named after her, was built and completed in 1260 and her remains were interred beneath the altar, where they lay for the best part of six hundred years before it was decided to dig her up and place her on display in a crystal case. The same fate that befell Lenin. He never asked for it in his will, either.

***

The main reason for stopping at Assisi on our way to Rome is to visit the grave of my uncle Edward, the eldest son of my grandad – the one who led his mule across Sulva Bay in Gallipoli. Grandad John was conscripted into the Army during the First World War. Twenty-eight years later, Edward shared the same fate in the Second but, sadly, the outcome for him was very different. According to family history, he died close to the shores of Lake Trasimeno, the victim of a booby trap left by the German army. Our family have never forgotten Edward, or his brother George, who survived the war, only to die of appendicitis shortly after its end whilst serving in the Royal Navy. My grandfather and grandmother visited Edward's grave here in Assisi in the 1950's as part of a government scheme that supported such visits, and quite a few of the next generation of the family have been here too. I made a point of stopping here to visit his grave in 2007 on the 63rd anniversary of his passing.

Assisi is the site of a British and Commonwealth war cemetery. It lies out in the plain below the town. The campsite has instructions on how to find it and provides us advice and assistance in locating a flower shop, telling us we'll find one in the town centre of Perugia. So, the plan for today is to ride there, buy a wreath, then head to the war cemetery. Having ridden the short few miles from Assisi to Perugia, we park the bike with a few two-wheeled friends under the shade of some trees and walk into the town centre.

Perugia is another example of a grand old Italian town, the ancient centre of which is situated on the crown of a hill, with gorgeous views of the countryside beyond. We find the florists very quickly in the old town centre. Unfortunately, we've been a trifle tardy and it appears to be closed for (what turns out to be) a very extended siesta. There's nothing for it but to have a coffee, wait a bit, then wait a lot more. Then we explore around the streets and back alleys of the old town, practicing a spot of photography before returning to the florists, which surely must now be open. They're still closed. We take to waiting in the shade opposite. Eventually, after what seems like hours, a lady arrives and unlocks the shop. We saunter over as nonchalantly as possible and wander into the cool interior.

I explain to the lady that I would like to buy a wreath with a predominantly white theme, including some white roses, the symbol of mine and Edward's native county. She advises us that she doesn't have white roses and makes a few satisfactory alternative suggestions, telling us that it will take a while to put together. So, we head off for more photography. An hour later, we are on our way, heading towards the village of Rivotorto, which lies a mile or so south of Assisi.

**

The British and Commonwealth war cemetery is situated on a road called the Via del Sacro Tugurio, which translates to the *Road of the Sacred Hovel*, running parallel to the main dual carriageway from Perugia to Spoleto. The name only makes sense if you park up in the convenient car park of the church that lies on the western fringe of Rivotorto and then take a peek inside. It's a basilica of relatively modest size and appearance, clearly of some age, but by no means an extravagant building, attached to a complex of other buildings of similar age that jointly comprise a real-life convent. I'm quite eager to visit the cemetery first and don't reveal to Diane the little secret that lies in the church. Instead, we ride round to the cemetery gates.

The plot of land on which the cemetery sits is quite sizeable, surrounded by a neatly clipped hedge and accessed through a set of iron gates, which are flanked by pale stone pillars. The site is an offset square, with the headstones arranged in ten blocks, all facing uniformly towards a large circular feature, at the centre of which rises a tall cross, embellished with a sword. Behind this is a small building designed to resemble a classical temple; inside are details of the battles that took place in the region, along with a guide to the location of the fallen soldiers' graves.

My uncle's headstone sits at the end of one of the neat rows. It bears the badge of his corps, the Reconnaissance Corps, and his service identity number: 14507133, Trooper E Earnshaw, 4th Regiment, Recce. Corps. RAC. Then the date of his death: 30th June 1944, age 20.

The Reconnaissance Corps was incorporated into the Royal Armoured Corps during 1944, having been previously formed from mainly infantry anti-tank units. It was a corps with an elite ethos, equipped with armoured cars, with a primary purpose of feeling out weak spots in the enemy lines that could then be exploited by heavier armoured units in tanks. In the campaigns in Italy though, with the difficult hilly terrain limiting such opportunities, the armoured cars often found themselves playing a leading role for infantry units, trying to spot evidence of minelaying from the turret. It was an incredibly dangerous task by all accounts. The attrition rate was apparently one of the highest in the army.

***

I found out the following in my research for this book.

The war diary of 4 Recce records that the regiment lost seven soldiers on the 30th June 1944, during the battle on the Trasimene Line.

The German army carried out a series of planned withdrawals to fortified lines as part of their strategy of slowing the Allies almost to a standstill in their invasion of Italy. One of these, called the Trasimene Line, was thrown across Italy, passing through the centre of Lake Trasimeno to the north of Assisi and was used to hold up the allied advance as it made its way towards the intendedly more permanent Gothic Line, to the north. Between the 28th and 29th June, the 1st German Parachute Corps withdrew from their HQ, situated in the Villa Paolozzi, which lies between the villages of Gioiella and Pozzoulo, to the west of Lake Trasimeno. 4 Recce occupied the villa and set up their own regimental HQ in it, hot on the heels of the Germans, settling in on the 29th and joined overnight by a detachment of airmen, who planned to set up a forward observation post in the loft of the building.

One of the airmen was an Australian fighter ace called Jack Doyle, who had spent time on flying missions before being dispatched to help set up the forward control site. Thinking that the upper part of the building would make a good vantage point, the airmen went up to the loft on the 30th and were in the process of removing some tiles from the roof when suddenly the whole villa blew up beneath them. Doyle's life was saved by a roof beam that broke his fall. The cause of the explosion was a 500 kg aircraft bomb, hidden by the German Paras in the cellar, with a timed fuse. It exploded at 3:30 in the afternoon. 4 Recce's official war diary was destroyed in the blast. Their commander, who presumably wasn't in the villa at the time, had to write up a new diary for the whole of June from memory. In the entry for that fateful day, the 30th, he noted in handwriting that the 'delayed mine' had killed seven, wounded three and that one man died later of his wounds. The eighth man is thought to have been a signaller from another regiment. Some of the airmen died too. I haven't been able to find out how many.

So, all the casualties of the regiment on that day, including Edward, perished in the bombing of the Villa Paolozzi. Tragically, it also claimed the lives of eleven civilians, including two children belonging to the family Paolozzi, after whom the villa was informally named. The family had remained in the house after the Germans left. Squadron Leader Jack Doyle DSO, DFC and Bar survived the war and visited the area in 1999, identifying the villa from aerial photographs that he had in his possession. He positively identified the rebuilt villa, aided by locals who had photos from before the war. Jack didn't know the name of the British unit that had occupied the house alongside his airmen, but the details were pieced together by a local historian, a British expat, author and historian called Janet Kinrade, who met Jack when he visited the site. That chance encounter led to her documenting the events described, making it possible for me to discover what had happened, for which I'm very grateful.

Edward was initially buried in a battle grave outside the villa. He carried a small, knitted teddy bear in his tunic pocket, made for him by my Aunt Sylvia, his elder sister. The burial party placed his personal tin and the teddy bear on top of the grave. By a quite incredible coincidence, his cousin passed the temporary grave while moving with his unit up to the lines and recognised the teddy bear. He paused to take a photo of Edward's temporary grave, with the little package on top. The photo found its way back to Yorkshire and into the possession of Sylvia who showed it to me a few years ago. Assisi was nominated as the final resting place for the men buried in the temporary Villa Paolozzi battle cemetery, which leads us back to today.

***

We lay our wreath on the immaculately clipped grass in front of the headstone and observe a minute's silence for Edward and his comrades who are buried in different parts of the cemetery. His headstone bears an epitaph written for those who died in battle:

Went the day well?

He died and never knew

well or ill,

Freedom, he died for you.

I read an article in a newspaper a couple of years ago. It reported that locals around Assisi had chosen to 'adopt' a soldier or airman in the cemetery, recognising that, as time passes, relatives are likely to lose touch with the men who lie there. Once a year, they place flowers on the grave of their adopted fallen soldier or airman. Initially, this caused some controversy amongst older residents, who may be less likely to see the men as liberators. The organiser said that, in carrying out this act of remembrance and compassion, the historical scars of war are gradually being healed.

Chapter 32
The Saintly Hovel

We're standing on the Road of the Saintly Hovel. I think it's time for Diane to witness the hovel in all its saintly glory. It lies within the church, just up the road. The Church of Saint Maria of the Angels is the Gothic, larger basilica that is built above and around the original dwelling and chapel occupied by St Francis of Assisi. The small cell in which St Francis died is included in this tiny complex of ancient buildings within Saint Maria. The first time I came here, I accidentally discovered the tiny building on wandering into the larger one, seeking a minute or two's respite in the shade. The pair of ancient, rectangular stone buildings with tiled roofs sit slap-bang in the middle of the basilica. It reminds me of a gigantic matryoshka doll. Strange to say, but true I think, that the real surprise of Assisi isn't to be found in the glorious town on the hill but, rather, right here – sitting amidst the flat farmland below it. It's comforting to think that Edward is at rest so close to the tiny buildings occupied by St Francis, eight hundred years ago. As we depart the hovel, a pair of hang gliders circle silently above us in the pale late afternoon sky, sufficiently low that we could probably shout a greeting to them, or hit them with a well-placed catapult shot, neither of which we do. Perchance, something of a missed opportunity.

I can confirm from first-hand experience that catapult shots hurt quite a lot. I was once hit squarely on my right buttock by a very clever shot, delivered by a time-served scally as I rode past him on my bicycle near the Pottery Pond fields, Swinton. He used a very skilful ricochet technique that must have taken hours of practice to master, aiming at the road surface in just the right place and correct angle to ensure vicious contact with said buttock at high velocity. Even though I was smarting badly, I had to ruefully admit that it was a fine shot against a difficult moving target. The perpetrator was ecstatic. I would have gone back to punch his lights out, but he was older than me, was council, and was armed. I was about ten years old at the time and a bit of a pacifist. I was armed with a plastic Norwegian troll in my saddle bag. It just didn't cut the mustard. Not long after this, I dumped the troll and surreptitiously acquired a BSA Airsporter air rifle. Life, henceforth, became increasingly difficult for the local mouse population.

* * *

Our next destination is Rome. It's just a modest ride away, 175 kilometres to be precise and the morning dawns bright, promising a fine ride. Hopefully we'll avoid catapult-bearing scallies. The evening presents an opportunity to go through our gear and fine-tune our packing. The bike is given a careful once-over and our clothes-washing is brought up to date at the excellent facility on-site. Biking and camping go so well together – when it's not cold or raining, and when the camp site is as good as this one.

Departing in the late morning, we ride the short distance down to the SS75, the highway that passes Assisi along the wide valley. The walls of the town shine a pale ochre in the morning sun. We catch a glimpse of the war cemetery, the headstones casting morning shadows on the bright green grass as we flash past, bidding farewell to Edward. When we departed the Basilica in the late afternoon yesterday, we decided to take a ride on a fantastic little road that circumnavigates Mount Subasio. It climbs in switchback fashion through dark woodland that grows on the perilous slopes, ascending high above the surrounding plain until it arrives at the tiny village of Armenzano, clustered around a ruined castle that dates from the thirteenth century. The community living there exist in a state of solitude and grandeur that probably feels like a form of heaven on earth; apart from the persistent attention of tourists, such as ourselves.

When I last navigated this road, back in 2007 on my little Yamaha, I nearly didn't make it to Armenzano, having not one, but two mishaps. The first one occurred about half-way up the serpentine road through the cool, damp forest. I needed a pee and decided to stop to relieve myself in the shrubbery. Big mistake! To the left of the road rose a vertical wall of dark rock covered in moss and lichen; to the right, a steep descent to the intended toilet facilities and the deep valley beyond. I clambered down and immediately realised I was in trouble. I could hardly stop myself from tumbling down the hill. I managed to cling to a tree whilst doing the necessary, then tried to ascend back to the road. Initially, I merely managed to slither downwards, making like a hamster in a wheel. With a pang of dread, I realised that if I couldn't make it up to the road then I'd be consigned to navigating my way down the side of the mountain, passing into a huge wilderness, leaving the bike stranded on the road above. It took a humungous effort, scrabbling my way upwards, clinging to the roots of bushes and strands of vegetation to finally, breathlessly, heave myself over the natural ledge back onto the road, where I all but fainted.

Mightily relieved (in every sense), I climbed back on the bike and sped off in the direction of the summit, feeling a bit of a wally. Leaning enthusiastically into the first right-hand corner that presented itself, I suddenly lost the back end of the bike, as if I'd hit a glass-smooth sheet of ice. Almost as quickly as this happened, the back wheel found grip and I managed to recover the slide without high-siding the bike. I'd hit a wash of almost microscopically fine sand that had been spread by water over the surface of the road. I remembered this incident very clearly last night, and rode the beemer carefully this time, taking it easy around corners that would normally be a delight. We duly arrived at the village without incident, and spent an enjoyable twenty minutes exploring the charming combination of cobbled streets, overlooked by tightly packed houses and courtyards, resplendent with potted flowers.

***

You may recall that I was somewhat flummoxed when we arrived in Italy by the dramatic conversion of the average Italian car driver from his (or her) lunatic former self into something bordering on sanity. The tell-tale boxes sitting on top of poles by the roadside might explain the phenomenon. Just a few short years ago, Italian drivers used to be as mad as a box of frogs. Now they've gone and spoilt it all by plonking cameras on the main roads and (presumably) nicking every Fangio who presses his accelerator pedal to the mat. Ok, I know he was Argentinian, but you know what I mean. Gone are the days when you'd be undertaken by a Punto-driving granny as she navigates three lanes of autostrada flat out, weaving through the trucks, tractors, and Lamborghinis or, worse still, find yourself chased across a mountain (as happened to me) by a deranged farmer in an ancient Fiat 500 with bald tyres – more of which later. I find myself wistfully hoping that Rome has retained some of its insane madness – because right now, without it, Italy just doesn't seem the same. In the meantime, we make our stately progress towards the fabled city.

Just a few short years ago, the idea of riding through Rome on a motorcycle might have brought a nervous twitch to the brow of even a seasoned traveller. Whilst staying at Camping Assisi in 2007, I found myself in conversation with a Dutch couple who had driven right through the centre of the city whilst towing a caravan (the Dutch are traditionally nowhere near as barking mad as Norwegians, but some of them do exhibit a smidgen of nuttiness). The husband admitted that the experience had probably aged him a couple of years. But my abiding memory at that time was just how rough the place was. I arrived in very heavy traffic, travelling in from the northern suburbs of the city. In doing so, I managed to get a trifle lost and pulled over at a riverside restaurant to ask if there were any hotels in the vicinity.

'You need get outta here now!' was the waiter's helpful reply. 'Di stadio oer der issa de stadio di Roma. All hated, especially you. Motos thrown over walls. Go now!'

I was a bit nonplussed. Why especially me? I don't support Leeds United. More than that, it seemed like quite a nice neighbourhood to me, at least compared to some I'd just travelled through. But I thought I should follow his guidance and I hopped back on the bike and sought safety in the comfort-zone offered by swarms of trendy people riding scooters in suits and the rest of the population driving mostly Fiats, feeling a bit like a sardine in a massive shoal, just prior to a gannet and dolphin feeding frenzy. I've seen one of these, by the way, in the seas close to Morocco and they are a totally awesome spectacle, Richard Attenborough is entirely correct to wax lyrical about them, but I digress…

Then there were the accidents. Every five minutes or so, an ambulance would race past, sirens piercing through the noise of the traffic, rushing to the inevitable scene of scooter-on-Alfa Romeo carnage. The sound of these ambulance sirens was almost constant. Welcome indeed to Roma.

I haven't bothered to tell Diane any of this.

* * *

Our journey today is in complete contrast to the navigational mayhem suffered five years previously. Our route is a different, more direct one. It passes through the more sedate, western outer suburbs, populated by relatively modern buildings. As we near the centre of the city, the streets become grander, with mature trees lining them and long lines of larger, older, fine houses, built in a variety of neo-classical styles. Despite this rise in the quality of the buildings, graffiti is never far from sight. Modern Romans have enthusiastically maintained the penchant of their forebears to decorate every possible wall-space with their angular monikers. Gradually, the road funnels us into the city without any real trial or tribulation, allowing Diane to sightsee from the pillion. She doesn't need to make like a banshee-meerkat on hotel watch duties today because I recall, quite clearly, the location of the hotel that I stayed in last time and am keen to see if we can find it. The Hotel St Angelo is situated quite centrally, very close to the Piazza Cavour and the Supreme Court, which, if memory serves me correctly, looks remarkably similar to the yorkstone fireplace that adorned the front room of my house in Ormesby St Margaret, back in the '80s. Clearly, it too was built by someone lacking taste.

The road around the piazza is surfaced with shiny black cobbles (possibly made of basalt) that are mighty slippery when wet and challengingly uneven in all conditions. Many of central Rome's roads are clad thus. The other navigational clue is that the piazza is situated just a block away from the River Tiber, which wends its meandering way on a very rough north to south trajectory right through the centre of the city.

Our audacious plan is to ride straight into the city and locate the river, at which point I'll head along its banks towards the city centre, whichever way that appears to be, most likely to the south. At some point, we'll then either: arrive at the Roma footie stadium and be ceremonially sacrificed, or: avoid it and fall off on the slippery cobbles, whichever happens first. Amazingly, it is the sight of a telephone box that stirs the memory. I recall its location by the river, just down the road from the hotel. Shortly after executing a sharp right, we emerge onto the piazza, cautiously navigating our way around to a point where we can park up on the uneven cobbles. From here, I can walk to the hotel to check on room availability, leaving Diane to take photos of the local Carabinieri who are parading around the square, pistols in holsters, in their sky-blue and white finery, which I think looks a bit camp. I'm quite astonished at how easy that was.

The telephone box that signals our arrival. Slippery cobbles it is!

As Dorothy said, 'there's no place like Rome'. It takes a few minutes on the stroll to the hotel just to savour the magic of the place. The Hotel St Angelo probably ranks as an ordinary 3-star hostelry by Roman

425

standards, but I loved staying there on my previous visit. The main part of the hotel is located on the first floor of a grand old building situated on the Via Marianna Dionigi, just across the river from the Mausoleum of Augustus, the Emperor formerly known as Octavian. The hotel reception is accessed by entering through a high-arched doorway and climbing up two flights of wide marble stairs. The doors on the street have decorative handles that are near replicas of the ones we saw in the Winter Palace, in the form of a clawed foot holding a ball, providing a clue to the age of this building. At the reception desk, I'm pleased to discover that there's a room available, albeit in an annex down the street.

The annex is situated in a tall building a couple of hundred yards from the main hotel, accessed through a huge door that is sectioned by a smaller one to provide normal human access. The hotel occupies half of the fourth floor, serviced by a wonderfully creaky old lift with narrow, double wooden doors sitting behind an external metal cage door with a clunky latch that closes heavily. The lift inside is a vintage Otis, built of thin polished wooden panels, with glass windows. You can just fit two adults inside, with a minimum of luggage.

In the early evening, we wander out for a meal, strolling along the via Marianna Dionigi. It is named after a quite remarkable lady from the late eighteenth/early nineteenth century who managed to be a skilled artist, musician, writer, archaeologist, and mother of seven children, all at once. Goodness gracious!

***

We only have one day to spend sightseeing the vast treasure house that is Rome, wishing to reserve sufficient time in our itinerary of the next few days to take in the sights of Pompeii and its close neighbour, Herculaneum, which lie a couple of hundred kilometres to the south. When I last visited Rome, the crowds to visit the interior of the Colosseum were horrendous and I only managed to view the exterior. We're keen to remedy that omission today.

We have a choice of two bridges to cross into the heart of the ancient city, the nearest being the Ponte Cavour. From there, it's a reasonably short walk to meet up with one of the main shopping streets, the Via del Corso – the 'Oxford Street' of Rome. It runs straight as an arrow, flanked on both sides by various shops and stores, requiring a small amount of gentle steering in the pillion rider department.

The directional propriety of the Via del Corso points to its Roman origin, but it gained its current name later in its career when it was used as a racetrack for riderless horses – the point of which quite escapes me. Riderless horses always look a bit lost and inclined towards a lazy canter when you see them on the Saturday afternoon horse-racing on ITV. After a short walk along this crowded homage to materialistic excess, we hang a left, following a tourist map purloined from the hotel, seeking out the first destination on our cultural whistle-stop tour: the world-famous Trevi Fountain.

The name 'Trevi' is derived from the word for 'three roads', named after the district in which the fountain stands, a place where three roads once came together. The fountain is fed by waters that were originally discovered by the ancient Romans, originating in springs located about ten kilometres outside the ancient city. The waters are transported to the city by the pull of gravity along the gentle slope of the ancient Aqua Vergine aqueduct, terminating quite forcefully at multiple fountains, one of which is the Trevi. Consequently, this is a very ancient water source, originally providing fresh, pure water to the thirsty Roman populace. Quite amazingly, it still uses the technology installed nearly two thousand years ago along much of its watercourse. What elevates it, perhaps above all others though, is the stupendous Baroque grandeur of the makeover it received in the eighteenth century.

The water cascades in a dramatic fall over a massive wall of rocks forming a reef carved from travertine limestone, above which rides Oceanus in a chariot constructed of shells, pulled by a pair of hippocamps – aka wild sea horses. The hippocamps are being led by a pair of Tritons, one of whom is blowing a shell to announce the arrival of Oceanus. The other Triton is having a mare of a time trying to control a very unruly hippocamp who, quite frankly, needs to be sent for a strong dose of behavioural training. Apparently, it's an allegory for the wild nature of the sea. Alternatively, it might just be a common-or-garden teenage hippocamp.

The backdrop to the fountain is formed from the edifice of a large neo-classical building, the Palazzo Poli, the main archway of which provides the entrance for Oceanus emerging in all his riotous glory. I don't know of any other palace that provides a supporting backdrop for the fountain in its front garden, but this one had a complete makeover to do just that; as a result the palace is part of the fountain. It sits in a relatively small piazza and totally dominates it. The rush of the water terminating here after its passage from the hills fills the air with a tumultuous cacophony of sound and the sight holds the gaze of hundreds of visitors.

***

After chucking a couple of coins over our shoulders into the fountain, guaranteeing that we will return here one day (probably in a couple of hours on our way back), we head off in the direction of Trajan's Forum, passing the huge monument to Vittorio Emanuele II, the first king of Italy, which is unfortunately undergoing restoration and is covered in scaffolding. When we arrive at the edges of Trajan's Forum, we encounter one of the gorgeous gelato vans that are to be found parked in strategic areas of the city. They're a paragon of Italian chic, dressed up in classy colours – tempting, even for a diabetic like me. Our next destination is Trajan's famous column which stands nearby.

The column glorifies the campaigns of the emperor against the Dacians, the tribe of people who occupied what is now Romania who nowadays manufacture badge-engineered, reasonably-priced Renaults. The Dacians were no pushover. Initially, when the Romans tried to forcibly introduce them to the Pax-Romana, they gave their Latin visitors a bit of a surprise and sent them home to think again. Undeterred, Trajan went back a few years later to finish the job off properly. The column celebrates both his campaigns. Surprisingly, it doesn't show too much fighting, preferring instead to show the day-to-day activities of the Roman Army: manning ramparts, manoeuvring siege engines and machines designed to fire huge projectiles at the unfortunate Dacians. The figures on the column, cut in deep relief, provide the onlooker with a fine impression of what the Romans and their enemies looked like: how they dressed and the equipment they used. From this primary source of information, we can deduce that the Romans tended towards the cocky and their enemies were inclined to look a bit cowed and dejected in defeat. It also appears that most self-respecting barbarians sported very impressive beards, a fact that shouldn't come as too much of a surprise. It's doubtful that the Romans would sell them razors.

As you stare up the column, you notice thin, elongated rectangular holes cut into it. These were designed to light the interior, which is hollow and has a circular staircase cut into it, allowing ancient sightseers to climb up and view the forum from a viewing platform at the top.

***

Our next whistle stop is the Colosseum, perhaps the most famous building in Rome and one that I'm not going to wax over because its fame doth go before it. We pay our entry fee, mingle with the crowds, carry out the obligatory photo calls and then spill back out again. Where to go next?

Well, the Palatine hill is a short distance away. It's the oldest part of the city of Rome, the place where (in Roman mythology) Romulus and Remus, the founders of the city, were discovered in a cave by the she-wolf Lupa who suckled them until they were rescued by a lowly shepherd. I'm not sure that being suckled by a wolf counts as being lucky, but there we are: any port in a storm as they say.

The archaeology of the city indicates that the hill is the birthplace of what would eventually become a super city state. The later emperors recognised this and chose to build their sumptuous residences upon the Palatine, providing the root of our word 'Palace'. But my favourite sight on the hill doesn't rest on the monumental ruins of the various palaces. The sight that transfixes me are the weirdly-shaped fir trees that grace the park around the ruins. The Pinus Pinea, sometimes called the *Stone Pine* or the *Umbrella Pine*, can be found scattered around various Mediterranean countries and further afield, but it is shown in all its glory here. As it becomes mature, it develops an uncanny likeness to tender-stem broccoli.

***

It's often difficult to imagine what the original buildings were like when all that remains are fragments. This is particularly true of the Forum and the buildings that line the Via Sacra, the Sacred Way, as it passes through the Forum. An example is the House of Vestals, where the eternal flame once resided, tended by ladies of exceptional repute. The fragments of walls and pillars give some idea of what the building looked like, but they seem modest in size, which comes as a bit of a surprise. The same can't be said for the monumental arches, through which victorious troops and emperors paraded all those years ago. They are truly magnificent. And the renditions carved upon them of barbarians being led in chains by triumphant legionaries are both poignant and compellingly lifelike. But, if you want to see a real Roman building, intact in all its glory, there's only one place to head for, and that's our final destination on this one-day, whistle-stop tour. The building in question is the Pantheon. It's getting a bit late and the rapidly gathering clouds bode rain, so we hurry along, chased by Jupiter, following our map and arriving at the appropriately named Piazza del Rotunda just in the nick of time. A sharp crack of thunder in the near distance signals our hasty arrival.

My interest in the Pantheon was sparked by a programme on TV describing its construction. Unlike so many of its brethren, it stands intact – nearly two thousand years after it was completed. If that isn't astonishing enough, the brilliance of its construction is truly incredible. The rotunda, from which the piazza takes its name, is the main body of the building, with the other element being a huge, oblong portico which houses the grand entrance. Nowadays, the building is a church but, in Roman times, it was a temple; to whom isn't clear.

We arrive at the building just before the gathering storm breaks, joining the throng of visitors within, many of whom are standing in a rough semi-circle, staring at the ceiling. Above them is a perfectly circular hole in the roof called an oculus, through which the (soon to be departed) sun beams down, lighting the people below. The oculus sits atop a perfectly symmetrical dome. If you measure from floor to ceiling, including the walls, you can fit a 43.3 metre sphere in the building, half of which would sit within the dome itself, which is made from concrete. It's still the largest unreinforced concrete dome in the world, a technological marvel. The cement at the base of the dome is mixed with travertine, which is denser than the mixture higher up, made with much lighter volcanic pumice.

Notwithstanding the fact that the Romans gave the world many things (to quote Monty Python), but not cement, they did a brilliant job with the Pantheon roof. The interior is made up of sunken rectangles (called coffers), which is very striking and almost overwhelming, when viewed from below. The walls of the building have the effect of appearing on two levels, with many alcoves and highly decorated supporting columns. Some of the decorations are later additions, carried out during the life of the building as a church. But I think it gives you a fine impression of what a Roman temple would have looked like, too, because the interior resembles Roman architectural wall paintings found in various sites and especially in Pompeii. To top it off, the Pantheon is the final resting place of the famous Renaissance artist Raphael. Being a long-standing admirer of the work of the Pre-Raphaelite Brotherhood, who detested Raphael's work so much that they named themselves after the period before him, finding oneself so close to the object of their derision is a mite uncomfortable. Perhaps we ought to make our exit.

Just before we depart, the skies above the oculus turn a darker shade of grey-bordering-on-black and the heavens open. The downpour descends straight through the hole and down through the building, falling with an increasing rhythm on the floor, causing people to stand back a little. The Romans obviously had this eventuality covered. They designed the floor with a slight degree of slope, allowing rainfall inside the building to wash away into cunningly designed drains. I think we would benefit greatly if we could design a time machine and spirit them into the boards of the companies that build modern British housing estates. We still haven't had the drains fixed outside our house, five years after it was built.

***

Saturday 13th October 2012.

We've drawn up by the roadside in a rather swanky, partially completed housing development. It sits right on the edge of the city.

In the far distance, across a patch of countryside, I can see the main autostrada that runs north-to-south past Rome, the E45, but I'm not sure how to get from here to there.

Initially, we made a surprisingly successful exit out of the city centre, crossing the Tiber. We took a wrong turn quite shortly thereafter and now here we are, lost again. There's nothing for it other than to back-track and try to pick up the signs for the road south, which we eventually do successfully. The parts of Rome that we passed through on the way to the housing development were part of the inner suburbs of the city, quite attractive, leafy streets interspersed with bustling commercial localities that felt well lived-in and generally quite clean. Now, for the second time of asking, even the traffic behaves itself; children in passing buses fail to snarl at my pillion passenger and we managed to pick up signs for the desired route.

When we eventually arrive at the E45, an hour later than planned, I find myself suffering a pang of regret at having to leave Rome after just one day. We both voiced the opinion, whilst tucking into our mandatory Prosciutto e Melone last night, that it would take at least another four visits just to scratch the surface of what's to be seen there. I guess we'll just have to keep coming back. In the meantime, we've set a steady course for Napoli, with every intent of studiously ignoring it and settling instead for somewhere near Sorrento.

The bike seems to have enjoyed its day off, tucked up beneath its lightweight cover on the street in the company of a bunch of tatty, feral Vespas. It has settled into humming along very nicely, lapping up the kilometres with a degree of Bavarian relish. The autostradas in Italy are toll roads, not dissimilar to those found in France, with the exception that the French take better care of their toll roads than the Italians. As chief trip administrator, it's Diane's job to muster up the spondoolies and pay the chap or chapess at the toll booths, not as easy a task as it sounds when you're burdened by a surplus of pockets, with hands wrapped up in gloves and the occasional pesky stray coin from Georgia or Russia attempting to disguise itself as a Euro. But Italians are nothing if they're not biker friendly. The toll persons wait with patient amusement as we fumble for our change before waving us off cheerily with an 'arrivederci', once the transaction is complete.

The scenic hills experienced a couple of days ago as we travelled down the spine of Italy, have now given way to a more open and slightly flatter, rolling countryside, bordered in the distance by relatively low-lying hills. It's by no means as flat as the north of the country, but it is easy going as we drone along at the legal limit of 130 kilometres per hour, a very sensible and reasonable 81 miles per hour. You don't really need to go any faster than this to get to your destination in a decent timescale. The traffic is quite light too, which helps keep everything nice and relaxed.

I think this is one of the reasons that I find myself falling for Italy once more. Once you've got over the grit, grime and the generally poor state of some of the infrastructure and once you've conditioned yourself to the enthusiastic driving, you gradually become immersed in the culture and the rich texture of everything around you. You start to appreciate the fabulous food, the attention given to design in the cars, boats, clothes, motorcycles and houses, even down to the sanitary ware and light switches in the hotels. I keep pointing these out to my travelling companion when we arrive at each hotel. Then there's the countless lovely old towns and villages clinging to hillsides and hilltops. And to cap it all off, they have sensible speed limits on their motorways. After a couple of days of this, the effect on me is quite cathartic.

*** ***

Roughly half-way into our journey, we pass the town of Cassino, famous for the desperate siege that took place there in 1944. I have it in mind to visit the legendary monastery on the hill when we return northwards. Today though, we pass by on the autostrada, catching the briefest of glimpses of the hill where most of the fighting took place, which is shielded from view by the roadside trees and the motorway embankments. From Rome to this point, the road has been heading in a south-easterly direction but, a few miles further, it starts to swing more determinedly to the south as it enters the final stretch towards Naples, at which point the traffic becomes a lot more congested and we grind to the occasional halt.

We catch our first glimpse of Vesuvius as we approach the great and ancient city. It rises above the eastern fringe, pressing against the built-up suburbs. The road passes through the suburbs then skirts around the brooding volcano. Ahead of us, we can see a towering range of hills, which I know to be the start of the Amalfi Peninsula, our target for today. The junction we're looking for appears just south of the modern town (and ancient ruins) of Pompeii, where the E45 bids farewell to us and cuts east on a trajectory towards the port of Salerno. Initially, we miss the turning to Sorrento and end up in the back streets of the surrounding town, arriving there as the clouds burst open, washing down the streets. Having navigated our way back to the junction, we join the road that hooks sharp right towards the northern coast of the peninsula. When it arrives there, it climbs in a most pleasing manner through a series of tightly sweeping and precipitous bends that carry it to sufficient height to permit magnificent views across the bay, back towards Naples.

We've arrived in good time and the rain has abated sufficiently for us to enjoy the views as we ride at a gentle pace along a road called the Corso Italia (hinting at riderless horse racing? Surely not!), which snakes its way along a precipitous coastline through various small towns before arriving in the larger and altogether splendid town of Sorrento. On arrival, we grind to a rush-hour halt, allowing us to peer around at the eclectic jumble of grand classical and more traditional commercial buildings that crowd in on our route. Sorrento deserves its upmarket reputation – it exudes the air of a fine resort, sitting on the northern coast of the peninsula above the pale towering cliffs, overlooking the bay. Eventually, the traffic eases, allowing us to filter our way through a slightly more modern section of the town. The road climbs up the western fringes through stone-lined cuttings towards a high, tree shaded, promontory where we pick up signs for camping. All of a sudden, as we round a bend, we spot a sign adorned with a mermaid and the words *Santa Fortunato Village, Camping Campogaio* which (I think) translates to something like 'Lucky Holy Village Camping'. We execute a prompt right turn through a rather grand walled entrance and pull up outside the reception office. It's time to break out the tent (again).

⤙⟨ ⟩⤚

Chapter 33
Up Pompeii

The Lucky Holy Village is a campsite of considerable distinction. It nestles in a mature olive grove on top of the cliffs overlooking Sorrento, enjoying some of the finest views of any campsite that I've ever camped in. After securing a pitch and signing in, I manage to almost drop the bike whilst executing a tight 'U' turn outside reception. It's one of those situations where the bike's top-heavy loading causes the handlebars to tuck under unexpectedly, almost catching me out. A more skillful rider would just lean the bike, apply some power and accelerate through the turn, but I've ended up wobbling embarrassingly around instead. Feeling a bit of a plonker, I ride the bike down the narrow road to a tidy little site in a square alcove bordered by a rustic fence constructed from slender sections of trees. A pair of fine olive trees provide multiple options for locating a washing line.

The peninsula is famous for its citrus fruit trees particularly, lemons, giving its name to a popular variety. Originally settled by the Greeks, Sorrento provided a naturally safe and secure site for the town to grow and trade with other parts of the Mediterranean Sea. Our intention tomorrow is to visit Pompeii. I'd also like to treat Diane to some of the views of the Amalfi coast. I know a terrific road for this purpose, having ridden it in 2007, but I think that might have to wait for later. I think we'll have a full day tomorrow visiting the famous, ruined town.

A little later, we wander up to the restaurant that sits up the gentle hill, close to the office, typical of the many decent eateries to be found on Italian campsites. What is unexpected is the quality of the entertainment, provided by a ballroom and latin dance school enjoying their weekly class in an area of the restaurant cleared to provide a dance floor. Watching them relish their lesson results in a pang of regret that I've had to desist from dancing due to the arthritis in my foot, losing the endorphin release that comes with such a pleasurable pastime. I do enjoy watching other people dance but find such enjoyment oft-tempered by a mild dose of envy.

***

It's the morning of Sunday the 14th October. The weather has improved quite significantly today following the rain showers that worked their way down Italy over the past two days. The dawning of clearer weather garnishes the dramatic view across the bay of Sorrento. A deep blue sky provides the backdrop for high cirrus clouds that cast a wispy veil. In contrast, powerful rolling cumulus formations cling to the furthest hills of the peninsula at the far end of the bay. It feels like there could be rain later today.

We pack our Finnish wet weather suits as an insurance policy and head along the peninsula in the direction of Naples. The bike is unencumbered with the paraphernalia of camping equipment and clothes and is pleasantly nimble to throw around the tight corners. The tyres that were fitted in Ankara are now well worn-in and starting to square off – an inevitable result of day-in, day-out high mileages. Tyres remain fresh for just a few days when your daily mileage averages around three hundred miles and the effects of wear are more readily sensed when it takes place over such a compressed timescale. I recall the feeling of pleasure, sampling fresh tyres on the sweeping corners following our exit from Ankara just one month ago. Now the ride is slightly less precise and prone to occasionally tracking minor irregularities in the road. It's still a shed load of fun though!

Pompeii sits in a wide, flat, congested valley to the south-east of Naples about one kilometre inland from the bay. Mount Vesuvius sits to the north-west of the town and the Lattari Mountains to the south-east. Our ride from the western side of Sorrento is the reverse of our arrival yesterday, dropping down from the hills into the valley. As usual, we manage to get a bit lost. For a world heritage site, Pompeii is slightly lacking in signage, and the roads around it are a modern Italian version of our own Spaghetti Junction, surrounded by a tired urban sprawl that fills most of the valley. It reminds me a bit of Rochester: a cultural gem squeezed between Gillingham, Chatham, and Strood.

After a considerable amount of navigational faffing, we eventually manage to locate two signs in relatively quick succession, landing ourselves in an area that becomes more familiar to me (having been here before). Five years ago, similarly lost, I rode into the modern town of Pompeii and stopped at a ladies' hair stylists to ask where the ruins were. Everyone looked blank and shrugged – I left, none the wiser. I think they were all confused, stylists and customers alike, by the intrusion of a bald, male foreigner entering the salon and babbling incoherently. This time around, despite being armed with a lady pillion rider sporting a much-improved hairstyle and colouring, I've opted to avoid such embarrassments and just ride around lost, until we manage to find ourselves un-lost.

Locating Pompeii on Google maps satellite view is an interesting way to spend a few minutes, when you have time to try it. If you ignore the obvious pointers provided by the application, the ruins are almost as difficult to spot from the satellite image as they are in real-life. When you do discover them, they appear almost as if they're a suburb of the modern towns, hidden in the clutter of the surrounding conurbation. The main clue to finding the town is that most of its buildings are sliced off at roof level, making them slightly less distinct than those around them. The large, ancient amphitheatre is also something of a giveaway.

The entrance to the site is situated on a road called *Via Plinio*, which I assume could be named after Pliny the younger who provided the most vivid eyewitness account of the eruption of Vesuvius in letters to his friend, the historian Tacitus. Then again, it could be named after Pliny the elder, who didn't. The car park resides opposite the entrance in a small, semi-circular road called *Piazza Anfiteatro* (Amphitheatre Square). The entrance to the ancient town is just across the road, a ticket office partially hidden by the trees in a strip of park that separates the old from the new, so we'll leave our trusty travelling companion right here, slouched on its side-stand and slightly squared off rear tyre, dig out our cameras from the top box, and mosey on over.

***

I once bought a large format book about the treasures of Pompeii. It had many beautiful photographic plates, in full colour, showing the amazing, occasionally rude, and sometimes quite gruesome artifacts found during the extended excavations of the town, which started in the mid-eighteenth century and continue to this day. The impact of viewing the town first-hand doesn't really hit you when you stroll along from the ticket booth, but it's just a short distance to the first set of streets. Once there, you are drawn into a world that is both starkly different from ours and yet eerily familiar, a world of well-constructed streets, raised pavements, temples, shops, bakeries, and substantially built houses. One thing I love about it is that it isn't a theme park. It's an immersive museum.

The material that buried the town came from a combination of falling ash from a cloud of gas and volcanic debris and from a series of catastrophic pyroclastic surges, similar to the event that occurred at Mount St Helens in the United States, in 1980. In that event, the surge was measured at a maximum speed of 290 mph, travelling along the ground and annihilating everything living in its path. Pompeii was buried in this debris to a height of six metres, which is now the ground level for the modern towns that surround the site. Viewed from the excavated ruins, it's as if someone has sliced off the buildings at that height, like topping-off a boiled egg.

The population of Pompeii at the time of the eruption in 79 AD is thought to have been around 15,000. Two thousand souls are thought to have perished, but it may have been far more – only part of the town has been excavated. Many of those lucky enough to survive returned some days or weeks after the eruption, trying to recover at least something from their homes, finding parts of the town rising from the smoking ash that had buried it. When the more recent excavations took place, they found evidence that people had dug into the ash trying to recover valuables. Gradually, over time, any visible signs of its existence disappeared, and it remained lost until 1592 when re-discovery occurred during the digging of a watercourse.

Pompeii is a fortified town, built predominantly in stone and brick. The town walls and towers are substantial and the gates into the town impressive. It is built on a north/south, east/west axis, very slightly skewed (if measured by the compass) in an anti-clockwise direction. The streets run in a grid pattern formed by minor streets and major thoroughfares, a bit like back home in Milton Keynes. Many of the smaller streets show a lower level of archeological excavation, whereas the major streets are a treasure-trove of highly preserved buildings, with fascinating details of daily life within them; in many cases, visitors can simply walk into a building and explore it. One of the first things you discover when you arrive at one of the main thoroughfares is the proliferation of commercial units, predominantly shops.

The general layout for a Roman shop was an oblong or square unit at street level, with a stone counter facing the street, often in a 'U' or 'L' shape. Many of these appear to be thermopolia: cooking shops that sold hot food, evidenced by large circular holes cut into the counter where receptacles would have held the produce being sold. The counters are often decorated by a kind of 'crazy-paving' pattern of polished marble slabs, variegated in their colour and shape, but perfectly laid – much better than my attempts at tiling. The remains of wall art in some of the shops, houses, and public buildings testify to how vibrant these buildings were. The walls were rendered in lime plaster, often with paintings applied on the top surface. The quality of the paintings vary greatly, but even some found in the thermopolia are quite elaborate. Red ochre is one of the predominant colours. It's very easy to imagine the hubbub of activity as you wander into and past these buildings. It puts me in mind of the wonderful atmosphere of the Grand Bazaar in Istanbul.

The grand houses of the town have understandably grabbed much of the attention of generations of archeologists and visitors alike, a bit like bees to the honey pot. Of course, we're no exception – we spend quite a lot of our time wandering around the terrific examples that exist, marveling at some of the details that have survived. Amongst my favourites is a house with its garden recreated as it would have been just before the eruption. How they managed this is explained in an exhibition that describes the archeology of seeds, studies of surviving tree root systems and also evidence from wall paintings. If anything can capture the feeling of living in the distant past, it's being able to stand in someone's garden, staring back at their house. You get the feeling that it would be quite a fine life, so long as you weren't one of the slaves...

A typical high-status house, called a *Domus* would be accessed from the street through a single, substantial door. You would walk through an entrance hall called the *Vestibulum* into the first major area of the house, the *Atrium*. The experience is not far removed from walking into a small hotel. The Domus, being high status, was equally a meeting place for visitors and clients of the head of the household, who would almost invariably be the male owner. The rooms surrounding the Atrium are called the *Cubiculum*. They were used as private rooms, often bedrooms. The centre of the Atrium held a pool to gather rainwater, which collected there after falling from an opening in the roof.

The next part of the house is the *Alae*, an open area where the busts (and sometimes even death masks) of ancestors of the family were displayed. The connection with past family members was, apparently, very strong in Roman times, as if they were still living with the family. It is also common to find the remains of household shrines, either in the Atrium or sometimes at the end of the courtyard behind this part of the house. The *Tablinium* was usually the next room, sitting at the far end of the Atrium in a large space, commanding a view of the entrance to the Atrium. This was the 'office' space, used to conduct meetings with guests and also as a 'command station' for the owner to manage the house. As such, it was often a very elaborate room, with high decoration on walls and floors. Beyond this command centre is the *Peristyle*, which took the form of a colonnaded walkway that surrounded a courtyard, much like a cloister in a cathedral or an abbey.

This design was common to Greek houses of an earlier period. It wasn't invented by the Romans, and it carried on after the Roman period too – cloisters being an example of its survival. The Peristyle surrounded the gardens. Various additional rooms were accessed from the walkway, including bedrooms, the dining room *(Triclinium)* and the kitchen *(Culina)*. In the Roman Domus, the cook was a slave who worked, lived, and slept in what was a small and, by all accounts, very smoky room.

***

We gradually work our way towards the municipal centre of the town, the forum, where we pause at the modern café for a bite to eat. By now, we've managed to take in the ruins around the forum and also the baths, which are very well preserved, with high arched roofs richly decorated with beautiful wall art. Also preserved are the water systems that supplied fresh water to the richer houses and the fountains: lead water pipes and drains. The method of building is interesting, too. Often, the columns that you would imagine to be fashioned from solid blocks of marble or stone, turn out to be built of brick, which has then been faced with cement or plaster, very similar to the utilitarian methods used in the rebuilding of Stalingrad, with one glaringly obvious difference: the brickwork at Pompeii, even when it was hidden, was perfectly executed.

Of course, to describe the full experience of discovering Pompeii would take up many pages, so I'll just mention two further features that I particularly enjoy looking around. The first is one of the numerous bakeries that can be found scattered around the town (around 35 have been excavated). They vary greatly in scale, and the one that impressed me most leans heavily towards the grand, with a huge oven, housed in its own building, sitting in close proximity to a sizeable milling yard. It was to Pompeii what Warburtons is to British crumpet manufacture. The corn mills have a circular base with cobbles laid around it and a cone shaped-stone called a *meta* mounted on top. Above this sits the *catillus*, an hour-glass shaped stone that resembles a waisted cotton bobbin with square holes cut into its middle. The millstones were made from basalt and the power to turn them was provided by donkeys harnessed to wooden stakes that were mounted in the square holes, plodding around the cobbles. Grain was fed into a funneled hole at the top of the catillus, to be ground by the two stones, before being collected in a tray that sat around the top of the circular base. In at least one bakery, a batch of loaves had been loaded into the oven, presumably just before the eruption. And there they remained until their eventual discovery during the excavations, a reminder of the immediacy of the catastrophe that hit the town.

The amphitheatre is the last stop on our tour. Situated on the western corner of the excavation, it is remarkably complete, surrounded by a broad expanse of park populated with lovely umbrella pine trees and overlooked by the brooding summit of Mount Vesuvius. Pliny the Younger described the eruption in detail noting that the massive plume of debris arose in a column to a great height, with different branches splitting from the central column, and a huge cloud spreading above forming the wide canopy in the shape of an umbrella pine.

Pompeii's amphitheatre is the oldest stone-built example in the world, beautifully executed. Even now, it serves as an example for the management of large groups of spectators, especially those partial to the odd brawl. Viewed from above, it describes the shape of a human eye. From the outside, it offers the viewer perfectly formed and elegant stonework, with a series of arches tracing the outer wall, punctuated by triangular staircases that give access to the upper levels. Nowadays, entry into the stadium is gained by passing through a tunnel. Further tunnels provide a glimpse of what it was like for the 'performers' as they waited to enter the arena – it's quite sombre to contemplate the purpose of this building, yet difficult not to appreciate the quality of its construction. Once inside, you can wander around the elliptical stage upon which gladiators fought to the death. The terraces, once crowded with rowdies, are now peaceful and overgrown with bright green grass, but it is easy to imagine the febrile atmosphere that once dominated this space.

The Romans were not averse to punitive measures in cases where crowds had got badly out of hand. There was a massive fight between the spectators from Pompeii and their neighbours from the nearby town of Nuceria during one of the gladiatorial games in AD59, resulting in the death of some of the spectators. The authorities imposed a ban following the mass brawl, which was to stretch for a full ten years. It raises the question as to what they did with the stadium during the downtime? Maybe they switched to Saturday chariot boot sales.

Pompeii is quite an extraordinary place to visit. My normal attention span of 1-1/2 hours is stretched like a well-kneaded dough when visiting places such as this, but it's time for us to head back to Sorrento. So, we'll just leave with one sobering thought: Pompeii is suffering terribly for being such a popular tourist venue. The town is deteriorating faster than it can be preserved. As in the case of the Vasa in Stockholm, or the Mary Rose in Portsmouth, it is such a fragile artifact that it needs extraordinary levels of care to ensure it can be witnessed by future generations. And how do you manage to preserve something that is at the mercy of the elements? I guess the obvious answer is that it needs to be covered and protected to reduce the footfall upon its streets. I hope they sort that one out before it's too late. On that slightly sad note, we make our departure.

***

Our entertainment for the evening is provided courtesy of our neighbours on the camp site – a German family comprised of parents and three teenage children. The expected level of Teutonic efficiency is present and correct, evidenced by an inordinate neatness around their pitch and the almost military precision to their morning and evening routine. But that aside, the family are also practising Christians, with grace being said before meals and the singing of hymns in the evening. It reminds me of the family Von Trapp – in a nice way. I do hope they pipe down before 11 p.m. though, or they may find themselves in trouble with the site authorities. If makeshift puppet theatres come out, then I'm definitely reporting them.

***

Today, we will visit Herculaneum. If anything, it is tucked away more secretively than Pompeii; in fact, we manage to ride right past it without noticing it. We are incredibly inept! The result is that we end up passing through a very downbeat, graffiti-ridden area of the Neapolitan suburbs. Once we've ascertained that we've missed the site, we about-turn and head back, striking lucky on the second attempt, arriving at an almost deserted car park.

I've been wanting to visit this site for many years, having read that it is, if anything, better preserved than Pompeii – much smaller and more of a personal experience. The first thing that strikes you, after you've paid the entrance fee and wandered around to a modern bridge that gives access to the ruins, is the location. Herculaneum has clearly been dug out of the ground. It sits in a vast hole, ensconced in towering walls

443

of rock formed from the volcanic ash. It feels as if an ancient town has been deposited inside the remains of a sizeable quarry.

The town sits a couple of hundred metres inland from the present shore. The front of the site consists of the ancient beach, an indication of the vast output of material from the eruption, raising the level of the land and pushing the sea backwards. The effect on Herculaneum was different to what happened to Pompeii. The ash fallout was lighter, with the result that the roofs didn't collapse. A modern pedestrian bridge leads to one of the main streets, which runs down towards the ancient seafront.

Despite its relatively small size, Herculaneum provides a richer experience than Pompeii on two major counts. The upper sections of many of the buildings have survived, and whilst there has been some decay, what remains has been preserved by careful reconstruction. In Pompeii, the nature of the destruction led to most of the wooden artifacts being destroyed. In contrast, many of the wooden structures here have survived in carbonised form. In many shops and houses, you can witness the division of the building through the use of wooden screens, with mezzanine floors, balustrades, and the charred remains of wooden supports in the walls. It's quite incredible that it survived, especially when the fate of the town and the people who remained in it is considered.

Herculaneum was hit by a series of surges that measured (it is thought) around 500 degrees Celsius and travelled at breathtaking speed. For those people who hadn't managed to evacuate, death was instantaneous, even for those who were sheltering and weren't hit by the actual blast. It had the effect of charring the wood in the town, but not destroying it completely. Human bodies fared far worse than wood. The soft tissue was instantly burned away leaving just the skeleton remaining. Yet it wasn't hot enough to melt jewellery (gold melts at 1064 degrees Celsius), so rings were still found on skeletal fingers and one victim, who I'll mention a bit later, a soldier, was found with his sword intact and the metal dressings on his belt remaining, too. In Pompeii, the archaeologists famously made casts of the victims by pouring plaster into the voids formed when the ash and pumice buried the body, creating a fascinating (and morbid) representation of the victims in their final moments. In Herculaneum, this wasn't possible. Only the skeleton remained.

The streets here feel smaller and more crammed-in by the buildings than those we saw yesterday. It is probably illusory because the buildings are more intact. The road paving is formed from large, irregularly laid blocks of basalt – some are fashioned into pentagonal shapes, sometimes a less regular piece has been added in. The result is a finely constructed road that is impressively devoid of potholes (Milton Keynes Council, please take note). As in Pompeii, the roads are lined with substantial pavements, built using very sturdy edging stones that contain aggregate used to complete the pathway. The theme of diagonally rendered stone extends to the buildings, where many walls are either built of diamond-shaped bricks or rendered with facings following the same theme. It really is lovely and feels quite homely. The town was apparently considerably richer than Pompeii, the houses grander in the main and, consequently, the artwork to be found in houses and public buildings is often superb (and most likely executed by Greek artists, from my recollection of old history lessons).

One of my favourite sites is the baths complex, which is situated on the north-western corner of the excavation. The baths are smaller than the ones in Pompeii, but make up for their lack of size in being beautifully preserved. They are split into separate baths for men and women, the women's baths being considerably smaller than the one serving the men. Having entered the complex through the male entrance, the client would have the opportunity to relax in a pleasant, open area called a paleastra, where a spot of light wrestling could be engaged in with like-minded, vigorous types, should the whim drift you in that direction. After spending a bit of time in the paleastra, you would then walk into the first room of the baths, the changing rooms. This is quite a spacious room with a vaulted ceiling and a washbasin (called a labrum) in an alcove at the far end of the room and latrines nearby if you need a tinkle. It feels like visiting a modern spa-gymnasium nowadays.

Once devoid of day-to-day clothing, which was handed over to the safe-keeping of a slave, the bather would enter the tepidarium, which was gently heated by underfloor channels to provide a transition from the conditions found in the hot and cold rooms. The floor of this room is decorated with a blue and white mosaic showing a Triton surrounded by dolphins. At least, we're told they're dolphins, but they look more like catfish to me. The room has benches for the bathers to sit and relax (and perchance debate the appalling rioting at the Pompeii games).

And so on to the caldarium, the hot room. This room was heated to a considerable temperature to induce perspiration, allowing the body to be cleansed by the application of olive oil, which was then scraped off (and apparently recycled for use as a hair product for ladies!). This caldarium is the least well-preserved room in the complex, having suffered the collapse of a section of the roof. Once cleaned, the bather would progress to the frigidarium, a circular room containing a plunge pool. Personally, it sounds like a form of torture to me, but it was apparently intended to close the pores following the rigours of the caldarium. The faint-hearted could stop off at the tepidarium on the way to the frigidarium, permitting an altogether gentler experience.

As previously mentioned, the ladies' baths are considerably more compact than those of the men. I imagine that hair drying would have been a bit of an issue. But the rooms are even better preserved and are quite beautiful, a notable example being the floor of the changing room, which is decorated with an exquisite blue and white geometric mosaic.

* * *

At the time of the eruption, Herculaneum was initially spared the dense fall of débris that badly affected Pompeii. It gave sufficient time for the townsfolk to realise the enormity of the catastrophe and for many of them to evacuate the town. One of the escape routes was by sea. Pliny the Younger described the actions of his uncle, with whom he was staying at the time, aged eighteen. His uncle commanded the fleet at Misenum (situated on the northern side of the bay). When his wife brought the cloud from the eruption to his attention, he initially intended to muster his ships to get a closer look. His plans changed when he received a letter imploring him to aid a friend who was trapped in her house, close to Vesuvius. He ordered the ships to be launched and for them to proceed to the heavily populated areas that were now in great peril. When he arrived at his friend's house, he became stranded, remaining in the house (and even having a nap) while the ash and pumice rained down and gradually buried the house. And there, supported by two slaves, he eventually expired.

The record of these events are vividly documented in letters to Pliny's friend Tacitus, written some time later. He went on to recount the effects of the eruption on people in Misenum, of the falling ash, people desperately trying to survive: men, women, and children overcome by dread as they thought their whole world was coming to an end. In Herculaneum, this fate was shared by around three hundred people who took shelter close to the beach, including the soldier mentioned earlier. There must have been survivors who were with Pliny's uncle, because his record of his uncle's courageous actions and untimely death are very detailed. When he arrived at the shoreline, he was unable to land his ship, due to the deposits of ash already blocking an approach from seaward. So, in similar fashion, at Herculaneum, evacuees who were in the final groups to leave the town were doomed. The ships were probably mostly stranded, grounded by the creation of a rising new land by the fall of ash. Many of those who had not been evacuated were found in the boat houses that line the original seafront of the town, facing the beach. The soldier was discovered lying face-down on the beach, lying in the direction of the sea. All of them were killed instantly by the pyroclastic holocaust when it ripped through the town.

The beach and seafront of Herculaneum.

Standing on the ancient seafront overlooking the beach is quite a surreal experience. It's easy to imagine it as a place bustling with activity in the days before the eruption, with fishing boats and pleasure craft pulled up onto the beach, people strolling down to take in the sea air, stopping by at the marble altar that still resides on an elevated terrace above the boat houses, overlooked by a fine statue of proconsul Marcus Nonius Balba, after whom the terrace is now named. He was a great benefactor and resident of Herculaneum, and popular enough to have no less than ten statues raised in his honour. From this terrace, you can look down at the ancient beach, which is now traversed by a modern watercourse and consequently covered in greenery. Despite this, it's easy to imagine the waves rolling up the beach. From here, you could stand alongside Marcus and stare out over the bay. Nowadays, his outlook is limited by the wall of rock that surrounds the whole site, but it's a distinct improvement from being buried forty or fifty feet underground. Select visitors to the site are escorted to the boat houses to view the skeletal remains of those who were trapped there, men and women, old and young, sitting propped against the walls, children laying in postures that suggest they were mercifully asleep when the final blast hit them.

The violence of their final second or two was so extreme that it is thought the children never awoke, and the adults barely moved a muscle. The terrific heat overcame them so quickly that we can only hope they felt no pain or suffering. After a moment of reflection, we watch as a small group of people are taken down to view the scene, then we walk over the modern bridge that crosses the beach, passing into a long tunnel that cuts through the wall of solidified volcanic ash, heading towards the exit. What a fascinating heritage site!

***

We wander out into the light and make our way to the car park. The weather has deteriorated over the course of the day, with grey clouds blanketing the sky and darker ones brooding in the direction of Vesuvius. We have a couple of hours to spare before heading back to Sorrento. My map shows a road that climbs the flanks of the volcano. It would be great to take a spin up there and view the caldera.

When we visited Pompeii yesterday, the volcano was an ever-present reminder of the source of the catastrophe that befell the town. And it is still active today. The last major eruption occurred in March 1944 – the most recent of many eruptions that date back thousands of years. Some of the surrounding villages were destroyed in that eruption. Consequently, Vesuvius is considered one of the most dangerous volcanoes in the world, not least because it continues to carry the risk of a massive eruption, similar to the one of 79 A.D. The difference is that, nowadays, more than three million people live right on its doorstep. A truly scary situation, not dissimilar to living on the San Andreas Fault.

The route from Herculaneum to its nemesis is reasonably direct, passing underneath the main highway to Naples and Rome and wending its way through the built-up, modern suburbs on a road called Via Vesuvio, which, I think, is fair warning to travellers of a nervous disposition. Eventually, the town thins out and the road starts to climb, passing isolated homesteads that are increasingly derelict in nature, and occasionally abandoned, with lots and lots of rubbish strewn around and the liberal application of graffiti to any standing walls. The road gradually narrows and morphs into a fine series of switchback bends as it climbs the shoulders of the volcano.

As we negotiate a series of 180° bends, we eventually reach the cloud base, arriving at the terminus of the road, pulling into a wide and very damp car park. Access to the higher reaches of the volcano is restricted to those who pay. Unfortunately, though, we discover that we've arrived too late. Vesuvius is shut, just like the Lonely Mountain in *The Hobbit*. So, after spending a short while taking in the sight of the cloud-wreathed heights, we climb aboard the bike and head back down. When we arrive back at the campsite, we find that our German friends have departed, leaving the entertainment options a tad limited. On the plus side, the weather has improved and the opportunities for a spot of landscape photography are almost limitless.

***

Tuesday 16th October. Time for us to depart this lovely part of Italy. We plan to take our time, though; there isn't any immediate rush. But it does feel like the beginning of the ride home. I've factored two days into the route plan to our next major destination: Florence. The journey will, in part, be a reversal of our trip down the boot of Italy, before it cuts westwards to the famous renaissance city.

We can't leave Sorrento without sampling another dose of this intoxicating place and its magnificent roads, though, so we hang a right at the campsite entrance and head in the opposite direction to the one that would whisk us northwards. This way will hopefully take us along the coast past the towns of Amalfi, Minori, and Maiori, whereupon we will take a left and ride on the terrific road that I know traverses the mountains of the peninsula, joining the E45 at the wonderfully named Sant 'Egidio Del Monte Albino – Saint Giles of the White Mountain (or something like that).

Much to my surprise, we find ourselves in a rush-hour crush, mingling with traffic composed mostly of scooters, with the odd motorcycle, bus, and Fiat Cinquecento mixed in for good measure. And the scooter riders aren't hanging around. A couple of the faster ones are piloting hotted-up Vespas and are scraping them around the corners in a very entertaining fashion, mostly on the wrong side of the road. It's most impressive to behold the degree to which you can lean a small-wheeled machine that possesses the handling qualities of a Tesco trolley. My personal favourite in this Italian version of Wacky Races is a very cool chap who is riding a modern scooter, just a little more sedately, accompanied by his Basset Hound, who is balancing somewhat precariously on the footboards of the scooter enjoying the ride, ears flapping merrily in the breeze. The sight proves one thing: Basset Hounds are not the ideal hound to accompany you on a scooter's footboard. A Jack Russell would be an altogether better fit, and there would be a much lower risk of ear on rear-wheel carnage. With a Basset Hound, such an eventuality doesn't bear thinking about.

The weather today is a great improvement to the overcast day yesterday, a pleasant mixture of blue sky and fluffy white clouds. Perfect for enjoying the extraordinary views and the chicanery of the road. It delves and soars high above the azure sea, burying itself in tunnels and hugging the pale, rocky cliffs – skimming through villages and small towns with their pantile roofs and white walls. It's a tiny area really, just a few kilometres long, but it is gorgeous. We pass through Amalfi, a beautiful town, once the playground of the rich, Diane shooting photos on her little Panasonic camera as we meander through the streets, chuffing quietly on our way.

***

The terminus of our joyride along the Amalfi coast is the small town of Maiori, the larger sister to Minori, which resides around the corner of a small headland to the west. Originally called Rheginna Maior by the Romans, the town sits on a fan delta – a common feature of the peninsula. A sizeable stream winds down from the hills over a series of man-made weirs, passing through the town, carrying sediment from the hills above and depositing it in quite a slapdash fashion into the sea, forming a modest delta (which isn't really visible to eye, at least not as far as I can see). The stream has been concreted over for quite significant stretches of its passage through the town. Severe flooding in 1954 led to the spectacular 'explosion' of the main street, due to the pressure of the water. Despite suffering fatalities in the incident, the townsfolk weren't dissuaded from continuing to build above the watercourse and parts of the town remain situated on top of the stream. Taken in the round, I think the Neapolitan region of Italy must be an insurance underwriter's nightmare.

I stayed here in 2007, finding a room in a hotel called the Torre di Milo, a modest 3-star establishment that seemed to be a favourite with native pensioners. The hotel is situated on one of the main streets that leads up the hill from the seafront. The room wasn't anything to write home about, but it was clean. The hotel didn't have a restaurant but recommended a reasonably priced one down the road near the seafront. Despite the modest surroundings, the meal I had there was terrifically good, both in terms of the quality of the food and the price. The portions were enough to feed an army. The next morning, at breakfast, I found myself the object of considerable curiosity, being stared at a lot. It didn't worry me too much. I didn't feel in any immediate danger.

As we pass up the hill, heading out of town, I point the Torre di Milo out to Diane. If we had more spare time, I'd be tempted to pull over and see if they have a spare room just for old times' sake, perhaps risk another dose of being stared at, but we don't, so I don't. Maiori is an attractive yet workmanlike town when viewed from the saddle. The area around the seafront is populated by restaurants, shops, and hotels and the road out is lined with white-rendered apartment blocks and houses crowding in on the street. We ride up the hill and out of town, the road gently snaking as it follows the contours of the narrow valley alongside the stream. Gradually, the habitable buildings start to thin out and we pass an industrial complex, sitting below the level of the road, half-hidden by a wall. The weirs that control the stream pass by at regular intervals and terracing is evident on the hillsides; both of these measures are evidence of mankind slowly losing the battle to control nature.

Apparently, Maiori is suffering from the pernicious effects of global warming, causing increased erosion of the cliffs and the valleys – some schools of thought suggest that this could accelerate to such a degree that the whole area will be decimated very quickly if our efforts to avoid climate change aren't successful. It seems difficult to believe, quite frankly, as you ride through this lovely place, one that has survived thousands of years in much the same state as it is now. But, like many other areas of outstanding natural beauty that we've visited, it's sad to consider man's destructive effect on the natural landscape. Vesuvius is a reminder that nature herself can be ultra-destructive. Payback is inevitable.

Once out of town, the narrow road becomes ever more twisty, and lively, clinging to the hillside as it passes through a series of small settlements, overlooked by craggy, tree-covered hills. We're riding along a long valley that stretches across the mountainous area to the north of the Amalfi coastline – the Lattari Mountains. It takes a while for me to realise that this is not the same road that I enjoyed five years ago. I recall that the road ridden back then was altogether wilder and more remote than this one (it was actually the SP1, and it runs parallel to this one and hits the coastline at Amalfi). Another cock-up. What a disappointment!

My journey along the SP1 in 2007 was punctuated by two incidents, the first of which I've mentioned very briefly in the previous chapter. It happened shortly after negotiating the magnificent series of switchback curves that climb the mountain above Sant 'Egidio Del Monte Albino. I became aware of a gentle purring, which seemed to emanate from behind me. When I glanced in my mirror, I noticed a completely beaten-up and ancient Fiat 500 clamped to my tail. My little Yamaha TT600RE was heavily loaded and very slightly unwieldy, but I was confident that I could stretch its legs around the tight bends and shake off this unwelcome interloper. After all, my engine was bigger than the one in the Fiat. So, I upped the pace. To no effect.

However much I tried, I could not shake off the lunatic behind me. Despite its asthmatic tendencies, the little TT could just wheeze its way to gaining a few tens of yards on the short straights, but around the corners the Fiat was king and when I exited each one, a quick glance in my mirror revealed the demon driver hunched over his steering wheel, having a whale of a time. In the end, I just had to admit to myself that I'm a crap rider. In a moment of desperate humiliation, I decided to give way and let him 'roar' past me trailing a pall of blue(ish) smoke. I might be the only motorcyclist in history to have been burned off by a Fiat 500. It's number one in my (rather large) litany of shame.

Every cloud has a silver lining though. After waving my nemesis 'goodbye', I lessened the pace (if that were possible) and took it easy, and I'm glad I did so, too. Because not much more than a mile had passed under the wheels before I exited a tight corner and came face to face with a very large dog, calmly walking down the middle of the road. It's not a common occurrence to meet a dog taking a gentle stroll down the middle of the road, at least not in the UK. It's even less common that the woofer in question refuses to give way and studiously ignores you as you putt past him then coast to a halt to swivel your head around, just to ensure that you aren't dreaming. Then, as I turned my head back around and started to ease out the clutch, I heard a faint tinkling. The road ahead suddenly filled with a flock of straggly-looking sheep, driven by a shepherd. I turned back around to acknowledge the dog, but he'd passed around the corner, dutifully maintaining his mission. His road manners were impeccable, despite a notable lack of high-visibility safety clothing or lollipop.

The two roads across the Lattari Mountains eventually meet up at a point half a kilometre east of the switchback down to the wide valley below. The view from the heights is spectacular, spoilt only slightly by the monumental amount of trash, fly-tipped in the lay-bys provided as viewing points. After winding down through the series of 180° bends, the road levels out in a suburb close to the E45 autostrada, which whisks us rapidly on our way, passing Pompeii, Herculaneum, and Vesuvius, heading northwards back up the boot of Italy.

⸺⸻◆⸻⸺

Chapter 34
Florence

We didn't ride very far yesterday. After taking the 'scenic route' on the first part of the day's journey, we soon bored of riding the autostrada and called it a day when we reached the town of Cassino. It's quite an attractive town and we spent some time bimbling around searching for a hotel, eventually finding quite a large touristic one with a spacious car park. I managed to engage in conversation with an old man in the car park who spoke not a word of English, whilst I responded likewise with zero Italian. He clearly appreciated our motorcycle and chattered away to me very amiably. It was very similar to the regular morning conversation I had with my parents' neighbour, Dickie Bishop, in Bodham, Norfolk in the 1980's. We'd moved there from Yorkshire.

Every morning I would wheel my bike (a Yamaha XS650) out of the shed in preparation for the ride to work. Dickie would often pass by the garden gate and engage me in conversation in his broad North Norfolk accent. I never understood a word that he said to me, but I always got the impression he was commenting on the weather, so I always replied in kind. On reflection, he could have been saying anything. He might have considered me a certified idiot and decided it would be amusing to talk complete gobbledegook every morning, just for a laugh. If he did, then he wasn't alone. Dickie was a true legend of his time. He used to drive a pony and trap at breakneck speed up the main Cromer-Holt road, signalling with his whip to the cars behind before executing a right turn into the village almost on one wheel. Dickie was our very own local Ben Hur. Prince Phillip would have loved him.

***

Cassino is famous for the events that occurred in 1944 during the allied push towards Rome. When we were in Assisi, I mentioned how the

Germans cast defensive lines across Italy in a very successful and skillful strategy to slow the allies down. One of these defensive lines was set up across this part of Italy.

Just behind the town of Cassino lies the hill of Monte Cassino, upon which an abbey was built, dating back to the sixth century A.D. The Germans didn't initially occupy the abbey, but the allies suspected that they were using it as an artillery spotting point and decided to bomb it to oblivion. The Germans then occupied the ruins and used them to great effect as a defensive strong-point, causing many thousands of allied casualties. Monte Cassino proved the lesson learned in Stalingrad: bombing buildings before a siege is often a big mistake.

When I was a teenager, our local priest, Father Leslie Harris, surprised me by asking if he could borrow a copy of Sven Hassel's book *Monte Cassino* from me. I read most of Sven Hassel's books as a youth. Like many lads of my age, I was interested in military history and his books appeared to be both autobiographical and very vividly written. The first book, *Legion of the Damned* covers the invasion of Russia. Subsequent books cover battles in various locations, always with the same regiment: the 27th Penal Regiment. It gradually dawned on me that Sven the Danish runaway had simply served in too many places at roughly the same time and by the time I read *Monte Cassino* I knew for certain that it was fiction. Anyway, never mind, I did lend the book to Father Harris with the warning that the language in it was pretty ripe. He said he wasn't too worried about that. He was partial to popping over to the King's Head to sink a couple of pints with the local miners, so it wouldn't be anything he hadn't heard before. When he returned the book to me, he said that he'd enjoyed it quite a lot.

'I was at Monte Cassino, during the battle,' he explained. 'I remember giving a sermon standing on the hull of a Sherman tank on a Sunday morning.' This earned him considerable kudos from the fifteen-year-old me. Unlike Sven, our parish priest had actually been there. He told me that the battle was truly horrific, going on to explain that the book didn't seem historical, but that didn't detract from his enjoying it. He'd never mentioned his own back-story before, the fact that he'd been an army padre in the war, and this was the only time he ever mentioned it.

He was a modest man, and a humorous, personable one, too. Someone I respected greatly.

The Nazis stand condemned (not least) for stealing historic treasures from the people and countries across Europe that they invaded – Herman Göring being a notably enthusiastic perpetrator in the mass crime. A master thief and scumbag, bar none. But the story of the treasures of the Abbey of Monte Cassino provides a surprising twist. Two German officers negotiated with the Vatican for the removal to safety of the abbey's treasures and provided the carpentry, labour, and transport resources to carefully pack the artwork and priceless library, then to ship them to the Castel Sant'Angelo in Rome, accompanied by monks to ensure nothing went missing. You may recall that we stayed just around the corner from the Castel, a few days ago. In a nice twist of irony, the German officers served in the Herman Göring Panzer Division. I'm sure he would have been furious at their honesty and common decency.

The abbey was completely rebuilt after the war and, I hope, reunited with its ecclesiastical treasures. Unfortunately, we don't have time to visit it as I'd wished, but I did so in 2007 and was amazed at how steep the climb was that faced the allied soldiers.

***

The weather has been quite changeable of late. Autumn is easing its way gently down Italy, cooling it with drifting weather fronts that augur clouded skies and showers. Today is a fabulous day, though, with clear blue skies, allowing us to enjoy the sun as we load up the bike. Our destination, Florence, is about four hours ride away, with one fuel and food stop on the way. It promises to be an easy leg, riding up the autostrada, bypassing Rome and heading steadily northwards. Time for a spot of in-helmet singing. I can bellow as much as I like – no-one can hear me, not even Diane.

Once we've passed the town of Caldere, we're in new territory, transiting a flat plain, with hills in the distance over to the right. The area appears to be primarily agricultural – a mixture of fields, fruit orchards, and strips of vines. The occasional speed camera crops up, providing a calming influence on the traffic. The autostrada through these parts is mostly of a high standard, with a smooth, well-maintained road surface. One nice feature of Italian motorways is the occasional use of a raised flower bed in the central reservation – a gardener's nightmare.

We ride past the western side of Lake Trasimeno, then gradually start to see hills rising blue on the horizon. These are part of the northern arc of the Apennine Mountains, which we rode through on our way south. They cradle Florence on their sweep around to the west, touching the Alps at their north-western geographical apogee. The Apennine Mountains are home to a very rare species of European bear. They live deep in the hills to the northwest of Cassino in the Parco Nazionale D'Abruzzo Lazio et Molise. A bit of a mouthful of a national park. This critically endangered sub-species of brown bears, called the Marsican brown bear, is unique. Their numbers have dwindled to critical levels, at one point reaching about fifty individuals. At the point where extinction looked inevitable, it was finally appreciated that they needed urgent protection – leading to a range of positive environmental measures. In bear terms, they are a particularly peaceful bunch of omnivores that leave humans off the menu, and they're rather beautiful too, so well worth the effort. Unlike their Chinese cousins, they mature very quickly, giving them a fighting chance of increasing their population. Fingers crossed for the Marsican brown bear.

* * *

Thursday 18th October. The hotel staff at the Ibis we landed at last night helpfully assist us in our plans to visit Florence today. They point out a bus stop across the road and promise us that the buses are reliable and regular. It turns out that they're correct. The bus negotiates the snarl of traffic at the intersection behind the hotel, then progresses through the outskirts of the city. It passes an interesting-looking Harley-Davidson dealership called the *Speed Shop Firenze* on the way, piquing my interest in snagging another 'T' shirt to accompany the one we purchased in Moscow. A mental note is taken to stop there on the way home, either today or tomorrow.

Our introduction to the city is less than salubrious. The bus drops us off outside a line of shops around the corner from a modern shopping mall. Not quite the Renaissance architecture I was expecting. Having said that, some of the shops are quite interesting. Florence is well-known, though not by me, for its fine writing paper. Consequently, the incidence of shops selling all manner of items pertaining to transcription is exceedingly high. We spend a while window-shopping, then entering one of the more up-market shops, leafing through beautifully bound notebooks, before clocking the price and beating a hasty retreat.

We eventually work our way around to the Piazza del Duomo, which translates to *Cathedral Square,* according to Google. The Piazza houses the Cattedrale di Santa Maria del Fiore alongside which lies the Battistero di San Giovanni – the Baptistery of Saint John. Having arrived at the cathedral, we just stop and stare at the Gothic splendour of its façade. In truth, it is so elaborately executed that the eye struggles to take it all in. There are three buildings in the complex. The largest is the cathedral, then there's the Baptistery already mentioned and, finally, a beautiful square bell tower of considerable height. Each building complements the other. One of the common themes that binds them is the use of coloured marble to face the buildings – a mix of creams, greens, blues, greys, and browns. The other buildings reflect this but are subtly different, too. The statues on the cathedral are incredibly crisp and perfectly preserved whilst the use of pale brown relief panels on the Baptistery presents a further nuance to stare at. If I'm completely honest, I think I've reached a point of cultural overload and am struggling to take even a small percentage of it all in. We decide to have a look around the inside of the cathedral.

The stunning carvings on the Cathedral of Santa Maria del Fiore, Florence.

What a surprise! Having suffered a bombardment of the senses whilst viewing the outside of the building, it's a small shock to discover that the inside is inordinately plain. I was of the misapprehension that churches and cathedrals of the Catholic faith are always brimming with elaborate decoration, part of the ritual that induces a heavenly trance on those who worship within. But in the case of the Cathedral of Saint Mary of the Flower, it seems that most of the pomp and circumstance was reserved for the outside of the building, leaving the interior to remain stubbornly unadorned. Maybe, as with Westminster Catholic Cathedral, they just ran out of money. Whoops! Hang on a minute! A sizeable group of visitors have gathered at the far end of the nave and are staring up to the heavens. We make our way down there and peer up into the vaulted ceiling.

The dome of Florence Cathedral was the final part of the building to be completed. The cathedral replaced an earlier one, with work commencing in 1296. The dome wasn't completed until 1469. It remains the largest brick-built dome in the world and owes quite a lot to the Pantheon in Rome, because it was decided from the outset that the dome would not be supported by buttresses. The designers studied the work of their Roman forebears with great care, trying to work out how to build an unsupported structure.

There's something awe-inspiring staring up at the interiors of Gothic cathedrals. This one is no exception. The original plan was to decorate the interior with mosaic. But that plan was binned during the passage of time and they just painted it with whitewash, for a while. Then, it was decided to paint it with a fresco. Not your common-or-garden fresco, mind you, but rather a violent and turbulent representation of The Last Judgement. Towards the centre of the painting, a few lucky souls are heading up to the heavens; very few of them will be motorcyclists or ex-matelots. But all around the base of the dome, sinners are getting their come-uppance and are being dragged down to the fiery pit of hell by demons, overseen by a character with horns and a pointy tail. It's mesmerizing, and not just due to the gory subject matter. The dome is octagonal in shape, bestowing upon the painting a kind of kaleidoscope effect. It feels as if it would change shape and pattern if you could just twist it, like so.

Having marveled at the fresco, we gradually make our way out of the cathedral and take another look at the bell tower – otherwise known as Giotto's Campanile. Giotto was clearly a multi-talented person, not just an artist credited as being a genius, but also an outstanding designer of notable buildings too. His bell tower was built between 1334 and 1359. Its designer didn't live to see it completed and work was also rudely interrupted by the Black Death in 1348. It's a beautiful, slender, square structure that reaches a height of just under 278 feet, one foot short of the second largest statue on earth, last seen in Volgograd. The tower is open to visitors and promises spectacular views from the top deck. So, with a deep breath, we pay the entrance fee and commence the wheezing ascent of 414 steps. Fortunately, there are stopping points at the different levels on which the tower was built, so it isn't a case of tackling all the stairs at once. They built the Campanile in stages and we make sure we climb it in stages, too.

The view from the top of the tower is probably one of the best you will find in Florence and is often seen in photos posted both online and in books. Not only does it offer a wonderful view of the cathedral dome, but it also stretches right out across the rooftops to the horizon and the dreamy hills of the Tuscan Apennine Mountains beyond.

On the way back to the hotel, we hop off the bus at a convenient stop close to the Harley-Davidson shop, ostensibly in search of a couple of 'T' shirts. I'm not sure if it's due to natural Italian flair, or their national enthusiasm for motorcycles, but the Speed Shop appears to me to be a cut above your average H-D retail outlet. It has the feel of a 'real' motorcycling enthusiast's shop, despite being a franchised clone. This is partly down to the friendliness of the staff. Put simply, they're a lot more welcoming than the ones we met in the Moscow concession, which is strange, because Russian motorcyclists were some of the friendliest ones I've ever met.

While I'm browsing, my attention is drawn to a detail on a customised bike, which I think might have started life as a Street Bob. It's a cam cover, a small circular cover that fits on the right-hand side of the engine, which does what it says on the packet. You can buy various versions of this cover from both Harley themselves and the plethora of aftermarket accessory dealers worldwide. But you can't buy one of these particular covers because it is bespoke to the shop that we're standing in. It's quite crude, really. The background is black with a spanner picked out in silver along with the words 'Speed Shop Firenze'. Curiosity tweaked, I approach the guy at the spares counter and ask him if I can buy one of their cam covers.

'We 'ave only made a few, to fita to de bikes we 'av customised,' he replies.

'But, 'ang on a minute…. I think we 'ave one in de workshop…'

He disappears, leaving me waiting with breath all bated. Most people wouldn't give a monkey's whether they 'ave one or not. But my Harley is black and silver, and I bet no-one in the UK has a cam cover like that one.

A few minutes later, he returns triumphant!

'Iss a leetle scrape-ed,' he says, doubtfully.

It is too. Just a little bit second-hand, but I don't care.

'Can I buy that, and the 'T' shirt please?'

'To you, de cover issa free.'

On the short stroll back to the hotel, we search in vain for a local restaurant (for local people) and draw a major blank. But I don't mind eating a microwaved pizza tonight. I've got my cam cover *and* a new 'T' shirt.

Chapter 35
From the Apennines to the Pyrenees

Saturday 20th October. It's going to be a short jaunt across Tuscany today, heading towards the city of Pisa. This will be our final destination in Italy, and we intend to spend just one night there. Hopefully, the short riding distance will allow us time to view the famous leaning tower. Then, we will ride up through the Italian Riviera and will pass into France, heading for Spain. I'd love to spend a while exploring the south of France, but we find ourselves somewhat time-constrained, so I think we'll restrict any dalliances to popping into Monaco. Hopefully, we can swing around a few bends of the famous road circuit, studiously avoiding the temptation to visit the casino. Then, perhaps we'll chink champagne glasses with a wealthy, sporting tax-avoider or two before heading for pastures new. In the meantime, with our chattels firmly strapped aboard the Mutt, we make our departure at 11 a.m.

**

The road to Pisa passes along a broad valley that is intersected by the meanderings of the river Arno, a body of water that, frankly, sounds a bit hard, one that might suffer from a split personality disorder. And such is indeed the case. Oft-times in the past, it would appear to be bone dry then, after a few sips of rain, it would become a tumultuous monster, bringing death and destruction to the great cities in its path. It is to rivers what Oliver Reed was to unfortunate bars. They should've introduced a few industrious beavers to sort it out but, instead, they dug a canal and did their own bit of dam building, upstream of Florence. It seems to have worked and, like the post-operative R P McMurphy in *One flew over the Cuckoo's Nest*, the river behaves itself nowadays. Beavers would have been cheaper.

Our route takes us along a toll road – the SGC Firenze-Pisa-Livorno or Strada di Grande Comunicazione to give it its full title. The Highway of Great Communication – it sounds like something from North Korea. In our part of the world, it would be called a dual-carriageway and, in America, a service road. It's quite slim, yet perfectly functional. I don't mind paying to use it because I'm sure we'll find a service station somewhere along its length and, as I've mentioned before, I'm a bit of a fan of Italian service stations. Sure enough, at a point roughly mid-way between Florence and Pisa, we happen across an example of the breed. Time to thumb the right-hand indictor and enter the slip road, clacking down the gears as we sweep into the car park that fronts the service area. BMW's, by the way, have an indicator switch on each handlebar cluster and a cancel switch on the right handlebar cluster. It makes as much sense as lederhosen, but you do get used to it after a period of hitting the horn accidentally.

It's pleasing to note that the service establishment is up to scratch but, while we're contemplating our refreshment, we find ourselves distracted by a touch of car park commotion. A large coach has pulled to an urgent halt directly opposite the shop/café entrance and the passenger door, which is situated centrally along the length of the bus, has swung open with a series of jerks, allowing the mixed contents of beer cans and bottles to spill out onto the concourse, in advance of a bunch of people who appear to be in varying stages of inebriation. This human detritus heads in a determined (yet occasionally weaving) fashion straight for the door and thence to the toilets. Shortly afterwards, the driver of the coach alights from his charabanc, surveys the scene of desolation, lights up a fag, and heads indoors for a strong infusion of coffee. Our initiation into the world of the Italian football fan is imminent.

Following the mass assault on the urinals, a slightly tense and edgy atmosphere descends on the service area, bringing with it a fog of uncertainty as to how things might turn out. We finish drinking our coffee and eating our pastries before venturing out through the throng to the bike. A crowd of smokers are standing close by. One of them speaks English and we strike up a conversation.

'Which team do you support?' I ask.

'We are Verona,' he responds. 'We play in Serie B.'

'Who are you playing today?'

'We go to Pisa.'

I explain that we too are travelling to Pisa and that I visited Verona in 2007 and found it to be a fine city. Well, at least the centre was very fine, although I thought it was a bit rough around the edges. Probably best leave that bit out.

'You'll win today. The score will be 2-1 to Verona.' This is how to win friends and influence people. Except with Rotherham United supporters, in which case they will take you for a fool.

He smiles and turns to his mates to pass on the good news. And, with that, we climb aboard our sturdy mount, wave goodbye to our new friends, and head towards the slip road, avoiding the empty cans and bottles.

***

Pisa is a modestly sized city, with a population of just over 90,000 people, roughly the same size as Chester. It sits a couple of kilometres inland from the Tyrrhenian sea. Locating the city centre is perhaps one of the simplest navigational missions of the trip so far. In fact, we manage it completely by accident, finding ourselves outside a tall, square building that declares itself to be the Hotel Roma, which is handily situated almost a stone's throw from the famous tower. Not that I would cast a stone in its direction; it might cause a catastrophic collapse.

The receptionist is a middle-aged man who might be the owner. He confirms room availability and secure parking for the motorcycle in a lovely courtyard behind the hotel that is shaded from the dappled sunlight by tall trees and vine trestles. The hotel isn't cheap. It's one of the most expensive nights we've booked so far. But the room is very good and the location superb, so a Nelsonian blind eye is turned and the cost is added to the credit card, which is fair bursting its seams and needs to stagger back into the wallet for a rest. After a quick freshen-up and change of clothing from skanky riding gear to very well-worn casuals, we head downstairs and ask for a map at reception. The receptionist asks us what we are intending to do, adding that he knows of a superb restaurant that is very reasonably priced and further adding that he is not related to the owners, or on any commission. He makes no mention of the tower. A pen is drawn out and 'X' very quickly marks the spot on the map. We leave with the distinct impression that he's on commission.

***

Normally, you would expect the cathedral of Santa Maria Assunta to be *the* centre-piece touristic attraction in Pisa. It is, after all, a rather beautiful and elaborate building that dates from before the Norman invasion of England, when most of our ancestors were living alongside their domestic farm animals in modest wooden houses that didn't even have chimneys. It is also notable for standing upright.

The layout for the cathedral complex is similar to the ones we found in Venice and in Florence, with a circular baptistery, bell tower and the main cathedral building, all situated in large oblong grounds that are mainly laid to (slightly parched) lawns. The tower sits at the far end of the site. To get to it involves walking past a long line of souvenir stalls, most of which are selling tat.

We were warned about the unauthorized selling of merchandise by the hotel receptionist. He advised us that there were a large number of 'foreigners' scamming legitimate tourists, such as ourselves. I don't think our receptionist would be very impressed with me. I've already bought a nifty little laser device from a non-Italian gentleman in Venice. It works like a battery-powered kaleidoscope, making patterns on the floor or the nearest wall. Unfortunately, it can also be used to dazzle pilots of airliners on final approach to airports. For safety reasons, I've stumped up my ten euros and taken one of these dangerous devices off the street. My cats will be delighted when I offer them hours of pleasure chasing multiple dots of light on the wall, taking care not to blind them.

***

After taking a few photos, including the obligatory one of Diane holding up the leaning tower, we weigh up the pros and cons of paying a few euros to ascend to the top. Now this might sound like me being a bit of a wuss, but I genuinely find myself weighing up the odds that the tower might give up the ghost at the precise moment that we reach the top. I think the odds might be lower than winning the national lottery back home but, mark my words, one day that tower is going to fall. Braving the mathematics of such a catastrophe occurring, we pay our entrance fee and park ourselves on the grass above the entrance, awaiting our turn. It's quite reassuring that they limit the number of visitors who can clamber up the 294 stairs to the top.

Eventually, the current crop of visitors spews forth out of the tower and we are invited to proceed through the door to its interior, which curiously resembles the inside of a grain silo. After a short opportunity to take photos, we head for the stairs in a gaggle of other visitors and commence the laborious slog to the summit. It readily becomes apparent that the angle of lean plays strange tricks on the physiology of human beings. We experience a bizarre feeling associated with climbing uphill on the outer section followed by (apparently) climbing downhill on the inner section of the lean. It really feels extremely weird. The view from the top is well worth the climb. Peering over the edge at the people below in the square, which is called the Piaza dei Miricalo, the Square of Miracles, then drinking in the gorgeous views of the cathedral, the baptistery and the city.

***

Having topped up on a dose of culture, we decide to hunt down the 'highly recommended' restaurant, departing the miraculous square via the back entrance and wandering along an attractive set of streets that are typically Italian – with tall, pastel-painted buildings crowding the street, forming a pleasant mix of small retail outlets, town houses and apartments. I imagine Pompeii looked something like this a couple of thousand years ago. We manage to locate the restaurant in short order and find the place to be open, so we wander in.

A couple are tucking into an early evening meal. They turn around and stare at us mid-munch. After forcibly swallowing her mouthful, the lady of the house tells us, in English, that they are closed and won't open for an hour and a half.

'We eat first, then prepare food,' she explains.

We make our apologies and say we'll come back.

***

Three hours later, I place my cutlery on the empty bowl in front of me and take another sip of red wine, reflecting on the fact that I've just finished what I consider to be the finest dish I've ever eaten in a restaurant. And I don't even particularly like ravioli – not normally. I would also be relatively ambivalent about the stuffed sardine starter, but it was also truly stupendous. While we were choosing our dishes, the chef's wife strongly recommended the ravioli, saying that it was all prepared freshly by hand, including the pasta. It was a fine recommendation. And, in a rare break from normal tradition, Diane didn't order the same dish as me. She doesn't rave quite as wildly about her hand-made lasagne. She missed a treat.

The wander back to the hotel in the gathering dusk is brightened considerably by the dozens of bright LED-equipped gadgets being catapulted skywards by the illegal street vendors in the square of miracles, mimicking a multi-coloured firework display as they spin like tiny helicopters to the ground. The temptation to buy one is almost overwhelming, but the souvenir stalls are still open and beckon us with their siren call. An Italia bumper sticker manages to wriggle its way into my pocket. A successful end to a pleasant early autumn day.

Verona were victorious in their match against Pisa. The score was 2-1 to the visitors. It's difficult to imagine the state of the fans' bus on the return journey to their fair city in the north. As for me – I picked the wrong day not to fill in the football pools.

***

All aboard the Hesperus. There's a bit of a 'Bond' feel about today's journey. We'll be sampling sections of both the Italian and the French Rivieras, heading towards the north-west, beneath warm, autumnal skies. Departure from Pisa is as straightforward as it was on arrival: turn left out of the hotel, first left after the Square of Miracles around a small roundabout and hang a right at the junction with the SS1, following signs for Genoa. The only complication is that I accidentally take a right out of the hotel in some fit of navigational dyslexia. Never mind, we're soon back on track.

I mentioned earlier that we were intending to pop into Monaco en-route to Spain. In the wider scheme of things, we're aiming for Gibraltar, which lies around 2,000 kilometres away – quite a surprising distance. It looks a tiny stretch in my Times atlas. Barcelona lies at roughly the mid-point, so we'll definitely pop in to have a look around there. When we arrive at the rock, we will find ourselves close to the southernmost tip of Europe. I harbour a mild tinge of regret that we didn't press on to the Nordcap when we rode through Finland, because touching the northernmost point in Europe and then the southernmost would have been quite neat. Failing to do so leaves a bit of a gap – one that might need filling sometime in the future.

Before that happens, though, we will almost certainly be attempting to complete the bike's journey around the world. I have it in mind to ride from Milton Keynes to Vladivostok in the Russian Far East. And to really be able to claim that the bike has travelled around the world by land, we probably need to visit the eastern coast of Japan. I've already started Googling 'road across Siberia'. The resulting information suggests that Mr. Putin is building a road and it 'might be completed in 2016'.

Leaving such thoughts aside, the first section of our journey today isn't much to write home about. We've found ourselves on a decent stretch of motorway that cuts along a flat coastal stretch of land twixt sea and a range of hills further inland. These constitute the final northward fling of the Apennine Mountains. The coastal strip is well-populated, a fact marked by a series of towns ending in one called Sarzana, which lies to the east of the larger city of La Spezia, a city with a deep-rooted naval and shipbuilding past. It marks the start of the Italian Riviera (actually, I think it starts a bit further south, but it's not entirely clear to me, so I'll avoid being too pernickety).

North of La Spezia, the road heads into increasingly hilly terrain, avoiding the coast in the process. We're riding under a pale blue sky flecked with high cirrus clouds that increasingly draw a veil over the heavens as we progress to the northwest. Our route of choice is called the SS1. It spends an increasing amount of its time linking the coastal towns to one another, providing a fine view of this part of Italy, passing the great shipyards and terminals of Genoa and the lively seafronts of many of the smaller towns, where pleasure craft bob in up-market marinas. Before we get to Genoa, we pull over in the resort of Rapallo for lunch at a seafront restaurant. It's a pleasant place to hang out for an hour or so, full of younger people.

A little later, we approach the town of Savona, coming face-to-face with one of the leviathans that so impressed us both when we spotted them in Montenegro and Croatia. The vessel in question is the Costa Serena. As we ride into the eastern fringe of Savona, we pass along a pleasant stretch of road that cuts through the rocky cliffs, providing occasional glimpses of the vivid blue sea out to our left. Then, it plunges into a cool tunnel before spitting us out, back into the bright sunlight, heading into the town through attractive, tree-lined streets with apartment blocks, shops and houses, typical of many others that we've passed through already. Arriving at the docks, we suddenly come face-to-face with a massive ship, which feels like it is almost touching distance away, the size playing a tromp l'oeil on us. Diane is clicking away on her camera as we sweep past.

The Costa Serena is truly huge, with a gross tonnage of just over 114,000 tons. Even so, she is merely a middleweight when compared to some. She's too big for Diane's little Panasonic camera, that's for sure. Her wide-angle lens is neither wide or angled enough to capture the full extent of Serena. She'll need Photoshop to fix that one! Costa Serena was the second of the six Concordia class to be built. Her sister ship, the name of which is given to the class, ran aground off the island of Giglio in January, when she hit rocks and capsized with the loss of 32 lives.

The final section of our journey through Italy takes place on the Autostrada, the E80. It runs a couple of miles inland, parallel to the SS1, carving through many tunnels and over numerous bridges in the process, providing fine views of the towns on the coast. The tunnels follow, one after the other.

Suddenly, almost without noticing it, we pass out of an Italian tunnel and find ourselves in France. It goes without saying that we've had a fantastic time in Italy. Is any other country so rich in cultural splendour? It really is one of my favourite places to visit. Arrivederci Italia; 'allo 'allo France.

***

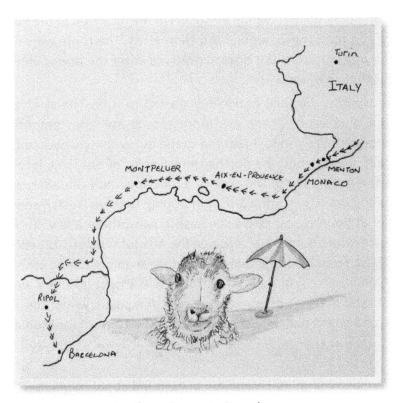

Southern France to Barcelona.

Breakfast in France is always a pleasure. They're completely useless at rustling up a fried English, but they do make the best croissants and their bread is always excellent. Interestingly though, Menton, the town we pitched up in last night, hasn't always been French. It was once owned by a wealthy Geonese family and then by the Grimaldis of Monaco. After a few shenanigans concerning the taxing of lemons, Menton decided to go it alone. Then, a plebiscite led to incorporation into France. Lemons were always an important factor, and they remain so to this day. The annual lemon festival in March draws huge crowds from all over the world. So that's a month to avoid if you want a cheap hotel room. On the other hand, if you like sucking on raw lemons, it's a must go-to event. It is a very pleasant town with lots of parkland and a proper Riviera feel to it.

On departure, we re-trace our steps of the previous evening's arrival, heading up the Avenue de Sospel in the direction of the hills. It's a short hop to Monaco, around ten kilometres. The route we've taken isn't the most direct, but it does allow us to enter the principality from the hills that soar above it.

The weather has just noticeably started to turn. The skies are no longer a blue vault. There are more clouds and the temperatures have dropped. We can feel autumn in the air. When we passed Genoa yesterday, we touched the northernmost point of our long, lazy curve across the geography of the region. From now until Gibraltar, we will be working our way southwards. I'm hoping that we'll catch some fair weather in the process, so we can bask in warmth for a few more days before we return home. We've joined the A8 motorway, a truly excellent road. If the French do one thing well, other than bread and croissants, then it's investment in their infrastructure. It's right up there with the best, at least in terms of our voyages over the past few months. In two shakes of a gnat's nadger, we've arrived at the turn-off for Monaco.

***

There are two things that stand out in my mind about Monaco. The first is the almost pointless nature of the Grand Prix, bearing in mind that it's almost impossible to overtake in the narrow streets that are blocked off to make up the circuit. Despite this, the section that runs through the tunnel is, I think, quite iconic, as are the yachts of the wealthy that pull up to watch the procession. The second thing is that Princess Grace's favourite car was a Rover P6. Out of all the cars she could have driven, she chose an eleven-year-old Rover. Why?

Monaco is the second smallest sovereign state in the world and has the shortest coastline of any. It is the densest in population and the wealthiest. I was hoping that I'd be able to get a feel for the circuit whilst riding around the city but, sadly, I don't. Instead, I find myself feeling quite claustrophobic. The trappings of wealth are unsurprisingly obvious (including my first glimpse of a Bugatti Veyron). But I can't say I'm particularly smitten by Monaco. It feels tiny, grid-locked, and very hemmed-in. I imagine a lot of Ferraris overheat in the persistent traffic queues, keeping the Monaco branch of the AA very busy. After a short ride around, we pop into a normal looking shop, buy a sticker for the panniers and head *tout de suite* for the exit roads. I think, personally, were I a Formula One pilot or tennis player, I would tell the accountant to stuff it and would opt to pay my taxes and live *anywhere* rather than here. Menton, just down the road, is much, much nicer.

Having rejoined the motorway that passes high above the tiny principality, we head resolutely towards the south-west, skirting the towns of the French Riviera and the big cities too. Nice and Cannes pass by to our left, then slip away in our wake. The road remains excellent and our progress is steady. In the late afternoon, we spot signs for a service area with a motel close to Aix-en-Provence and decide to call it day. My attempts at speaking French at reception are met with a knowing smile and replies in English. At least I tried.

Over the past few miles, the A8 has gradually worked its way inland, cutting a dash across a great curve in the coastline where Toulon lies. A separate motorway cuts down to Toulon and thence on towards Marseille, but we've deliberately avoided that longer route. Tomorrow we will need to be on our toes to ensure we stay on track, negotiating a series of motorway intersections that will take us towards Nimes and then Montpellier. Our eventual target is to overnight in Perpignan, close to the Spanish border, but I'm hopeful we can do better than that and perhaps make our way across the border into Spain.

***

An inspection of the bike in the morning reveals the evidence of the miles travelled on it so far, which have just ticked beyond 17,000 on this trip and 50,000 in total. The rear quarter looks slightly odd now that the crud-catcher has gone AWOL and the rear tyre is looking distinctly worn and squared-off. Most of the (formerly) shiny bits have dulled and the nooks and crannies are filled with ingrained dust. Back in the '70's and '80's, BMW engines were crafted from quality aluminium, which was free to oxidise in the air, unencumbered by any form of coating. Nowadays, they paint everything, which I personally consider a retrograde step. It's fine when the bike is new, but once a few miles have passed under the wheels, the paint starts to lift and peel off – the worst cases look horrendous. Also, there's the lingering suspicion that the alloy is of lesser quality than that lavished upon the marque in days of yore, hence the need for paint and lacquer. The intensive mileage of this trip has accelerated the process of decay on Mutley. Little blisters have appeared around most of the joints and fixing points at the front of the engine and the paint on the main stand has been removed by thousands of small stone impacts, turning it to rust in places. I continue to clean and occasionally add polish, but my attempts increasingly resemble those of King Canute.

It isn't just the long mileage and climatic wear and tear that have contributed to the ageing process of the machine. The bike is very rarely kept in a garage, back home in Blighty. It is more often to be found stored under a cover and is in regular use between longer trips. But the conditions of this journey have caused the decline to accelerate both cosmetically and mechanically.

The two main sources of concern mechanically, as previously mentioned, are a distinct rattle from the area of the clutch, and the declining efficiency of the suspension. Both of these will need attention when we get home.

On the positive side, I've been pleased with how well the bike has performed, generally. It has started reliably every time the little grey button has been pressed and, apart from a period of wheeziness in the low-RON regions of the east, the engine has been faultless. Perhaps most surprisingly, the complicated electrics have held up in tough conditions without a single sign of gremlins or short-circuitry – to make a passing reference to two 1980's films in one sentence. I didn't carry out too many improvements to the bike before setting off on the trip, but one or two things are worth mentioning.

I fitted a heavy-duty battery when the original BMW-badged one gave up the ghost. The new battery has the kick of a rampant mule to it but doesn't quite fit as well as the original in the space provided. Two areas of the bike have been given added protection: the front of the engine has its own crud-catcher, an aluminium plate made by a company called Cymark. This helps protect the engine from filth thrown up by the front wheel, which already has a fender extender. I think the engine cases would be completely grit blasted but for the fitment of these two items. The second item of protection is an alloy contraption that protects the throttle potentiometer.

Wrecking the potentiometer in a spill could cause a serious period of down-time. In fact, it's probably worth carrying a spare one on a long trip, just in case – but then there are plenty of other parts that are probably worth carrying too. On Mutley, the potentiometer, which monitors the throttle position and feeds information to the engine management system, is located in a very vulnerable position indeed, on the left engine intake, where formerly would have sat a nice Bing carburettor. I'm sure there are other areas of the bike that could benefit from additional guards and many of the adventure bikes you see nowadays are festooned with all manner of protection, but the summary of all the guards on our bike are: headlight, front of the engine and potentiometer, with the last of these fitted for this trip.

The one thing that is seriously missing from our parts catalogue is a spare gear lever. The existing original one could be broken very easily in a spill, and we would be royally stuffed if that happened. So that's going on the shopping list for the next trip!

✳✳✳

The long drone across southern France is similar to the transit south of Moscow, where serious mileage had to be covered and the only option happened to be a motorway. In this case, it is exclusively on motorways and toll roads. The initial shock of hitting a toll road, and not being prepared for the fumbling required to gain a ticket and pay for it at the other end, has given way to a slicker operation, where tickets are snatched from machines and funds deposited at pay stations in the blink of an eye. Not.

The landscape is different from the Moscow to Volgograd leg though. Inland of us are rolling blue and grey hills. I'm always struck, when riding through France, by the feeling of expansiveness, at least compared to the feeling you get riding in the UK. But there's no joy covering distance on motorways, not unless you are passing through truly mountainous countryside, with decent bends and lots of tunnels. Then, it can be quite entertaining.

Over in the UK, we seem to have a collective anathema to the concept of toll roads. We are a toll road averse nation. Which is fine if that's how you feel. Personally, I can see some sense in them. For one thing, here in France, the roads are way better than the ones we have back home and the regularly spaced public rest spots, called aires, are world class. I haven't seen anything better than them on my travels, apart from a few of the state rest stops in the US, which are found far less frequently than their French counterparts. You get plenty of warning that an aire is approaching and can pull up for a nice leg-stretch and a leak in a clean toilet. The rest area will be in a pleasant spot of park land, nicely landscaped and, apparently, many of them are havens for plant life and fauna. If Capability Brown did autoroute rest stops, they would look something like this. I read somewhere that it is a legal requirement for them to be placed around twenty kilometres apart on the autoroutes – mandatory. Well done, les Francais.

Gradually, the signs show that the number of kilometres to Perpingnan are reducing. Then, as that passes by on the left, we find ourselves catching our first enigmatic glimpses of the mountain range on the horizon, with grey-blue peaks appearing far ahead. Time for a decision.

I've always wanted to see the Pyrenees, and I don't want to see them from a motorway, despite the fine road surface and regular aires. So, I'm contemplating hanging a right and riding a dog leg on minor roads across the mountains. Quick glimpses of the map, when it is relatively safe to do so, reveal a wriggly little road called the D115, that branches off and snakes its way in a determined fashion, heading in a west-south-westerly direction. I'm not quite sure what it does once it gets into Spain, but my guess is that all roads lead to Barcelona, because they have one of the best football teams in the world. So, when junction 43 arrives, we hang a right and then a right again and breathe a sigh of relief that the long motorway miles are suspended – at least for a day or two.

⸻◆⸻

Chapter 36
Barcelona

It's been a long time since the bike enjoyed a proper mountain ascent. I think the last one occurred in Montenegro. Sorrento was hilly too, but not in the manner that we're experiencing right now.

The road climbs through a fine selection of bends. In doing so, it passes through a series of charming villages that are situated in the French Pyrenees, or to be more precise, French Catalonia (Catalogne), including the quaintly named Amélie-les-Bains-Palalda, one of a number of Spa towns that are dotted around the region. Eventually, after a considerable amount of fun for the rider (could be a tad stressful for the pillion), we arrive at what seems to be the road's highest point, at a place called Col d'Ares, which sits just to the south of the amusingly named village of Prats de Mollo la Preste. I'm not sure what a Prat is in French; my Google translator doesn't appear to recognise a Prat when it sees one, but a col is apparently a mountain pass. This is positively educational for me, because I always thought it meant 'mountain', I'm not sure why.

We decide to stop to take a few photos, quietly observed by a small herd of high-altitude cattle of a long-horned variety. The mountains, hereabouts, are not particularly high. The Haut Pyrenees rise some way out to the north-west. So, we have to content ourselves with ones that are 'only' 5,000 feet high. Apparently, cattle don't normally thrive at high altitude. They're susceptible to altitude sickness and prone to an early demise. If you experience the need to take a cow to altitude, make sure it's a Hereford, because they are quite good at surviving up to 9,000 feet. Beyond that, you need to consider goats or sheep. And it's with sheep that our tale will shortly take a slightly surprising turn.

***

An hour or so later, we've descended to a lower altitude on the Spanish side of the range. The initial feeling, riding into Spain from France, is similar to arriving at Dover after a spell on the 'other side'. Things appear less pristine. The houses in the villages appear to be different from those in France, with shallower roofs and a variety of colours on the external rendering. In France the colours are more uniform, often white, and everything feels a little more orderly. And the roads are superior too.

In passing over the border, we've arrived in the region of Spanish Catalonia. Working out the allegiance of residents and governmental buildings is initially somewhat confusing, because there is more than one flag. The official Catalonian flag consists of four red horizontal stripes on a field of yellow, called a Senyera. It reminds me of the flag of Northumberland but is simpler in its execution. Some Catalans aren't content with this official rendition of their flag and have decided to add a blue triangle on the left, bearing a white, five-pointed star. This flag advertises the owner's commitment to independence from Spain, the blue and white addition providing a reference to the independence of Cuba in the early twentieth century. There is also another version of the star theme, which is red on a yellow background. This one is much loved by those of a more left wing, revolutionary tendency. It's pretty rare and we haven't spotted one yet.

The flag of the European Union is also quite prominent. I guess the hope of those striving for independence is that they can settle their nationhood under the sovereign umbrella of the EU. There are many other regions of Europe with similar aspirations, none of whom seem to hold an absolute majority in their region – at least not quite now. But their numbers seem to be growing.

The towns of Catalonia have held a series of referendums over the past three years which have returned a significant majority in favour of pressurising the regional government to begin moves for independence. However, the turnout for these unofficial mini referenda appears to have been only around 30% of the total eligible electorate. It appears that there is an underlying majority who aren't voting in the unofficial elections. Despite this, it's interesting how powerful a symbol a flag is. With the notable absence of the Spanish flag, it promotes the impression that everyone wants out!

***

I'm surfing the internet after dinner in our hotel room, discovering some of these facts on Wikipedia. We're in a town called Ripoll, having arrived here after descending from the mountains, riding along a picturesque curvy route, through hilly uplands. We passed through the town, scouring the slightly faded streets for a hotel or campsite and then found one to the left of a route out of town, on the road to Barcelona: a modern boxy establishment with substantial, well-kept grounds that house tennis courts and a sizeable swimming pool (which is less than enticing in the grey, cooler climes we find ourselves in). Diane accompanied me into reception since the car park was deserted and the bike seemed perfectly safe.

The lady in reception was of middling years, with brown hair and an unsmiling, yet not unpleasant countenance. My first attempt at conversing with a Spaniard (could be Catalonian) was close to pathetic. I don't know a word of Spanish and apologised for the fact in advance, in English. It turned out that she spoke passable English and quickly confirmed that a room was available. I complemented her on the quality of her English, to which she replied modestly, 'I lived and worked in Gibraltar and improved my English there.'

A flag of caution waved vigorously in my subconscious. As I've mentioned previously, we're heading for Gibraltar, but I felt that stating so might be a touchy subject if you're discussing it with a Spaniard — considering the state of relations between the UK and Spain on the subject. So, I proceeded with care. This is quite unusual for me as I do occasionally suffer from 'bull in china shop syndrome'.

'Oh, did you like living in Gibraltar?' I enquired.

'Yes, I did,' she replied. 'It was nice, but I didn't like the dirt on the beaches.'

I cast my mind back to the few beaches I'd frequented in Gibraltar when the various ships I served on visited the rock. I spent a lot more time in bars than on beaches, but, as a fully time-served member of the ship's demolition team, I spent a very enjoyable time on one stretch of sand, making up explosive charges and blowing things up. It seemed like a nice beach, apart from a rash of dead seagulls. Seagulls don't have many natural enemies, but TNT is highly efficacious in culling them up to a height of a hundred feet or so. Anyway, other than the dead shite-hawks, I didn't spot any particularly dirty beaches. Things in the Gibraltarian public sanitary department must have deteriorated quite badly over the past thirty-five years.

'Really! Are the beaches dirty?' was my riposte.

'Yes. Very dirty. On account of the sheeps.'

I was now becoming increasingly confused. Visions of peasant shepherds herding their sheep, or maybe goats, to the golden sands of Gibraltar momentarily flitted through my mind. I could only recall seeing Barbary apes…. It was all very confusing.

'I didn't know there were any sheep in Gibraltar,' I responded, wracking my brain over where on earth they would find sufficient grass to eat. After all, it's just a rock. A bloody big one, but 99% rock nevertheless. Perhaps the sheep eat seaweed.

'Oh yes, very many sheeps,' she assured me with a very serious, concerned expression on her face.

'They leave hoil on the beach. Is against the law, pump hoil from their tanks in the water, but they do.'

I was still chortling when we exited the lift and dragged our bags to the door of our room. I slid the key in the lock and opened the door.

The room was clearly occupied. No one was *in flagrante* but, regardless, we beat a hasty retreat back to reception, where our friend was still puzzling on why the issue with dirty sheeps caused so much confusion and hilarity.

***

In the morning, we continue our ride towards Barcelona in the direction of the ancient town of Vic. The road is following the meanderings of a river called the Ter, which has usefully managed to carve its way south through a series of hills that run on an east-west axis, forming its own valley in the process. I imagine that people have used this valley for millennia when making their way north or south, just as we do today. If they needed food, they could dip a line in the water. The Ter is notable for its excellent trout and its stony beaches are largely free of sheep hoil.

The distance to be covered today is modest, not much more than a hundred kilometres and a couple of hours at most, maybe two and a half, if we take into account searching for accommodation. We're travelling under the vault of a pale blue, autumn sky. Suddenly, the traffic, which was previously quite light, starts to slow, becoming noticeably denser, until we find ourselves crawling towards a standstill. The suspicion is that there's been an accident.

I could opt to filter through the gap in the lanes but decide against it. I'm not sure if it's legal in Spain to do so. We move forward in short hops. Then, the reason for the standstill becomes apparent. Both sides of the carriageway are being blocked by a group of men dressed in dark blue overalls, shades, flak jackets and black boots. They're toting very serious-looking machine guns. Questions are being asked through lowered windows before vehicles are allowed to pass and continue on their way. As we approach, we make ready to stop and recover our passports from the top box, but the nearest policeman waves us through. I get the impression that they know what they're looking for and it isn't a couple riding a motorcycle. To the side of the road, vans are being searched.

It's a reminder that the world has changed since the 9/11 attacks. Spain suffered terribly in the attack on the Madrid train network in 2004 and, before that, at the hand of ETA, the Basque separatist group. What precipitated this stop-and-search isn't clear to us, but it is a sobering feeling as we pass through the cordon. It prompts the thought that it could be associated with sectarian issues rather than the international war on terror. We arrive at the suburbs of Barcelona about forty-five minutes later, descending from the hills that surround the city. It feels like a descent into normality after the mildly unsettling experience back there in the hills.

**

Here's an admission! Up until very recently, I didn't really know where Barcelona was situated! My old geography teacher, Mr Church, would be mortified. I didn't know it was part of Catalonia, or that Catalonia was a region of Spain. I think I had some concept of it being on the Atlantic seaboard. Maybe I confused it with Lisbon. I *did* know that Freddie Mercury and a lady opera singer sang a song about it for the 1988 Olympics, which were held there.

We pass through the outskirts of the city, catching glimpses of it sprawling over to the south of us. Without too much ado, we arrive at a large roundabout that has clearly seen better days. Following the signs for the city centre, passing an impressive building to our left that is almost identical to the 'Gherkin' in the city of London, before we arrive, a few minutes later, at an older part of the city where hotels start cropping up in satisfying abundance. The first attempt at finding a room draws a blank. Undeterred we climb back on the bike and trundle around, quickly locating the harbour area where we find room in a very modern, boutique-type hotel that has the faint whiff of the one we frequented in Ankara when we first arrived there. Unusually, this hotel has no parking space whatsoever, so the bike is left to languish in the street beneath a youthful tree, close to a bus stop, sharing its new home with a very nice old 1970's Bultaco, which is interesting to me, because it is a roadster. I'm only familiar with that brand's off-road machinery.

Once we're settled in and have had chance to grab a shower and a change of clothes, we wander out and acquaint ourselves with our new surroundings. Our normal, haphazard navigation has reaped a rich reward. When we arrived, we pitched up at an area called the Gothic Quarter, the heart of the medieval city of Barcelona. We're a two-minute walk from there and it draws us like a magnet. At first sight, Barcelona appears to be a very laid-back city, full of young people and very cosmopolitan to boot. Strange to say then, that finding an eatery is not as easy as you would think. We're forced to put a degree of effort in before we find a place that specialises in selling home-made beefburgers, huge things dripping with juice, begging the question whether we should use cutlery to eat them, or risk dribbling fat all over the place. Now, where are the napkins....

Hunger abated, we take a stroll around the streets of the Gothic Quarter. It isn't huge, as far as medieval city centres go, but what it lacks in size, it makes up for in the quality of the buildings and their... erm Gothiciness. We have one full day in the city tomorrow and, unusually for me, I've agreed to join Diane on a red bus tour. We plan to mingle bus riding with walking to take in as much as possible of the city. I'm very keen to visit the Sagrada Familia, the wacky, unfinished basilica that sprouts somewhere on the far side of the Gothic heart of the city. I'd also like to see the Camp Nou, Barcelona FC's stadium. I've heard they're quite a good football team but, since they play outside the English Championship, I don't know much about them.

***

Our trendy hotel might look nice, but it isn't ultra-comfortable. Our room is quite small and the walls turn out to be paper thin. I awake in the morning wholly unrefreshed, mainly on account of the nocturnal goings-on in the room next door. I won't go into the details, other than to say that it was patently a liaison of complete strangers, one of whom was less enthusiastic than the other. My partner snored quite noisily right through it all, whereas I wanted to bang on the wall and tell them to get on with it, or go to sleep, for goodness' sake!

Prior to heading off in search of a red bus, I pop down to check the bike out. A couple wander across the pavement for a chat, introducing themselves as Roy and Vivien Perkins.

Roy, a well-dressed and well-spoken Englishman who reminds me of the gents we met at Anzac Cove in Gallipoli, asks me if we've travelled far. I reply with a brief synopsis of the trip so far, including our journey through Russia.

'That's fascinating,' he says. 'We were in Russia recently shooting a film. Do you know anything about Hawker Hurricanes being sent to Russia in the war?' I reply that I did read about that many years ago as a teenager, and that I seem to remember they were sent there via Murmansk.

'That's exactly right,' he says, seemingly encouraged that I know a little about the subject. 'We've made a film about it. It's called

'Hurricanes to Murmansk'! We released it last year, you should go and see it when you get the chance. Those boys who took those aircraft over and fought with the Russians did an amazing thing.' We chat a little longer and he writes the name of his film company's website in my little black notebook before they say cheerio and head on their way. Www.atollproductions.co.uk.

I love the way people come over to pass a few words with you when you're stood by your motorcycle. In the course of our travels so far, we've met many interesting people, a proper cross-section of humanity. Apparently, 70% of the 'news' we're fed by the media is of a negative nature. In contrast, our travelling experience of people has been 99% positive. Perhaps we should stop listening to the news.

***

Duly ensconced on the top deck of a tour bus, with informational devices pressed to our ears, we head off on our little trip, wending our way past a few parks then heading in towards the city centre. I can't say that the route we've chosen is particularly exciting; we trundle past the 1988 Olympic village, and further along the seafront before turning back in towards the city centre. Perhaps the most noteworthy building thus far is the Torre Agbar, the 'gherkin' tower we passed yesterday, which is similar to the one in London. If anything, it's not quite as shapely as our gherkin. I'm sure cities get a feeling of one-upmanship if their gherkin is of greater shapeliness (and height) than the competition. And imagine the horror of the architect, when both gherkins are built at roughly the same time, and the more voluptuous one is gradually revealed in all its curvaceous, twist-effect beauty. It must be like getting the runner-up rosette at the Bognor Regis small dog breeds kennel championship.

I'm still playing my own private game of top trumps, city of London versus Barcelona, when the bus arrives at the Sagrada Familia and we are forced to make a hasty exit. We do so under increasingly gloomy skies.

The basilica of the Sagrada Familia is truly dramatic when you see it in the stone and glass, a quite extraordinary outgrowth that rises above the surrounding buildings like an architectural alien. But, when you arrive this close to it, viewing it properly becomes quite difficult. We'd love to see the interior, but the queue to do so is huge, meaning that we would probably queue for hours and miss the opportunity to see more of the city. So we limit ourselves to walking around the outside and partaking in a bout of photography. We've marveled at more than one religious building on this trip, but we haven't seen anything to match the figures that grace the front of this one. The statues of Roman soldiers resemble troopers from Star Wars. Or maybe it's the opposite that is true, it's a bit hard to tell, I'm not sure which came first. They haven't finished building the Sagrada Familia and George is still churning out his inter-galactic epic.

Shortly after departing the basilica, the heavens open. We're caught out, inappropriately attired, and are forced to seek the shelter of a doorway on the Avinguda Diagonal. This is one of the main thoroughfares that bisect the city. We were riding along it earlier on the tour bus. The buildings on that earlier part of the route weren't particularly interesting. But, as the rain subsides and we wander along in the direction of the Camp Neu, it gradually reveals a fabulous mixture of architectural styles, ranging from tastefully ornate Art Nouveau frontages, to the modern mixture of nature and concrete that is the Jardí Tarradellas, a stunning living wall, planted with trees and shrubs that forms one side of an otherwise unremarkable, modern building. I think this is the future of building in cities. A haven for insects, birds, and swampy environmentalists.

The rain has abated properly now and we're able to wander into an area called Les Corts, discovering Barcelona's take on a Harley-Davidson dealership, which boasts a fine café as well as the usual line of 'T' shirts. The famous Camp Nou, home of Barcelona Football Club, is a short walk away. Fortified by provisioning at the HD café, we walk the final leg to the Stadium, plastic bags crammed with 'T' shirts and pin badges in hand.

***

My first experience of a football stadium involved a secretive visit to watch Barnsley FC at Oakwell. It was secretive because my father wasn't too keen about my obsession with football and didn't want to encourage me. My mate, Edward, suggested we should support a local team and we decided to try Barnsley first (although I was already fairly determined to follow the Owls, over the hills at Hillsborough). I recall paying at the cramped turnstiles before walking, wide-eyed, through the entrance to the stands, which were rocking. The crowd had broken out into chanting and swinging their scarves and rattles. They were stamping their pit boots in rhythm to the bawdy songs they were singing. They were literally shaking the wooden floor of the stand. I recall that the lush green of the pitch was what really impressed me. I don't think I'd experienced anything like it before.

I don't think any amount of stamping would rock the Camp Nou. It's a massive concrete oval structure, capable of holding just shy of 100,000 people. You need to dig back quite a long way into the history of Barcelona FC to find it playing in a stadium of the ilk of Oakwell, circa 1972, but it did so, once upon a time. The stadium in question was the Campo de la Calle Indústria, which held a capacity crowd of around 6,000 fans and was the home of Barca until 1922. In grainy, online photos of the Campo, the stands appear to be of wooden construction, absolutely perfect for a bout of pre-kick-off pit boot stamping, one can imagine.

**

We hop on the bus for a lift back to the Sagrada Familia, then walk back to the hotel by way of the Gothic quarter, which has a pleasant, cosmopolitan feel to it. We wander past busy cafes and coffee houses, bars and shops, through broad alleyways and past small, secluded squares, heading in the direction of another of the main city streets called La Rambla, a wide thoroughfare with a long pedestrian walkway down its centre, planted with trees and bordered by elegant buildings. It terminates close to the harbour in the environs of an impressive column dedicated to Christopher Columbus, one of the city's most famous visitors.

The view across the harbour is dominated by the Transbordador Aeri del Port, which, roughly translated, means the Port Aerial Ferry; an icon of Barcelona. It travels from the port to the top of the mountain of Montjuïc, which, at an elevation of 184 metres, probably qualifies as a sizeable hill, rather than a mountain. In Sheringham, Norfolk they would probably call it a *very big bump*. In similar fashion to the Palatine hill in Rome, Montjuïc is the birthplace of Barcelona. I was surprised to discover that it is also the birthplace of the measurement that we call a metre, defined by two French astronomers who measured the latitude between Dunkirk and Barcelona and then extrapolated from that the distance between the North Pole and the Equator. A metre is that distance divided by ten million. They did all of that in 1792 without the assistance of Casio.

Like a scene from 'War of the Worlds'. The Transbordador Aeri del Port.

The name of the hill is famous in motorsport. I became aware of Montjuïc in 1979 when Roger Slater of Slater Brothers in the United Kingdom developed a raw and intoxicating 500cc twin cylinder version of the Laverda F500 racing motorcycle and named it after the circuit that wound its way through the city streets and wooded slopes. It prompted one of the best motorcycle magazine cover pictures in history when *Bike* magazine pictured a rider extracting his brain before riding the beast. The circuit was the venue for the Spanish Grand Prix for many years, until the fatalities were too much to bear. The cable car heads up to the summit of this hill via two large towers, its red cars dangling precariously from the cables as they make their way over the harbour. We complete our tour of the city by walking around the harbour's edge, taking in the sight of a huge luxury yacht, then a smaller one of more practical, compact size. It's a strange looking vessel with a reversed chisel bow that is reminiscent of the Aurora in St Petersburg. I'm not sure of the value or kudos gained from owning a modest super-yacht, other than it might fit in Bridlington harbour. The one around the corner would be way too big.

Our final, bizarre, sight on this whistle-stop tour of this great city, comes when we stumble upon a certified lunatic who has taken it upon himself to hand feed the local population of juvenile seagulls. He's being mobbed by hundreds of them. He may perish in the course of events, so we bravely leave him to his tomfoolery and head back to the sanctuary of the knocking-shop... sorry... boutique hotel. As we say in my home county, 'there's now't so queer as folk!'

Chapter 37
On towards the Atlantic

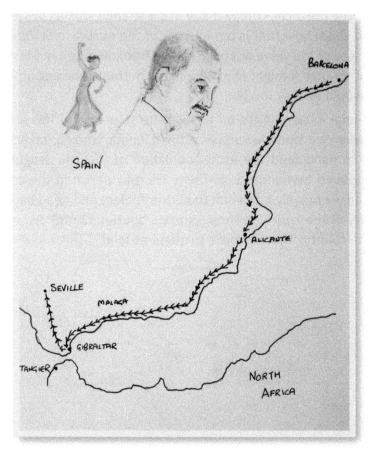

Ernest, Flamenco, Macaques and expats: Spain and Gibraltar.

Friday 26th October. The road out of Barcelona heads in a south-westerly direction, once we've managed to navigate our way to the outskirts of the city. On clearing the urban sprawl, it passes through a green landscape, surrounded by the low-lying cousins of Montjuïc.

As the miles clock up, we find ourselves passing through an area of intense agriculture with a mixture of crops and large plantations of fruit trees, a reminder of the origin of a large slice of the produce on our supermarket shelves back home. The green-clad hills remain in the distance, but the general feeling is one of increasingly parched earth as we head further away from Barcelona. We're riding along a decent motorway, allowing for steady progress as we track along the Mediterranean coastline, skirting around the city of Valencia.

So far today, we've been following the original path of the Via Augusta, built by the Romans to link their ill-gotten territory of Hispania to the rest of the Empire. Now we've reached a point where the ancient road took a turn inland and headed in a typically Roman series of straight lines towards the city of Gades on the Atlantic coast, nowadays called Cadiz. This was a bit of an oversight by the (usually very thorough) Romans, because they missed building a highway to the delightful area that we nowadays call the Costa Blanca; they seem to have by-passed it. When Rome fell, the Germans invaded *tout de suite* in the shape of the Visigoths. It took the British another 1,500 years to realise that the Germans had got to the poolside first.

Arrival at Alicante coincides with the late afternoon, prompting a decision to call it a day and attempt to locate a vacant hotel room. I didn't know what to expect arriving here, but I'm pleasantly surprised to find that it isn't a building site. In fact, truth be told, it seems to be quite a pleasant town. After riding a little further, we spot a likely candidate. The restaurant options in the hotel are zero, but there's a Chinese restaurant a hundred yards away across the street. The perfect scenario for the weary traveller. And I have to admit that I do feel quite weary and fancy a chicken fried rice.

***

Four months on the road have taken their toll. The face staring back at me in the mirror this morning is looking somewhat careworn. Worse still, I think I've put on weight. The food options in Europe, whilst being variable in nature from country to country, have often tempted me away from a healthy, fat-free diet. Adding to the distress in the waistline department is the wine. The local wines everywhere, from Russia to

Spain via Greece and Georgia, have often been notably good. We've barely sampled a single duff bottle – something I find quite remarkable. *Le Piat D'or* and *Laski Reisling* have been notable for their absence.

Alicante is a sizeable city, with a population of around half a million people in its wider municipal environs. It dates back to the days before the Punic wars, when the Carthaginians ruled the roost in this part of what is now called Spain. Nowadays, it is part of the Valencian Autonomous Community, which is recognized as a nationality in its own right. The Valencian Community flag is very plush, with the now familiar red and yellow Senyera stripes and a very fetching azure stripe at the flagpole end. This, in turn, is richly decorated with an ornate flourishing in yellow, called a lambrequin. A vertical red stripe divides the other two parts, decorated with pearls and emeralds. It's as fine a flag as you'll find anywhere, I believe. The Catalonians might be more famous on account of the brouhaha that goes with independence movements, but the Valencians have stolen the lead in the flag department.

The Carthaginians weren't the only visitors from North Africa to make a mark on Alicante. It attracted the regular attention of Barbary Coast Pirates in the years between the 16th and 19th centuries. Despite the presence of the impressive castle of Santa Barbara, the town was often raided and its inhabitants dragged off into slavery. On that cheerful note, we'll pack the bike and mosey off on our way.

***

We commence our ride today with the same level of uncertainty regarding our destination as we did yesterday. According to Google maps, Gibraltar is 600 kilometres away, and that's taking the shortest route via Granada, a town that sits quite a long way inland. Following our intended route along the coast will add at least another fifty kilometres to the total distance.

It's a very pleasant day, with blue skies and a few scattered clouds. The air temperature gauge shows twenty degrees as the bike chuckles into life, not bad for a late October ride. Our journey begins with us departing the city and joining a road called the AP-7. The feel of the countryside is much drier than in the north as we head into the region of Murcia. We pass by the ancient city of Cartagena, a famous old port that, to this day, houses substantial naval and shipbuilding facilities.

There are seventeen regional autonomous communities in Spain. Power is devolved from the central government to each of the communities, differing in degree, depending partly on the separate national identity of the community in question. I guess it's not dissimilar to our own country, with regional councils in England and the devolution of power to Scotland, Wales and Northern Ireland. Spain has had a history of conquest and consolidation going back to pre-Roman days, being occupied by the Carthaginians, Romans, Visigoths, the Byzantine Empire and the Moors of North Africa. The communities that we are passing through all evolved through a complex mix of events before, and during, the reconquest of the peninsula by the Catholic faith. Once they had secured their homeland from invaders, the Spanish decided to embark on a spot of conquistadoring themselves.

We find ourselves passing through a landscape that is semi-arid, comprising a mix of long flat plains near the coast and more mountainous terrain inland. It's no surprise that a lot of the films dubbed 'Spaghetti Western' were filmed in Spain (despite the Italian sounding name and connection). Passing by Almeria, we catch glimpses of an area that is often called the *Mar de plástico*: the Sea of Plastic – a vast network of plastic-covered greenhouses covering a large promontory that juts out into the Alboran Sea. The result can be seen clearly from space, resembling a huge area that is covered by 'snow'. A large immigrant population lives in this area, working in the greenhouses. Strangely though, we pass it by without hardly seeing a soul.

We've arrived in the community of Andalucia, the second largest of the autonomous communities. It stretches from Almeria in the east, to the borders of Portugal in the west and is the cultural epicentre of many of the traditions that we see as quintessentially Spanish – flamenco dancing (which I love), bullfighting (which I don't) and the guitar (which I definitely do). Without Andalucia, Carlos Santana would be plucking *Samba Pa Ti* on something resembling a lute.

An increased frequency of hills leads to an entertaining ride, with the road snaking along the coastline, passing over bridges when it meets a valley and diving into tunnels to carve through the rocky hills. On some stretches, it becomes astonishingly good, resembling a racetrack, with tight sweeping bends that can be taken at speed, with the bike heeled right over, bend after bend. It's one of the most entertaining stretches of road of the whole trip, a pleasure to ride.

After five hours in the saddle, stopping only for a fuel break and snack, we eventually arrive at the popular seaside destination of Malaga, stopping off at a petrol station to carry out a quick top-up and to attend to the annoying re-appearance of the (sadly, by now) familiar *Lampf* warning on the LCD display panel adjacent to the speedometer. One of the lights has blown. While we're investigating which pesky light has gone AWOL, a stream of adventure bikes pull into the station, led by a rather charismatic individual who is clad in proper desert riding gear and mounted on a BMW GS that is resplendent with exotic stickers. Once he's topped up with fuel, he wanders over to us with a few of his compadres.

He asks us where we've been so far and we explain in brief, without trying to sound too extravagant.

'I rode to Ukraine two years ago,' he says. We ask him whether he liked it.

'I had very serious problems at that border, they caused me a lot of trouble. They didn't like me because I am Spanish,' he answers, bristling with indignation. Diane comments that we didn't really have any problems with Ukraine and recounts the issues we had in comparison entering Transnistria. Mention of the rebellious, self-proclaimed republic draws a blank. It sounds like he rode into Ukraine by a different route than the one via which we exited.

A few of the other riders come over for a chat. A couple of them are expat Brits. In attempting to locate the spare headlight bulb purchased in Greece, I've had to empty some of the contents of the panniers and my toolkit is opened across the seat of the bike. The idea of an on-road repair being attempted seems to be a focal point for everyone to gather, despite the basic nature of the said repair. The group appears to be an informal club of bikers who intend to carry out long-distance trips sometime in the future. Most of their bikes are almost brand-new, apart from the travel-worn GS owned by their head honcho. I explain to them that replacing the light bulb on the Mutt is not a task for fat fingers like mine, but, having carried out the evolution relatively recently in Corinth, I manage to slot home the new bulb and hook on the retaining wires with a semblance of calm professionalism that, frankly, takes me a bit by surprise. By the time we're ready to leave, I feel that I have upheld the honour of Mr. Pavey and the BMW Off-road Adventure Maintenance school. It's taken 43,000 miles, but I think I've risen off the baseline setting of 'rank amateur' in the hallowed world of long-distance motorcycling. I just need to stop cleaning the bike so often and maybe drop it on its side a few times.

After fixing the light bulb, we climb aboard and ride down from the surrounding rocky hills into the city. The streets of Malaga are quite pleasant to ride through. As with many other cities, the walls are liberally plastered with graffiti on the outskirts, but when we arrive at the *Paseo Del Parque*, the Park Lane of Malaga, the impression is of a very pleasant place to hang around, lined by towering palm trees and shaded parks, with wide walkways and grand, white buildings. At the far end of this road lies an attractively planted roundabout, where we do an about face for a second pass at trying to find a hotel. We eventually arrive at the slightly less salubrious end of town outside the door of a hotel that offers extended views over the town's docks from its rooms. The bike is tucked up in the spacious underground car park.

Malaga is simply a convenient overnight stop for us. But it would be remiss of me not to mention a couple of interesting facts about the city (other than its residents' penchant for spraying graffiti on their walls, which they do). It is one of the oldest currently occupied cities in the world, with a history dating back nearly 3,000 years. Neanderthal remains point to human habitation going back as far as 42,000 years. The graffiti artists are merely following in the steps of one of the city's most famous sons: Pablo Picasso. Best of all, Ernest Hemmingway celebrated his final birthday (his 60th) in Malaga, with a great party and a spectacular firework display that set fire to one of the palm trees and resulted in the fire department being called out. Once the firefighters had put out the fire they joined in the celebrations and got royally drunk.

***

We depart in the morning, anticipating a relatively short hop to Gibraltar – around 85 miles. The twisty, entertaining roads of yesterday afternoon have given way to a more mundane drone along the motorway. When we arrive close to where Gibraltar should be, we search each major blue road sign for mention of the rock, only to be disappointed at the response. As far as the Spanish mainland is concerned, Gibraltar doesn't really exist. Then, finally, when we arrive at a point very close to our destination, we spot a sign that grudgingly advises us to hang a right (if we really wish to visit such a hotly disputed rebel territory, possessor of dirty beaches).

The road heads down to the town of La Línea de la Concepción where the famous, towering, pale limestone buttress of rock appears gloriously before us. Gibraltar is a magnificent natural phenomenon that dominates everything that surrounds it, even the nine-mile wide straight between Africa and Europe. Accessing it is not a simple matter. Despite a gentle thawing of relations between Spain and Great Britain under the auspices of the EU, there remains a hard border between La Linea and Gibraltar and local relationships remain testy, so we are forced to join a lengthy queue that slowly edges its way to the border post on the Spanish side. After what seems an interminable wait, we eventually arrive at the said post and our passports are checked; then we are waved through.

This is a strange moment. The first time I've visited Gibraltar since 1978. We find ourselves riding along *Winston Churchill Avenue,* passing straight across the runway of what is still a military airfield and a civilian one too. The runway is shared between the two, although the RAF don't maintain any permanently based aircraft here any longer. It is plain weird driving across the runway of an active airport. You feel singularly exposed. A bit like crossing a main line railway level crossing.

Very little is immediately familiar upon our arrival. I guess, back in the 1970's, I mostly travelled on foot, and my journeys were typically limited to walking from the naval dockyard to the main strip of shops, pubs and clubs in the town centre. I recall taking a taxi to the Catalan Bay Hotel, which had a lively bar in those days. I also remember a taxi ride to a night club that was located near the lighthouse at the tip of the Peninsula, driven by a knife-wielding maniac who's sister had been 'disrespected' by a matelot, whatever that entailed. When we got there, the nightclub was closed, so we had to hire him to drive us back. But that's another story. The short story is that I'm not finding any instant familiarity with either the streets or the buildings located on them. Before you can say 'sheeps on the beach', we've passed beyond the main town and are climbing up a steep curving road. Then something familiar finally jumps out at me. It's called the *Rock Hotel*.

The classic art deco lines of the Rock Hotel testify to the fact that it has stood here for many years. Despite that, I've never visited it. It was way too posh for the average matelot, back in the day. The Rock was the preserve of the wardroom, a place where pink gin was sipped and white-jacketed waiters served early afternoon canapés, a fading vestige of an empire that had already slipped quietly away.

It is a very beautiful building. The broad, white frontage sits on an elevated position, nestling in the lee of the towering limestone rock face. Built in 1932, it has built a solid reputation through the years as one of the iconic Mediterranean hotels. The question is: can two derelict tramps afford to stay here?

***

An early evening stroll into town takes us into recognisable territory (for me, at least). The road and path into town are steep, even at these lower altitudes, but it's mostly downhill on the way into the town centre.

We were pleasantly surprised by the price of a double room at the Rock. The bike was ridden into the shaded car park at the front of the hotel, unloaded, and our gear was shuttled up to our slightly faded, totally chintzy room, taking careful note of printed instructions regarding window security. The said window provides a spectacular view over the bay. I noted that it was an original 1930's steel-framed window, possibly manufactured in Witham, Essex by a company called Crittall.

The only known problem with Crittall art deco metal windows, apart from a tendency to rust, lies in their latches. They lack a 100% security guarantee, covering against the invasive attention of small, dexterous hands and fingers. And, in Gibraltar, that can pose something of a problem. But let's not worry about that small detail, right now. The warning message in the room is clear enough: KEEP THE WINDOWS SHUT! Personally, I think they should have welded them. Meantime, we're safely installed and heading into town for a bite to eat. A reminder of the garrison's past springs up as we enter the town. Just before passing through a gate in the fortified town wall, we pause at the entrance to a small cemetery named after the battle of Trafalgar, which took place on the 21st October 1805. Fittingly, a small troop of apes are searching for food at the edge of the cemetery.

For many years, I was under the impression that the cemetery was full to brimming with the men who died as a result of their battle wounds, but this isn't true. In fact, there are only two men buried here from Trafalgar, the rest of the graves are for victims of other mishaps, notably outbreaks of yellow fever. The headstone of Captain Thomas Norman, a Royal Marine officer who passed away in the Naval Hospital, records that he died on the 6th December, "having suffered several weeks with incredible Patience and Fortitude under the Effects of a severe Wound received in the great and memorable Seafight". He served aboard HMS Mars, a 74-gun ship of the line that was in the thick of the battle, engaged by five French ships of similar size. The Mars lost 29 crew (including her captain) in the battle and 69 were injured, presumably one of whom was the unfortunate Thomas Norman.

Walking through into the town, it's pleasing to find that it is still recognisable. Gibraltar was one of my first experiences of travel beyond the shores of Great Britain and, at the time, it felt quite exotic, not least because there are palm trees planted in various locations – including the Trafalgar cemetery, which is very green and pleasantly shaded by a variety of mature trees. Beyond the cemetery, the path to the high street passes through the gate. The southern end of the high street has a Mediterranean feel to it but, further along its course, the street becomes more of a hybrid. If you employ a slight squint, you might feel as though you're in a town-centre in Devon. Red post-boxes and English club football shirts abound. But when you glance up one of the side alleys (alternatively, ginnels or snickets in my native dialect), the view seems altogether different.

I always enjoyed shopping for presents in the town. The shops were quite different from those back home and it was possible to pick up watches and cameras at knock-down, duty-free prices with a smidgen of bartering. The high street remains something of a treasure trove for the army of tourists who are disgorged from passing cruise liners. We take careful note of the prices in the windows and decide to return tomorrow for a more serious mission. Diane is taken by the need to buy a new, improved camera.

The variety of public houses add to the split personality of the town. I recall some of them from my youth, particularly one that we decide to pop into to sample the brew. It's called the Angry Friar and I have a recollection of once spotting the comic legend Tommy Cooper sitting at the bar, large as life. He was being fed beer by a crowd of sailors, some of whom were from our ship. The mess deck jokes improved noticeably for a few days following that incident.

***

Some hours later, we find ourselves partaking in the revelries of a mixed bunch of British expats in a bar called The Horseshoe. It turns out to be a bit of a mistake.

We haven't met many Brits on our travels, with the notable and excellent exception of Reg in Melitopol, Roy and Vivien in Barcelona and the well-dressed chaps at Gallipoli. Everyone in the Horseshoe seems friendly and we engage in a bit of banter with them. Included in the group to my right are a couple who are getting royally drunk. It transpires that they live outside Gibraltar and commute in for work and for a spot of expat social life. The husband holds quite a senior position in a utility company that keeps Gibraltar running. To my left, Diane gets into quite a deep conversation with a Scottish guy who seems friendly enough.

Then, after the course of an hour or so, Diane's new friend questions her about her accent, then berates her for having 'poshed it up' to accommodate living in the South. Diane has always spoken with the same accent. She was brought up in Africa. It makes me quite angry that someone would try to judge another person based on their accent or, for that matter, where they choose to live. When we eventually leave the bar, I find myself in two minds as to whether I've enjoyed the experience of expat socialising. It feels strangely inward-looking and claustrophobic.

* * *

My first stint in Gibraltar was in 1976 whilst serving on HMS Rothesay; the second was with HMS Euryalus, a couple of years later. If I remember correctly, we replaced HMS Fife as the guard ship. Apparently, the Fife had a reputation of causing trouble ashore wherever it went, but I don't think they ever attempted what happened shortly after we took over...

I gained an appreciation of cocktails in Gibraltar. It was a nice change from my standard fare of bitter-tops. On one particular night, I'd had more than my fill of Tom Collins and decided to split from the crowd and head back to the ship. The rest of the party continued until closing time and then opted to try a Gibraltarian form of 'hedge-hopping' on the way back to the ship, finding themselves on an elevated garden patio facing the (all too) tempting sight of a fully loaded rabbit hutch. Within seconds the contents of the hutch were emptied and a new recruit was press-ganged into the navy.

Animals, stolen or otherwise, were banned from Royal Navy ships due to rabies restrictions. So, a degree of ingenuity had to be employed to spirit away any spurious pets that found their way into the mess deck. Fred the gerbil was quite easy to hide from the daily routine of officer's rounds, but a fully-grown rabbit was an altogether different proposition. The ship was under sailing orders and the die was cast. Bugs became an Able Rating and took up residence in the mess lockers, being fed mainly with carrots wangled from the galley. After a couple of days cruising the Mediterranean, a crisis meeting was held. Under considerable pressure, the rabbit-nappers agreed that, when we returned to port, a secret mission would take place to return the bunny to his rightful owners. And so it was that the lost rabbit mysteriously re-appeared in its hutch, four days after vanishing, slightly thinner and with two pairs of furry little sea-legs.

* * *

Although the Mediterranean climate is gradually cooling, the new morning dawns bright. We've decided to carry out a spot of sightseeing today, hopefully with a visit to the tunnels that Gibraltar hides within her bowels. The bike resides outside the hotel with three new friends of similar species. They sport British Legion and other veteran organisation stickers, so I guess their riders are also visiting a previous military stomping ground. The Rock Hotel serves up an outstanding full English breakfast, the first of the trip, leaving us well set-up when we depart on the bike for the first stage of 'rock climbing', which involves the lazy method of riding the bike up the winding streets to the ticket office for the tunnel experience. The view from the higher section of road is spectacular, with the town and ancient dockyard below and a wide panorama over the straights, right over to Africa in the distance.

Having purchased our tickets for the tunnel tour at a ticket office, we find out that there's going to be a delay before our tour commences – it isn't much of an inconvenience. For one thing the views up here, overlooking the airport, are outstanding and, as an added bonus, there's a young mother and infant hanging around, sitting precariously on a wall, overlooking the town. The mother in question is a Barbary ape.

The term 'ape' is incorrect. As Inspector Clouseau of *Pink Panther* fame would point out, it is not an ape, it is a minkey, and as such it should require a leesense, but I digress. Barbary apes are actually Barbary macaques, a species of wild monkey that inhabits North Africa and Gibraltar. A young girl nearby briefs us on a few facts about wild macaques, explaining that they live in small gangs led by the dominant male, who is currently absent without leave. They tend to spend the nights in the higher reaches of the rock, then head down towards the town for a spot of rubbish rifling and outright robbery. The authorities try to discourage this with a mixed measure of success. The girl explaining this holds the title of 'Monkey Warden'. She explains to us that feeding them is illegal, part of quite strenuous efforts to avoid them becoming too familiar with humans (something that must be a losing battle with so many human monkeys being crammed onto such a small patch of earth).

The mother of the pair is a pretty little thing, with spiky brown hair and a flecked face with pursed lips. The baby that clings to her has a curiously wrinkled face and wiry body. The feature that fascinates me most is the mother's hands, which are resting on the wall in front of her, helping her balance their combined weight as she sits there calmly taking in the attention. Her hands are so similar to our own. In fact, her nail manicure is impeccable, much better than mine. Whilst most of the rest of their bodies are covered in fine long hair, the skin on their fingers is partially hairless and coloured a dark, leathery brown. In their company, I find myself experiencing a strong feeling of evolutionary proximity. Primate solidarity!

***

The tunnel network in Gibraltar is huge. I knew that already, even though I didn't get the chance to view it when I served here. During the Second World War the native population was evacuated and the rock was garrisoned by many thousands of troops. Engineers extended the existing tunnels to a network that was almost 35 kilometres long, linking the whole of the rock and enabling all the garrison to be accommodated within. Such was the strategic importance of the site. The modern tour isn't particularly long, nor does it give access to an extensive set of tunnels, but it does give an excellent flavour of the conditions and the haste with which the digging took place. The walls are, in the main, rough-hewn and the conditions relatively primitive.

The garrison was stocked with provisions for an eighteen-month siege. One can only imagine the privations that 16,000 people would have suffered living underground for that period if the worst came about. The suffering of other places under siege bears witness to the wisdom of carrying out the tunneling. It is difficult to understate the importance of Gibraltar in maintaining the convoys that re-supplied Malta. I read an article recently suggesting that the battle of Crete played a critical part in the outcome of the war. The author of the article argued that the resistance put up by the defenders not only crippled the strength, and limited the future deployment of Hitler's airborne troops (who later in Italy laid the bomb in the cellar of the Villa Paolozzi), but it also led to a month's delay in launching Operation Barbarossa, the invasion of Russia. That delay, in turn, led to the German army arriving at the gates of Moscow just as winter broke. The battles in the Mediterranean and North Africa are often seen as something of a side-show, but the author of the article argued otherwise.

* * *

We've ridden half-way up the steep incline that climbs above the town, but I think we should attempt the rest of the climb to the top by foot. There's an old set of stairs that have recently been refurbished. After riding along a narrow lane called Queens Road and arriving at a convenient car park, we locate the said stairs. They climb the rock along the top of a wall that dates from the mid-16th century, built by the Holy Roman Emperor, Charles V. Peering up at the seemingly endless set of steps, it feels like a) we are not of an age where we should be attempting this and b) we aren't that fit, even for our age. It feels like we're about to attempt to free solo El Capitan in Yosemite park. Neither of us wants to admit defeat, right at the beginning, so we commence the ascent. I'm not sure what the weather is like on the summit, or whether we have enough daylight left to make the hazardous trip back to base camp, but hey-ho, we're on our way. Also, I forgot to bring oxygen.

The assault on the western face of Gibraltar.

I walked to the top via the much longer route called Engineers Walk, a long time ago. I recall the spectacular view. And it's none the less spectacular now. From a point matter-of-factly called Monkey Feeding Station at the top of the steps, it's a short wheeze (and I do mean wheeze) round to a point where you can peer down the western side of the rock. Far below nestles the Catalan Bay Hotel and beach.

The eastern side of Gibraltar is dominated by a very steep slope that extends from the base of the cliffs we now stand on, down to a point close to the sea at a place uninspiringly called Sandy Bay. It is part of an ancient sand dune, the size of which is almost beyond comprehension. There is evidence all around the rock of enormous change in the landscape around it, including caves that were once on a shoreline and are now stranded high above the sea. The Great Gibraltar Sand Dune was formed when the eastern side of the rock became a catchment area for sand blown from a huge, pre-historic savanna landscape. Gibraltar was populated in these times by Neanderthals. Indeed, some of the last remaining Neanderthals remained here as their population dwindled towards extinction. Some of them may have been Royal Marines.

Much later, in 1903, work commenced to cover the dune with corrugated steel and concrete, providing a method of water catchment that was gradually expanded until it covered 34 acres. The water ran off the slope into channels that fed reservoirs constructed within the rock. This method remained in use until it was decommissioned and subsequently dismantled between 2001 and 2006, in favour of desalination plants. The corrugated slope was a feature that I remember well. Nowadays, the dune has been stabilised and restored with native vegetation, a distinct improvement on what was, frankly, a bit of an eyesore.

***

Whilst we're on the subject of eyesores, the monkey feeding station leaves a bit to be desired. There's a good deal of excrement around and the smell is particularly ripe. Not a place to hang around for a touch of primate spotting, should you be so inclined. Instead, we take to walking back down the wall, marveling at the view of the old dockyard below. Beyond that is a huge harbour, which was extended by the British with the building of three moles, the last of which was designed to protect shipping from torpedo attacks. The bay outside the harbour is an anchoring point for many ships. It also forms the playground for the odd nautical 'handbags at dawn' between the rival authorities of Britain and Spain – little tiffs that have been played out over the years.

On one occasion, when we were acting as the guard ship, we were put on high alert and sailed out into the bay to a point that was right on the territorial border with Spain, quite a provocative act. The ship was called to 'action stations' and we were informed over the Tannoy that there was a red air raid warning. It was quite alarming. Then, after a while, we were told to stand down. It was only then that we were informed that it was an exercise and we sailed back into Gib. I took a dim view of this because it was always the case that the Tannoy announced 'for exercise, for exercise', when calling us to Action Stations. It seemed that the captain left the 'for exercise' out to shake us all up a bit, either that, or I was starting to go a bit deaf.

However, this wasn't the most exciting event of our stay as guard ship. And a little boat, nestled alongside the jetty far below us, serves up a vivid reminder of a wee adventure and diplomatic incident, wrapped up into one. One weekend, our navigating officer managed to blag the loan of a port auxiliary vessel with a view to sailing it over to Morocco for a banyan (a beach party). A large contingent of the ship's off-watch crew applied and a few of us who were from the seaman branch were given first dibs because they needed us to crew the boat, which was a Cartmel class tender, I think called the Ettrick, quite seaworthy and a very common sight in naval ports at that time. At 143 tons and with a length of 80 feet, it was more than capable of traversing the nine-mile-wide straight between Gibraltar and Africa. The plan was a good 'un: load up with burgers, beers and combustible materials, sail over the straight on Saturday morning, have a party into the wee hours and sail back on the Sunday afternoon, ready for muster on Monday morning, everyone to take their passports with them. What could go wrong?

The Moroccan authorities had apparently been notified. But what went wrong was that our navigating officer decided to run the white ensign up the flagstaff instead of a civilian red ensign. This technically turned us into a warship and transmogrified our 'banyan' into a 'Longest

Day' type invasion of North Africa. As soon as we entered Moroccan waters, we were intercepted by a quite serious-looking gunboat and escorted to the nearest fishing port for detention.

After a couple of hours' negotiation, the Moroccan authorities agreed to let the party animals stay, while governments negotiated. They even agreed that we could have our banyan, although it took part under the watchful eye of a posse of armed Moroccan sailors. In return for their generosity, they insisted that the fake warship had to go. I did the brave thing and volunteered to crew the boat. We sailed off with our tails between our legs and piddled around in international waters where we met a British couple who were sailing their yacht around the Mediterranean Sea in happy retirement. They hove alongside for a cup of tea and a chat and told us about their adventures, free of a house and the worries of ordinary life. I drank it all in and thought, 'I'd like to do something like that, one day.'

On Sunday morning, we received a call on the radio to say that we could go back and pick up the hung-over detainees. Apparently, they'd caused a bit of a stir and had been visited by a steady stream of sightseers from the nearby city, arriving by car to witness the sight of a bunch of British matelots dressed in pirate rig, dancing around a big bonfire on the beach. One Petty Officer managed to get arrested for a second time for taking photos of something official. It wasn't the Royal Navy's finest hour.

The little boat tied up in the harbour below is un-mistakenly a 1970's-era port auxiliary vessel, virtually identical to the one in our little adventure. I wonder if it is one and the same.

∗∗∗

Following a day's R&R involving a hairdo for Diane and a spot of shopping, it's time to depart Gibraltar and head back into Spain. In doing so, we face the minor inconvenience of crossing a border again. The queue to leave is very similar in length to the one we faced on arrival. Nothing is happening very quickly. We have time to peer back at the outstanding rock and marvel at its creation, when a massive tectonic plate crashed into Europe 55 million years ago, sending the monolithic lump of limestone skywards. If you've seen the launch scene in the film *Apollo 13*, it was probably very similar, albeit much, much slower.

One of the effects of this slo-mo collision was the drying up of the Mediterranean Sea, which remained above water until the Atlantic finally breached the Straights of Gibraltar five million years ago, giving the emerging mankind somewhere to go on their holidays and reintroducing turtles to the shores of Greece. Oops! It's time to nudge the bike forward a few metres. We eventually reach the two border posts and gain entry back into Spain.

The navigation out is a reversal of our arrival and quite easy to follow. We eventually hook up with the N340 and are rewarded with spectacular views of the gateway to the Atlantic, the coast of Africa stretching away on the grey-blue horizon. It really is a wonderful sight: two continents, an ocean and a sea. The road follows a set of lovely, twisty bends as it carves its serpentine route around the tip of the Iberian Peninsula. To our left lies the town of Tarifa. A small strip of land links it to the former island called Isla de Las Palomas, the tip of which is the southernmost point in mainland Europe. The road follows the coast closely until it arrives at Casas de Porro, then it cuts inland, leaving the spectacular views behind us.

The time spent crossing the border has presented us with a small dilemma. Our nominal target destination is the city of Seville. It isn't too far away, perhaps about a hundred miles or so. But the afternoon is wearing on and we both feel a bit lackadaisical today. An opportunity for an overnight stop presents itself in the form of a hotel complex about ninety minutes into our journey. We decide to call it a day and pull in to check out room availability.

***

Some time later. We emerge from our room, a motel cabin arrangement with a double room at the front and a bathroom at the rear. The Mutt has been joined by a partner – a Triumph Explorer.

We make our way towards the restaurant, meeting a fellow traveller heading in the opposite direction, a European rhinoceros beetle, genus Oryctes, male of the species, walking determinedly up the path. He's an impressive creature, measuring at least 35 millimetres long and possessing a fearsome-looking horn, from which he gets his name. Sadly, he's almost reached the end of his own particular road. He probably lived for three or four years as a larvae and just a few months as an adult beetle, during which time he hasn't eaten at all. Most of his compadres will have expired now that autumn has arrived. Rhinoceros beetles are flying insects and typically head for the nearest light when they fly at night. If that light happens to be placed above the front wheel of a two-wheeled contraption, travelling at a reasonable lick, with the rider's visor sitting in the raised position... well, the consequences don't really bear thinking about. Having marveled at this extraordinary insect, we head down to the restaurant in the main building. As soon as we sit down at a table with a nice glass of red, we find ourselves loudly greeted by a semi-inebriated German, the rider of the Triumph, no less. Whenever motorcyclists meet like this, a friendly conversation is almost inevitable. The brother and sisterhood of bikers transcends nationality. Notwithstanding this default camaraderie, it quickly transpires that this motorcyclist is possessed of a slightly strange sense of humour, involving telling exceptionally lame jokes and then laughing almost hysterically at them.

A hazard to the motorcycling fraternity (when airborne).

He insists on buying us drinks at an alarming rate, something that helps a lot. In fact, the more wine I consume, the funnier his jokes seem to be or, to be more precise, the more his outrageous behavior becomes mildly amusing. After a while, we agree to join him for a meal. More drinks are consumed, and Diane and I both plump for the local fish dish.

At moments like this, a recollection of events in Tblisi, bolstered by the cockpit scene in the film 'Airplane', might avoid catastrophe. The pilot and co-pilot should *never* consume the same dish. In our case, unfortunately, we aren't carrying an auto-inflate motorcycle rider to save the day if everything goes wrong, which it does quite spectacularly. We manage to complete the meal in the company of our loud companion and we also consume an unhealthy volume of post-meal spirits (whisky for me and a snifter of cognac for Diane). I even remember to do the decent thing and split the bill. But, beyond that, other than noticing on the way back that Marvin the beetle has managed to safely negotiate the dangers of the pathway and has left the scene, it's basically 'lights out' for me as soon as I hit the bed.

I awake in the early hours of the morning with an immediate and urgent need to sprint to the bathroom and stick my head down the toilet bowl, to make a re-acquaintance with my good friends Burt and Huey, last seen in Georgia. Sadly, I only make it as far as the washbasin, whereupon I manage to aim (projectile fashion) the contents of my stomach in the general direction of the porcelain. At some point in the proceedings, I become vaguely aware that Diane has joined me.

***

The hours between 8 a.m. and 10:30 are mostly spent in a state of painful semi-slumber. I'm vaguely aware of our companion of the previous evening starting his bike and riding off. Surely, he's in no fit state...? When we do manage to arise, sometime around 11 a.m., we find the bathroom to be in an appalling state; so much so that we undertake to give it as thorough a cleaning as possible. I'm very apologetic, thinking that I was entirely responsible for the catastrophic mess, but Diane comes clean and tells me that she, too, consulted the great white oracle. The over-riding smell pervading our nice cabin is a sickly-sweet reminder of the tomato-based sauce that the fish was swimming in last night. We desperately try to clean up the mess by using wet towels, then resort to washing the towels in the shower before repeating the process. At a time like this we could benefit hugely with some guidance from Harvey Keitel's Mr. Winston Wolf.

A few hours later and we find ourselves on the bike, passing through a small, innocuous town. Diane has been fast asleep on the back of the bike almost since we departed the hotel/motel. We paid the bill and sloped off, hoping that the chambermaid was able to clean the room without being overcome by nausea. Despite our best efforts, we were unable to completely eradicate the scene of carnage. There was just too much evidence to get rid of. But in true *Pulp Fiction* fashion, we did manage to improve the situation 'at a glance'. It's just that the towels turned pink in the process. Boiling them might help. In the words of the Kate Nash song, *Foundations* (with a slight amendment), 'our faces are pasty, 'cos we went and got so wasted'. We deserve no sympathy.

We pull into a petrol station to top up the Mutt, purchase an intake of Diet Coke and to check the map, removing it from the clear panel on top of the tank bag. We're heading towards the city of Seville, which is just a couple of hours away. It's quite a nice day today, despite our both being a trifle green around the gills. Diane is looking a lot greener than I feel, it has to be said. Not wanting to rub salt into the wound, I mention to her that my head is remarkably clear, all things considered. The tactic works and she goes visibly a shade paler and mumbles something about feeling extremely sick. I hope she can hold it, because she's spending a lot of time staring at the back of my head. There's an underlying feeling that maybe, just maybe, our drinks were spiked last night. Putting that conspiracy theory to one side, though, I think the fish was off (it smelt strange), and, since I was the first to bring mine up, most of the alcohol that I'd consumed was probably duly 'evacuated'. Every cloud has a silver lining.

***

We are transiting a dry area of Andalucia, heading for Seville. Despite the dry conditions, there is plenty of agriculture in the region. Spain is the world centre of olive oil production, generating over a million tons a year. The production of this quintessentially Mediterranean crop dates back over two thousand years in this region. Trees can be found here that date back hundreds of years, and there are some in the northern mountains of Spain that date right back to Roman times. The region is also famous for an abundance of other tree species, notably almond trees, olives of the wild variety, lemons, junipers and oaks.

A little further along the road, whilst traversing a wide plain, we pass Jerez de la Frontera, one of today's waypoints – famous for its equestrian school, the production of sherry, and a rather twisty racing circuit. Despite having a soft spot for sherry, especially when it's floating around the soggy bottom of a well-made trifle, it's the race circuit that brings the city's name to my attention. It's a relatively new circuit, having been completed in 1985 and is probably best known for Moto GP racing and for motorcycle testing and new model launches. The local winter climate is perfect for these activities, being predominantly dry and warm(ish), a perfect climate, in fact, for the production of sherry, which is named after the town (it's an anglicised version of 'Jerez').

We arrive at the outskirts of Seville in the late afternoon, pitching up in a district called *Dos Hermanos*: Two Brothers, which I think is quite a nice name. After pulling up for a consultation with our paper map, we discover that the route into town is very simple. The road we're following is called the Avenue de Jerez, which makes sense because that's where we've come from. To reach the city centre, we just need to keep following this road. I'm feeling reasonably confident that we'll locate some form of accommodation when we arrive at the heart of the city. My pillion has awoken and is on full alert.

Initial impressions of Seville is of an attractive, modern city. The road along the river is tree-lined and pleasant, passing an attractive park as it heads towards our destination. But the streets are unusually traffic-free and quiet for a city of this size. It's the first place we've arrived at since departing Greece that feels like this. Is this the effect of the financial crisis? I suspect that it is. We arrive at an intersection, with cafés to our right. Thankfully, they appear to be open and doing at least some trade, though not a lot. Everywhere else seems either shut, or not particularly busy.

Following signs for hotels, we pull off to our right and head into a labyrinth of narrow back streets, spotting a promising-looking establishment on our left. It's a three-star joint and it looks quite cheap, which fits our mission. The only minor issue is the car park, which is situated beneath the hotel and is accessed by an inordinately steep ramp with an incredibly tight turn at the bottom, even for a motorcycle. A family, who's arrival coincided with ours, head in before me and have great difficulty in parking their car. Once parked, I'm not sure they'll ever get it out again.

Having decanted the luggage mountain, we decide to wander out in search of food. We're still feeling quite subdued from the excesses of the previous night and decide that a break from wine might be advisable tonight. Neither of us have any idea where the city centre is, but we spotted a few shops on the narrow street that the hotel is situated on, the Calle San Vicente, so we head off in search of mini-market sustenance. After strolling a short distance, we pass a small square, noticing that a crowd of people are gathering. Not sure what that's all about.

On the return journey, victuals secured, it's apparent that the crowd has grown somewhat larger and is being addressed by a speaker. The vibe is a lot calmer than the one we experienced in Athens, but there's little doubt that the subject matter is, in some way, related to Spain's dire economic circumstance. Unemployment has gone through the roof and many of the local banks have collapsed (having lent money to just about anyone who wanted to build or buy a property). Very recently, the European Central Bank stepped in with a 100 billion euro re-capitalisation of Spain's banks. But, despite this, youth unemployment is entrenched at the 50% mark. Young, educated Spaniards (of which there are many) are leaving the country in droves, a deep loss that will surely affect Spain for many years to come.

Travelling through countries that have been so badly affected by the global economic crisis is an experience of mixed emotions. On the one hand, there are opportunities: cheap hotels, businesses that are desperate to sell to you, and lighter traffic to negotiate a path through. But the crisis has also damped down the vibrancy you would expect to find visiting a place like Seville, and ultimately that leaves a feeling of sadness and regret. We've discovered that the amount of traffic on the road, particularly trucks and other commercial traffic, is a key economic weather vane. In Greece, the roads were virtually deserted outside of Athens. In Spain, the story is similar, but, perhaps, slightly less so. It feels as though Spain is surviving on the very edge of the abyss. I guess, when all's said and done, it's just too big an economy for the EU to allow to collapse completely.

***

Friday 2nd November. Seville is situated at a major crossroads in the south-eastern part of Spain. The road to the north travels in the direction of the ancient, walled city of Cáceres, then on to the north coast via the equally photogenic city of Salamanca. We haven't visited either of them before, but they look very beautiful on the internet. The road east would take us back to the coast, towards Murcia, and south would, of course, take us back to Gibraltar. Our path today heads to the west, though, following the A-49, a dual carriageway that will run for (perhaps) just shy of 100 kilometres to the border of Portugal. Our intention is to progress beyond the border and find accommodation somewhere in the Algarve; exactly where, I'm not certain right now, but I'm sure it will become apparent to us when we get there.

Before we can depart Seville, I need to negotiate the perils of the pocket-sized car park and its near-vertical access/escape ramp, a torturous event for both rider and the poor clutch on the bike. There's the distinct stench of fried friction compound when we arrive at the door, waiting for it to open, hard on the front brake then revving the engine and slipping the poor old power-engagement device relentlessly before emerging, triumphant, onto the street. I tend to use the front brake in these situations which demands dual action of both the brake lever and the throttle with the right hand. Professional riders would scoff at this method of egress. They would point out that the rider should engage the *rear* brake pedal with their foot, retaining full control of the throttle. Amateurs such as myself would point out that they would definitely fall off while attempting something so stupidly un-natural on such a top-heavy machine, and would subsequently look a complete knob. It occurs to me that I really should load the bike *after* exiting the garage in these situations!

Things could be worse. I could be riding my Ducati Monster. It would have been barking like a frisky bull elephant seal and would surely have set fire to itself, if it faced the same punishment. By comparison, the beemer settles into its usual (reasonably) quiet rhythm, once it's taken a breath of fresh air. And fresh the air is too. It's a grey, overcast day, here in Seville. The cloud base is decidedly low.

We eventually locate our intended route, with a little luck and very little map-reading. I just mentioned that the bike is 'reasonably' quiet on tickover. The truth is that the clatter it has developed when stationary with the clutch out is intruding on my sensibilities. It is definitely different from the quiet efficiency of earlier days. I need to investigate this when I get home. I'm increasingly fearful that the clutch is knackered. It certainly has good reason to be so. On the positive side, though, there is no sign of slip or drag and the take-up is at the same point at the lever.

This part of Andalucia is every bit as dry as the area we rode through yesterday. The land is mostly flat. A signpost declares that we are about to cross a river: the Rio Guadiamar, which provides a thin sliver of relatively green vegetation before we head back into drier, more scrubby parts. Gentle slopes of pale brown earth are planted, as far as the eye can see, with short, stumpy olive trees. The groves of olives are interspersed with ploughed fields. I imagine that the Spaniards must be masters of irrigation.

One of the products of the region, grown in abundance in these sun-kissed lands, is the Seville orange, which became much favoured by the Scots in the production of marmalade, one of my favourite preserves, not least because my great grandfather used to manufacture it. According to popular history, a Spanish ship found itself marooned in Dundee with a cargo of Seville oranges that needed to be consumed. An enterprising merchant bought the job lot and his wife turned the oranges into a preserve, thus inventing marmalade. Apparently, marmalade is going through a bit of a lean patch, nowadays, because only older people appreciate its sharp tang. This is a double whammy for Andalucia because sherry, of course, is the favoured drink of maiden great-aunts. And on that slightly bleak note concerning the economic future of Spain, we arrive at the Portuguese border.

Chapter 38
The World's End

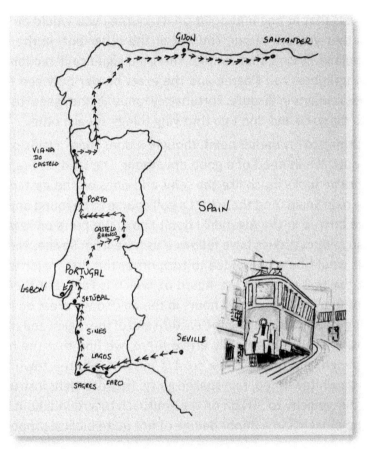

It's November, it's cold, and we are on our final leg of our journey.

When anyone mentions the Algarve to me, I immediately think of golf courses. Since hearing about it, I've always thought that it must be a particularly green part of the world. The border between Spain and Portugal hereabouts is transited by crossing an impressive, modern bridge that throws its concrete span across the river Guadiana, a mysterious watercourse, the source of which has been the subject of intense debate amongst geographers and similar anoraks for millennia. We might not know where it springs to life, but we can be reasonably certain that it completes its journey to the sea just a couple of kilometres south of our wheels as we pass over its central span.

The river is an international one, providing the border between Spain and Portugal. You would think that a river is a perfect natural border and that at any mid-point on its journey you would be able to say whether you are in one country or the other but, in the case of the Guadiana, it isn't that simple. There's a significant section where the cartographers can't agree and the exact border between the two countries remains in dispute. Fortunately for us all, they seem to merely agree to disagree and don't go throwing things at each other.

Returning to my earlier point, though: it does seem a trifle parched, hereabouts. It's in need of a good downpour. The land on the far side of the bridge looks much like the semi-arid ones on the eastern bank, back there in Spain. And there isn't a golf course to be found anywhere. Have we arrived in the Algarve? I don't know. We press on regardless. The drab, overcast skies have followed us here from Seville. Part of me thinks it would be a good idea to turn off at the first major town, or at least the first one that I've heard of, which is Faro. But there's still plenty of fuel in the tank and hours in the day, so we press on into the gathering gloom, heading for the eastern end of the region and the town of Lagos. When we eventually arrive there, we find that the heavens have opened, big time. As we crest a modest hill, the town reveals itself in its whitewashed, rain soaked glory. The road signs instruct us to reduce our velocity to 50 kph on the approach to a roundabout and we enter the outskirts in a minor deluge of not quite biblical proportions.

Lagos is a town of around 22,000 residents; quite small, with a long, fascinating and sometimes dark history. Its population grows hugely with the invasion of tourists in the summer months, something that also happened a couple of thousand years ago when the Carthaginians came over to cause trouble. It happened for a second time a few hundred years later with the arrival of the Visigoths and, still later, the Moors from North Africa. Nowadays, the modern town is quite sprawling, radiating out from the ancient centre situated near the harbour. Having located a vacant holiday apartment to rent, we decide not to roam far this evening, with the weather so inclement and cold. We discover a very handy bar situated close to the apartment and settle for a few glasses of the local red to warm our spirits.

***

When we finally manage to drag our bones out of bed, pretty late, we find that the resort is being lashed by heavy rain. The bike is snuggled up under its cover outside the front of the apartment and there isn't much to be done, apart from mooching around a bit in our chilly surroundings. The weather starts to clear in the late morning, so we decide to take a walk into the old part of the town.

The streets that we discover are very quaint, with narrow roads, cobbled squares and brightly painted low-rise houses and shops. The shops are mostly closed and it's remarkably quiet. Hedgehogs could jaywalk very safely, hereabouts. There's an open coffee bar at the top of the town and a couple of restaurants that show some signs of life on the walk down towards the harbour. We aren't going to starve. What a relief! Meanwhile, the skies are threatening to deliver another deluge when we arrive at the waterfront. An opportunity to shelter presents itself in the shape of a tiny fort.

An exhibition in the Fortezela de Lagos pays homage to one of the most important historical aspects of the town, of which I was only vaguely aware in very general terms. Simply put, Lagos was one of the most important towns in the world during the 15th century. And it had nothing to do with the beaches or reasonably priced villas. Following the invasion of the town of Ceuta in what is now Morocco by his father, King John 1st, Prince Henry became fascinated with Africa. Based in Lagos, he initiated the period that was subsequently called the *Age of Discovery*. Portuguese ships explored the coast of Africa, seeking the source of the trans-African gold trade.

The Portuguese were able to exploit their prowess in navigation with the development of a new type of vessel called a caravel, a small ship equipped with triangular lanteen sails, rigged on up to three masts, depending on the size of the vessel. Based on existing Portuguese fishing boats, the caravel could sail into the wind, meaning that it could navigate coastlines and rivers with comparative ease, venturing where other vessels simply couldn't go. In short, it was a maritime version of a BMW GS motorcycle.

On a much darker note, the exploration of the west coast of Africa led to the introduction of the African slave trade to Europe. The caravels started returning to Portugal with human cargo, and a slave market was established in Lagos, providing slaves to Portugal and to a wider, hungry market across Europe. The original market building survives to this day. Over time, the Portuguese navigators pushed further away from friendly shores, through seas that were believed to be populated by monsters. Eventually, Vasco de Gama and his crew sailed around the Cape and on to India, the first Europeans to do so.

To reinforce the incredible navigational achievements of the sailors of Lagos, the port is home to an exact replica of the Caravel *Boa Esperança*, which translates in English to *Good Hope*. It is berthed across the river from the fort, a very basic, clean design of vessel, without any of the adornments that were scattered over the Vasa and missing the high forecastle of that vessel. Somewhat surprisingly, our land journey around the European periphery has developed something of a nautical theme. From the beautiful Viking longboats of Roskilde, via the *AF Chapman* and *Vasa* in Stockholm, the cruiser *Aurora* in St Petersburg and the frigate *Frisky*, languishing hundreds of miles from the sea in Moscow, to the magnificent lines of the *Moskva*, witnessed from our bobbing launch in Sevastopol. The replica caravel is a fitting addition to that seaward facet of our little adventure.

The Fortaleza de Lagos is an interesting building. When it was built in the 17th century, it was considered a marvel of modern military architecture, perfectly designed for its intended purpose of guarding the entrance to the port. Later in its life, it was heavily modified, especially in the interior, and nowadays it is a delight to wander around, not least because there are a number of very photogenic, modern, metal sculptures scattered around the exterior, wind-powered art by an artist called Jose Maria S. Pereira, a very Portuguese-sounding name, if ever I heard one.

Continuing with our artistic theme, the graffiti artists of Lagos seem to have been influenced by Banksy. Or maybe he's got a holiday villa out here. Either ways, their output is extremely fine by graffiti standards. There's one spray-painted masterpiece of the face of an old man that is particularly excellent. I don't know who he is. Well done rattle can-shakers of Lagos!

The work of a master.

***

Bonfire night in Blighty.

After spending a languid Sunday sampling the delights of Lagos café culture, the time has arrived for us to pack our mule and inch our way a bit closer to home. Our next destination is Lisbon, the famous old capital that has been close to the top of my list of cities that are desirable to visit.

There are a few directional options, but we have decided to stick as close as possible to the coast and to visit, en-route, the small town of Sagres, home of Henry the Navigator when he wasn't exploring the oceans. After that, we'll dial in magnetic north and, most likely, get lost on the back roads. I wonder which route would tickle Henry's fancy?

The exhibition in the fort yesterday, emphasised the importance of Sagres in the story of the Portuguese navigators. For many years, it was taken as a historical fact that Henry the Navigator built a school for navigation there; children were taught it by rote in school, but the information cards in the exhibition debunked this as a myth. In more ancient times, it was thought that Sagres was the most westerly point in the whole world, a place where the setting sun boiled the sea. Nowadays, it's a known fact that it is almost the most westerly point in Europe, but not quite. The boiling maelstrom of the Atlantic Ocean is now heaven on earth for surfers. Consequently, Sagres is a natural breeding ground for the lesser, fried-out Kombi. As if to emphasise this fact, we pass a surf shack to our right as we ride into town. The place is deserted. I think we're sat upon the only vehicle to arrive for a day or two. A rolling ball of tumbleweed passes across our path as we continue into town and vultures circle the rotting carcass of an unfortunate property investor. Eventually, the road expires at the impressive gateway to what appears to be an expansive fortress.

The fort lives on a promontory to the south of the town, flanked by two beaches. A wide bay stretches out to the north with Cape St. Vincent at its furthest reach. It is windswept and magnificent, even on an overcast day like today. The promontory is remarkably flat, sitting on the top of high cliffs. It was known to the Romans as the holy promontory, using the Latin word 'sacrum', from which the town derived its name. Early mariners used the promontory as a sheltered anchorage when the winds coming off the Atlantic were unfavourable. They feared the rocky shoreline around Cape St Vincent and likely thought they'd sail off the end of the world if they ventured too far out to sea. So, they would 'tarry here for a while', waiting for the winds to change before they set off on their perilous journey around the Cape.

Henry the Navigator built the original fortress, along with his house and a church. But much of it was destroyed in a great earthquake that ravaged Portugal in 1755. Most of what remains was built in the eighteenth century. One of the dominant features inside the fort is a massive compass rose, which is forty-three metres in diameter. It adds to the mystique surrounding the school of navigation, but historians think that it was added at a later date, no doubt by someone having a laugh: 'I'll just pop this compass here... that'll confuse the plebs.'

Having wandered around the grounds of the fortress and its church, we head over to the edge of the cliffs that tower high above the ocean, staring out across the bay to the headland of St. Vincent. Tiny upper torsos can be seen bobbing in the sea, beyond the point where the waves break. Surfers are a hardy and committed breed of lunatics, almost as barking mad as motorcyclists. There they are! Waiting for that perfect wave. Paddling furiously when one comes along. Some miss it and are left bobbing, but one or two manage to catch it and clamber onto their boards, cruising in on the power of the curling breaker. Part of me hankers for my kayak but, in truth, these waves are way too big for me. I would get totally wiped out, without a doubt. My kayak-surfing skills can just about handle Gorleston beach in a slightly frisky swell. Better to watch this lot from afar. Safe in our fortress.

A brief, unexpected distraction draws me away from surfer twitching: I notice a quick movement just below the cliff top, just a few feet away, the flutter of a sleek-looking bird, the like of which I don't think I've seen before: a dapper little fellow with grey-brown plumage and a sharp, pointed beak that testifies to a primary diet of insects. It's a rock pipit, *Anthus Petrosus*, a relative of the more commonly seen pied wagtail, one of my favourite garden birds. I've never seen a rock pipit before and become mildly excited in doing so. I had to come to the end of the world to see one. Apparently, rock pipits also wag their tails with gay abandon, just like their pied and grey cousins, but this one holds a pose long enough for a photo opportunity and gives it a miss.

A handsome little chap. Might be a chapess. The Rock Pipit.

***

Back on the road. We head northwards along a gently winding single carriageway road. The landscape feels old and weathered. The slightly stunted trees that we pass lean dramatically away from the Atlantic, appearing to be in the process of tearing themselves from the earth to escape the worst of its weather. For a while, the land is greener. We pass semi-derelict stone farms with fields that grow fallow. Our passage north is very slow, but I'm glad we took this route. It wafts us gently through small villages as it makes its way toward the town of Aljezur, past houses that cling to the hillsides and a windmill that looks exactly like the one in paintings of Don Quixote.

Sometime later, we pitch up in a rather strange town. It seems to spread itself along the road, probably something it has done for centuries. In fact, it feels as though it is living in another century. If you were to remove the tarmac and the odd vehicle scattered here and there, it would probably be *exactly* the same as it was a hundred years ago. And, speaking of odd vehicles, when we roll up to a stop outside the local shop in search of cola and crisps, we (I should say I, really) find ourselves transfixed by an old classic motorcycle. One that I know a little bit about, being quite ancient myself.

The motorcycle in question is a very battered Casal, a brand that was manufactured in Aviero, Portugal, just up the coast from Lisbon. The little bike parked in front of the shop is liberally covered in brown dust, beneath which the original dark blue paintwork can just be discerned, along with a smattering of light rust. It displays that rare-to-find patina that should never be restored. The rust is far from terminal and the little machine's history is carried in every filthy nook and cranny.

Casals were not uncommon in our neck of the woods when I was making the transition from pedal power to the heady realm of Mobylette ownership. Two of my friends had them. One of them had a 49 c.c. sports model that was tatty, slightly fragile, but reputedly 'very fast'. The other lad, David Coy, had a more mundane 'cooking' model that was brand new when he turned sixteen. It had three gears, operated by hand change. I really liked it. In fact, I was deeply envious. It was finished in a very attractive metallic-red and silver paint scheme. Try as I might, I've struggled to track down the model, but I now think that it was a K181, notable for an elaborate shroud that encased the top end of the engine. Identifying the model of the bike in front of us is much easier because the name is emblazoned across the tank and the side panel. It's a Macal M70.

I realise, in discussing this with you, that I've descended perilously close to motorcycle anorak territory. Diane is suffering the monologue about David's weird and wonderful machine from the mists of time with good humour and a countenance of, 'enough already'. The fact that this bike sports a German Sachs engine, which is, frankly, a bit of a surprise to me, it's the icing on the cake. Suffice to say, that if I had my van handy, I would linger with intent, waiting for the unsuspecting owner to arrive and would make an immediate offer that couldn't be refused. It would be loaded into the van and whisked off to England *mega-pronto*. It's my favourite motorcycle discovery of the trip so far.

***

Our chosen route, the N120, eventually reaches the outskirts of a coastal town called Sines, which sits on a small promontory jutting out into the Atlantic in a reasonable representation of a recalcitrant Yorkshireman's chin. The key landmark feature on arriving at Sines is an ugly red-brick power station with two chimneys painted with red and white stripes in a failed attempt at prettification. The next sight that heaves into view is a line of dockyard cranes.

In the case of many towns, now might be a good time to start looking for a bypass. But, in the case of Sines, successfully locating one would be a shame, because the centre of the town is worth visiting even if, like us, you're just passing through.

The port is Portugal's largest commercial dock. Thousands of Casals must have been exported from this very place to an expectant world of hormonal juveniles. It is also the birthplace of the great explorer and navigator Vasco de Gama. After riding past the port, we find ourselves tracing the edges of a small bay with a beach. The road then climbs in serpentine fashion around the angular battlements of a large fortification, the *Castelo de Sines*. After getting hopelessly lost, passing the same petrol station three times, we eventually find ourselves back on track for Lisbon. I hate to think what Vasco would make of my map reading.

The skies have remained grey today. The sun has been attempting to valiantly break through from time to time, but now it has given up and is descending towards the Atlantic horizon in a huff. In the final throes of the afternoon, its fading light turns the sky into a gorgeous, pearlescent grandeur that I suspect will be quite short lived. We arrive at a 'T' junction opposite a closed restaurant and hang a left in the direction of the small town of Comporta.

The rugged coastline that we saw in the south of Portugal has given way to an area that sits almost at sea level. A thin band of cultivated fields stretches to our left, running along the coastline. The road runs virtually straight, heading northwards through small villages with single-storey houses painted in white and blue. The contrast between the green rice fields to our left and the drier, more scrubby land, populated with scatterings of young pine trees to our right feels strangely un-balanced. But, before I become too engrossed in it, we arrive in Comporta, a village originally populated by African slaves.

We are well overdue a look at the map, which is tucked away in the top of the tank bag. After whisking past the village, we spot a hotel to our right called the *Comporta Village Hotel – Apartamentos* and decide to pull over and investigate. We both notice some movement in the building as we climb off the bike but, when we arrive at the reception door, it is found to be stubbornly locked, however loudly we bang and stare through the glass, hands shading our eyes. Back to the map.

It is apparent that we are still some distance from Lisbon. Between that fine city and our current position are two large river estuaries, separated by a sizeable stretch of land. There is an alternative route to the capital that skirts around both estuaries, but also involves trekking quite a long way inland before turning towards the great city. The first estuary has no bridges and can only be traversed by taking a ferry from a point at the tip of a long spit of land called the *Peninsula de Troia,* arriving at the town of Setúbal.

We decide to give up on the hotel and to head for the ferry, without thinking it through too much. On the ride up to Troia, things take a swing towards the modestly wild. Extensive sand dunes appear on both sides of the road, with occasional lay-bys for parking and many informal pathways winding their way through the tall clumps of grass towards the sea. I imagine the beaches are spectacular. After a short while, we pass a few houses and then a sign for the ferry.

The ticket salesman informs us that we are in for a long wait. The ferry has just slipped its lines and departed; it won't be returning any time soon. He tells us to head down past the car park and to wait in a shelter on the jetty. This is a 'cup half-full situation'. Despite the long wait, we will at least manage to take the next step in our journey tonight. Hopefully, we can find a hotel on the far side. When we arrive at the jetty, we park behind a small van in the gathering dusk. A pastel-pink sunset glows through the darkening clouds, etching the conifers that line the beach in stark relief. The beach curves gently to the right, its tip appearing to point at the ferry as it plies very slowly away in the distance, lights twinkling. A few cables away, an empty container ship called the Temara rides high at anchor, silent in the dusk.

After an hour or so, the tiny trickle of new arrivals increases modestly as the more informed passengers arrive at an appropriate time to catch the ferry, joining those of us who are starting to resemble frozen corpses. A tiny glimmer of hope appears on the far horizon: a set of navigational lights that grow out from the mass of sodium light pollution on the distant shore. It seems to take an age for the approaching vessel to arrive, but it starts to gradually morph into the recognisable, dark shape of a squat passenger-and-vehicle ferry. Everyone heads for their vehicles. Twenty minutes later and we're all aboard, the ramp is raised, and the vessel departs the jetty. Very, very slowly.

The journey to Setúbal seems to take forever. But it isn't boring. At least, not when we draw closer to the northern bank of the river. The city has close links to the sea, dating back many centuries and the estuary of the river Sabo is a parking lot for a fascinating collection of ships that are riding at anchor. The ferry winds its way between them, heading for the fluorescent light bathed terminus that is now rapidly approaching. We've been standing by the bike all the way across – there's no lashing down of vehicles and it's not worth risking an accidental crunch this late in our journey. But, for a few minutes, I relinquish my guard duties to watch the stately procession of ships go by. Setúbal was once the centre of the Portuguese sardine industry and a large fishing fleet sallied from the port into the Atlantic in search of their quarry. Nowadays, fish has given way to tourism and the city is famous as a resort. This presents an unexpected bonus – as we depart the ferry terminal, heading to our left towards what is hopefully the town centre, we spot a hotel called the *Luna Esperança* (Lunar Hope) on the avenue Louisa Todi. In these desperate financial times, they are almost empty and delighted to welcome a pair of cold, late arrivals into their warm and well-kept rooms.

✳✳✳

Tuesday 6th November. Back in England: the last forlorn wisps of smoke will be rising from the larger and more persistent bonfires of the night before. Empty firework cases will be strewn here and there and a few people will be heading to work with a hangover from over-indulgence of Aunt Fanny's punch bowl. For us, it's a case of having a bit of a lie-in. We only have a short distance to travel today and there's no point in busting a gut.

We managed to find somewhere to eat last night, despite our late arrival – a pleasant little taverna just down the road from the hotel. The dish of the day was clams with rice; very nice too. We couldn't see much of the city in the dark, but the area around the hotel seemed pleasant: a long road, lined with shops, bars and restaurants with two carriageways in either direction divided by a slim park. The road is named after a famous opera singer and actress from the eighteenth century, who was born in Setúbal. Having risen to the status of celebrated actress and singer, she travelled to St. Petersburg and spent four years there. Her biggest fan was Catherine the Great, who showered her with fabulous jewels. She lived to the grand old age of 80 and was buried in Lisbon. Over the years the graveyard she was interred in was built upon. Nowadays her final resting place is beneath the floor of a cellar – an ignominious ending for a glittering star of the Regency period.

Today is a landmark day. Diane has offered to pick up the tab for the hotel. I'm being cheeky; she's done so on many an occasion. After humping all the gear down to the bike and having carefully loaded it, I spend a casual few minutes observing the morning street life on the avenue Luisa Todi, unaware of the minor drama that is about to unfold before my very eyes.

A man appears in front of a building adjacent to the hotel and commences hollering up at an open window. Nothing much happens. He starts to become agitated, cursing and swearing (at least I think he's swearing – I have no knowledge of Portuguese) and hammering on the door. Then he starts kicking the door. In fact, he appears to have gone completely *berserk*. This is mildly alarming, since the bike is parked a little too close to him for comfort; he might come over and kick it. I decide to hover around it, just in case. After an extended period of hammering and kicking the door and screaming at the open window, he suddenly grabs hold of a drainpipe and starts climbing, all the way up to the window, where, with an impressive turn of agility, he swings his legs over and manages to scramble in. Spiderman could not have improved on this performance.

Before I can make any sense of this blatant example of entering without much breaking, Diane appears at my side ready for the off.

'I just watched a bloke break into that building,' I explain, somewhat nonplussed. 'We should call the police, but I don't know how.'

Before she can reply, the door swings open and the madman emerges, having miraculously recovered his decorum. He closes the door and locks it before heading demurely off down the street. I guess he just locked himself out, after all.

✳✳✳

The ride to Lisbon is merely a short hop today. It involves simple navigation: heading eastwards towards the main Lisbon-Algarve motorway then taking a left to ride northbound across one of two long bridges that cross the Tagus estuary, arriving in Lisbon on the south-eastern side of the city.

The first stage involves taking a right down the one-way Avenue Luisa Todi, then executing a 'U' turn to head back past the hotel and the ferry terminal, skirting the river's frontage along the way. The little harbour that we pulled into on the ferry last night is part ferry port, part marina. The ferry to Troia – painted garishly in a red and white Coca Cola logo – is berthed at the ramp, awaiting its next crossing. A large commercial car transport ship has weighed anchor and is being towed by a tug towards the docks, which lie a short distance upstream from the marina. A gorgeous, pale blue sky arches over the scene, a pleasant change from the grey clouds that have beset us ever since we arrived in Portugal.

Our exit is executed along a road called the avenue Jaime Rebelo. It celebrates another notable citizen of Setúbal, an anarchist and anti-Fascist who actively supported the trade unions during strikes in Portugal in the early '30s and fought against Franco in the Spanish Civil War. He cut his own tongue to avoid divulging secrets when captured by the authorities in Portugal following the strikes. I once had a sizeable slice taken out of my tongue for a biopsy and it was absolute agony once the local anaesthetic wore off! I'm not sure that it rivalled delivering a baby but, in man terms, it was dreadful. I, too, couldn't talk for days! Some people were probably relieved at this misfortune. Mr. Rebelo was clearly a proper nutter; someone to have on your side in a pub fight.

After a short while, we arrive at the Ponte Vasco da Gama, a hugely impressive bridge, the longest one in Europe at over ten miles long.

***

We're arriving in Lisbon with a feeling of high expectation, carrying, as it does, something of a reputation for classical grandeur. Historically, it joins Ankara as one of the oldest surviving cities in the world. The sun is still shining when we arrive, providing a grand entrance to a dramatic view of the various neighbourhoods of the city, draped over the hills that overlook the river Tagus estuary, resplendent in a shade of beautiful, deep blue. One of the stand-out features of the city, the Parque Eduardo VII, leaps out at us and takes our breath away as it descends steeply towards the centre of the city. In terms of wow-factor, arriving in Lisbon is only rivalled by the sight that greeted us in Volgograd.

We ride alongside the park, around a huge roundabout and quickly spot a hotel. After settling into our room, we decide to take a stroll into the city centre.

The large roundabout that we negotiated on arrival houses an underground station and is surmounted by a large column with a statue perched on the top. The statue is dedicated to the Marquês de Pombal. As Prime Minister of Portugal, he was hugely influential: rebuilding Lisbon after the catastrophic earthquake of 1755, embracing the fundamental changes that were sweeping Europe during the age of reason and repelling the invasion of Portugal by France and Spain, acting in alliance with Britain. In an age when it is customary to heap criticism on our forebears, it is nice to discover someone who, despite being from the elite, seems to have been quite an admirable character. Nowadays, though, he presides over a steady string of drug pushers in the streets below, who approach us quite brazenly once we've crossed the square. Lisbon is clearly experiencing hard times.

Having firmly told a couple of drug pushers 'no', we wander along a street called *Liberty Avenue* and, passing a corner, are drawn to the sight of an oddly-shaped, bright yellow tram that sits waiting for passengers at the end of a steep side street, covered liberally in graffiti.

It isn't really a tram. The correct term is a *Funicular*, a cable-operated carriage that climbs and descends steep gradients using the weight of a second carriage attached to the other end of the cable.

We make our way further towards the city centre, which is home to a fine array of architectural gems. The cream of the crop for me is the *Estação do Rossio*: Rossio Railway Station, a stunning building that dates back to 1890. Its design is in a style called Neo-Manueline, drawing from a form of Gothic architecture that dated from much earlier in the 16th century. The stand-out features are the two main doors, which are both gigantic and exquisite, formed in the shape of elaborately decorated horseshoes. I've never seen anything like it before. Simply beautiful.

Having marvelled at the sight of the train station, we take a long stroll through the city, eventually arriving at an area where colourful old houses and shops reside at the crest of a steep hill. A standout shop is one selling outstanding (and very expensive) African art, a reminder of the close links that still exist between Portugal and the west coast of that continent. From there, we head back under gathering clouds that portent rain. By the time we pass through the centre of the city, the heavens have opened. Arriving at Liberty Avenue, we take shelter briefly in a small shop that is crammed with antique collectables (and not-so-collectables). After browsing with very little intent to purchase, we arrive at the main counter where my eyes zoom in on a small display case full of vintage enamel motorcycle badges. I notice very quickly the Bultaco, Montessa and Ossa badges –favourites amongst the bikes I've never owned. Then my gaze is arrested by the sight of a Casal badge, nestling in amongst the others. The shop owner is very savvy. He spots my attention to the weathered little badge and addresses us both in English.

'Casal motorcycles were made here in Portugal.'

'Yes,' I reply. 'We had them in the UK. I like them a lot.'

'I have owned many Casals,' he goes on wistfully. 'They are fine motorcycles.'

I tell him about our encounter with the lovely patinated example yesterday, showing him the photograph I took on my little Panasonic camera. I'm sorely tempted to buy the badge, but it's slightly expensive and I baulk at making the purchase. The shop owner doesn't seem too bothered. I think he's just chuffed that two Brits turned up and recognised his treasured brand. Shame we're skint. We depart the shop with me reminiscing to myself about the addictive waft of blue smoke emanating from the exhaust of 1970's two-stroke Portuguese motorcycles.

***

We wake up to a dismal day – at least in weather terms. Despite the sun trying to occasionally peek through, grey clouds are scudding across the skies ushering in periodic heavy showers. Let's hope it improves tomorrow, because we'll be back on the bike. In the meantime, we buy tickets for the local city bus tour at the reception desk, after mulling over which colour route would be the most interesting.

Once aboard the bus, we head for the upper deck and grab a front bench seat under the small portion of roof that hasn't been cut away. The bus provides audio devices for those of us who wish to listen and learn, notably Diane, while I relax and enjoy the scenery in blissful ignorance of the marvellous, historic buildings that we pass by. Roughly halfway into the outbound journey, the skies open and a temporary deluge commences.

My attention is grabbed quite late into the outbound leg when the bus passes a very beautiful, long building. Diane has the audio device glued to her ear. She advises me that this is Jerónimos Monastery. I thought he was an Apache Native American, but never mind. It is built in the original Manueline style, started in 1501 and completed one hundred years later. The train station that I raved about yesterday took its cues from buildings like this Monastery. Despite being very delicate and ornamental in execution, the building survived the earthquake of 1755 almost intact and, nowadays, it's the last resting place of many of Portugal's most notable people, including Vasco da Gama.

Poor old Vasco contracted malaria in Cochin, India in 1524. He was buried there for fifteen years before being disinterred and returned to Portugal, where he was buried for the second time in the town of

Vidigueira. You may recall the fate of poor old St. Clare back in Assisi, the follower of St. Francis, who was dug up and ended up being displayed in the basilica that bears her name. Well, Vasco was even more unfortunate. He was disinterred for a second time in 1880 and transferred to the monastery, where he resides in a decorative tomb in the nave of the church. At least he isn't on open display.

All of this connectivity with India reminds me of the book *The Moor's Last Sigh* by Salman Rushdie, which tracks the fortunes of a family in India who are of mixed Portuguese and Jewish descent. When I read the book, I found the link to Portugal to be somewhat surprising but, in discovering a little about Vasco da Gama, it now makes a lot more sense. I was intrigued to discover that the Portuguese population who settled in India made up an entire, ethnic branch called Luso-Indians and Luso-Goans. Many of them were descended from the Portuguese aristocracy. Their trading communities in India pre-dated the arrival of the British and French by 150 years and never left.

The bus is passing through an area called Belém, famous for the monastery and for a tower that sits on what was once a small island on the River Tagus. It, too, is an example of the Manueline style. The bus terminates at this point, so we alight briefly to view the tower and a superb, riverside statue. It takes the form of a perfect replica of an old biplane (a seaplane), raised in commemoration of another pair of Portuguese adventurers: Gago Coutinho and Sacadura Cabral who, in 1922, became the first aviators to fly across the South Atlantic Ocean. It was an epic flight, involving the unfortunate loss of two aircraft. After ditching for a second time in the middle of the ocean, they were picked up after nine hours by a British vessel. They eventually managed to blag a third identical seaplane to complete their mission.

The aircraft in question, sculpted here in exquisite detail is a Fairey IIID MkII; the original aircraft, called *Lusitânia,* was a specially adapted version. The third aircraft landed at Rio de Janeiro on the 17th June 1922. It had taken them 79 days, yet the actual flight time was a mere sixty-two and a half hours!

Gago Coutinho was born here in Belém and was a career naval officer and inventor. He developed a version of the sextant that used two spirit levels instead of requiring sight of the (real) horizon. This allowed him to navigate in conditions of limited visibility– something that apparently happened for much of their time in the air on the flight to South America. Gazing upon the beautiful representation of the Fairey seaplane brings home just how adventurous people like Gago and Sacadura were – the equivalents, I think, of the astronauts who first ventured into space. It is fitting that the statue of the plane, with its intrepid explorers strapped firmly in the cockpit, resides here, pointing at the sea. For it is from this very spot that they departed on the 24th March, 1922.

Chapter 39
Smoke the Kippers

The bike is loaded in the hotel garage and we're ready to depart Lisbon. We're heading out on our final few days of the trip, striking northwards in the general direction of Bilbao in Spain. The route plan should be to continue following the coast, but we've decided unanimously to head into the dark, mysterious interior of Portugal to discover whatever can be found there: hopefully uplands of the rugged, sheep-infested category beloved of Yorkshiremen and the Welsh (roughly in that order). The overnight ferry to Portsmouth is booked for Monday, so we have four days in which to cover the distance to Bilbao, which is about 900 kilometres, as the crow flies.

As we hit higher ground on the outskirts of the city, the hills become increasingly wreathed in tendrils of smoky, low clouds. It doesn't take too long for the skies to open. A few spots splatter on the screen in front of my nose as the view ahead gradually greys-out, steadily increasing to a point where the water is being diverted above the screen by the wind blast and into the space twixt visor and helmet chin bar, giving the old goatee a right old rinse.

There was a distinct autumnal edge to the temperatures in Lagos, a few days ago, and today is similar. We haven't travelled far into the afternoon before the skies give up the pretence of daylight. We've struck eastwards, heading towards a small town called Zibreira. The road drifts a broadly easterly course for about forty kilometres then swings gently towards the northwest, whereupon the rain increases to a right old lashing; most uncomfortable. Having passed a town called *Castelo Branco,* we start to think about calling it a day. Twenty-five kilometres further along the road, the opportunity arises to exit the dual carriageway at a sign saying *Covilhã Norte* (North). A few minutes later we sweep into the car park in front of a large, monolithic, concrete and glass block of a hotel. Our suits are dripping wet on the outside but have gamely held the deluge at bay.

Covilhã is known as the city of snow and wool and sits in the highest, most mountainous region of Portugal. It boasts having more than one climate at any given time, depending on where you are in the city. Snow in the nether regions, tropical heat in the depths of the valley and monumental downpour, right above our heads. Ok, that's a slight exaggeration. About ten kilometres from the town lies the highest point in continental Portugal, a mountain called *Torre*: Tower. It rises to a height of 6,539 feet to the northwest of the town and can be accessed entirely by road. If conditions were more clement, we might attempt an early evening ascent, but they aren't, so we won't. Over our evening meal, we discuss the options for combating the increasingly chilly climes.

Numero uno in our armoury for protecting us from freezing to death are our electrically-heated jackets, procured on the strong recommendation of our friend, Ed, in America. They're nestling at the bottom of one of the bags that sits on top of the panniers. Diane is keen to start wearing hers. I'm with her on this proposition, but have neglected to mention that I haven't wired up the connections to the bike. I know I have the necessary kit somewhere in the depths of the baggage. After a quick search back in the room, we locate the jackets at the bottom of one of our red Ortleib bags, neatly rolled up and strapped with rubber bands by my lovely navigator/organiser. They've been sitting in there for seventeen thousand miles of (often) extreme heat and consequently they smell like a pair of foisty hamsters. Further rummaging around locates the wiring. Now, all I have to do is to pull off both of the seats, disconnect the mass of wires that are attached to the battery and reconnect them, along with the jacket wires. After that, I will have to route the jacket wires to a suitable location for plugging-in and tie-wrap them into place. Then, finally, I will have to reset the digital clock on the bike. Before nodding off, I decide that it might be easier to stay quiet in the morning, mention now't, and see how we get on....

Despite the weather outlook, the surroundings in this part of Portugal appear to be very attractive: a mix of rolling hills, wide valleys dotted with farms, and trees that are in the midst of their autumnal splendour. The recently tilled earth provides a patchwork quilt of differing shades of brown which match with the russets and yellows of the leaves. The low hills that we pass have many small, rugged peaks, perfect sites for rows of wind turbines and the famous leaning trees of Portugal. As the ride progresses in the morning, the clouds begin to roll back and patches of blue make a welcome appearance. Despite this brightening up of the weather, there remains a definite chill in the air.

It isn't just an autumnal chill – there's a severe economic one too. Having located the dual carriageway that we rode along yesterday, the paucity of fellow travelling companions becomes readily apparent. It's not quite completely deserted, but the weight of traffic is a lot less than in Spain, and that wasn't exactly buzzing with activity.

By my count, we have travelled through twenty-one countries, one rogue state and one British Overseas Territory on our journey around the edge of Europe. In population terms, Portugal is the tenth largest of those destinations and in economic terms it ranks eleventh, with a GDP of 216 Billion USD. It was suffering from economic stagnation prior to the financial crisis of 2008 and remains on the critical list, mired in deep, deep financial trouble. In April, 2011, the situation became so bad that Portugal had to apply for a 78 billion Euro bail-out from various parties, including the International Monetary Fund. The result is that crippling austerity has been imposed on the populace with high unemployment and many businesses folding. At least, with the bailout there is some hope that the country can start rebuilding and haul itself back to some semblance of prosperity. I certainly hope so.

***

We've been tracking alongside the splendid hills of the *Serra da Estrela* Natural Park for about 40 kilometres, with the hills of the park to our left. At the town of Guarda, we arrive at a major crossroads. Continuing ahead would transport us towards the very top north-eastern-most corner of Portugal, if we chose to take it, allowing a more direct route to our eventual destination. Alternatively, we can opt to turn off and head westward towards Aviero and the Atlantic coast.

We decide to head in the latter direction. The pleasant, hilly countryside remains with us for a while, then it gradually eases back into the distance behind us. We're heading through a region called *Centro*: Central Portugal, passing into a municipal district called *Viseu*, named after the city that lies in its centre. Viseu is thought to be the birthplace of the first King of Portugal, Afonso Henriques, a colourful twelfth century character who defeated his own mother in battle before banishing her from the newly created kingdom, an action that guaranteed no further washing of his smalls. Much revered in Portugal, he was famous for having something of a temper and for bearing a sword that took ten men to carry when he wasn't wielding it in battle. Wimps.

Beyond Viseu, it's an 85-kilometre hop to Aviero but, before we arrive there, we hang a right onto the A1/E1 motorway, running promptly into a line of toll booths. Off with the gloves for Diane and a spot of rooting around for dosh. Then, we're on our way again. Through hours of practice and many repetitions, Diane has managed to reach the fine-tuned adroitness of a Formula 1 pit crew at tyre-changing time. Not a single cent has recently slipped through her dextrous digits.

* * *

Our right turn onto the E1 means that we're now heading northwards towards Porto, just two or three kilometres inland from the Atlantic Ocean. The coastal strip that runs northwards from Lisbon to Porto is home to a denser scattering of towns compared with the rain-lashed hinterlands that we passed through yesterday. At a point just south of Porto, the motorway takes a lazy turn in towards the centre, heading through the built-up suburbs of the city and passing over the rather beautiful Ponte da Arrábida, a bridge of quite glorious proportions and form. It was completed in 1962 and, at the time, was the largest concrete-arch bridge in the world. It provides fine views across the city and the River Duoro as it winds its final couple of kilometres to the ocean. Shortly after the bridge, we change onto the A28, riding past blocks of high-rise apartments and then across a short stretch of road that passes the very edge of the main docks of the city, feeling almost within touching distance of the huge container ships unloading there.

The River Duoro gives its name to the valley that is the home of port wine, named after Porto, which was the loading point for exporting the finished product. I used to enjoy the odd glass of aged tawny port, accompanied in the traditional manner with a selection of cheeses. In fact, I liked the sweet side of the equation far too much and often swapped the cheese for a hefty slab of Cadbury's finest milk chocolate. My doctor was confused why I'd developed type 2 diabetes at such a young age. 'Were you ever obese?' he asked. I replied that such was never the case, but, as the great-grandson of a line of well-known confectioners, I developed an addiction to chocolate at an early age.

'That'll do it,' came the reply.

* * *

We have reached the outer suburbs of the city, an area called Perafita, which is Portuguese for the things you have at the end of your legs... It seems to be a pleasant, modern area – increasingly green. I've been forming the impression that Portugal would be a reasonable place for a Brit to settle in retirement. I like the feel of the country and feel quite at home here. It is, after all, England's oldest ally, the oldest surviving alliance between two countries in the world. It has a nice mix of old-world charm and relative modernity and the people seem to be very polite. Our alliance dates back to 1373. Since then, the two countries have never engaged in acts of aggression towards each other and have never fought in an opposing alliance either; quite remarkable since the English are, in global peace terms, a bit like Animal from the Muppets. Despite our upsetting everyone else at some time or another (to varying degrees), Portugal has our back. And, if that isn't enough, they introduced us to peri-peri chicken.

By my calculations from the map in front of my nose, the distance from here in the northern suburbs of Porto to the Spanish border is about 120 kilometres (75 miles), a distance that can be covered in just over an hour if the traffic and weather conditions remain as they are. It would be nice to spend one more night in Portugal, leaving us two further nights before we catch the ferry. So, I think we'll commence the hotel search somewhere ahead, close to the border. It turns out that there's a destination with an attractive name on the road signs called *Viana do Castelo* – something to do with a castle. I think we'll search for accommodation there or thereabouts.

We're now heading into the *Região do Norte*, the Northern Region of Portugal. Not a very inspiring name, but, on the bright side, it isn't grim up Norte. It's the most populous part of Portugal and, in common with many other areas of the Iberian Peninsula, the history of human habitation goes right back to neolithic times. The land is quite intensively farmed and slightly undulating. We pass through a few miles of this pleasant countryside before arriving at the town of *Vila do Conde,* which translates to Villa of the Count.

Passing through the municipality, we enter a region that is slightly hillier. North of the town, the road increasingly carves its way through the hills, passing rock faces that appear hard, gritty and igneous. When we arrive at the outskirts of Viana do Castelo, we find ourselves entranced by an enormous mushroom cloud, rising from behind one of the surrounding hills in a pale blue, late autumn sky. It even has a grey, crescent-shaped, smaller cloud surrounding the stem of the mushroom, mimicking the effects of an atomic shock wave.

With this spectacle still visible to our right, we pass over another modern bridge spanning the River Limia, hanging a left at a major intersection beyond the bridge and heading westwards towards the town centre. The first hotel that we chance upon looks quite impressive in a boxy way. It's called the Axis Vianna – a fine, four-star, executive establishment intended, no doubt, for well-heeled businessmen and their wives who may, perchance, wish to frequent the spa.

✳✳✳

We awake to a dingy, leaden morning that promises drizzle. After breakfast, we carry out the familiar routine of departure. Yesterday was quite a modest hop in terms of mileage, but it still took us most of the day to accomplish it; we dawdled somewhat. Today, we will head for the northern coast of Spain. We need to spend the night within an easy day's ride of Bilbao.

I was cautiously optimistic about the weather conditions last night. It was quite a beautiful evening, with blue skies, the awesome mushroom cloud, and the lovely, autumnal colours of the leaves on the trees, set alight by the late afternoon sun slanting through them. This morning, the uneven base of the grey clouds are caressing the peaks of the hills that surround the town. We don our electric(less) jackets under our riding suits and wriggle into the Finnish waterproofs. We've decided to strike inland, along a picturesque minor road that follows the gentle meanders of the River Limia.

Shortly after departure, the skies start to clear a little, with patches of blue peeping between the clouds. With the roads still damp, and most likely a trifle slippery with freshly deposited leaves, we pass through a charming landscape of stone walls, rustic farms, small villages and stretched, regimented rows of vines. This is the home of Vihno Verde, Portuguese green wine – the largest area of wine production in the country. The region is split into nine sub-regions, this one being named Lima. Contrary to my expectations, I discovered that Portuguese green wine can be white, rosé, or red. It is famous for being a crisp, young wine, with high acidity and a very gentle fizz. We tried a bottle of the local red variety last night with our meal and I can report that it cut the mustard and was entirely tiddely-pom. I think that's the correct, technical wine-tasting term.

After a few miles of wafting serenely through this idyllic landscape, we arrive at a village called *Santa Comba*, named after Saint Columba. Anyone who considers saints to be all peace and light should check out Santa C. The Galician version of her tale describes her as a witch. One day, she was walking along a road – could even be this road – minding her own business, nipping off the odd ear of a bat, when she happened upon a vision of Christ who told her that she could remain a witch, continue with the bat abuse, or she could convert to the path of righteousness. Having chosen the latter and thus being saved from a warm reception in the hereafter, Comba became the patron saint of witches and had more than one village named in her honour, this being one of them. The alternative to this story is quite visceral, involving a rampant bear and the executioner's axe, so we'll leave that one for another day.

We presently find ourselves crossing the river and arriving at a junction, in the form of a roundabout at the town of Ponte de Lima. Ahead of us lies the road to the city of Braga that lies to the south. The road to our right would take us southwards to the town of Barcelos, home of a famous rooster that advertises the Portuguese love of life. It's tempting to head in that direction but we must resist and turn left, for that way lies the E1 motorway, which we will re-join on our quest for the Spanish border.

***

The time passes by slowly and uncomfortably as we leave Portugal in our wake and pass into northern Spain. We catch odd glimpses of quite a wild landscape but, beyond that, we remain focused on life within the confines of our helmets as the rain, which arrived as we crossed the border, lances down mercilessly. Our trajectory is towards the city of *A Coruña*, the second most populous city in the ancient autonomous Celtic region of Galicia. After an hour or so of riding, we find an opportunity to cut eastwards, heading towards the northern coast of Spain. The rain finally abates as we approach a service area and decide to seek warmth and a meal. After topping up with fuel we head into the restaurant area, which is almost deserted.

'You've got to plug the electrics in. I'm freezing!' An ultimatum from my better half if ever I heard one!

It's not difficult to graciously surrender. I'm pretty cold too, and it's started raining again outside. We decide on a team effort: Diane will hold the brolly, I'll do the wiring. It's not a job to be relished but, on the plus side, I was given plenty of warning two days ago and I know where all the necessary cables and tools are. Out by the bike in the car park, we unload the gear and locate the necessary bits and bobs. Then, it's off with both seats to commence disconnecting the battery. This isn't quite as simple as it seems, because the satnav and the trickle charging wires are also connected up to the battery. It's a proper fiddle with cold fingers, trying to avoid dropping one (or both) of the battery nuts or bolts 'twixt engine and frame, once the terminals have been disconnected. Doing so in these conditions would prompt a *monumental* fit of swearing. There's a tendency, with all the connections hooked to the terminal bolts, for the wires to ping around once the bolt has been slackened. But, with a measure of care and attention, we avoid any such drama and manage to fit on the extra wiring with a just few threads to spare on the terminal bolts. It's a close-run thing, but we've managed that stage of the task.

I could just botch the rest of the job and find a quick way of routing the cables so that we can plug in and be on our way. But I decide that the job is worth doing well. So, it's out with the cable ties, wire clippers, penknife and tape. With cold, wet fingers, a proper route is found for the wires so they won't rub on the frame and the terminals will be in the optimum location for connecting up our suits, which seems to be at the point where the two separate seats meet. The big questions are: *will they work?* And*: will the wet wires short circuit and electrocute me when I plug in?*

I concede that the risk of electrocution is minimal. Electrical science is mostly a mystery to me, but the sight of a pair of modestly-rated fuses in the suit wiring loom is confidence-inspiring. I owned a Kawasaki Z900 back in the 80's that had the regrettable tendency to short circuit through the back of the fuel tank when the starter motor was engaged in rainy conditions. The resulting spark invariably leapt across into my nether regions. It's the kind of experience that garners a degree of caution when plugging into electricity for the first time in the wet.

With the bike chuffing quietly away, I plug in the jacket connector and fumble around for the large control box that has three buttons on it: gently warmed, quite hot and flaming red chillies in your pants. Let's go for broke...

A huge grin spreads across my fizzog as a rush of warmth instantly eases me into a temperate comfort zone. Diane is bursting at the seams.

'What's it like?'

'FAB-U-LOUS!' I declare, almost entirely without mimicking Craig Revel Horwood.

'Plug me in! DO IT NOW, OR DIE LIKE THE DOG YOU ARE!'

With Diane duly plugged in we both just stand there, with our bags and the bike seats scattered around us on the ground, gently steaming, Diane wielding the brolly. Before us lies a deserted car park in the grey north of Spain, lashed by the bitter chill of approaching winter, here we are, in heaven, standing on a tropical beach – soaking up the life-giving rays of a mid-summer sun as baby turtles scurry past our toes in a flipper-flapping race towards the bright blue ocean. Lovely. Until one gets snapped up by a patrolling frigate bird. Best be on our way.

***

A little later in the afternoon, we hit roadworks and find ourselves diverted on to a single carriageway road, which slows the pace down significantly. The kilometres, which were formerly clicking by at a satisfying rate, are now dragging interminably as we progress at a snail's pace just inland of the coast, heading east. Despite this, we're in good spirits because we're warm and dry, snug as a pair of bugs in a rug. Our rising core temperature is politely allowing the blood to flow to the extremities. In my case, the main effect is on the feet. My pinkies are already kept toasty by the bike's electrically heated handlebar grips. Thus ensconced, we watch northern Spain slip quietly by on either side of the skinny little road.

We have gradually made our way into the principality of Asturias, the princedom of which is bestowed upon the heir to the Spanish throne, currently Felipe Juan Pablo Alfonso de Todos los Santos. Asturias is a mountainous province, a fact that isn't lost on us because the mountain range at its heart tracks along the coast, looming to our right. These are the Cantabrian Mountains, a range that extend from the edge of the Pyrenees for 180 miles to the Galician Massif Mountains. Both these mountain ranges rise to nearly 7,000 feet. It's a fabulously beautiful area.

I was of the view this morning that we would easily make Bilbao today if we pressed on with modest dose of vigour. A couple of days in that area would permit one final day exploring. Top on the agenda was a daytrip to Bayonne in Southern France. This would add one final region to the list of those visited and would satisfy a temptation to re-visit a town I last frequented in the 1970's. An alternative would be to visit the Guggenheim Museum in Bilbao. But, by the time we manage to reunite ourselves with the dual carriageway, we find that the afternoon is wearing on and, with it, the light. Ahead of us lies the city of *Gijón* and the promise of hotel salvation and respite from wondering whether we will weather the relentless weather.

***

By my rough calculations, we've travelled just over 18,000 miles since June, covering 204 miles a day on average. A quick tot-up of diary entries reveals that we've spent 49 days at rest out of the grand total of 137 days. It's a very modest achievement, taken at a leisurely pace, if truth be told.

We exit the Hotel AC Gijon into a dull and slightly damp late morning. The ground glistens following a fresh fall of rain, but the weather appears to be holding off as we exit left out of the car park and head towards the main coastal route, east. The blanket of cloud has had a mild, warming effect on the climate, such that plugging in our newly found source of warmth is deemed, by the boss, to be unnecessary. Once we've settled into our stride, the weather gradually clears. The clouds start to break, with increasing patches of pale blue peeking through, slowly conglomerating as the clouds draw back like a veil, revealing an increasingly mountainous view with snow on the high, triangular peaks.

We continue our eastern trek along the coastline of the Bay of Biscay, riding just a couple of kilometres inland, occasionally managing to catch glimpses of that oft-tempestuous body of water to our left. The Autovia 8 curves lazily around the contours of the hills, occasionally resorting to burrowing its way through them. We pass the smaller towns of Ribadesella and Llanes, making decent time, passing into the region of Cantabria at the village of Unquera, which sits on the eastern shore of the mighty River Deva.

Cantabria is the third smallest of the seventeen autonomous communities in Spain, covering a smidgen over 1% of the total land area of the country. One school of thought suggests that the name of the region comes from the same Celtic root as Kent and Canterbury, meaning on, or close to, the edge. It shares a few other things in common with one of my favourite counties too. The landscape is very lush and green, similar in this respect to the garden of England. And the mountains are built of limestone, as are the chalk downs in Kent. It may also have links to Morris dancing, which can often be witnessed in the festivals of Kentish towns and villages, providing a rich seam of ribald entertainment for anyone who isn't English and most of those who are, too. But, I have news for those of you who mock so cruelly...

Morris dancing is practiced in many of the countries we've visited on our travels, including America, Canada, Sweden and Finland, in St Petersburg too. But the links to Spain are the most intriguing. There is quite strong evidence that Morris dancing is an evolution of a dance practiced by the Moors in Spain – Moorish dancing.

With that tantalising, cultural gem revealed, we arrive in our final autonomous region: the country of Basques. We coast down the exit road into the centre of Bilboa, greeted by a monumental thunderstorm. I would love to ride past the Guggenheim Museum, to present the opportunity for Diane to photograph it on her trusty little Panasonic camera but, with lightning chasing us, when we spot a convenient Holiday Inn, we screech to a halt and make a rush for the entrance.

Chapter 40
Next stop Tokyo

Travelling around the fringe of Europe has been our own little voyage of discovery. The early stages of our journey took us into areas of spatial remoteness that are rarely found in our own little island and the vast tracts of Russia were a stark reminder of the distance we must cover to arrive in Vladivostok on our next little jaunt.

We discovered a wealth of cultural experiences that were quite unexpected: the beauty and richness of Russia and the humour of its citizens, which extended to the other countries we visited in eastern Europe. The wild glory of Georgia and its roadside menageries. Hanging teddies, mad motorists and the sanctuary of hostelries, found in the nick of time. The most obvious divide between east and west was, for me, the stark comparison between our reliance, in the west, on rampant materialism, versus the sense of community and the vestiges of collective goodwill that exist in the countries to the east. I loved the austere functionality of the machinery and the tendency towards self-reliance. I fear that they will lose this in many countries as the EU spreads its market influences into pastures new. It begs the question: what matters most, perpetual growth and shareholder value, or maybe less growth and communal value?

Our mission, on departure, was ostensibly to test our endurance. To see how we would cope in regions remote. On that score, I think we've managed to pass muster. Occasionally, by the skin of our teeth. I feel as though my riding and mechanic-ing skills have popped their head modestly above mediocre, but I don't wish to get ahead of myself. I'm still far from sure how I'll fare if, and when, the road disappears completely. Constant monitoring on the internet reveals that Mr. Putin is indeed building a road across Siberia. Completion date is still estimated to be 2016. Imaginary dates are being pencilled into calendars that are yet to be printed. As in 2009, we now need to find work to recover from our own impending austerity.

My travelling companion has carried out her duties stoically. She is my navigator. And, by that, I mean that she keeps a sharp weather eye on me and makes sure I don't wander too far from the straight-and-narrow on the path of life. She is, truthfully, quite challenged in physical stamina, but draws from a deep well of resilience that often leaves me amazed. My little voice of sense and reason. An indispensable companion for a hopeless drifter and tilter of windmills.

We arrived home on Thursday, 15th of November, having sailed overnight across the Bay of Biscay, spending an extra day sightseeing in Portsmouth. We pulled up outside our house, ragged in our attire but with a wealth of treasured memories of the countries we had visited and the people we met on the way. Perhaps the most hopeful thing we discovered, in the patchwork quilt of nations that we visited, tiny and huge alike, is that nearly everyone we met wished us well. We only had one stone cast in our direction. And it missed.

Milton Keynes UK
Ingram Content Group UK Ltd.
UKHW021833031123
431812UK00014B/427